OBJECT-ORIENTED PROGRAMMING: AN INTRODUCTION

Greg Voss

Osborne **McGraw-Hill**
Berkeley New York St. Louis San Francisco
Auckland Bogotá Hamburg London Madrid
Mexico City Milan Montreal New Delhi Panama City
Paris São Paulo Singapore Sydney
Tokyo Toronto

Osborne **McGraw-Hill**
2600 Tenth Street
Berkeley, California 94710
U.S.A.

For information on translations or book distributors outside of the U.S.A., please write to Osborne **McGraw-Hill** at the above address.

Object-Oriented Programming: An Introduction

34567890 DOC 998765432

ISBN 0-07-881682-3

Figure 1-1, "Evolution of structure in architecture," is a computer-generated drawing after Fig. 0-16 in *Art Through the Ages, Fourth Edition*, by Helen Gardner (New York: Harcourt, Brace & World, Inc., 1959).

Part opener art is by Janie Wooldridge.

To Melissa
for her love

To Janie
for her courage

To Bret
for making me a member of the tribe

Publisher

Kenna S. Wood

Acquisitions Editor

Jeffrey Pepper

Associate Editor

Vicki Van Ausdall

Project Editor

Judith Brown

Copy Editor

Paul Medoff

Proofreading Coordinators

Bob O'Keefe
Ann Krueger Spivack
Kelly Barr

Proofreaders

K.D. Sullivan
Mick Arellano

Artists

Janie Wooldridge
Greg Allen

Indexer

Sharon Hilgenberg

Computer Designers

Judy Wohlfrom
Mickey Salinaro

Cover Design

Bay Graphics Design, Inc.

CONTENTS

ACKNOWLEDGMENTS

As always, the more creative ideas must be credited to Melissa Milich, who has an eye and an ear for the funny things that most of us never see or hear. Melissa also edited, proofed, and typed thousands of strange little words—without complaint—and kept me laughing through it all. She never ceases to amaze me.

Thanks to the folks at Osborne: Judith Brown for never-ending patience as production editor; Vicki Van Ausdall and Emily Rader for manuscript preparation and revision; Ann Pharr for keeping us all in touch; and Jeff Pepper for keeping me on target and giving me rope when I needed it.

Bruce Clift played a critical role as developmental editor and Microsoft Windows guru. Not only did he read and critique several drafts of the manuscript, Bruce translated most of the ObjectWindows example programs for Chapter 14 into C++. Jeff Hsu read every word and program of a manuscript that grew to astronomical proportions before his very eyes. He has no idea how much I depended on his technical commentary and review. Readers can thank Paul Medoff for improved readability of the text and elimination of many errors that would have resulted in frustration and misunderstanding.

I thank Janie Wooldridge for her wonderful drawings and Judith Brown for insisting that they had a place in this book. Greg Allen lightened a heavy discussion of encapsulation with his slovenly cook cartoon.

Not all of the contributions to this book were technical. Cindy Borjon made sure the manuscripts got to Osborne on time. Priscilla kept me from swearing and made sure I got my exercise. Once again David, Martha, and the little Intersimones opened their home to us in time of need. I thank members of the Santa Cruz City Council and municipal offices for their support. Louis Rittenhouse and Sharon Saldavia were knights in shining armor.

Most of all I would like to thank the Santa Cruz Police Department. Without their protection and professional services this book would never have been completed. They gave us the spirit and backbone to stand up to a nightmare. Particularly I want to thank Mike Dunbaugh, Jeanne Morningstarr, Randy Harris, Todd Dickson, and the undercover officers who helped a neighborhood say no to drugs. Chief Bassett, you have reason to be proud.

PREFACE

This book introduces the concepts of object-oriented programming using a variety of languages. The principles of object-oriented programming are language independent. In fact, object-oriented programming can be practiced, although awkwardly, in traditional languages such as ANSI C or standard Pascal. This book, however, uses only languages that provide special features designed to make object-oriented programming easy, natural, and reliable. The languages covered include C++, object-oriented Pascal, Actor, and Smalltalk.

GOALS OF THE BOOK

A great deal of confusion has resulted from inadequate explanations of object-oriented programming. Programming language features have been emphasized almost exclusively while larger structural issues of object-oriented systems have been ignored. Some programmers have been led to believe that the principles of structured programming are obsolete and have been replaced by object-oriented programming. Today, more than ever, the principles of structured programming hold firm. Object-oriented programming supplements these principles. The expert programmer will merely add the tools of object-oriented programming to the professional toolbox, and through experience and training know how to select the appropriate tool for the job at hand.

As much as possible the exercises in this book convey realistic and exciting object-oriented application programs that prepare you for problems currently being explored in industry and education.

Starting with the concepts of object-oriented programming the book shows complete working example programs that are made easier to build and understand precisely because they use object-oriented programming techniques. Seeing how the general concepts of encapsulation, inheritance, polymorphism, and message passing simplify program construction provides the motivation for study of language features. Not until the general concepts are thoroughly discussed in the context of working programs does the book go on to a detailed discussion of the manner in which various languages provide features to support the object-oriented style of programming.

In the second part of the book the implementation of object-oriented language features is compared and contrasted in C++, object-oriented Pascal, Actor, and Smalltalk. In addition to language features, the significant features of programming environments are discussed, including the presentation of powerful programming tools introduced by object-oriented programming environments like Smalltalk, which invented browsers, inspectors, and debuggers to provide development tools that were as sophisticated as the new concepts introduced by objects.

The third part of the book is devoted to a specific type of class library called an application framework. Application frameworks show the power that object-oriented structure can give to users by making code reuse possible.

Every effort has been made to make example programs as realistic as possible. For this reason the initial programs are larger than those you will typically see used to introduce object-oriented programming. The size and complexity of the initial programs is not accidental. Realistic programs of moderate size provide better illustrations of object-oriented programming principles.

PROGRAMMING LANGUAGES, ENVIRONMENTS, AND TOOLS

As mentioned, this book covers four popular object-oriented programming languages: C++, object-oriented Pascal, Actor, and Smalltalk. The main operating environments for both program development and program execution include MS-DOS and Windows. Programs developed for Smalltalk can run almost without modification on the Macintosh and under UNIX X-Windows, as well as under MS-DOS in graphics mode and under Windows and the OS/2 Presentation Manager.

Much of the code presented for C++ will run under any operating environment that supports the standard iostream library. However some of the lower-level graphics output requires the support of graphics primitives to draw lines and ellipses. All modern graphics environments support such primitives. To make the programs as portable as possible, an abstract screen class is developed and used for graphics output. All you need to do to get the programs to run in your specific environment is define the line and circle drawing methods inside the abstract screen class.

As a specific example, complete implementations of the abstract graphics screen class are provided for the Zortech C++ Flash Graphics library, for the Borland BGI, and for Microsoft Windows. Adapting this class to run under X-Windows should be a project that will take you from an hour to a half-day, depending on your level of familiarity with X-Windows.

The specific language products used for development include:

- Borland C++ and Turbo C++ (all versions)

- Zortech C++

- Digitalk Smalltalk/V 286

- Digitalk Smalltalk/V Windows

- Turbo Pascal (5.5 and later)

- Turbo Pascal for Windows

- Microsoft QuickPascal

- Actor from the Whitewater Group

Other language products were also used to develop example programs. These include standard tools for Microsoft Windows, such as the Software Development Toolkit (SDK) and add-on class libraries designed to enhance the basic products just listed. These include

- C++ Views

- Turbo Vision

- ObjectWindows

- Whitewater Resource Toolkit

- Microsoft Windows 3.0

- Microsoft Windows SDK

C++ Views is an application framework and class library by CNS, Inc. for developing Microsoft Windows applications. C++ Views works with both Zortech C++ and Borland C++. Turbo Vision is an application framework and class library developed by Borland that works with Turbo C++, Borland C++, and Turbo Pascal. Turbo Vision provides support for character-oriented window systems (COWS) running under MS-DOS.

ObjectWindows is an application framework and class library developed by the Whitewater Group in cooperation with Borland International. Object-Windows runs under Microsoft Windows and works with Borland C++, Turbo Pascal for Windows, and Actor. ObjectWindows uses a class hierarchy and class naming conventions that are nearly identical to Turbo Vision. The Microsoft Windows SDK is required only if you are using Zortech C++. Borland C++ provides its own version of the Microsoft Windows standard library, Windows-compatible linker, header file, and resource compiler. Actor and Smalltalk/V Windows do not require the SDK. The Whitewater Resource Toolkit is handy for developing resources such as menus, dialog boxes, and bitmapped images such as icons and cursors. The Whitewater Resource Toolkit comes with Actor, Borland C++, and Turbo Pascal for Windows.

You do not need to have all these products to follow this book. In fact you do not need to have any software if you are simply trying to learn the basic concepts of object-oriented programming. If you are shopping for languages or tools for an object-oriented programming project, this is a good place to start. You'll get a solid feeling for what it is like to use all of the products just mentioned. By the time you are through with the book you should be able to adapt any program you find to the desired target language by seeing the different approaches each of these products takes to solving a similar problem.

All program listings have been submitted to the appropriate compiler or interpreter to verify their correctness. However, you may be using a different implementation of one of these languages than was used for the development of this book. This is only likely to be a problem with Smalltalk other than Digitalk (that is, Parc Place System's Smalltalk) and with very special-case issues for object-oriented Pascal.

Note that the term used in this book is *object-oriented Pascal*, not Object Pascal. Object Pascal is a specific product of Apple Computer, originally called *Clascal*. Both Borland and Microsoft followed the basic implementation of Apple's Object Pascal when they extended standard Pascal to support object-oriented programming language features. The term *object-oriented Pascal* is used in the broadest sense to include Turbo Pascal 5.5 (and later), Microsoft's QuickPascal, and Apple's Object Pascal.

WHAT YOU SHOULD KNOW

You should have a basic familiarity with at least one procedural language such as C or Pascal. If you have worked with the newer varieties of BASIC, which support the definition of data structures and named subroutines, you will do fine. You should be familiar with basic program structure such as conditional statements, loops, and callable subroutines, as well as basic input and output mechanisms for printing strings and reading input from the keyboard. A good understanding of structural programming would be helpful, but is not essential.

APPLICATION FRAMEWORKS

Application frameworks are a special type of class library used in the quick construction of application programs. Application frameworks provide menus and dialogs, and use built-in event-driven input to simplify the construction of window-oriented programs. Application frameworks are presented that use character-oriented windows in MS-DOS as well as the Microsoft Windows graphical user interface. The third part of this book should be approached as an example of how object-oriented programming can extend power and flexibility to programmers through class libraries. Class libraries for standard C, Pascal, and FORTRAN can extend power, but seldom flexibility. Because standard libraries do not support inheritance and polymorphism, they cannot be extended and specialized by the programmer. Application frameworks are more than an example of the power of class libraries. Application frameworks will change forever the way you program systems that require sophisticated user interfaces. You should read this section as an example of things to come and as proof that continuing to design your own user interface code is an obsolete practice.

OBJECT-ORIENTED PROGRAMMING AND WINDOWS

Windows and objects are natural companions. This is true whether you are talking about a character-oriented window system for MS-DOS or a graphical user interface such as Windows. Windows are by definition complex data structures manipulated through a variety of standard operations. In other words, windows are objects.

The windows theme recurs frequently throughout this book—it is a good approach for pulling together a diverse set of languages and topics under one umbrella. The windows theme also guides and unifies the example programs to demonstrate a natural progression of basic concepts. By the time you have worked through the examples you should find it easier to approach any window system or application framework, even if the window system is not explicitly object-oriented. It is surprising how much this approach can prepare you to understand the inner workings of Microsoft Windows and the SDK, even if you are programming in C.

BIBLIOGRAPHY

Booch, Grady. *Object-Oriented Design with Applications.* Redwood City, CA: Benjamin/Cummings, 1991.

Cox, Brad J. *Object-Oriented Programming: An Evolutionary Approach.* Reading, MA: Addison-Wesley, 1986.

Ellis, Margaret A., and Stroustrup, Bjarne. *The Annotated C++ Reference Manual.* Reading, MA: Addison-Wesley, 1990.

Franz, Marty. *Object-Oriented Programming Featuring Actor.* Glenview, IL: Scott, Foresman, 1990.

Fuller, R. Buckminster. *Synergetics: Explorations in the Geometry of Thinking.* New York: Macmillan, 1975.

Goldberg, Adele, and Robson, David. *Smalltalk-80: The Language and Its Implementation.* Reading, MA: Addison-Wesley, 1983.

Hansen, Tony L. *The C++ Answer Book.* Reading, MA: Addison-Wesley, 1990.

Meyer, Bertrand. *Object-Oriented Software Construction.* New York: Prentice Hall, 1988.

Peterson, Gerald E., ed. *Object-Oriented Computing.* Vols. 1 and 2. Washington, DC: IEEE Computer Society Press, 1987.

Petzold, Charles. *Programming Windows.* Redmond, WA: Microsoft Press, 1990.

Schmucker, Kurt J. *Object-Oriented Programming for the Macintosh.* Hasbrouk Heights, NJ: Hayden, 1986.

Stroustrup, Bjarne. *The C++ Programming Language.* Reading, MA: Addison-Wesley, 1986.

Get the Disk!

Companion Disk for

Object-Oriented Programming:
An Introduction

$12.95

Source code for example programs

Complete source code for all programs in the book. Includes makefiles and project file lists.

Additional ObjectWindows examples

Advanced examples of the Borland/ Whitewater application framework. Examples are in Actor, Pascal, and C++.

Smalltalk/V Windows

Now Smalltalk works with MS-Windows. As a prototyping tool Smalltalk is unsurpassed. See Smalltalk/V Windows examples in action.

Advanced graphics examples

Rotate three dimensional shapes. Source in C++, Pascal, Smalltalk, and Actor.

WindowFrame demo programs

WindowFrame is a separate product available from SoftSmith. This disk includes sample programs demonstrating the convenience and power of the *WindowFrame* application framework.

($12.95 each, postpaid. Tax included. Foreign orders add $10 shipping/ handling and use a check from a US bank or a credit card.)

Please send me _____ copies of the companion disk for *Object-Oriented Programming: An Introduction.*

Name		
Address		
City	State	Zip

IBM PC Diskette Size (check one): 5-1/4"_____   3-1/2"_____.

Method of Payment: Check_____   Visa_____   MC_____.

Credit Card Number	Expiration date
Signature	Telephone

SoftSmith Publishing   **P.O. Box 1124**   **Soquel, Ca 95073**

I

INTRODUCTION TO OBJECT-ORIENTED PROGRAMMING

WHY LEARN OBJECT-ORIENTED PROGRAMMING?

If you don't build a bridge, a dam, or a building through sound design, planning, and construction, it will crumble under stress. This idea is so obvious in the field of architecture that it's a wonder we have such a hard time accepting the notion in the software field. While you can build a shed without knowing a great deal about engineering or design, you cannot build a cathedral without mastering more sophisticated construction and planning techniques.

To build today's complex software it is no longer sufficient to glue together sequences of machine instructions, high-level language statements, or even sets of procedures and modules, hoping to find a way to weave through the maze of variable names, procedure names, and filenames to string together a robust program. Today's sophisticated programs require practical construction techniques along with guidelines for laying down a sound program structure that is easy to flesh out, comprehend, and modify.

THE ARCHITECTURE OF SOFTWARE

Alan Kay, the principal designer of Smalltalk, once said "As complexity increases, architecture dominates material." Kay uses the example of spanning two columns, or an opening in a building, using bricks. Although you might know a lot about the material properties of bricks—how to bind them together, how to build walls, floors, and other common structures with them—unless you know the principle of the arch, you are going to have trouble spanning a large opening with bricks. If you are practiced in the principle of the arch, the problem is trivial. Discovery of the arch made it possible to span greater distances with less material and led to a renaissance in architecture resulting in construction of buildings that were not only larger, but also capable of supporting greater loads.

That is the point at which we've arrived in software. The way we put software together is now dominated more by structural organization than by raw material. You might think of machine language statements or high-level language statements as the raw material of software. Data structures, procedures, and functions provide a way of packaging raw material. The structures built from such components can be quite sophisticated. But ultimately, as systems grow in size and complexity, the approach of laying one brick on top of another strains the integrity of the entire structure and a fragile system results.

There is still much to learn about the structure and composition of software systems. A lot has been discovered over the past ten years about structuring techniques that eases the construction and maintenance of large programs. The idea is not to ignore raw material and packaging in order to concentrate on structure and composition. The basics must still be mastered: forming expressions and statements, so that you can predict the values they will return; grouping statements into subroutines to create abstract procedures; setting aside storage for variables; creating complex data structures from the basic data types of a programming language. But mastering raw material is not enough. Anyone who has tried to program knows that there is more involved than simply gluing together sequences of machine instructions or high-level language statements to create a program that will even run—much less a program that will do something useful or interesting.

Evolution of Design

Structured programming has given programmers a tool of immeasurable power. Most programmers today are schooled in structured programming techniques and take the architectural principles introduced by structured programming for granted. Structured programming can be equated to the discovery of the arch—it allowed the engineers and architects of software to build constructs that were not only stronger and more stable, but that were built with less effort and material. It allowed them to do more with less.

Accomplishing more with less is possible through the discovery of general principles and applying those principles to the construction of systems. Principles must first be discovered, articulated, and tested. If a general principle survives the rigors of testing, and proves to be a useful tool, then it is foolish not to apply the principle in practice. Structured programming lays down a set of principles for the construction of software systems resulting from years of observation and study of program construction techniques.

The arch has been part of our engineering and design vocabulary for so long that we take it for granted. But the arch was not always used in the construction of large buildings. The arch solves a practical problem: spanning an opening in a building while providing structural support for the building. The problem of spanning an opening was not always solved using an arch. Figure 1-1 shows the evolution of ideas in architecture for solving the problem of spanning an opening while providing sound structural support for bearing heavy loads.

The arch is an example of doing more with less: more structural integrity with less physical material. The truss and the cantilever show another step forward in the evolution of architecture and building construction. Object-oriented programming is the next evolutionary step in the design and construction of software.

The Promise of Object-Oriented Architecture

Object-oriented programming was one of the first programming systems to acknowledge that change and evolution in a program are not only inevitable, but desirable. Object-oriented programming seeks to minimize the impact of change through the technique of *encapsulation*. Object-oriented programming also encourages the reuse of existing code and makes code reuse practical.

Although structured languages acknowledge code reuse as a goal, they have not been able to deliver code that can be easily modified. Even though

Figure 1-1. Evolution of structure in architecture. Advanced structuring principles reduce the effort and material required to solve a specific problem.

libraries are cited in structured languages as a means for reusing code, the stability required by libraries is an impediment to adapting them easily to special case problems. Object-oriented programming circumvents this restriction through *dynamic binding*.

Programmers used to thinking in terms of procedures often feel disoriented when trying to understand the purpose of objects and the structure of object-oriented programs. They hear over and over that object-oriented programming requires a whole new way of thinking—forget everything you already know. Nothing could be further from the truth. Regardless of what anyone says, the better practiced you are in principles of good structured design and coding, the easier it will be for you to make the transition to objects.

Object-oriented programming simply formalizes practices that good programmers already use with structured languages. If you already know you should try to limit the use of global variables, or at least isolate and group together procedures that do share data, you are already practicing many of the principles of object-oriented programming. Even with objects, coding ultimately boils down to the construction of procedures, or *methods*. It is simply the packaging of program components that is different. Object-oriented programming requires that you explicitly describe relationships between procedures and shared data.

Many programmers already package shared data and procedures in separately compiled modules or files and restrict access to those modules to a small set of interface procedures. Defining such a module is the same thing as defining an object. Object-oriented languages simply formalize the structure and provide a way for the compiler to ensure that your code does not violate access restrictions that you specify.

There is nothing new in object-oriented programming, and yet everything is new. This paradox prevents programmers from knowing when and how to use object-oriented programming. Today, more than ever, the principles of structured programming hold firm. What is new, is a slight mental twist—a shift in perspective that lets you see a structure found in most well-crafted procedure-based programs.

The difference with object-oriented programming is an equal emphasis placed on data and actions. Structured programming tends to emphasize actions. Functions and procedures are viewed as the basic units of construction. This perspective gives rise to the technique of top-down stepwise refinement originally championed by Nicklaus Wirth, the inventor of Pascal. Abstract actions are broken down into more and more concrete steps until each step can be specified as a programming language statement.

However, many problems are better resolved from the bottom up or from both directions at once—or using even a third system in which a structure does not even have a top (*event-driven systems*). The building of reusable components is just as important as the design of overall structure. Object-oriented class libraries provide truly reusable components without locking users into a limited set of data types.

LEARNING THE BASICS

This book takes a somewhat unconventional approach in presenting the concepts of object-oriented programming. Rather than introducing the language features of object-oriented programming languages one by one, this book starts with complete example programs introduced in the context of object-oriented concepts as a whole. Presumably you already know something about procedure-based programs. You can get hints about the purpose of new object-oriented language features when you see them used in context.

If you can read C or Pascal code, and you know the general structure of an object-oriented program, you'll be surprised at how much C++ code you can already understand. You'll find that expressions using new object-oriented features jump out and puzzle you. Often you can guess the purpose of new features and syntax because they automate or simplify tasks that were formerly accomplished manually or through use of awkward data structures and control constructs. Seeing new features used in context will bring to mind questions that will make you a better reader when language features are more formally introduced. The intent is to establish motivation before covering detail.

Most books on object-oriented programming focus on a single language. The typical approach presents each of the features of a given language. Once the reader works through the presentation of language features, object-oriented concepts are introduced and example programs show how to put the language features to work. Finally the theory of object-oriented program structure is presented. This order of presentation seems logical at first because it follows the natural progression of learning that is required to begin programming with objects: Start with building blocks, move on to structures, then show systems and construction techniques.

If we learned to speak the way most books present the principles of object-oriented programming, we would first learn how to identify nouns and verbs and then how to properly construct phrases and sentences. We would then move on to using groups of sentences to express a train of thought. Finally, we would get to see examples of how other people use these basic forms of speech to talk to each other. After mastering the basics, someone would sit us down, explain the theory of communication, the place of the basics we have mastered in that theory, and the reason for wanting to talk to someone in the first place. This is not natural. Motivation for expressing an idea is the *first* step of learning to speak, not the last.

Objects Alone Do Not Provide Structure

Many people become frustrated by the traditional approach to learning about objects. It takes a lot of time and effort to learn object-oriented language features and syntax. Programmers frequently question how new features make life easier when they are so hard to master. This feeling is natural when you approach object-oriented programming by first trying to learn about language features and the basic structure of objects. It's hard to stay motivated through this phase because you wonder if there is truly a purpose to it all. You might be inclined to reach the conclusion that object-oriented programming is just another flash in the pan being thrust upon us by an industry that is always looking for something new to sell.

Building Systems from Objects

Object-oriented programming is not a flash in the pan. Nor is object-oriented programming an impractical ivory tower idea—nice in theory, but useless in practice. The people who invented and developed object-oriented programming did not start with basic phrases and language features and then move on to establish a programming practice based on those phrases and features. They were expert programmers with a great deal of practical programming experience, and they used their experience and knowledge to look for ways to simplify the programming process and to address their frustration with existing tools and techniques. In short, they started with an overall concept and a motivation: make programs easier to build and understand.

Understanding, Design, and the Construction of Complex Systems

If the designers of object-oriented programming did not start from the bottom up, why should you? Try to look at object-oriented programs as a whole. Learn to work with objects the same way you learned to speak: by finding complete examples and learning from context. Seek out articulate examples and learn from them. If you take this approach, you will find that object-oriented programming is not that difficult. In fact, object-oriented programming should make life considerably easier. Don't try to grasp all the details. Look for the big picture. When you've got the big picture, you'll find the pieces fall into place quite naturally.

Today it's hard to imagine what the world would be like if the arch had never been discovered. It's likely that one day it will be equally hard to imagine how programs were once built without objects.

2

BASICS OF OBJECT-ORIENTED PROGRAMMING

Object-oriented programming is a structuring technique. In object-oriented programming, objects are the principal elements of construction. However, simply understanding what an object is or using objects in a program does not mean you are programming in an object-oriented fashion. It is the way objects are pieced together that counts.

In procedural programming it is possible to build a program out of procedural elements and still violate principles of sound construction. Simply knowing what a procedure is or how to build one doesn't guarantee that you will build a robust, bug-free program that is easy to use, easy to read, and easy to modify. The same is true of an object-oriented approach. That's why it's important to start with a perspective of the overall structure of object-oriented programming.

WHAT IS OBJECT-ORIENTED PROGRAMMING?

If one is to be strict about the exact meaning of object-oriented programming, it is programming by sending messages to objects of unknown type.

Such objects would be found in an array or in a collection such as a desktop. All objects in the collection share certain characteristics (such as knowledge of screen location and the ability to be repositioned, activated, or deactivated). From the programmer's perspective, selection of an object within the collection does not provide information about the object's exact type.

Since the type of an object is not known when a message is sent to it, the exact response of the object cannot be predicted. Again, sending messages to objects of unknown type is a powerful programming technique, and what is truly meant by the term *object-oriented programming*.

Windowing environments, such as Microsoft Windows and the desktop in the Smalltalk programming environment, provide examples where an object's precise type is not always known. For instance, the objects displayed on the screen might be scrollbars, text, windows, icons, menus, buttons, or other types of controllers. Each of these objects responds to messages sent by the user in the form of keypresses or mouse clicks, and different things will happen depending on which object is being pointed to when the message is sent. For example, if the mouse pointer is directed at the minimize button when the left mouse button is pressed, the window or application will be turned into an icon. If, on the other hand, the mouse pointer is directed at the file save selection of a word processor menu, then the file currently being edited will be saved to disk.

Polymorphism, Inheritance, and Encapsulation

The objects on a desktop, like the ones just described, are known as *polymorphic objects*. That means that they share certain characteristics in common, such as the ability to be put in a single collection (a desktop, for example), and the ability to respond to the same messages. Polymorphism is directly related to inheritance. Programming by *inheritance* allows you to define new objects by describing how they differ from existing objects. For example, in Smalltalk, a prompt window behaves just like a text editor window, except that the prompt window only holds a single line of text.

If you've been to any lectures or read any books on object-oriented programming, you've heard the terms *encapsulation*, *inheritance*, and *polymorphism*. You may have seen the ubiquitous encapsulation-inheritance-polymorphism triangle illustrated or projected on a screen. Inheritance and polymorphism are quite complex and require the understanding of some preliminary concepts. This chapter will use these terms in general, but complete discussion of inheritance and polymorphism is deferred until the next chapter.

Encapsulation, on the other hand, fits more easily into a discussion of preliminary concepts. This chapter introduces objects and classes, and explains how objects encapsulate data and procedure into a single entity. It also explains how objects are created from class definitions and how objects communicate. Though you must start with objects, the perspective to be emphasized is the framework, or program structure. Rather than being seen as a set of procedures, an object-oriented program is best understood as a set of communicating objects. Emphasizing objects, rather than actions, leads to a very different program structure than is typical of procedure-oriented programs.

Program Structure

Good structuring techniques for procedural programming are well established. Procedures are the basic building blocks in procedural programming. One commonly used technique is *top-down stepwise refinement*, in which you start with the most general view possible of the overall program structure and break the program up into smaller manageable pieces — procedures. That is, you begin by describing what you want the program to do in a single statement: "I need a program to count the number of words in a file." Next you express a preliminary abstract solution by describing the general steps required to solve the problem, for example:

1. Open the file.

2. Read the next word from the file.

3. Increment a word counter.

4. At the end of the file report the number of words read.

5. Close the file.

   The strategy is to keep breaking down each subtask until eventually you get to the point where you can express the steps for a given task with statements from the desired programming language.

Most procedural programs are more complicated than a word counting program, but the process for breaking a complex problem down into manageable subtasks is the same, regardless of complexity. Starting from general abstractions you break down the problem gradually into steps that become more and more concrete. From this analysis you develop levels of abstraction. In the final programming solution you will have more general procedures calling more concrete procedures (subroutines) until finally you reach the lowest level of abstraction, which can be expressed directly as programming language statements. This *hierarchical decomposition* of a problem gives rise to a structure like that shown in Figure 2-1.

The techniques of hierarchical decomposition and stepwise refinement are so common that most programmers use them without conscious effort—they automatically look for the procedures in a given problem. But two notions underlying these techniques are challenged by the object-oriented approach. The first notion is that programming should be approached from the top down, and the second is that a program is a series of procedures or actions invoked one after the other.

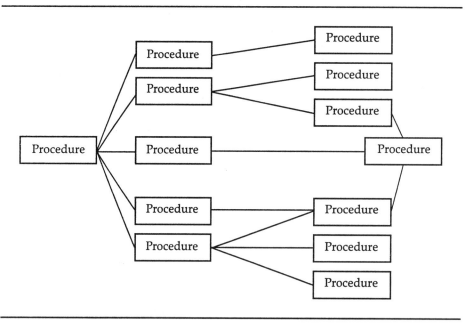

Figure 2-1.   Ideal program structure for procedural programming. Local data is hidden inside procedures. Shared data is passed in arguments.

Compare the representation of a procedural program in Figure 2-1 to the diagram of a typical object-oriented program in Figure 2-2. You can easily see the difference in structure. But Figure 2-2 also tells you a number of other things about object-oriented programming.

First of all, the figure shows that objects are the primary structural units in the program. This in itself doesn't tell you much since the exact structure of objects has not yet been covered. However, objects tend to be described by nouns rather than verbs. Objects in the problem space map more directly to objects in the program than to procedures. Object-oriented programs are often described as *simulations* because objects in the program usually mimic the behavior of their real-world counterparts.

A second observation, which is less obvious from Figure 2-2, is that objects can also be thought of as tasks or processes. In fact, two names

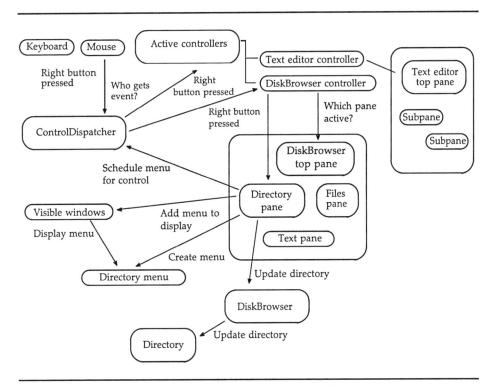

Figure 2-2.   Ideal program structure for object-oriented programming. A program is a set of objects that communicate through messages.

originally given to objects by Smalltalk developers were *task* and *activity*. Examples of objects in Figure 2-2 include "Keyboard", "Mouse", "Control Dispatcher", and "DiskBrowser".

Processing takes place inside of objects, and information is passed back and forth between objects. Objects can invoke processing in other objects by sending *messages*. Example messages in Figure 2-2 include "Right button pressed", "Update directory", "Create menu", and "Display menu". The main thing Figure 2-2 makes obvious is that an object-oriented program is a set of communicating tasks.

The program diagrammed in Figure 2-2 is a Smalltalk DiskBrowser. Actually, this is only a partial diagram of the program. A DiskBrowser consists of five windows, only one of which is represented in the diagram. The diagram shows the communication that would take place among some of the objects on the Smalltalk desktop if the right mouse button were pressed while pointing at the directory list pane of a DiskBrowser object. Figure 2-3 shows the Browser window.

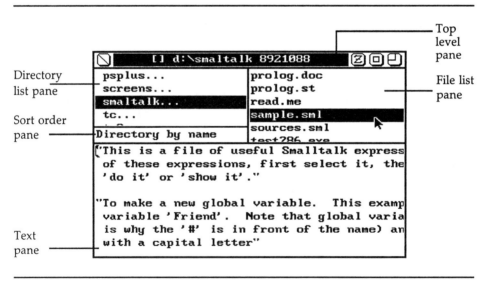

Figure 2-3.   A Smalltalk DiskBrowser is composed of dozens of communicating objects. The five visible window panes constitute the interface through which a DiskBrowser object can be manipulated.

It only takes a couple of steps to see how a procedural program structure evolves into an object-oriented structure. Take a look at Figure 2-4. Whereas Figure 2-1 represents the ideal, Figure 2-4 represents actual programming practice. The ideal advocates hiding information as much as possible to keep the components of a program modular. Local data is hidden inside of procedures, and information that needs to be shared by procedures is passed in the form of procedural arguments.

Sometimes, however, the number of procedures that need to share information is too large, or the data structures themselves are too large to be easily passed among procedures. In such cases, global data is used. The problem with using global data is that it can be altered by any procedure within the program. This makes it easy for bugs to creep in. And it makes it difficult to track down bugs because the scope of the statements that could possibly cause an observed problem is now the entire program.

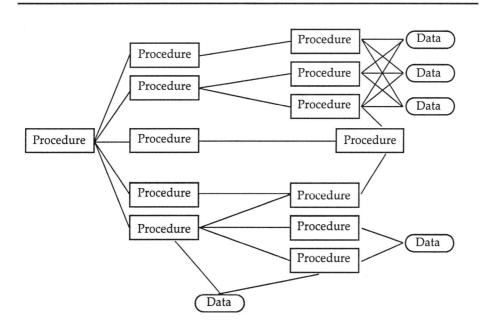

Figure 2-4.   Procedural program structure with global data. Global data structures are used frequently to provide access to information shared by several procedures.

The concepts of data hiding and data abstraction were introduced to deal with the problem of unrestricted access to global data. Figure 2-5 shows a structuring technique where the relationships between global data and the procedures allowed to alter global data are made explicit. It is possible to practice this form of organization without programming language features that enforce the boundaries drawn around associated procedures and data. However, the technique is much more effective when directly supported by the language.

Figure 2-6 shows a structural element from a procedural environment with support for data abstraction. The resulting component is an object. The object component or module is divided into public and private parts.

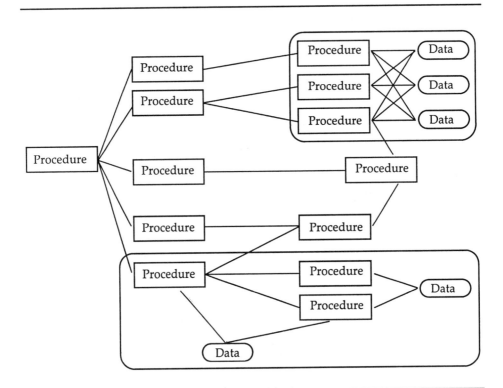

Figure 2-5.   Procedural program structure with data hiding. Object-oriented programming acknowledges the tendency to use global data and provides tools to make the relationships between global data and procedures explicit.

Only procedures within the object are allowed access to the private data elements. This ensures that data is not accidentally altered by procedures outside the structural boundary. If erroneous data is found when debugging the structure, it can be immediately traced to one of the three procedures that have access to the data. All processing inside the structure must be activated through one of the public procedures. This bundling of procedures and associated data is *encapsulation*.

Objects

You've already seen that objects are the primary structural units in object-oriented programming. Figure 2-6 gives you a pretty good idea of what an object looks like. Giving specific names to the data and procedural elements found inside an object helps clarify the representation and purpose of an object.

Figure 2-7 shows how a point might be represented as an object. Points turn out to be very useful objects in windowing systems, computer-aided design programs, and drawing tools. A real point object would provide

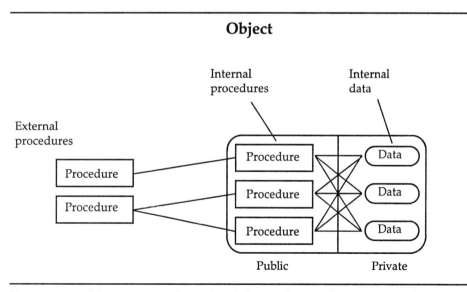

Figure 2-6.   Objects encapsulate related data and procedures and guard against unwanted access to data elements.

many more procedures in the public interface, but this simplified representation will give a better feel for the structure and behavior of a typical
object. The C++ definition used to create an object like that in Figure 2-7
looks like this:

```
class Point
{
    int x;
    int y;
public:
    void setXY(int a, int b)
    {
        x = a;
        y = b;
    }
    int getX () { return x; }
    int getY () { return y; }
};
```

This code is a template describing the internal data and procedural
elements of a Point object. In this implementation, point objects have two
data elements representing x and y positions on a two-dimensional grid.

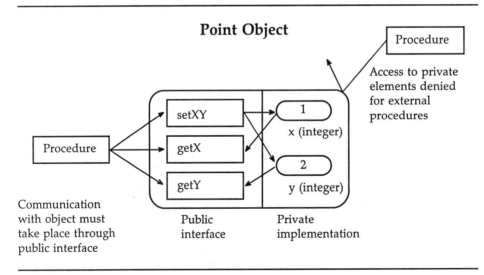

Figure 2-7.   A Point object demonstrates data hiding. Objects are characterized
by their public interface, which indicates what an object can do, not
how an object is represented.

Only one procedure, setXY, is allowed to modify these data values. The two other procedures, getX and getY, are used only to return the respective values to requesting objects and procedures.

Data and procedures are encapsulated in a protective shell to prevent unwanted modification. Objects also remember things. This means objects have a *state*. The state of an object is remembered by its data components. In addition, objects can process information, although there is not much processing that goes on within the point object shown in Figure 2-7. The procedures merely set the values of the private data and return those values upon request. Real objects, however, generally have more sophisticated processing ability.

The last thing to note about objects that particularly distinguishes them from procedures is that objects have a life cycle. They can be created and destroyed. As long as an object is alive and active, you may access any of its public elements. After it has been destroyed, any memory used by the object is reclaimed, and it is no longer possible to communicate with the object.

Figure 2-8 shows the actual representation of a Pane object, which is one of many reusable components found in the DiskBrowser object diagrammed earlier. Recall that the DiskBrowser has five panes. Any one of those panes will respond to messages directed to the public procedures in Figure 2-8. Rather than showing each public procedure in a separate box, Figure 2-8 groups related procedures. One of the things you can learn from this diagram is that every pane has a private menu associated with it: paneMenuSelector. However, you do not need to know about paneMenu-Selector in order to activate the menu associated with a given pane. You would simply send the message popUpAt to the desired pane.

Classes

Classes are templates for objects. Classes are like types in a traditional programming language. The difference is that users can define new types in an object-oriented programming language. Types that most programmers are familiar with include integers, characters, floating point numbers, and strings (in Pascal). If a class is like a type in a traditional programming language, then an object is like a variable. Sometimes objects are referred to as *instances* of a class.

Pane Object

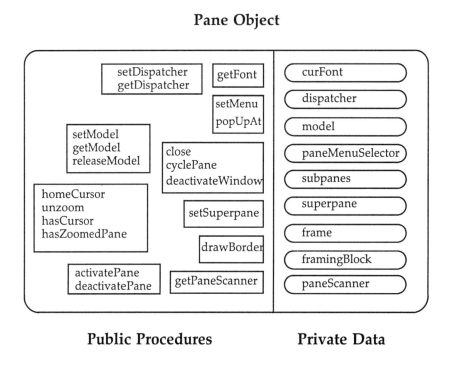

Public Procedures   **Private Data**

Figure 2-8.   A Smalltalk Pane object shows a more elaborate interface protocol.

The code listed earlier for creating a Point object is a *class definition*. A class definition by itself does not create any objects. However, the class definition can be used like a type to create an object.

```
Point p;
```

This code creates a single object, p, which is a point having undefined values for its internal data elements, x and y. Classes are sometimes called *user-defined types* because the types defined by classes behave like the built-in types of a programming language. Notice that the syntax used to create a point object is no different than the syntax used to create an integer object with C's built-in type int.

```
int i;
```

This code creates a single object, i, which is an integer having an undefined value. The process of programming in an object-oriented language is characterized by:

1. Creating classes that define object representation and behavior
2. Creating objects from class definitions
3. Arranging communication among objects as a sequence of messages

The following listing shows a simple program that uses the Point class.

```
#include <stdio.h>

class Point
{
    int x;
    int y;
public:
    void setXY(int a, int b)
    {
        x = a;
        y = b;
    }
    int getX () { return x; }
    int getY () { return y; }
};

main()
{
    printf("A simple Point class\n");
    Point p;
    p.setXY(1,2);
    printf("p==>%d,%d\n", p.getX(), p.getY());
    p.setXY(3,4);
    printf("p==>%d,%d\n", p.getX(), p.getY());
}
```

In this program, a point is created and then assigned the value 1,2 with setXY. The first printf statement retrieves and prints the respective x and y values of the point. Next the value of the point is changed to 3,4. The second printf statement again retrieves the values of the point with getX and getY, printing the result. It is debatable whether this program is truly object-oriented, but its main purpose is to demonstrate the role of classes in the creation of objects.

Figure 2-9 shows a class definition for a Waiter object. The important thing to understand is the difference between the class Waiter and the objects pierre and helga, which represent instances of the class. *Instances* are created from the class template and contain private copies of the variables defined in the class. These variables are frequently called *instance variables* because they exist in the instance and not in the class itself.

Procedures associated with the class, however, do not really exist inside the object instances. It would not make sense to duplicate these over and over again, since they are the same for all objects of a given class. Diagrams will frequently list these procedures inside the object itself, but technically they reside elsewhere. However, access to these procedures is always mediated through objects created from the class in which the procedures are defined.

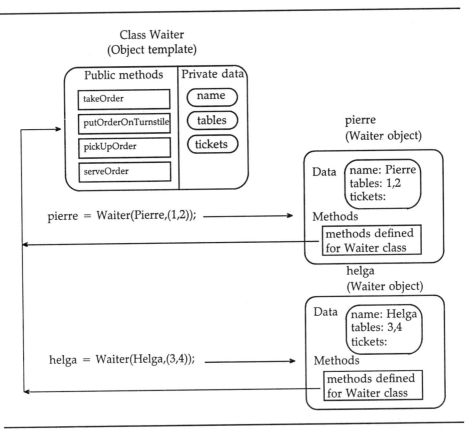

Figure 2-9.   Classes are templates for creating objects. Each object retains a private copy of the data defined in the class template. Code for class methods is shared by objects of the same class.

Communication

Objects communicate with one another by sending messages. You've seen an overview of how this works in Figure 2-2. The term *messages* has been used somewhat loosely up to this point. In fact, many of the terms of object-oriented programming represent only slight refinements of their use in everyday language. This was a conscious choice on the part of the designers of Smalltalk, one of the first object-oriented languages. It was intended that Smalltalk be used by children as well as adults. Thus, the metaphors used to express basic programming concepts had to come from experience that children could grasp. At the same time, however, the metaphors could not restrict the expressive power of the language required by advanced adult users.

One of the basic metaphors developed was the notion that objects communicate by sending messages. Objects send and receive information by passing messages much the way people do. One example is the turnstile in a restaurant, used to pass information about an order from a waiter to a cook. Messages have a counterpart called methods. Messages and methods are two sides of the same coin. *Methods* are the procedures that are invoked when an object receives a message.

In traditional programming terminology, a message is a *call* from one procedure to another. A method is the actual code or procedure definition that is invoked. At first this change in terminology appears arbitrary, even trivial. But that's because traditional languages do not support polymorphism and message dispatching handled by the objects themselves at run time. These subjects will be taken up at the appropriate time. In the meantime, the message-passing terminology makes it easier to talk about building systems that directly model or simulate their real-world counterparts.

Methods and messages help enforce division of labor. The turnstile message-passing system in the restaurant draws a boundary and defines functional responsibility. The boundary keeps a clean division between the work done by the waiter or waitress and the work done by the cook. The waiter sends a message to the cook by way of the turnstile. A method is carried out by the receiving object in response to a message. A method is like a recipe. The cook has a number of methods for preparing various orders. The cook follows a method for preparing an order of scrambled eggs upon receipt of the appropriate message. The distinction between methods and messages keeps the waiter in the dining room and the cook in the kitchen.

Figure 2-10 shows a simulation of activities or tasks that take place in a typical restaurant. The basic objects in the simulation are tables, customers, waiters, cooks, the turnstile, and a counter. The main thing to make note of is that all objects in the simulation are connected through messages. Messages provide communication through narrow bandwidth interfaces to objects- .Message passing reduces the number of connections among system components. Reducing the number of connections increases the modularity of system components.

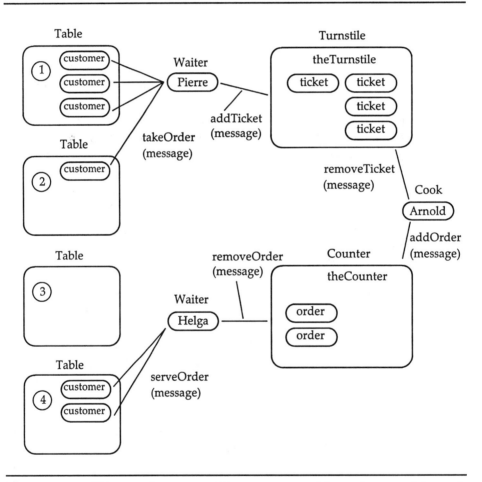

Figure 2-10.   Objects and messages. Objects are created from class templates and communicate by passing messages.

Another thing that may not be immediately obvious is that objects can contain other objects. For instance, a table contains a collection of customers, and a turnstile contains a collection of order tickets. How one object communicates with another depends on the interface. For example, a waiter can directly communicate with each customer at a table. In the simulation the table would tell the waiter how many customers are at the table by returning a list of customers to the waiter. The waiter would then take the order from each member of the list.

The interface to the turnstile is slightly different, however. The only thing that a waiter can do with a turnstile is add an order ticket. The only thing a cook can do with the turnstile is remove the next ticket. This turnstile functions more like a stack than a true turnstile because individual elements of the turnstile (tickets) cannot be accessed directly.

So far you know that objects send and receive messages. You also know that messages are procedure calls. In addition, messages carry information. They do so through arguments and return values, just as procedures do. For instance, Pierre the waiter might send a message carrying information in the form of an argument to the turnstile:

```
theTurnstile.addTicket(aTicket);
```

In this expression, aTicket is an argument to the message addTicket, which is sent to the object theTurnstile. Messages might also return information. For instance, a waiter might look at the counter to see if an order is ready. This activity would be simulated by having the waiter ask the counter if an order is ready.

```
if (theCounter.isOrderReady())
  anOrder = theCounter.removeOrder();
```

Both the messages isOrderReady and removeOrder return information to the waiter. The former returns a boolean value indicating whether the order is ready. The latter returns an actual object, which is the order. The waiter can now carry out another method to deliver the order to the appropriate table. In addition to carrying information, messages can also invoke processing.

Processing

Processing is directly associated with methods. As mentioned above, *method* is just another word for *procedure*. Sometimes methods are referred to as *member functions* because they are members of an object. So far, all the methods you have seen are public. But methods may be private as well. Public methods are not generally associated with the concept of processing. The usual function of public methods is to provide access to an object's instance variables and to receive messages, as you have seen. Requesting access to private data is a form of processing, but only in the technical sense of the word.

A very complex process may be invoked through a simple message. For instance, a Directory object may be asked to update itself. Such a message request would invoke processing inside the object that is much more complex than merely fetching the values of instance variables. In such a case a public interface method might call one or more private methods that do all the dirty work. For example, processing inside a DiskBrowser object takes place through private methods that find all the directories on the currently logged disk, sort the entries, update the presentation in the window, and inform other windows that a change has been made.

Figure 2-11 shows the methods inside objects as well as the messages passed by objects. The waiter, for example, has a method, putOrderOn-Turnstile. This method sends the message addTicket to the turnstile object. The turnstile object has a method addTicket, which responds to the message addTicket. The external message and the internal method have the same name. Again, it may seem trivial to make the distinction between the message received and the method invoked since both bear the same name. However, when polymorphism and function overloading come into play, a message could possibly invoke one of many different methods with exactly the same name.

Figure 2-11 also shows an example of private methods inside the cook object. No one can communicate with the cook directly. The cook keeps checking the turnstile for a ticket. Once a ticket is on the turnstile, it is up to the cook to take the ticket. He then has three different private methods he can carry out based on the information contained in the ticket. This is exactly the type of processing objects were designed for.

The interface to the cook object is narrow. There are only two channels through which information (or objects) can flow. A narrow interface keeps lines of communication from becoming crossed in a complex system. Once

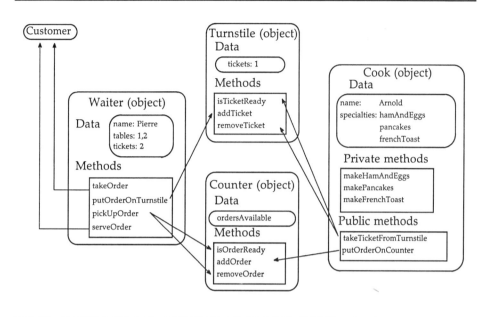

Figure 2-11.   Messages invoke methods and methods send messages.

an object takes control for processing a message, it is that object's responsibility to carry out the appropriate method in response. Objects outside can't know and don't care how this processing takes place, as illustrated in Figure 2-12.

Processing and its relationship to message passing among objects can be understood in terms of traditional programming concepts. Objects contain procedures. Procedures inside objects are called methods. Methods respond to messages. Methods process information. Methods are executable code.

WHY IS OBJECT-ORIENTED PROGRAMMING IMPORTANT?

Object-oriented programming tools help manage complexity. Making software that is easy to use makes software hard to build. Sophisticated user interfaces, windowing systems, and multitasking programs are making software more complex than ever. What object-oriented programming tools do

Figure 2-12.   Once a message has been passed to an object, objects outside can't know and don't care how processing takes place.

is help manage that complexity. The whole raison d'être of object-oriented programming is to provide a way to structure and manage complex relationships among a large number of system components.

Object-oriented structuring reduces the number of connections among system components. Forcing objects to communicate through a narrow public interface makes it is easier to isolate bugs and determine which methods are responsible for the bugs that do occur.

Objects themselves protect private data from unwanted modification. Explicit definition of communication protocol allows compilers and interpreters to warn users about illegal access and even to prevent unwanted modification of system components.

One of the greatest benefits of an object-oriented structure is the direct mapping from objects in the problem domain to objects in the program. This direct mapping is a consequence of having a structure based on objects. If programming is viewed as simulation, it's much easier to pick objects out of a simulated world than it is to develop a programming solution based entirely on procedures and actions.

CHAPTER HIGHLIGHTS

To summarize the basic principles of object-oriented programming:

Program Structure

- Objects are primary structural units.
- Objects are tasks or processes.
- A program is a set of communicating tasks.

Objects

- Objects bundle data and procedures.
- Objects remember information (data).
- Objects process information (procedures).
- Objects have a life cycle.

Classes

- Classes are templates for objects.
- Objects are created from class specifications.
- Classes are types.

Communication

- Objects send and receive messages.
- Messages carry information.
- Messages invoke processing.
- Messages are procedure calls.

Processing

- Objects contain procedures.
- Procedures inside objects are methods.
- Methods process information.
- Methods are executable code.

3

INHERITANCE, POLYMORPHISM, AND OBJECT-ORIENTED PROGRAMMING

Objects encapsulate data and action and communicate by passing messages, as shown in the preceding chapter. But, as was also mentioned, simply using classes to create objects and sending messages to objects does not comprise object-oriented programming. In addition to encapsulation, object-oriented programs make use of inheritance and polymorphism. *Inheritance* involves classification of objects according to shared properties. *Polymorphism* involves sending messages to objects of unknown type.

The previous chapter defined object-oriented programming as programming by sending messages to objects of unknown type. This is a little imprecise. Object-oriented programs send messages to objects whose exact type is not known. However, the programmer sending these polymorphic messages knows that all the objects in a polymorphic collection have something in common. At a minimum, polymorphic objects share a common set of names in their public interface. This common set of names is referred to as the objects' *communication protocol*.

Objects can be classified according to the features they share. Even though a set of objects might define a common set of method names for a communication protocol, some objects might provide methods that other objects do not. Further, even when method names are the same, method definitions might differ. For example, a draw method for a circle object would have to be implemented differently than a draw method for a rectangle.

Polymorphism exploits the features shared by a set of objects. Thus, if you have a collection consisting only of circles and rectangles, you can safely send a draw message to any element in the collection. The response, however, will be slightly different depending on whether the message receiver is a circle or a rectangle. Inheritance provides the tool for expressing the properties or communication protocol common to a set of objects. Polymorphism assures that objects respond to general messages in their own unique ways.

POLYMORPHIC COLLECTIONS

Consider how polymorphism applies to a collection of windows on a computer desktop. Windows come in a variety of shapes and forms. That is to say, there are many different types of windows. In Figure 3-1 you can see several different types of windows.

One of the first things you do when you see a set of new things is fit them into a framework that makes sense to you. You try to find a way to classify new information in ways that help you attach meaning to it. One way to do this is to look for similarities in objects. What properties do the objects in Figure 3-1 share?

Loosely speaking, all five items on the screen are windows. You may hesitate to call the File Manager and Paintbrush icons windows since they do not have the same shape as the other windows. But they do have other properties that let them be classified as windows. The other three display objects in Figure 3-1 clearly are windows: they are all rectangular, and they all have title bars and a surrounding frame border. In addition, each of these three windows has a control-menu box in the upper-left corner, as well as minimize and maximize buttons in the upper-right corner.

All of these are *observable* properties—properties you can see without interacting with the windows directly. Other properties define the way windows behave. Examining the *behavioral* properties of windows gives a clue as to why the File Manager and Paintbrush icons can be classified as windows.

One common property of windows is control menus. All top-level windows contain menus and respond to messages that are sent when a menu

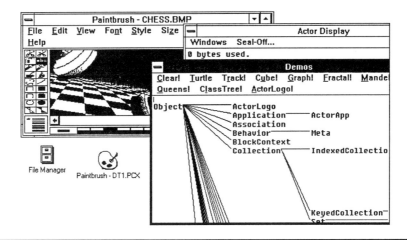

Figure 3-1.   Windows come in a variety of shapes and forms.

selection is made. Figure 3-2 shows four windows in the form of icons. Clicking a mouse button on the Program Manager icon causes the menu shown in Figure 3-2 to appear. (In fact, clicking the left mouse button on any of the icons in the figure would cause the same menu to appear.) The

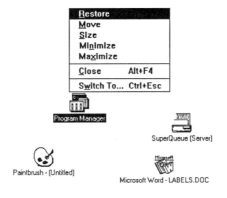

Figure 3-2.   Icons have behavior that classifies them as windows.

menu associated with a particular icon will always appear directly above that icon. So one way icons behave differently is by specifying different locations for presenting their menus. Although it's a minor difference in behavior, this nuance is important if you want to understand a window system, and critical if you are trying to program one.

A menu is also a form of window. However, menus behave very differently from icons. If you point to the first entry in the menu in Figure 3-2 and press the left mouse button, you will get a very different response than if you point at the Paintbrush icon and do exactly the same thing. Pointing to the menu choice Restore and pressing the left mouse button causes the corresponding application window to be restored to the size and position it occupied before it was turned into an icon. Pointing to the Paintbrush icon, on the other hand, and pressing the left mouse button will cause the menu above the Program Manager icon to disappear and cause another menu exactly like it to appear above the Paintbrush icon.

The menu shown in Figure 3-2 is a *control menu*. Such a menu is associated with every top-level window, whether the window is displayed as an icon or as a full-sized window. One difference between an iconized window and an expanded window is that the expanded window's control menu won't allow Restore to be selected. This is communicated to the user by displaying the menu entry in gray rather than black.

As seen in Figure 3-3, the same menu that was available to the Program Manager icon is available to the Program Manager window. The difference in behavior is that in the icon you can produce the menu by pointing anywhere inside it and pressing the left mouse button, whereas in the expanded window you must point specifically to the control-menu box in the upper-left corner of the window.

The menu itself gives you another hint about the behavioral properties of top-level windows. Each window must be able to handle the messages that result from selecting menu choices. At the very least, window objects must know how to restore, move, size, minimize, maximize, and close themselves. In addition, windows must provide a way for control to switch to other window applications.

The last several paragraphs could serve as the beginning of an introduction to working with Microsoft Windows. The reason for pointing this out is that introductory discussions, on almost any topic, are rife with material that explains how things work: how general classes of things behave in similar ways, and how specific things from the same class behave in different ways. This little hint can save you a lot of digging when initially

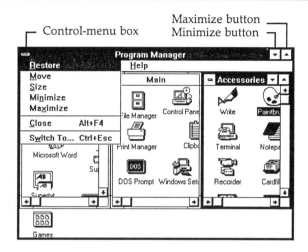

Figure 3-3.   Icons and windows have the same control menu.

tackling an object-oriented programming task. Look for introductory litera-
ture in the subject area of the programming problem for names and de-
scriptions of objects, classes, and methods.

For now, the main points of interest in the discussion on windows are
types of things, *classification* of things, and *properties* that things have in
common.

CLASSIFICATION

Object-oriented programming is a style of programming that seeks to minimize complexity by reducing the number of connections among the components of a software system. Message passing is one way this is
accomplished. Another way is the definition of a simple communication
protocol, which is channeled through a narrow public interface of component objects. For communication to be simple, it must be general—special-
case issues are temporarily ignored. The more general the communication
protocol, the fewer the number of special-case messages that need to be
sent to objects.

Consequently, one of the first things to think about, after determining the objects that will make up a program, is the general properties shared by objects. Objects that share common properties are grouped into *classes*. A base object can then be defined for each class.

Objects whose behavior does not exactly correspond to the general behavior of the base object become specializations of the base object's definition. These objects inherit the general properties of the base object and then are further defined by how they differ.

Special cases are handled by creating subclasses of objects from the base class. The *base* class defines general properties, the subclasses, or *derived* classes define the special properties.

Recall the activities required to build an object-oriented program:

1. Create classes that define object representation and behavior.

2. Create objects from class definitions.

3. Arrange communication among objects as a sequence of messages.

Classification relates directly to step 1, the creation of classes that define object behavior. The properties used for classifying objects will differ depending on the application. The purpose of classification is to impose some form of order on a group of objects and to define a common protocol for communicating with that group.

Figure 3-4 shows a group of shape objects for which no order has been imposed, and Figure 3-5 shows a classification based on object size. If one of the goals of the program were to manipulate all shapes according to size, size would need to be one of the properties defined in the general base class from which all specific shapes are derived, for example:

```
class Shape
{
    int size;
    // ...
public;
    void setSize(int s) { size = s; }
    int  getSize()      { return size; }
    // ...
};
```

You would then create Circle, Rectangle, and Triangle classes, which are derived from the Shape class. Automatically, without your doing any other

Figure 3-4.   Classification imposes order

programming, these derived classes inherit methods to set and check the size of a shape object.

Alternatively, if you did not plan to do any processing of shapes that requires knowledge of their size, you would not specify methods and data

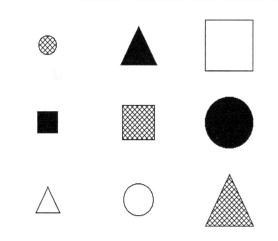

Figure 3-5.   Classification by size

in the Shape class for that purpose. Or, if you only needed to know size for certain special cases, the support for size information could be put only in the derived classes.

In another scenario, you might need to communicate with a certain subset of objects based on their color. Figure 3-6 shows such a classification. An organization like this might be necessary if you were designing CAD software for the layout of printed circuit boards. Circuit traces on the top of the board would be represented in one color, and traces on the bottom would be represented in another color. Multilayered circuit boards might require even more colors to designate each individual layer. In any case, when working on a drawing, you typically want to see only one layer at a time. The view presented on the computer screen would need to classify trace objects according to color. Consequently color information would be encoded directly in the Shape base class. The code for this would be written as follows:

```
class Shape
{
    int color;
    // ...
public;
    void setColor(int c) { color = c; }
    int  getColor()      { return color; }
    // ...
};
```

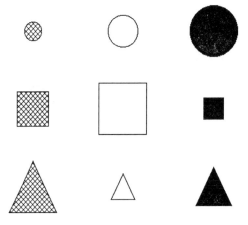

Figure 3-6.   Classification by color

Other criteria for classifying shape objects are also possible. For instance, Figure 3-7 shows the very likely situation in which it is necessary to organize or manipulate objects according to their shape. This poses a unique problem. Since the Shape class is implemented before the classes that are derived from it, the type of every shape derived from Shape cannot be known ahead of time. There are two ways to handle this. One way would be to include a field in the Shape class so that every object derived from it would know its type, as in:

```
class Shape
{
    int shapeType;
    // ...
public;
    void setShapeType(int st) { shapeType = st; }
    int  getShapeType()       { return shapeType; }
    // ...
};
```

Although this is one possible organization, programs that base message dispatching on the type of an object can quickly become a maintenance nightmare if they store type information explicitly inside of objects. True object-oriented programming allows message dispatching based on type. But what does this mean?

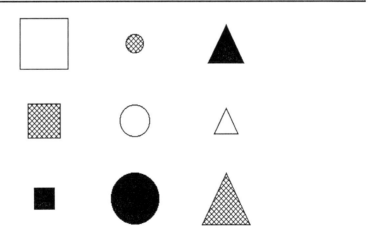

Figure 3-7.   Classification by shape

First, recall that the reason for classifying objects is to simplify message-passing protocol. For example, it would be nice if you did not have to remember a different method name for each type of shape object you might want to draw, hide, or move. Remember that when a user points to an object on the screen, such as a window or a shape, the program cannot predict the exact type of the object. The program simply guarantees that only a certain class of objects can be displayed, so you know that the object is ultimately derived from a particular base class.

Consider a scenario in which a user points to an object, clicks and holds the left mouse button, drags the object to a new location, and releases the mouse button. (To simplify the analysis, discussion will be confined to shape objects which include circles, rectangles, and triangles.) Among other actions, a moveTo message must be sent to the shape in question. Communication with the object is general.

```
moveTo(anObject,newLocation);
```

Message dispatching, however, is a special case. This is because the techniques for erasing a circle and drawing a circle are different from the techniques for erasing and drawing rectangles. How then can communication be kept general while still ensuring that message dispatching directs calls to the appropriate special-case methods?

With the techniques cited, in which type information is stored inside of shape objects, some kind of switch statement could handle the job.

```
void moveTo(Object anObject, Point newLocation)
{
    switch(anObject.shapeType)
        case circle:
            circleMoveTo(anObject, newLocation);
            break;
        case triangle:
            triangleMoveTo(anObject, newLocation);
            break;
        case rectangle:
            rectangleMoveTo(anObject, newLocation);
            break;
        default:
            error("Unknown shape type in moveTo");
            break;
}
```

However, as mentioned earlier, all the various types of objects cannot be known ahead of time. For instance, a programmer might want to extend the original shape class hierarchy. After Shape, Circle, Rectangle, and Triangle are implemented, the programmer may want to implement a Pentagon class. This is quite typical, and a class hierarchy that starts out with 5 or 10 basic types is often extended to include 50 or more special-case types. It would be a nightmare to have to remember unique function names for each of the types.

Remember that even a simple window system responds not only to a Move message, but also to Restore, Size, Minimize, Maximize, Close, and Switch To, for a total of seven possible messages. The number of communication connections needing explicit maintenance by the programmer would be 350—seven methods multiplied by 50 object types. However, by generalizing the communication protocol, the programmer only needs to maintain seven connections for any display object, one for each possible message.

Deciding to generalize and simplify the communication protocol does not eliminate the maintenance of seven switch networks. One switch is still required for each method group. True object-oriented programming eliminates these switches as well, by providing a feature known as *run-time binding*. Dispatch to specific methods is handled by the base class. The programmer states explicitly which base class methods should use run-time binding as the call dispatch mechanism.

INHERITANCE

Inheritance and polymorphism are tools to organize type hierarchies and simplify communication. Inheritance allows the formal definition of commonality to be expressed for a set of objects, whereas polymorphism allows a common protocol to be used when communicating with objects from the same type hierarchy.

As stated earlier, a class of objects is a set of objects that share common features and characteristics. These features and characteristics are defined in a base class. Subsequent classes or types are defined as specializations of the base class. As a programmer you create new types or classes that *inherit* the characteristics of the base class. The new classes are derived classes.

The process of defining new types and reusing code previously developed in base class definitions is called *programming by inheritance*. Classes that inherit properties from a base class may in turn serve as the base definitions for other classes. Hierarchies of types usually take on a tree structure, with the most general properties defined in classes at the root, and the more specific properties defined in the leaves. Such a tree is referred to as a *class hierarchy* or a *type hierarchy*.

Consider the development of a type hierarchy for a set of shapes. The ultimate goal is to be able to rotate a set of shapes on the display around a given reference point. For a first cut, the point of reference will be the origin, or Point(0,0). The program code for this example is presented in C++. To make the code for the Shape class hierarchy portable across different C++ compilers and graphics libraries, an abstract screen class is used. Only one instance of the screen class is used in a given program. The name given to this global instance of the Screen class is screen. The screen class defines an abstract graphics display screen whose x and y coordinates range from Point(0,0) to Point(100,100). Point(0,0) is in the lower-left corner of the screen, and Point(100,100) is in the upper-right corner of the screen.

The screen class provides methods to clear the screen, set the foreground and background colors, and draw lines. The screen class is a good example of how encapsulation of function and data can maximize the programmer's freedom—in this case to change the internal representation of the real screen hardware. The details of the screen class are irrelevant to the discussion of inheritance at this point, so complete analysis of the screen class will be presented when a more thorough discussion of encapsulation is presented. For now it will be obvious what screen class methods do from their names.

The Shape class hierarchy developed here presents a simplified example of dealing with screen display objects that have common properties. Although the examples are simplified, the principles discussed apply equally to coding for more complex graphics systems such as Microsoft Windows or the Smalltalk desktop environment.

The example objects in the simplified Shape class hierarchy are circles, rectangles, and triangles. Having identified the objects that will be found in the final application, you can move on to the next step: looking for common properties of circles, rectangles, and triangles in the context of drawing these shapes on the screen. Eventually they will be rotated around Point(0,0) by a specified angle.

Here is a first stab at expressing the common characteristics of circles, rectangles, and triangles in a base class called Shape. Figure 3-8 shows a base class definition for Shape objects. The following listing shows the C++ code that implements the class diagrammed in Figure 3-8.

```
class Shape
{
    Point       center;
    int         color;
public:
    Point       position()      { return center; }
    void        moveTo(Point p) { center = p; }
    int         getColor()      { return color; }
    void        setColor(int c) { color = c; }
};
```

The objects created from the Shape class template are not especially useful by themselves. Such objects can't do anything other than set and retrieve information about position and color. However, classes which are derived from Shape can provide a little more interesting behavior.

Figure 3-9 shows the class template for a Circle object. Circle objects inherit the private instance variables and the public methods for manipulating position and color from the Shape class. In addition, the Circle class provides a private instance variable radius and two access methods for checking and altering the value of radius inside circle objects getRadius and setRadius. These elements represent behavior unique to circles since circles need special methods for drawing and hiding themselves. Methods for

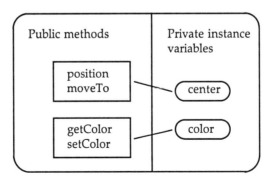

Figure 3-8.   A Shape object class template

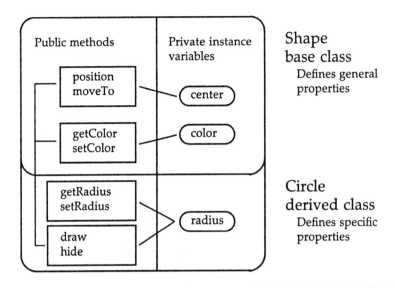

Figure 3-9. A Circle object class template

these behaviors are also provided. The following C++ code illustrates a possible definition for a Circle class that inherits properties defined in Shape.

```
class Circle : public Shape
{
    int        radius;
public:
    int        getRadius()     { return radius; }
    void       setRadius(int r) {  radius = r; }
    void       draw()
               {
                   int saveColor = screen.foreground();
                   screen.foreground(getColor());
                   screen.circle(position(), radius);
                   screen.foreground(saveColor);
               }
    void       hide()
               {
                   int saveColor = screen.foreground();
                   screen.foreground(screen.background());
                   screen.circle(position(), radius);
                   screen.foreground(saveColor);
               }
};
```

Rectangles, like circles, inherit their base properties directly from the Shape class. Figure 3-10 shows a Rectangle object template with the general inherited methods and data in the upper part of the object and specific methods and data in the lower part. The following C++ code implements these features by specifying inheritance from Shape.

```
class Rectangle : public Shape
{
protected:
    Point           extent;
public:
    Point           getExtent()              { return extent; }
    void            setExtent(Point ext)    { extent = ext; }
    void            draw()
                    {
                        int saveColor = screen.foreground();
                        screen.foreground(getColor());

                        Point a(position()-(extent/2));
                        Point c(a+extent);
                        Point b(c.x(), a.y());
                        Point d(a.x(), c.y());

                        screen.moveTo(a);
                        screen.lineTo(b);
                        screen.lineTo(c);
                        screen.lineTo(d);
                        screen.lineTo(a);

                        screen.foreground(saveColor);
                    }
    void            hide()
                    {
                        int saveColor = screen.foreground();
                        screen.foreground(screen.background());

                        Point a(position()-(extent/2));

                        Point c(a+extent);
                        Point b(c.x(), a.y());
                        Point d(a.x(), c.y());

                        screen.moveTo(a);
                        screen.lineTo(b);
                        screen.lineTo(c);
                        screen.lineTo(d);
                        screen.lineTo(a);

                        screen.foreground(saveColor);
                    }
};
```

Rather than requiring an integer radius in order to be drawn, rectangles require an extent specification. An *extent* is a point object that specifies the width and height of a rectangle.

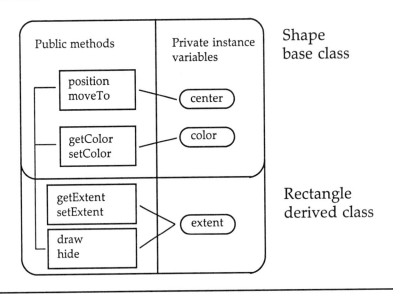

Figure 3-10.   A Rectangle object class template

Surprisingly, triangles are very similar to rectangles. It is tempting to classify shapes by similarities in appearance. For instance, an ellipse would appear very similar in form to a circle. But what you really need to look for when specifying common properties in a type hierarchy is the way objects will be *used*. Ellipses require more information than do circles. An ellipse needs two radii (one horizontal, one vertical), in addition to a center point. As another example, if a triangle is always to be drawn upright, then it only needs to have its height and its width specified—exactly like a rectangle, even though it doesn't look like a rectangle at all.

Figure 3-11 shows the representation of a Triangle object class. Since a triangle can be specified with an extent, just like a rectangle, the Triangle class inherits directly from the Rectangle definition. This means triangles inherit the characteristics of both the Shape and Rectangle classes. However, the methods to draw and hide triangles are different from those to draw rectangles. For this reason new definitions are provided for draw and hide. When this happens the new class is said to *override* the inherited definitions for the draw and hide methods.

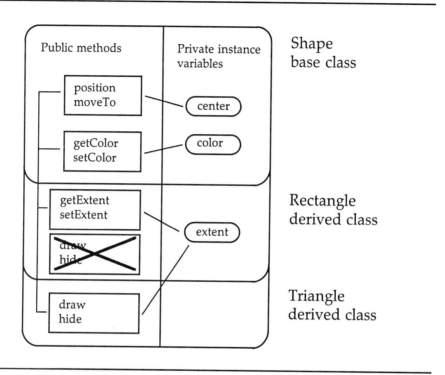

Figure 3-11.   A Triangle object class template. The Triangle class overrides
inherited methods, draw and hide.

The following listing shows the C++ definition for Triangle.

```
class Triangle : public Rectangle
{
public:
    void        draw()
                {
                    int saveColor = screen.foreground();
                    screen.foreground(getColor());

                    int w2 = extent.x()/2;    // half the width
                    int h2 = extent.y()/2;    // half the height
                    Point a(position()+Point( 0, h2));
                    Point b(position()+Point( w2, -h2));
                    Point c(position()+Point(-w2, -h2));
```

```
                    screen.moveTo(a);
                    screen.lineTo(b);
                    screen.lineTo(c);
                    screen.lineTo(a);

                    screen.foreground(saveColor);
                }
  void          hide()
                {
                    int saveColor = screen.foreground();
                    screen.foreground(screen.background());

                    int w2 = extent.x()/2;    // half the width
                    int h2 = extent.y()/2;    // half the height
                    Point a(position()+Point( 0, h2));
                    Point b(position()+Point( w2, -h2));
                    Point c(position()+Point(-w2, -h2));

                    screen.moveTo(a);
                    screen.lineTo(b);
                    screen.lineTo(c);
                    screen.lineTo(a);

                    screen.foreground(saveColor);
                }
};
```

Notice that only two new definitions are provided for the entire Triangle class definition.

Figure 3-12 shows the entire class hierarchy for Shape and its subclasses, and Program 3-1 shows how to use these objects.

The routine, main, is quite simple. The screen is initialized and a test pattern is drawn. The test pattern draws two diagonals and a frame around the screen—the diagonals give a point of reference for the screen's center. Next, three different routines are called to test the drawing, hiding, and moving of shapes. These routines are called testCircle, testRectangle, and testTriangle. Finally, the program cleans up the screen after receiving a keypress from the user.

Figure 3-13 shows the screen during execution of the testCircle routine. At this point, control is halted at the first getch statement in the following code fragment.

```
void testCircle()
{
    Circle aCircle;
    aCircle.moveTo(Point(50,50));      // general for all Shapes
    aCircle.setColor(Screen::red);
```

```
        aCircle.setRadius(4);              // specific to Circle
        aCircle.draw();
        getch();
        aCircle.hide();
        getch();
        aCircle.moveTo(Point(60,60));
        aCircle.draw();
}
```

After a key is pressed, the program tests the hide and moveTo methods before redrawing the circle at a new location. Figure 3-14 shows the screen after the original circle has been hidden, moved, and redrawn. The routines testRectangle and testTriangle in Program 3-1, do exactly the same for rectangles and triangles.

POLYMORPHISM

The ability to put objects of a common base type in a single array or collection, and then use the common protocol defined in the base class to communicate with the individual objects, is known as polymorphism. The

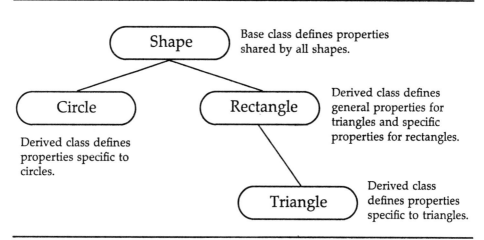

Figure 3-12.   A type hierarchy is usually called a class hierarchy.

```
#include "screen.h"

/////////////////////////////////////////////////////////////
// class Shape
/////////////////////////////////////////////////////////////
class Shape
{
    Point           center;
    int             color;
public:
    Point           position()          { return center; }
    void            moveTo(Point p)      { center = p; }
    int             getColor()           { return color; }
    void            setColor(int c)      { color = c; }
};


/////////////////////////////////////////////////////////////
// class Circle
/////////////////////////////////////////////////////////////
class Circle : public Shape
{
    int         radius;
public:
    int         getRadius()      { return radius; }
    void        setRadius(int r) { radius = r; }
    void        draw()
                {
                    int saveColor = screen.foreground();
                    screen.foreground(getColor());
                    screen.circle(position(), radius);
                    screen.foreground(saveColor);
                }
    void        hide()
                {
                    int saveColor = screen.foreground();
                    screen.foreground(screen.background());
                    screen.circle(position(), radius);
                    screen.foreground(saveColor);
                }
};


/////////////////////////////////////////////////////////////
// class Rectangle
/////////////////////////////////////////////////////////////
class Rectangle : public Shape
{
protected:
    Point           extent;
public:
    Point           getExtent()          { return extent; }
```

Program 3-1.   Using the objects in the Shape class hierarchy

```
void           setExtent(Point ext)    { extent = ext; }
void           draw()
               {
                   int saveColor = screen.foreground();
                   screen.foreground(getColor());

                   Point a(position()-(extent/2));
                   Point c(a+extent);
                   Point b(c.x(), a.y());
                   Point d(a.x(), c.y());

                   screen.moveTo(a);
                   screen.lineTo(b);
                   screen.lineTo(c);
                   screen.lineTo(d);
                   screen.lineTo(a);

                   screen.foreground(saveColor);
               }
void           hide()
               {
                   int saveColor = screen.foreground();
                   screen.foreground(screen.background());

                   Point a(position()-(extent/2));

                   Point c(a+extent);
                   Point b(c.x(), a.y());
                   Point d(a.x(), c.y());

                   screen.moveTo(a);
                   screen.lineTo(b);
                   screen.lineTo(c);
                   screen.lineTo(d);
                   screen.lineTo(a);

                   screen.foreground(saveColor);
               }
};

/////////////////////////////////////////////////////////////
// class Triangle
/////////////////////////////////////////////////////////////
class Triangle : public Rectangle
{
public:
    void           draw()
                   {
                       int saveColor = screen.foreground();
                       screen.foreground(getColor());
```

Program 3-1.   *Continued*

```
                    int w2 = extent.x()/2;   // half the width
                    int h2 = extent.y()/2;   // half the height
                    Point a(position()+Point(  0,  h2));
                    Point b(position()+Point( w2, -h2));
                    Point c(position()+Point(-w2, -h2));

                    screen.moveTo(a);
                    screen.lineTo(b);
                    screen.lineTo(c);
                    screen.lineTo(a);

                    screen.foreground(saveColor);
                }
        void    hide()
                {
                    int saveColor = screen.foreground();
                    screen.foreground(screen.background());

                    int w2 = extent.x()/2;   // half the width
                    int h2 = extent.y()/2;   // half the height
                    Point a(position()+Point(  0,  h2));
                    Point b(position()+Point( w2, -h2));
                    Point c(position()+Point(-w2, -h2));

                    screen.moveTo(a);
                    screen.lineTo(b);
                    screen.lineTo(c);
                    screen.lineTo(a);

                    screen.foreground(saveColor);
                }
};


/////////////////////////////////////////////////////////////
// main program
/////////////////////////////////////////////////////////////

#include <conio.h>

void testPattern()
{
    // Draw two diagonals to mark center point
    screen.moveTo(Point(0,0));
    screen.lineTo(Point(100,100));
    screen.moveTo(Point(0,100));
    screen.lineTo(Point(100,0));

    // Draw a border around the screen
    screen.moveTo(Point(0,0));
    screen.lineTo(Point(0,100));
```

Program 3-1.   *Continued*

```
        screen.lineTo(Point(100,100));
        screen.lineTo(Point(100,0));
        screen.lineTo(Point(0,0));
}

void testCircle()
{
    Circle aCircle;
    aCircle.moveTo(Point(50,50));          // general for all Shapes
    aCircle.setColor(Screen::red);
    aCircle.setRadius(4);                  // specific to Circle
    aCircle.draw();
    getch();
    aCircle.hide();
    getch();
    aCircle.moveTo(Point(60,60));
    aCircle.draw();
}

void testRectangle()
{
    Rectangle aRectangle;
    aRectangle.moveTo(Point(50,50));       // general for all Shapes
    aRectangle.setColor(Screen::red);
    aRectangle.setExtent(Point(8,8));      // specific to Rectangle
    aRectangle.draw();
    getch();
    aRectangle.hide();
    getch();
    aRectangle.moveTo(Point(60,60));
    aRectangle.draw();
}

void testTriangle()
{
    Triangle aTriangle;
    aTriangle.moveTo(Point(50,50));        // general for all Shapes
    aTriangle.setColor(Screen::rcd);
    aTriangle.setExtent(Point(8,8));       // specific to Triangle
    aTriangle.draw();
    getch();
    aTriangle.hide();
    getch();
    aTriangle.moveTo(Point(60,60));
    aTriangle.draw();
}

main()
{
    screen.initialize();
    screen.background(Screen::cyan);
```

Program 3-1.   *Continued*

```
    testPattern();
    testCircle();
    getch();

    screen.clear();
    testPattern();
    testRectangle();
    getch();

    screen.clear();
    testPattern();
    testTriangle();
    getch();

    screen.cleanup();
}
```

Program 3-1.   *Continued*

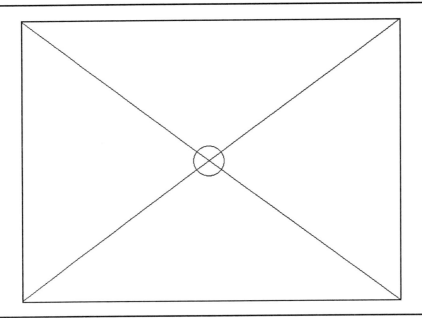

Figure 3-13.   Program 3-1 draws a circle object.

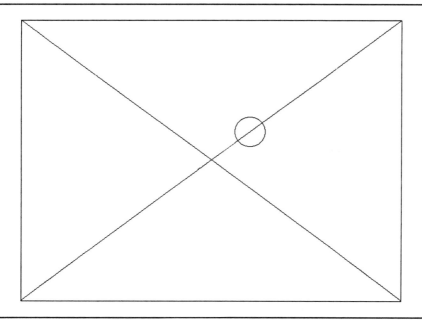

Figure 3-14.   Program 3-1 moves the circle to a new location.

term *polymorphism* comes from biology and means, literally, many forms. Biologists define polymorphism as variation in form and function found among members of a common species.

For example, in a colony of bees the queen bee is much larger than either the worker or drone bees. Her special function is propagation. The other bees are typically smaller and have specialized tasks or functions ranging from construction of honeycomb cells to gathering pollen and attending the queen. Even the shapes and organs of bees from the same hive may be different. For instance, only the pollen-gathering bees have pollen sacks on their hind legs. But the bees in a given colony are all members of the same species, despite their differences in shape and function. Thus the term *polymorphism* connotes both the characteristics shared by a species such as bees, and the properties by which members of the species differ.

Polymorphism requires inheritance. Polymorphism simplifies a programmer's task by generalizing communication syntax, which lets you treat objects of a different type in a similar fashion. That is, polymorphism uses

inheritance to express commonality in the form of a communication protocol for sending messages to objects of similar (but not exactly matching)
type.

It has been stated previously that object-oriented programming is programming by sending messages to objects of unknown type. Since the type
of an object is not known when a message is sent to it, the object's exact
response to a message cannot be known ahead of time. Object-oriented
programming involves putting many different objects of unknown but
similar type into a collection, and then activating the objects in turn by
sending each one the same message.

For instance, a video game might consist of a player's spaceship, laser
torpedoes, enemy ships, bombs, explosions, and parachuting humans. Each
of these objects shares certain properties: a screen position and a velocity.
Each object also has an image or shape that allows it to be drawn on the
screen. In addition to having properties in common, each of these objects
shares common behavior: they know how to move to the next position
indicated by their velocity, they know how to display themselves, and they
know how to check if their position coincides with the position of any
other object in the game. They also have a method, called "destroy", which
for most objects generates an explosion and removes the object from the list
of active game objects.

With polymorphism, each element in a collection is sent the same
message, but each one is programmed to react to the same message in a
different way. Each of the objects in the video game shares basic data
characteristics, and each responds to the set of messages required to simulate play. However, each class of object will respond somewhat differently
to the basic messages—create, destroy, checkCollision, display, and move.
For instance, a different method is required to draw a user's spaceship than
a photon torpedo or a parachuting human. Different actions are taken
depending on whether the player's ship position coincides with an enemy
torpedo or a parachuting human seeking rescue. This is polymorphism in
action. Polymorphism is the ability of similar objects to respond to the same
message in different ways.

How Polymorphism Differs from Inheritance

Inheritance by itself is simply a tool to support the reuse of code. Through
inheritance, objects may inherit all or only some of the characteristics of
other objects. Inheritance can also be used to take away or restrict access to
features provided by a base class. Polymorphism applies only to methods

inherited from a base class. Polymorphism is required, in addition to inheritance, to program in an object-oriented style. Inheritance is a more general tool than polymorphism; it is useful for modifying the behavior of a class that provides functionality close to what you want, but it doesn't go the whole nine yards.

Suppose you have both a Point class and a Rectangle class with limited functionality, and you want to add mouse support for moving objects on the screen. To do this, you will need to "ask" each object on the screen if it occupies the position the mouse is pointing to when the mouse button is pressed. A common technique is to assign a rectangular area to each icon and window, representing a *hot spot* that responds to a mouse button press. In Smalltalk, this area is called a *bounding box*. The collection of objects on the screen is a *polymorphic array*. That is, the elements within the array have many different forms or types, but each knows how to respond when asked to return its bounding box. What is needed in adding mouse support is a way to see if the rectangle (the bounding box) contains a specified point (the mouse pointer) for each element in the desktop.

The original Rectangle class provides no such method. However, all you need to do is derive a new class, called MyRectangle, that inherits all the methods of the base class Rectangle and adds a new method, containsPoint.

```
class MyRectangle : public Rectangle
{
public:
    int containsPoint(Point p) { /* ... */ }
}
```

This is the most basic use of inheritance—to extend or restrict the capabilities of an existing class. Polymorphism uses inheritance for a more special purpose—to express commonality. That is, polymorphism uses inheritances specifically to build polymorphic type hierarchies. *Polymorphic type hierarchies* are like normal type hierarchies, except that communication protocol for all types within a polymorphic hierarchy is established in the base class for the entire hierarchy. Polymorphism requires the definition of a base class that specifies a set of operations or procedures that all subclasses will use to communicate.

Polymorphism Generalizes Method Dispatching

Closer inspection of the routines testCircle, testRectangle, and testTriangle in Program 3-1 reveals that the code is nearly identical for each routine.

Aside from the use of a different variable name for the object being drawn, only one line differs in each routine.

```
void testCircle()
{
    // ...
    aCircle.setRadius(4);                   // specific to Circle
    // ...
}

void testRectangle()
{
    // ...
    aRectangle.setExtent(Point(8,8));       // specific to Rectangle
    // ...
}

void testTriangle()
{
    // ...
    aTriangle.setExtent(Point(8,8));        // specific to Triangle
    // ...
}
```

The similarities between rectangles and triangles are much more obvious from looking at the code than from looking at the shapes on the screen. At first glance, the similarity would seem to be grounds for code reuse and program simplification: you could combine the three routines into a single routine called testShape. The routine testShape would receive an argument of type pointer to Shape.

```
void testShape(Shape *pShape)
{
    //...
}
```

The actual shapes would be created in main and passed as arguments.

```
main()
{
    Shape *pShape;              // pointer to a shape

    pShape = new Circle;        // create a circle
    pShape->setRadius(4);       // specify circle's radius
    testShape(pShape);

    pShape = new Rectangle;     // create a rectangle
    pShape->setExtent(Point(8,8));  // specify width and height
    testShape(pShape);

    pShape = new Triangle;      // create a triangle
    pShape->setExtent(Point(8,8));  // specify width and height
    testShape(pShape);
}
```

Unfortunately, this won't work. The methods setRadius and setExtent are not defined in the base class Shape, so calling these methods would produce a compiler error. One way of getting around this problem is to use *constructors*. Most of the languages discussed in this book provide special methods for initializing the instance variables of an object when it is created. Constructors are defined for each special-case type — they allow creation of objects and assignment to instance variables in a single statement.

In C++, constructor methods have the same name as the class to which they belong. Without going into detail, constructors would let you get around calling setExtent and setRadius and keep the definitions for these special-case assignments in the derived classes where they belong. Using constructors would enable this revision of the previous listing:

```
main()
{
    Shape *pShape;                 // pointer to a shape

                                   // circle specifies
                                   // position and radius
    pShape = new Circle(Point(50,50), 4);
    testShape(pShape);

                                   // rectangle specifies
                                   // position, width, and height
    pShape = new Rectangle(Point(50,50), Point(8,8));
    testShape(pShape);

                                   // triangle specifies
                                   // position, width, and height
    pShape = new Triangle(Point(50,50), Point(8,8));
    testShape(pShape);
}
```

But there's still a problem. How do you dispatch to the appropriated draw method in testShape? Remember, each class defines its own specific method for drawing. The specific method called depends on the type of the shape being drawn. Consider a possible definition for testShape.

```
void testShape(Shape *pShape)
{
    pShape->draw();
    //...
}
```

The pointer, pShape, is a Shape, and no draw method is defined for the Shape class. This is a minor difficulty: you simply need to add a draw method to Shape. But how would this method be defined? Ideally, it would do nothing. The specifics of drawing the particular shapes should be defined in the derived classes.

```
class Shape()
{
    //...
public:
    //...
    void draw() {}          // do nothing
};
```

Since the only type information about pShape inside of the testShape function indicates that pShape is a Shape, how is the following resolved?

```
pShape->draw();
```

The only thing that a normal compiler can conclude from the available type information is that it should always direct this call to the draw method defined in the Shape class (Shape::draw). But that method does nothing.

Clearly, the advantages of communicating with polymorphic objects through a generalized dispatch mechanism are desirable. Such a generalization dramatically reduces the special-case knowledge of method types and names and greatly simplifies the use of polymorphic type hierarchies in application programs. One solution encodes type information inside objects.

```
enum ShapeType{ circle, rectangle, triangle };

class Shape
{
    int shapeType;
    // ...
public;
    void setShapeType(ShapeType st) { shapeType = st; }
    int  getShapeType()             { return shapeType; }
    // ...
};
```

Type information must be set when objects are created.

```
// ...
pShape = new Circle(Point(50,50), 4);
pShape->setShapeType(circle);
testShape(pShape)
```

```
pShape = new Rectangle(Point(50,50), Point(8,8));
pShape->setShapeType(rectangle);
testShape(pShape)

pShape = new Triangle(Point(50,50), Point(8,8));
pShape->setShapeType(triangle);
testShape(pShape)
```

You have two choices regarding the dispatching of the Shape::draw message to the appropriate special-case method. You could handle the dispatching in testShape as follows:

```
void testShape(Shape *pShape)
{
    // ====== draw shape ======
    if (pShape->getShapeType() == circle)
        ((Circle *)pShape)->draw();
    else if (pShape->getShapeType() == rectangle)
        ((Rectangle *)pShape)->draw();
    else if (pShape->getShapeType() == triangle)
        ((Triangle *)pShape)->draw();
    else
        error("You blew it.");

    //...

    // ====== hide shape ======
    if (pShape->getShapeType() == circle)
        // ...
    else if (pShape->getShapeType() == rectangle)
        // ...
    else if (pShape->getShapeType() == triangle)
        // ...
    else
        // ...

    //...

    // ====== move shape to new location ======
    if (pShape->getShapeType() == circle)
        // ...
    else if (pShape->getShapeType() == rectangle)
        // ...
    else if (pShape->getShapeType() == triangle)
        // ...
    else
        // ...

}
```

However, the whole purpose of generalizing communication protocol was to simplify things. Although the calling syntax in main has been simplified, the direction that testShape is headed in doesn't look promising.

The alternative is to handle the method dispatching in the Shape class itself. At least this approach follows the principle of hiding implementation detail at as low a level as possible.

```
class Shape
{
    // ...
public:
    // ...
    void draw()
    {
        if (shapeType == circle)
            // ...
        else if (shapeType == rectangle)
            // ...
        else if (shapeType == triangle)
            // ...
        else
            // ...
    }
    void hide()
    {
        if (shapeType == circle)
            // ...
        else if (shapeType == rectangle)
            // ...
        else if (shapeType == triangle)
            // ...
        else
            // ...
    }
    void moveTo()
    {
        if (shapeType == circle)
            // ...
        else if (shapeType == rectangle)
            // ...
        else if (shapeType == triangle)
            // ...
        else
            // ...
    }
    // ...
};
```

You can see that handling the message dispatching in the base class doesn't simplify things either. These two different ways of handling the dispatching bring up a very sticky question. In order to simplify use of objects from a Shape class hierarchy, someone must handle method dispatching. Is it going to be the person who builds the basic Shape class library? Or is it going to be the person who uses the Shape class library?

Raising such questions in design meetings has been known to result in persons and objects colliding in rather violent fashion. Why should the user have to do it? You contract or assign a builder to do the work you don't want to do or don't have the time to do. You have someone provide core primitives and libraries so you can concentrate on the higher level implementation issues.

But what if the designer can't predict every type of shape for which various messages will require special-case dispatching? In that case, every time you add a new type of shape to the class hierarchy, all the source code in the hierarchy needs to be recompiled — and that's the easy part. Finding every switch statement that is affected by the addition of a new type has sent many a programmer to a padded cell.

Evidently someone has to maintain those dreaded 350 sets of communication connections (7 methods times 50 types) for the typical class library — and that's for a very simple communication protocol. Although information hiding makes the application programmer's life easier, the library builder has it tough. Library builders usually try to shift the burden of managing type-based method dispatching to application programmers.

Unfortunately, the generalization that is allowed through type hierarchy definitions is not powerful enough to allow you to easily express generalization of communication protocol, specifically method dispatching. You can see how much code it would save if you could generalize the call dispatching mechanisms for the methods draw, hide, moveTo, and eventually rotate, for any shape object. What is needed is a special tool to allow this kind of call-dispatching generalization to be expressed: message dispatching at run time based on an object's type.

DYNAMIC BINDING

By now, you know that object-oriented programming is a structuring technique based on type hierarchies in which communication with anonymous objects occurs through a common protocol designed for the hierarchy.

Object-oriented programming also allows the addition of new types to the type hierarchies. Generalized message dispatching to the new types through base class methods works without a need for recoding or recompiling the base classes. This means none of the source code defining the original type or class hierarchy needs to be modified or recompiled to add new types—communication to objects created from the new types is carried out exactly the way it was carried out to objects of previously defined types.

In addition, message dispatching to the appropriate special-case methods is handled at run time. Dynamic binding is required to make this type of extension to class hierarchies without forcing recompilation of code and explicit maintenance of call-dispatching mechanisms through switch statements.

The programmer can specify that certain methods in a base class should use a dispatching mechanism based on object type. This dispatching mechanism is called run-time binding, *late binding*, or *dynamic binding*. Any classes that have a method specifying dynamic binding automatically maintain type information inside object instances of the class. This type information and management is transparent—the programmer knows nothing about invisible type fields maintained inside these special objects.

In C++, methods resolved by run-time dispatching based on type are called *virtual functions*. The compiler maintains a method dispatch table, often called a *virtual function table*, to dispatch to the appropriate methods at run time. Only the base method requiring run-time binding needs to add the keyword *virtual*. In derived classes, methods that override the base class definition of a virtual function are automatically assumed to be virtual.

```
class Shape
{
    // ...
public:
    virtual draw() {}  // does nothing
    // ...
};

class Circle : public Shape
{
    // ...
public:
    // override draw method inherited from Shape
    draw()
    {
        // code to draw a circle
    }
};

class Rectangle : public Shape
{
    // ...
```

```
public:
    // override draw method inherited from Shape
    draw()
    {
        // code to draw a rectangle
    }
};
```

In the listing, both the methods Circle::draw and Rectangle::draw are virtual methods (methods bound at run time), even though they do not specify virtual in their definitions. Specifying virtual in the base class method, Shape::draw, implies that the draw method in all descendants will be virtual. Since the compiler maintains type information and handles dispatching at run time automatically—by inserting a copy of the virtual function table in the executable program—no switch statements need to be maintained for method dispatching. Both the builder and the user of the Shape class library are free to worry about other problems: the builder about special-case Shape objects, and the user about the higher level implementation of the application.

An example program will show how dynamic binding simplifies program construction and maintenance. While you're at it, other routines from Program 3-1 can be generalized with the support of dynamic binding. If you look at the draw and hide methods for any class in Program 3-1, you'll notice that they, too, duplicate a lot of code. In fact these methods differ by only one statement. Both methods save the current drawing color upon entry and restore the color on exit.

```
void        draw()
            {
                int saveColor = screen.foreground();
                screen.foreground(getColor());

                // draw the object

                screen.foreground(saveColor);
            }
void        hide()
            {
                int saveColor = screen.foreground();
                screen.foreground(screen.background());

                // draw the object

                screen.foreground(saveColor);
            }
```

The code to save and restore the current drawing color is exactly the same in each draw and hide method in every class descended from Shape. Although draw sets the current drawing color to the color contained in the object,

```
screen.foreground(getColor());
```

hide sets the current drawing color to the background color for the screen.

```
screen.foreground(screen.background());
```

If you decide to change the way an object is drawn, you have to change the implementation of draw and hide, which is extra work. Once again generalization simplifies maintenance. It's better to have each class maintain only one copy of the code specific to drawing the actual shape. Express only the difference between drawing and hiding in the draw and hide methods.

```
void        drawShape()
            {
                // code to draw specific shape
            }

void        draw()
            {
                int saveColor = screen.foreground();
                screen.foreground(getColor());

                drawShape;

                screen.foreground(saveColor);
            }
void        hide()
            {
                int saveColor = screen.foreground();
                screen.foreground(screen.background());

                drawShape;

                screen.foreground(saveColor);
            }
```

Actually, now that run-time binding is possible, you could move the definitions for draw and hide directly to the base class, Shape, since none of the special-case shapes needs to redefine draw or hide. Shape can now be redefined.

```
/////////////////////////////////////////////////////////////
// class Shape
/////////////////////////////////////////////////////////////
class Shape
{
    Point center;
    int color;
    virtual void drawShape()=0;
public:
                Shape(Point p)                      // constructor
                  : center(p),
                    color(screen.foreground())
                            { }
    int         getColor()     { return color; }
    void        setColor(int c) { color = c; }
    Point       position()     { return center; }
    void        moveTo(Point p) { center = p; }

    void        draw()   {
                        int saveColor = screen.foreground();
                        screen.foreground(getColor());
                        drawShape();
                        screen.foreground(saveColor);
                    }
    void        hide()   {
                        int saveColor = screen.foreground();
                        screen.foreground(screen.background());
                        drawShape();
                        screen.foreground(saveColor);
                    }
};
```

The only things that need to be defined now in any of the classes derived from Shape are the instance variables needed to maintain the shape, the constructor for creating the shape, and the special-case method drawShape, which overrides the base class virtual definition. This makes the definition for a derived class such as Circle very clear.

```
/////////////////////////////////////////////////////////////
// class Circle
/////////////////////////////////////////////////////////////
class Circle : public Shape
{
    int radius;
    void drawShape()
    {
        screen.circle(position(), radius);
    }
public:
        Circle(Point p, int r)                  // constructor
          : Shape(p), radius(r) {}
};
```

Two methods are defined here: the private method to draw the shape
and the constructor. There's not much more than that to either Rectangle or
Triangle.

```
/////////////////////////////////////////////////////////////
// class Rectangle
/////////////////////////////////////////////////////////////
class Rectangle : public Shape
{
    void drawShape()
    {
        Point a(position()-(extent/2));
        Point c(a+extent);
        Point b(c.x(), a.y());
        Point d(a.x(), c.y());

        screen.moveTo(a);
        screen.lineTo(b);
        screen.lineTo(c);
        screen.lineTo(d);
        screen.lineTo(a);
    }
protected:
    Point extent;
public:
        Rectangle(Point ctr, Point ext)        // constructor
            : Shape(ctr), extent(ext) {}
};

/////////////////////////////////////////////////////////////
// class Triangle
/////////////////////////////////////////////////////////////
class Triangle : public Rectangle
{
    void drawShape()
    {
        int w2 = extent.x()/2;    // half the width
        int h2 = extent.y()/2;    // half the height
        Point a(position()+Point(  0,  h2));
        Point b(position()+Point( w2, -h2));
        Point c(position()+Point(-w2, -h2));

        screen.moveTo(a);
        screen.lineTo(b);
        screen.lineTo(c);
        screen.lineTo(a);
    }
public:
        Triangle(Point ctr, Point ext)         // constructor
            : Rectangle(ctr, ext) {}
};
```

Now it is also possible to implement the general version of testShape.

```
void testShape(Shape *pShape)
{
    screen.clear();
    testPattern();
    pShape->moveTo(Point(50,50));        // general for all Shapes
    pShape->setColor(Screen::red);
    pShape->draw();
    getch();
    pShape->hide();
    getch();
    pShape->moveTo(Point(60,60));
    pShape->draw();
    getch();
}
```

All calls to either draw or hide are directed to the base class implementations: Shape::draw and Shape::hide. Both of these in turn call the virtual base class method, Shape::drawShape. Since Shape::drawShape was specified as virtual, it waits until it is called (until it receives a message), and then it checks to see the type of the object for which the call was invoked. Depending on the type of the object, it automatically directs the call to one of the special-case derived class implementations: Circle::draw, Rectangle ::draw, or Triangle::draw. Dynamic binding makes this possible without forcing the programmer to explicitly maintain type information or switch networks to do the dispatching.

Now for the litmus test—how simple is it to use these generalized tools? Have a look at main.

```
main()
{
    screen.initialize();
    screen.background(Screen::cyan);

    Shape *pShape;

    pShape = new Circle    (Point(60,6), 4);
    testShape(pShape);

    pShape = new Rectangle(Point(70,6), Point(8,8));
    testShape(pShape);

    pShape = new Triangle (Point(80,6), Point(8,8));
    testShape(pShape);

    screen.cleanup();
}
```

Things look pretty good. This code produces exactly the same output as Program 3-1.

Figure 3-15 shows a diagram of the current implementation of the Shape class. Now draw and hide are public methods and need to be implemented only in the base class, Shape. Circle, Rectangle, and Triangle can eliminate specific implementation of draw and hide altogether. The private virtual method drawShape generalizes the actions that draw and hide shared in Program 3-1. Each class derived from Shape must implement its own version of drawShape. A call to this method from a general shape pointer will be directed to the drawShape method defined in the base class. Through dynamic binding, Shape::drawShape will dispatch to the appropriate special-case implementation of drawShape based on the calling object's type.

The entire listing for Program 3-2 is included here for reference. Note how it differs from Program 3-1, which does not use dynamic binding. Compare the two listings with an eye toward maintenance and readability.

Rotating Polymorphic Shape Objects

The original goal was to rotate objects about the origin on the screen. Program 3-3 does this, but first let's look at some examples from it. The

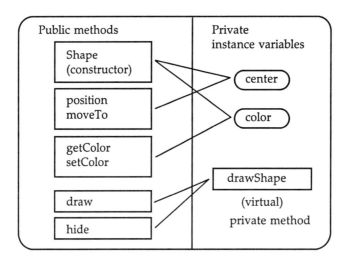

Figure 3-15.   Shape base class now defines hide, draw, and drawShape.

```
#include "screen.h"

/////////////////////////////////////////////////////////
// class Shape
/////////////////////////////////////////////////////////
class Shape
{
    Point center;
    int color;
    virtual void drawShape()=0;
public:
                Shape(Point p)                  // constructor
                  : center(p),
                    color(screen.foreground())
                            { }
    int         getColor()      { return color; }
    void        setColor(int c) { color = c; }
    Point       position()      { return center; }
    void        moveTo(Point p) { center = p; }

    void        draw()  {
                    int saveColor = screen.foreground();
                    screen.foreground(getColor());
                    drawShape();
                    screen.foreground(saveColor);
                }
    void        hide()  {
                    int saveColor = screen.foreground();
                    screen.foreground(screen.background());
                    drawShape();
                    screen.foreground(saveColor);
                }
};

/////////////////////////////////////////////////////////
// class Circle
/////////////////////////////////////////////////////////
class Circle : public Shape
{
    int radius;
    void drawShape()
    {
        screen.circle(position(), radius);
    }
public:
        Circle(Point p, int r)                  // constructor
          : Shape(p), radius(r) {}
};
```

Program 3-2. Dynamic binding simplifies program construction and maintenance.

```
////////////////////////////////////////////////////////////
// class Rectangle
////////////////////////////////////////////////////////////
class Rectangle : public Shape
{
    void drawShape()
    {
        Point a(position()-(extent/2));
        Point c(a+extent);
        Point b(c.x(), a.y());
        Point d(a.x(), c.y());

        screen.moveTo(a);
        screen.lineTo(b);
        screen.lineTo(c);
        screen.lineTo(d);
        screen.lineTo(a);
    }
protected:
    Point extent;
public:
        Rectangle(Point ctr, Point ext)      // constructor
          : Shape(ctr), extent(ext) {}
};


////////////////////////////////////////////////////////////
// class Triangle
////////////////////////////////////////////////////////////
class Triangle : public Rectangle
{
    void drawShape()
    {
        int w2 = extent.x()/2;   // half the width
        int h2 = extent.y()/2;   // half the height
        Point a(position()+Point(  0,  h2));
        Point b(position()+Point( w2, -h2));
        Point c(position()+Point(-w2, -h2));

        screen.moveTo(a);
        screen.lineTo(b);
        screen.lineTo(c);
        screen.lineTo(a);
    }
public:
        Triangle(Point ctr, Point ext)       // constructor
          : Rectangle(ctr, ext) {}
};


#include <conio.h>
```

Program 3-2.   *Continued*

```
//////////////////////////////////////////////////////////
// main program
//////////////////////////////////////////////////////////

void testPattern()
{
    // Draw two diagonals to mark center point
    screen.moveTo(Point(0,0));
    screen.lineTo(Point(100,100));
    screen.moveTo(Point(0,100));
    screen.lineTo(Point(100,0));

    // Draw a border around the screen
    screen.moveTo(Point(0,0));
    screen.lineTo(Point(0,100));
    screen.lineTo(Point(100,100));
    screen.lineTo(Point(100,0));
    screen.lineTo(Point(0,0));
}

void testShape(Shape *pShape)
{
    screen.clear();
    testPattern();
    pShape->moveTo(Point(50,50));       // general for all Shapes
    pShape->setColor(Screen::red);
    pShape->draw();
    getch();
    pShape->hide();
    getch();
    pShape->moveTo(Point(60,60));
    pShape->draw();
    getch();
}

main()
{
    screen.initialize();
    screen.background(Screen::cyan);

    Shape *pShape;

    pShape = new Circle    (Point(60,6), 4);
    testShape(pShape);

    pShape = new Rectangle(Point(70,6), Point(8,8));
    testShape(pShape);

    pShape = new Triangle (Point(80,6), Point(8,8));
    testShape(pShape);

    screen.cleanup();
}
```

Program 3-2.   *Continued*

main difference between Program 3-3 and Program 3-2 is the addition of
methods and data to the Shape base class to maintain information about
the current rotational angle of a given object.

```
/////////////////////////////////////////////////////////////
// class Shape
/////////////////////////////////////////////////////////////
class Shape
{
    // ...
    int angle;
    // ...
public:
                    Shape(Point p)              // constructor
                      : center(p),
                        color(screen.foreground()),
                        angle(0)    { }
    // ...
    int         getAngle()      { return angle; }
    void        setAngle(int a) { angle = a; }
    // ...
    void        rotate(int angle)
                    {
                        setAngle(getAngle()+angle);
                        draw();
                    }
    // ...
};
```

Figure 3-16 diagrams the resulting Shape class template.

Next, a general purpose routine is provided to rotate a given point
about the origin.

```
#include <math.h>  // required for rotations
Point rotateAboutOrigin(Point p, int angle)
{
    double theta = angle * M_PI/180;
    double cos_theta = cos(theta);
    double sin_theta = sin(theta);
    int x = p.x()*cos_theta - p.y()*sin_theta;
    int y = p.x()*sin_theta + p.y()*cos_theta;
    return Point(x,y);
}
```

The drawShape method in each of the derived classes is modified to
take the rotational angle into account, but only Rectangle::draw is shown
here. (See Program 3-3 for Circle and Triangle.)

```
/////////////////////////////////////////////////////////////
// class Rectangle
/////////////////////////////////////////////////////////////
```

```
class Rectangle : public Shape
{
    void drawShape()
    {
        Point a(position()-(extent/2));
        Point c(a+extent);
        Point b(c.x(), a.y());
        Point d(a.x(), c.y());

        a = rotateAboutOrigin(a, getAngle());
        b = rotateAboutOrigin(b, getAngle());
        c = rotateAboutOrigin(c, getAngle());
        d = rotateAboutOrigin(d, getAngle());

        screen.moveTo(a);
        screen.lineTo(b);
        screen.lineTo(c);
        screen.lineTo(d);
        screen.lineTo(a);
    }
    // ...
};
```

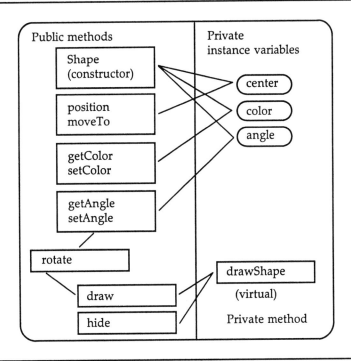

Figure 3-16.   Shape objects can now rotate themselves.

Finally, to show polymorphism in action, a polymorphic array is used to contain the objects displayed on the screen. The following code inside main declares an array to contain shapes, and then adds three shapes to the array.

```
ShapePointer shapeArray[10];
int size=0;

shapeArray[size++] = new Circle    (Point(60,6), 4);
shapeArray[size++] = new Rectangle(Point(70,6), Point(8,8));
shapeArray[size++] = new Triangle (Point(80,6), Point(8,8));
```

The array, shapeArray, is a true polymorphic array. It doesn't care what kind of things you put in as long as they are derived from the Shape class. (Actually, shapeArray contains pointers to Shape objects. In C++, run-time binding is closely associated with pointers.) Note that the variable, size, is originally set to 0 and incremented each time a new shape is added to the array. This makes it possible to tell how many items are currently stored in shapeArray. A general purpose routine is provided to rotate all the elements in an array of shapes.

```
void rotateArray(ShapePointer array[], int size)
{
    for (int j=0; j<size; j++)
    {
        array[j]->draw();              // original position
        for (int i=0; i<8; i++)        // rotate shape 8 times
        {                              // 10 degrees each rotation
            array[j]->rotate(10);      // rotate is relative to
        }                              // current angle setting
    }
}
```

The function, rotateArray takes an array of shapes as its first argument and the number of elements in the array as its second argument. It then rotates each element in the array eight times by calling the Shape::rotate method. This method receives the desired angle for rotation as an argument and is incremental. Each time rotate is called, it adds the specified angle to the current rotation angle and then draws the shape.

```
void        rotate(int angle)
            {
                setAngle(getAngle()+angle);
                draw();
            }
```

Note that this method is not dynamically bound. That is, the keyword *virtual* does not precede rotate's definition in the base class. However, because rotate calls draw, it doesn't need to be virtual. By the same token, draw is also not virtual, but draw does call the virtual method drawShape, which dispatches to the appropriate special-case drawShape method at run time. As long as new classes do not override draw, hide, or rotate, none of these three methods needs to be virtual.

Figure 3-17 diagrams the static binding mechanism used when a pointer to a Shape object receives either a rotate or a draw message. At compile time, all rotate messages are bound to Shape::rotate because Circle, Rectangle, and Triangle do not provide definitions for rotate. The same is true for draw and hide.

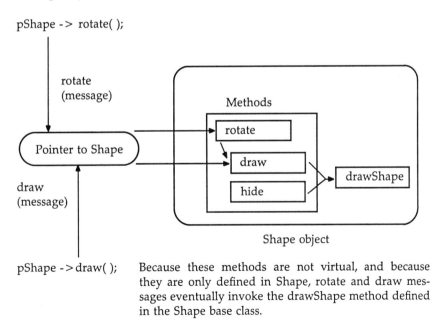

At compile time, rotate and draw messages to Shape objects are resolved.

pShape -> rotate( );

rotate (message)

Methods

rotate

Pointer to Shape

draw (message)

draw

hide

drawShape

Shape object

pShape -> draw( );   Because these methods are not virtual, and because they are only defined in Shape, rotate and draw messages eventually invoke the drawShape method defined in the Shape base class.

Figure 3-17.   In C++, static binding is used by default.

Deciding which version of drawShape to call is a different matter. Shape, Circle, Rectangle, and Triangle each implement their own version of drawShape. Since drawShape is specified as a virtual method in the base class, Shape, the program waits until run time to decide which version of drawShape to call when a pointer to a Shape object gets a drawShape message.

Figure 3-18 shows how the virtual base class method Shape::drawShape dispatches to one of the methods from a derived class that overrides it. When a base class specifies virtual methods, a virtual method table is built by the compiler and inserted into the executable program at compile time. All objects that descend from a virtual base class retain type information

A shape pointer receiving a drawShape message invokes a binding mechanism, which looks at hidden type information stored in all Shape objects.

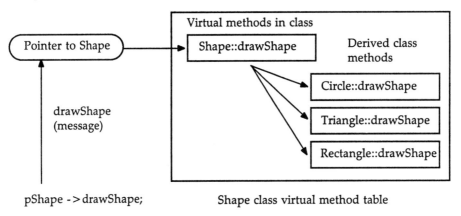

pShape -> drawShape;   Shape class virtual method table

The mechanism decides which drawShape method
to call based on the object's exact type at run time.

Figure 3-18.   Dynamic binding enables simplified polymorphic communication. In C++, dynamic binding requires a pointer compatible with the base class declaring the dynamically bound method.

about themselves at run time. When a pointer to an object receives a message to a dynamically bound method, the dynamic dispatch mechanism looks at the type information in the object pointed to and uses that information to look up a method in the virtual method table that matches the object's exact type.

Dynamic binding of messages to virtual methods allows a simple call in main to rotate the entire array of objects.

```
rotateArray(shapeArray, size);
```

After this statement is executed, the screen will look like Figure 3-19. Program 3-3 is listed here for your study. Try to relate the code in Program 3-3 to the dispatching mechanisms diagrammed in Figures 3-17 and 3-18.

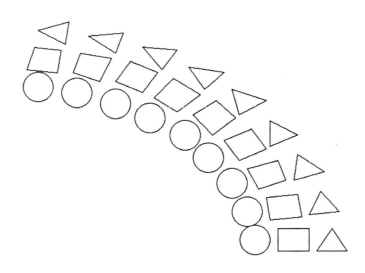

Figure 3-19.   Rotating three shape objects through polymorphic messages

```
#include "screen.h"

///////////////////////////////////////////////////////
// class Shape
///////////////////////////////////////////////////////
class Shape
{
    Point center;
    int color;
    int angle;
    virtual void drawShape()=0;
public:
                Shape(Point p)                 // constructor
                  : center(p),
                    color(screen.foreground()),
                    angle(0)    { }
    int         getColor()      { return color; }
    void        setColor(int c) { color = c; }
    int         getAngle()      { return angle; }
    void        setAngle(int a) { angle = a; }
    Point       position()      { return center; }
    void        moveTo(Point p) { center = p; }

    void        draw()    {
                    int saveColor = screen.foreground();
                    screen.foreground(getColor());
                    drawShape();
                    screen.foreground(saveColor);
                    }
    void        rotate(int angle)
                    {
                    setAngle(getAngle()+angle);
                    draw();
                    }
    void        hide()    {
                    int saveColor = screen.foreground();
                    screen.foreground(screen.background());
                    drawShape();
                    screen.foreground(saveColor);
                    }
};

#include <math.h>  // required for rotations
Point rotateAboutOrigin(Point p, int angle)
{
    double theta = angle * M_PI/180;
    double cos_theta = cos(theta);
    double sin_theta = sin(theta);
    int x = p.x()*cos_theta - p.y()*sin_theta;
```

Program 3-3.   Methods and data in the Shape base class maintain information about the current rotational angle and allow polymorphic communication with Shape objects.

```
    int y = p.x()*sin_theta + p.y()*cos_theta;
    return Point(x,y);
}

/////////////////////////////////////////////////////////////
// class Circle
/////////////////////////////////////////////////////////////
class Circle : public Shape
{
    int radius;
    void drawShape()
    {
        Point ctr = rotateAboutOrigin(position(), getAngle());
        screen.circle(ctr, radius);
    }
public:
        Circle(Point p, int r)                 // constructor
          : Shape(p), radius(r) {}
};

/////////////////////////////////////////////////////////////
// class Rectangle
/////////////////////////////////////////////////////////////
class Rectangle : public Shape
{
    void drawShape()
    {
        Point a(position()-(extent/2));
        Point c(a+extent);
        Point b(c.x(), a.y());
        Point d(a.x(), c.y());

        a = rotateAboutOrigin(a, getAngle());
        b = rotateAboutOrigin(b, getAngle());
        c = rotateAboutOrigin(c, getAngle());
        d = rotateAboutOrigin(d, getAngle());

        screen.moveTo(a);
        screen.lineTo(b);
        screen.lineTo(c);
        screen.lineTo(d);
        screen.lineTo(a);
    }
protected:
    Point extent;
public:
        Rectangle(Point ctr, Point ext)        // constructor
          : Shape(ctr), extent(ext) {}
};
```

Program 3-3.   *Continued*

```
//////////////////////////////////////////////////////////////
// class Triangle
//////////////////////////////////////////////////////////////
class Triangle : public Rectangle
{
    void drawShape()
    {
        int w2 = extent.x()/2;    // half the width
        int h2 = extent.y()/2;    // half the height
        Point a(position()+Point( 0,  h2));
        Point b(position()+Point( w2, -h2));
        Point c(position()+Point(-w2, -h2));

        a = rotateAboutOrigin(a, getAngle());
        b = rotateAboutOrigin(b, getAngle());
        c = rotateAboutOrigin(c, getAngle());

        screen.moveTo(a);
        screen.lineTo(b);
        screen.lineTo(c);
        screen.lineTo(a);
    }
public:
        Triangle(Point ctr, Point ext)       // constructor
           : Rectangle(ctr, ext) {}
};

#include <conio.h>

//////////////////////////////////////////////////////////////
// main program
//////////////////////////////////////////////////////////////

typedef Shape *ShapePointer;

void rotateArray(ShapePointer array[], int size)
{
    for (int j=0; j<size; j++)
    {
        array[j]->draw();            // original position
        for (int i=0; i<8; i++)      // rotate shape 8 times,
        {                            // 10 degrees each rotation
            array[j]->rotate(10);    // rotate is relative to
                                     // current angle setting
        }
    }
}
```

Program 3-3.   *Continued*

```
main()
{
    screen.initialize();
    screen.background(Screen::cyan);

    ShapePointer shapeArray[10];
    int size=0;

    shapeArray[size++] = new Circle    (Point(60,6), 4);
    shapeArray[size++] = new Rectangle(Point(70,6), Point(8,8));
    shapeArray[size++] = new Triangle (Point(80,6), Point(8,8));

    rotateArray(shapeArray, size);

    getch();
    screen.cleanup();
}
```

Program 3-3. *Continued*

CHAPTER HIGHLIGHTS

Inheritance and polymorphism are the keys to object-oriented programming. The following list summarizes the basic features of inheritance and polymorphism covered in this chapter.

Classification

- Classification imposes order.
- Objects are classified according to shared properties.
- Objects may have different implementations and still share properties.
- Objects' properties are highlighted or ignored depending on intended use.
- Objects with similar properties belong to the same class.

Inheritance

Hierarchical Programming

- Type hierarchies express common properties of objects.

- Type hierarchies express special-case differences among similar objects.

- Type hierarchies are class hierarchies.

- Ancestor classes define common properties.

- Descendant classes define special-case differences.

Base Classes

- A common ancestor in a class hierarchy is a base class.

- Base classes define a common communication protocol for descendants.

- Objects from a common base class respond to the same messages.

Polymorphism and Dynamic Binding

Object-Oriented Structure Regulates Communication

- Object-oriented programming encourages formal specification of communication protocol.

- Objects communicate through public interfaces.

- Object-oriented programming languages detect violation of interface protocol.

Dynamic Binding

- Dynamic binding dispatches general calls to specific methods.

- Dynamic binding selects specific methods based on object type.

- Dynamic binding resolves calls at run time.

- Dynamic binding eliminates programmer-maintained type information.

- Dynamic binding eliminates programmer-maintained method dispatch switches.

Polymorphic Collections and Containers

- Collections and containers hold unnamed objects.
- Objects with a common base class can be placed in the same collection.
- Method dispatching is handled by the receiver rather than the sender.
- Polymorphism generalizes communication and simplifies maintenance.

4

JUST ENOUGH SMALLTALK

Before moving on to the subject of class libraries, a little Smalltalk is in order. The primary examples in Chapter 5, "Class Libraries", are presented in Smalltalk, although many examples will also be presented in C++. The main emphasis throughout Chapter 5 will be on the function and usage of class libraries rather than on the semantics of either Smalltalk or C++. Examples are presented in both languages in order to highlight the common features of class libraries, which are largely language-independent. C++ will be used as the representative example for programming with the traditional compiled language. The process of working with such a language should be familiar to you. You work with an editor to create program source code. You then compile and link the program source to create an executable program image. The operating system then provides a means for loading and running the executable image.

The intention here is to provide just enough information about Smalltalk and C++ to enable you to follow the example programs in Chapter 5. In order for that presentation to be clear, you need to understand some of the differences between programming in Smalltalk and a more traditional language such as C, C++, or Pascal.

SMALLTALK VERSUS C++

Two features distinguish programming in Smalltalk from programming in
C++. First, the connection between the language and the programming
environment is much stronger in Smalltalk than in C++. Second, interactive
program development in Smalltalk blurs the distinction between the various programming steps. In Smalltalk, it is possible to enter program text
and execute and test a program without invoking a compiler.

In this respect Smalltalk is similar to BASIC, in that one of the primary
tools for interacting with the environment is an interpreter. The *interpreter*
will check the syntax of program source code and report errors. However, if
there are no errors, the program will execute immediately upon request. In
contrast, C++ syntax checking is handled entirely by the compiler, and
compiling is completely distinct from entering or editing source code and
from executing a program specified by source code. Let's look a little more
carefully at some of these distinctions.

The Smalltalk Programming Environment

Whereas C++ is a *compiled* language, Smalltalk is mainly an *interpreted*
language. Or, to be more precise, Smalltalk is an incrementally compiled
language—both the compiler and the interpreter are part of the Smalltalk
programming environment. The primary difference between working in
C++ and Smalltalk is that when you're working with Smalltalk, you never
leave the programming environment. When you submit pieces of your
program to the Smalltalk compiler, they become part of the environment.
Program code that is submitted to the Smalltalk interpreter, however, does
not become part of the environment. Instead, it is simply executed and then
discarded.

Actually, the text that you submit to the Smalltalk interpreter eventually
does go through a compiler. The compiler produces an intermediate form
of executable object code that is temporarily loaded into memory. The
executable object code is executed, and, if requested, the value returned by
this code is printed. As soon as the object code is executed it is thrown out,
and only the source code and the resulting return value remain in the edit
window.

Smalltalk's Incremental Compiler

In early stages of development you will work more with Smalltalk's interpreter than with its incremental compiler. However, it's still handy to know

how the Smalltalk compiler works and how it is different from a C++ compiler. When you submit program source code to the Smalltalk compiler, the executable object code actually becomes a permanent part of the programming environment. Thus, when you run a Smalltalk program, you actually run the program in the context of the programming environment.

This is different from a compiled language, such as C++, in which everything that is required to run a program is bundled into an executable file separate from the programming environment. The editor, compiler, and linker do not become a part of an executable C++ program. This means you cannot compile and test a C++ program in pieces. You must submit an entire C++ program to the compiler and linker at once, before you can execute and test any part of the program.

In Smalltalk, however, since the programming environment is always present (including library support, classes, and methods), you can test out even the smallest program fragment with the interpreter, or compile only a small piece of code so that it becomes a new component of the programming environment itself.

The program pieces you submit to the Smalltalk compiler actually change the programming environment or system image. Once the executable code becomes part of the system image, you may invoke the code interactively by evaluating expressions with the Smalltalk interpreter. This is done by typing in program source text and then highlighting the text you want to evaluate. Next you send a message to the programming environment indicating that you want it to interpret and respond to the highlighted text.

USING SMALLTALK'S INTERACTIVE INTERPRETER

You will hear many people say that Smalltalk is an interpreted language. This is only a half-truth. While you work primarily with the Smalltalk interpreter to develop Smalltalk programs, ultimately the source code will be compiled to become a permanent part of the system for large applications.

You can use Smalltalk's interpreter without using the compiler at all. This is how programmers work with older varieties of BASIC, which were strictly interactive and did not provide a compiler. In fact, BASIC was originally envisioned as an interpreter for FORTRAN. (The world has turned a few times since then.)

You could use the Smalltalk interpreter like a very sophisticated calculator, to evaluate mathematical expressions, as you'll see shortly.

Nearly all versions of Smalltalk provide a graphical user interface (GUI) and present a variety of different text and graphics windows for various programming tasks. Everything presented on the screen uses graphics — even the characters drawn on the screen to represent text are simulated using graphics. Graphical user interfaces allow the integration of text and graphics within the same window. This in turn enables the screen to more closely simulate a real-world desktop (where the primary objects are paper, pens, and typewritten text) with images, shapes, and lines frequently drawn on top of written text. Figure 4-1 shows how Smalltalk integrates text and graphics on the same screen.

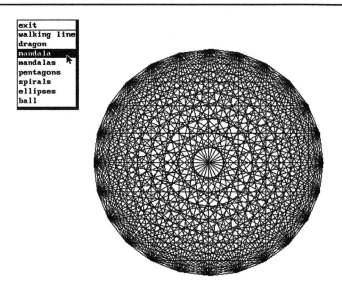

Figure 4-1.   Smalltalk's graphical user interface displays text and graphics on the same screen.

Entering and Selecting Program Text for Evaluation

Figure 4-2 shows how you would enter the expression 3 + 4 in a Smalltalk edit window. Most interaction with the Smalltalk environment takes place through the *Transcript window*, which is the main window for program output. To evaluate the expression 3 + 4, you would first type the expression into the Transcript window, as shown in Figure 4-2. Next the expression must be highlighted.

Note: Although it is possible to use Smalltalk without a mouse, it is awkward and therefore not recommended. The following discussion assumes you have a mouse and follows input-control conventions compatible with Digitalk's Smalltalk/V. If you are not using Smalltalk/V or do not have a mouse, consult your Smalltalk manual if you want to follow the example programs on your computer. This discussion is designed to give you a feel for working with Smalltalk even if you do not have access to a Smalltalk environment.

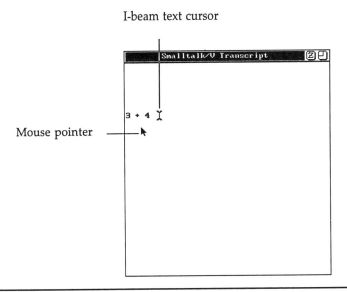

Figure 4-2.   Entering simple expressions in the Smalltalk Transcript window

To highlight the expression 3 + 4, move the mouse pointer so it is just touching the left side of the 3. Now press and hold down the left mouse button and, still holding it down, drag the mouse pointer to the right. As you do this, each of the successive characters under the pointer will be highlighted in turn, as shown here:

Continue dragging the mouse pointer until several blank spaces to the right of the expression are highlighted, as shown in the following illustration. Then release the mouse button. The expression currently highlighted in the active window is now "3 + 4".

Evaluating Selected Text

Next, you can tell Smalltalk that you want to evaluate the highlighted expression by pressing the right mouse button with the mouse cursor pointing anywhere inside the window that contains the highlighted expression. When you release the right button, a menu like this appears:

You can evaluate the highlighted expression by selecting either "show it" or "do it" from the menu. Selection of a menu command is made by pointing to the desired entry, then pressing and releasing the left mouse button. The "do it" command merely evaluates the expression; it does not show the result returned by the expression. The "show it" command, on the other hand, prints the result returned by evaluating the highlighted expression, as shown here:

3 + 4   ▊

The result is printed immediately after the highlighted text in the Transcript window.

Note that the original expression is no longer highlighted. Instead, the result of the evaluation is highlighted. This makes it possible to quickly delete the result or copy it to another window.

Multiple-Statement Programs

The Smalltalk interpreter will let you evaluate complex expressions and sequences of statements that can be thought of as programs. In Smalltalk, statements are separated by a period. For example, the following Smalltalk program consists of three statements:

```
1 + 2.
3 + 4.  5 + 6.
```

White space, including tabs and carriage returns, is ignored; it is used mostly to make Smalltalk programs more readable. Note that when a sequence of statements is evaluated, only the value of the last executed statement is returned. To evaluate more than one statement, you simply highlight all the statements you want to evaluate and then invoke the "show it" command, as shown here:

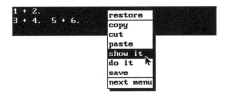

The result of the evaluation is shown in the following illustration:

```
1 + 2.
3 + 4.  5 + 6.
```

11

Note once again that the original program source text is no longer high-lighted; instead the result is. The highlighted value, 11, is the value re-turned by the expression 5 + 6, which is the last of the three executed statements.

Temporary Variables

You can use temporary variables if you want a program to return a value other than the one returned by the last statement executed. In order for this to work, temporary variables need to be declared before they can be used. Specifically, they must be declared at the beginning of the program block in which they will be used. You declare a temporary variable by typing its name between horizontal bars.

```
¦tempVariable¦
```

In contrast to variables in C++ or C, it is not necessary to declare the data types of temporary variables in Smalltalk.

Figure 4-3 shows how a temporary variable might be used to return the result of the first of a sequence of statements, rather than the last. In the figure, the program text to be evaluated is highlighted (in reverse video), and the result of the evaluation is shown immediately below the program, unhighlighted. The command menu is also shown with the command used to produce the result selected.

Note: Your screen will not look exactly like this if you are following along on a computer. Figure 4-3 actually combines two screens into a single image. (This book will frequently use this technique to reduce the number of figures required to show the result of an evaluation.) If you are interact-ing directly with Smalltalk, as soon as you evaluate the highlighted expres-sion, the menu will disappear, and the highlighting will move from the program text to the result expression.

Return Values

Note that the value returned by a sequence of statements must always be the last statement in the sequence. Even if you save the result of an earlier statement to a temporary variable, you need to place a statement returning

Figure 4-3.   Temporary variables can be used to return a value other than the one returned by the last statement in a sequence.

the value of that temporary variable as the last statement in the sequence. Frequently, the expression containing the return value is preceded by an upward-pointing caret (^).

```
^tempVariable.
```

If this is the last statement in the series, the caret is not strictly necessary, but it is a good habit to insert a caret before all returned values. The ^ is like a return statement in C or Pascal, and it can be placed earlier in a sequence of statements if an early return from a program is desired. Usually such an early return would be associated with some sort of conditional test.

```
| answer |
.
.
.
answer = 'yes' ifTrue: [^1].
.
.
.
```

The preceding program fragment assumes that other Smalltalk statements surround the single statement displayed. If the value of the temporary local variable, answer, is equal to the string, 'yes', then program control will exit immediately without executing the statements following the test. The value 1 then becomes the return value for the entire program block. This is indicated by the upward-pointing caret used to signal an early return from a program block.

```
^1
```

Understanding the details of conditional execution is not crucial at this point. The main idea is that early return from a program block is possible. Here is a complete program block that, when evaluated, will return one of two possible values:

```
| answer |
answer := Prompter prompt: 'continue?'
                   default: 'yes'.
answer = 'yes'
   ifTrue: [^1]
   ifFalse: [^0].
```

Either a 1 or a 0 is returned by this program block, depending on the answer a user types in response to the prompt.

Evaluating the highlighted expression in Figure 4-4 would cause a prompt window to be displayed.

The prompt window displays a title box containing the string 'continue?' and an input field for typing a response. A default response string, 'yes', is also provided, as shown in Figure 4-5. If the user types nothing but a carriage return, answer is set to 'yes'. The default string can also be edited before RETURN is pressed. This example program returns a 1 if the user accepts the default response to the prompt. Otherwise the program returns 0.

It is possible to have more than one temporary variable in a program block. Simply list all the variables you need, separated by spaces, inside the vertical bars in the declaration.

```
| var1 var2 var3 |
```

Figure 4-4. Early return from a program block is indicated by a caret. Early returns generally work with conditional statements.

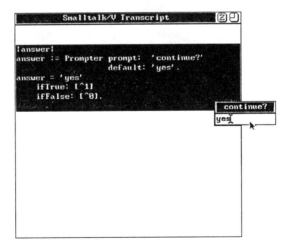

Figure 4-5. A prompt window with a default response string. Different values are returned by this program block depending on the user's response to the prompt.

You can also use temporary variables to build complex expressions.

```
var1 := var2 + var3 * 10.
```

Figure 4-6 shows several temporary variables used in a compound expression to return a computed value.

Working with Multiple Windows

It is often desirable to evaluate text in one window and send output to another window. Typically, when working in Smalltalk, you will have five or more windows open at a given time. One way to send output from text evaluated in one window to another window is to open a second editing window called a *Workspace window*. This is done by popping up the global system menu: point to the gray background area outside any windows open on the Smalltalk screen and press the right mouse button. You will see a menu like that in Figure 4-7. Select "open workspace".

Figure 4-6.   Several temporary variables may be used within a single program block. Compound expressions using variables and constants may be returned by the block.

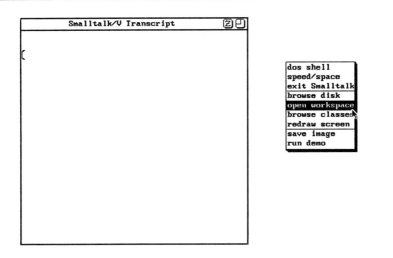

Figure 4-7.   Workspace windows can be opened through Smalltalk's global
system menu.

A new window will appear like that shown in Figure 4-8. You can now
type in the expression **3 + 4** in the new Workspace window and print the
result in the Transcript window by evaluating the following expression:

```
3 + 4 printOn: Transcript.
```

In some Smalltalk systems the result may not immediately appear in the
Transcript window when the expression is evaluated. Since the input focus
is not on the Transcript window (the Transcript window is not the active
window), the visual display of the Transcript window is not updated every
time an expression is evaluated. Only the active window is updated automatically when an expression is evaluated.

What actually happens when the visual display is not immediately
updated (because output is sent to a nonactive window) is as follows: the
data buffer for the window receives the text strings intended for display,
but the visual area itself is not updated until the window becomes active or

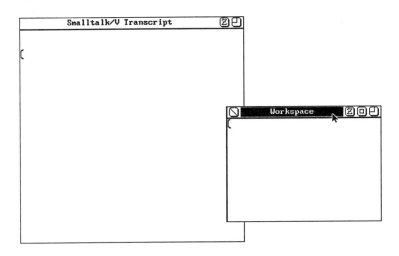

Figure 4-8.   The Workspace window, like the Transcript window, can be moved or resized by the user.

until it receives a message forcing update of the display. However, it is possible to force the update of the Transcript window by sending it a "show" message.

```
Transcript show: '<=='.
```

The show message takes one argument, which must be a string. Because you no longer need to display the result of evaluating the expression in the active window, you can now use the "do it" command instead of the "show it" command.

Figure 4-9 shows the result of evaluating the two preceding statements in the Workspace window. The two statements show two different ways to send output to the Transcript window.

The Transcript window is really an output stream, much in the same way that files are considered output streams in C. The first way to print an object on any stream is to tell the object to print itself, with the printOn message, and then give the name of the stream as an argument.

```
'Hello' printOn: Transcript.
```

All objects in Smalltalk know how to print themselves. The preceding expression tells the string object 'Hello' to print itself on the Transcript window.

Note: Strings in Smalltalk are surrounded by single quotation marks, whereas strings in C++ are in double quotes. Double quotes in Smalltalk are used to surround comments.

The second way to send output to a stream is to send a message to the stream object itself, rather than to the object to be printed.

```
Transcript show: ', World'.
```

This expression sends the show message to the Transcript window. The show message gets a single argument, which must be a string.

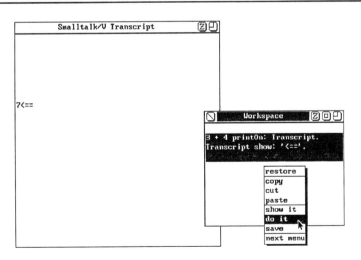

Figure 4-9.   Statements that send output to the Transcript window can be evaluated in a Workspace window.

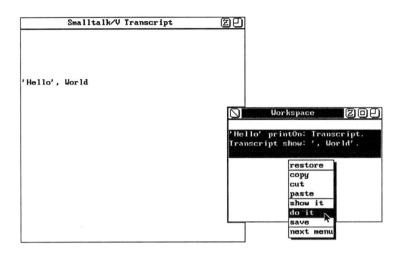

Figure 4-10.   Strings can be printed to windows in two different ways: by sending a printOn message to the string or by sending the string to the window as an argument of the show message.

Look at Figure 4-10 to see the result produced by each of the two output techniques. The first expression produces a string inside single quote marks, and the string in the second expression is printed to the Transcript window without surrounding quotes. The difference is that the first form of output is more general.

As stated earlier, all objects in Smalltalk know how to print themselves on an output stream. When objects are printed to streams using the printOn message, they often contain punctuation that helps identify their data type. For example, strings are printed with surrounding quotes; points are printed with x and y coordinates separated by an @ sign; rectangles are shown by printing the points of opposing corners preceded by the strings 'origin' and 'corner'.

Sometimes you may want better control over the format of strings than is allowed by the printOn message. In this case, the preferred technique is to send the show message to the stream. However, since show requires a string argument, only strings can be printed in this manner. Other output messages can be sent to streams in addition to show. For example, the message "cr" sends a carriage return to the selected output stream.

```
Transcript cr.
```

A tab can be sent in a similar manner.

```
Transcript tab.
```

Figure 4-11 shows one possible way to use combinations of show, cr, and tab messages to format output for a stream.

Concatenating Messages Sent to the Same Object

The object that results from evaluating an expression such as this

```
Transcript show: 'Hello'.
```

is the Transcript object itself. This means you could take the result of evaluating this expression and send that result another message. You do

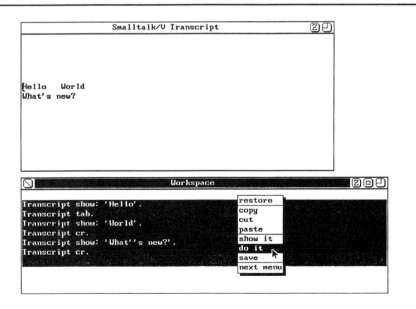

Figure 4-11.   In addition to printing strings with the show method, windows can print tabs and carriage returns through tab and cr messages.

this by separating expressions with a semicolon rather than a period. For example, you could string together four output messages to the Transcript window, as follows:

```
Transcript show: 'Hello'; tab; show: 'World'; cr.
```

This program consists of only a single statement. First the string 'Hello' is sent to the Transcript window, at which point, only the following fragment of the entire statement has been evaluated:

```
Transcript show: 'Hello';
```

The semicolon indicates that more messages are to be sent to the object that results from evaluating this fragment.

Since the result of evaluating output to a stream always returns the stream object to which the output is sent, the next expression,

```
tab;
```

acts exactly like the expression

```
Transcript tab;
```

This expression, like the two that follow it, also returns the Transcript object when evaluated. You can see this is true by noting the result of evaluating the entire statement in Figure 4-12. Note also that "show it" rather than "do it" was used, so that the object returned by evaluating the entire statement would be displayed in the Workspace window. The Workspace window shows that the resulting object is a TextEditor. A TextEditor is a form of window that contains an output stream object.

PROGRAMMING ENVIRONMENTS FOR COMPILED LANGUAGES

Output streams and windows in the Smalltalk environment will be covered in greater detail in Chapter 5. For now, you should know enough about the

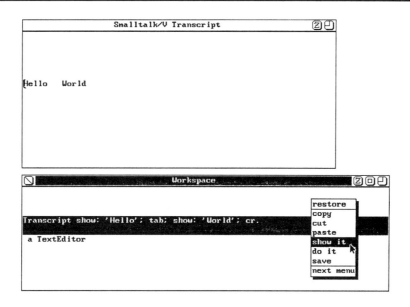

Figure 4-12.   Transcript output messages return the Transcript object itself as the result of evaluation. The Transcript object is a TextEditor, which contains an output stream object.

way Smalltalk operates to follow the examples in the next chapter. Though C++ examples are provided as well in the next chapter, an in-depth explanation of the process of programming in C++ is not as important as it is for Smalltalk.

First of all, working with C++, from the standpoint of editing, compiling, linking, and running programs, is no different from working with C or Pascal. It is easier to separate the C++ programming language from the environment used to construct and run C++ programs than it is in Smalltalk. Actually C++ defines no such programming environment. Although newer compilers, such as Turbo C++ and C++ produced by Zortech, do provide integrated development environments, you do not need to use these environments to create C++ programs. You can use your old familiar editor to create program source text and then submit the code to a stand-alone compiler.

Many people see the clear distinction between a language and its programming environment as a positive thing. Others see it as a drawback.

You'll have to decide for yourself. The integrated environment of Smalltalk and the stand-alone compiler for C++ represent the opposing poles of a continuum. It is becoming more and more common to find programming environments integrated into traditional procedural languages.

RUN-TIME SUPPORT FOR EXECUTABLE PROGRAMS

As mentioned earlier, Smalltalk provides both an interpreter and an incremental compiler in a typical environment. But all the Smalltalk examples in this particular chapter make use of only the interpreter. You cannot run programs in an interactive interpreted fashion without the support of either a programming environment or another supporting run-time environment such as a debugger. A debugger for C++ provides a limited sort of programming environment to run and test programs.

The ability to move quickly between editing text, compiling a program, and running, testing, and debugging the program—all from within a single programming environment—has been made possible with modern C, Pascal, and C++ compilers. This process, however, can largely be attributed to the influence of Smalltalk.

The distinction between an interactive interpreted language, such as Smalltalk or Actor, and a compiled language (C, Pascal, C++) changes the process of program development dramatically. Rather than considering that process at this point, simply keep in mind that the C++ program fragments and listings presented in the next chapter are intended to show similarities between the expressions and syntax used to solve a given problem in both Smalltalk and C++. The assumption is that you have worked with a compiler for some procedural language. The C++ examples simply put an object-oriented "spin" on some simple statements that you should already be able to read and understand, whether your background is in C or Pascal. Beyond this, the details of building C++ programs are not important right now.

That's just enough Smalltalk to get off the ground.

5

CLASS LIBRARIES

Object-oriented programming is characterized by programming in the presence of *class libraries*. Few of the real advantages of object-oriented programming are realized until you begin to build upon the work of others. You build upon the work of others by reusing code that has been developed, tested, and debugged before being placed in a class library.

At first it seems insignificant to say that class libraries play a central role in object-oriented programming. It could be argued that the use of standard libraries plays a central role for procedural programs written in C or Pascal. But there's a difference. Standard libraries for procedural languages are not nearly as flexible as class libraries for object-oriented languages. If you don't like the way that a procedure or function behaves in a standard library, you can't modify it. Even if the function handles 95 percent of your requirements for a given application, you still have to write the entire procedure over from scratch when it doesn't go the whole nine yards. This dilemma wastes both time and code. In most cases, the code for the standard library function is going to be linked into your executable program even if it is not called. This eats up precious memory. Further you have to rethink and recode a solution to a problem that has already been thought out and implemented. Because the procedure doesn't do exactly what you want it to do, you have no choice but to reinvent the wheel.

Object-oriented libraries give you a way out. First of all, inheritance allows you to redefine new classes based on previously defined classes. Inheritance provides a mechanism for code reuse that lets you specify only the code that needs to be different from an existing class implementation in order to get the behavior you want. You don't need to redefine entire functions or classes from scratch. Further, dynamic binding lets you build flexible dispatch mechanisms that make code easier to read and maintain by simplifying the way objects communicate and pass control.

The notion of a uniform mechanism for communicating with objects and dispatching control has been advocated for some time. The problem is that traditional procedural languages force the programmer to maintain switch statements to dispatch to the appropriate functions based on the type of the object for which the function is requested. This makes it nearly impossible for someone building a class library to put the dispatch mechanism in the library itself. Each time a new type is added to the system, the entire class library has to be recompiled. It would be impossible to stabilize a library that constantly needs to be recompiled. Even with disciplined maintenance and testing, bugs will eventually creep in as the capabilities of the library are stretched beyond the original design boundaries. The integrity and dependability of the library are compromised.

Dynamic binding allows users of class libraries to extend the class libraries without requiring access to source code. This makes third-party builders happy because they don't have to give up the proprietary secrets that make their libraries unique. Protecting proprietary code gives developers a better chance of recovering research and development costs. Giving users the power to extend the capabilities of a class library without source code means the builder of the class library can do the major work of defining the communication protocol without limiting the options of the user. Further, the builder of the class library doesn't need to try and foresee every use and special case that the class library will have to handle. Users adapt third-party class libraries to handle special cases by deriving new classes from the original classes in the library while still relying on the control dispatch mechanism provided by the library developer.

THE SMALLTALK CLASS LIBRARY

Class libraries come in two varieties: *general class libraries* and *application-specific class libraries*. General libraries include container class libraries and application frameworks. Application-specific class libraries are usually built and maintained in-house for the purpose of supporting deliverable application programs. Application-specific libraries are usually proprietary and not sold to the public in either source code format or object code format. Sometimes general libraries are called toolkits, or utility libraries. Often they are platform specific, such as window systems for a particular piece of hardware, or they might be more general interface tools such as dialog boxes, radio buttons, and scrollbars, which will run on a variety of different hardware.

Rather than try to understand the purposes of each of the different types of class libraries, it's easier to begin with general class libraries that are found in many different programming environments. The most commonly found and used class libraries are *container class libraries*. Most of these libraries are based on the original class library designed for Smalltalk-80.

There are a number of advantages in starting a study of class libraries with the Smalltalk container classes. First of all, you will inevitably encounter container class libraries as you work more with object-oriented programming languages. You will at least need to know how to use container classes if you don't need to build them yourself. Second, by understanding the design, implementation, and intended use of general container class libraries, you will learn techniques and principles that can be applied to building or using any class library.

You'll find the influence of the original Smalltalk class library everywhere. The container classes in Actor, for example, are taken directly from Smalltalk. Keith Gorlen's public domain NIH library is nearly a direct implementation of the Smalltalk class library in C++. Flavors of the original Smalltalk container class library are found in example libraries distributed with Turbo C++ as well as Zortech's C++.

Application frameworks such as C++ Views, which provides a sophisticated programming environment for developing Microsoft Windows applications in C++, descend directly from the Smalltalk container classes. These frameworks borrow a number of other concepts from Smalltalk such as the model-view-controller structure, which is now becoming a powerful and popular structure for organizing programs. Even Microsoft Windows derives a number of concepts from the Smalltalk class library, such as the BitBlt class for rapid transfer of graphic images and management of graphical user interfaces. Even though C is the language chosen to implement Windows applications, the organizational structure of Windows applications is dramatically influenced by Smalltalk.

Message passing and event-driven control mechanisms for today's sophisticated user interfaces require the support of object-oriented programming and polymorphic class libraries in order to give programmers the required tools to manage program complexity.

COLLECTIONS AND CONTAINERS

First of all, look at the class hierarchy for the collection classes provided by Smalltalk/V. With minor variations, most container class libraries follow the basic structure outlined by the following classes, and use similar naming conventions.

```
Collection
    Bag
    IndexedCollection
        FixedSizeCollection
            Array
            Bitmap
            String
                Symbol
        OrderedCollection
            SortedCollection
    Set
        Dictionary
            MethodDictionary
            SystemDictionary
```

Bags and Sets

Bags and Sets are the simplest forms of collections. Figure 5-1 shows a simple Smalltalk program to create a Bag object. Three strings are added to the Bag. Remember, a Bag object is a form of collection. After the program adds the strings to the Bag, the variable, aBag, is returned by the program. If this program is evaluated with the "show it" command, the Bag itself is printed in the same window as the program text. Take a look at the distinguishing lines in the program.

The first line declares a temporary variable that will hold the Bag collection.

```
| aBag |
aBag := Bag new.
aBag add: 'one'.
aBag add: 'two'.
aBag add: 'three'.
^aBag.
```

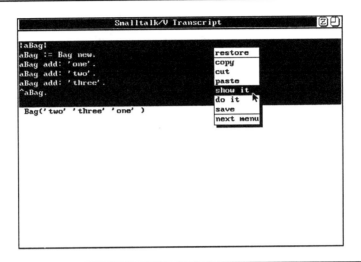

Figure 5-1.   A Bag represents a typical container class.

Remember that Smalltalk variable declarations do not specify type information. Calling the variable aBag simply gives the reader information about the type of data the variable is expected to refer to. There is nothing, however, that prevents the programmer from doing something confusing, like making aBag refer to a Point object at one point in the program, to a Rectangle at another place, and to a String in still a third place. Doing this would be an invitation to disaster, but it points out that there are both advantages and disadvantages to using such polymorphic variables in Smalltalk.

The next line in the program actually creates a new Bag object and assigns the variable aBag to refer to the new object.

```
aBag := Bag new.
```

The subexpression that creates the Bag object is

```
Bag new
```

In Smalltalk, classes themselves are objects within the programming environment. This is not the case with C++ and Pascal class libraries. In Smalltalk, the Bag object (which is a global variable representing a class) is sent the message "new". The new method for Bag is then invoked, which sets aside the proper amount of memory for a Bag collection and then returns a reference to the object that can be assigned to a variable.

The most common thing to do with any collection is to add items to it. The protocol for adding elements to a collection is the same for all collection classes. The add: method is sent to the collection with some form of object given as an argument.

```
aBag add: 'one'.
```

The variable, aBag, receives the message "add:". The colon following add indicates that an argument follows.

For most collections, the argument to add may be any type of object: a String, a Point, a Rectangle, a Character, an InputEvent, a Window, and so forth. In the case of aBag, only strings are added to the collection.

Finally, after three Strings are added to aBag, the value of aBag is returned by the program:

```
^aBag
```

If this program were highlighted and evaluated with "do it", you would not see anything. The program would go through the process of creating a Bag and then add three Strings to it. Since aBag is a temporary variable, it is discarded, along with its contents, as soon as the interpreter is through evaluating the program.

In order to see the actual contents of the Bag, you must evaluate the program with "show it". When you do this, the printOn message is automatically sent to aBag, and the argument for printOn is the output stream for the window containing the highlighted program text. When a Bag object receives the printOn message, it automatically prints the String, "Bag", followed by an open parenthesis. Then the printOn message is sent to every element in the collection, followed by a space to separate the output. Since all objects in the collection are Strings, they are printed inside single quote marks. Finally, a closing parenthesis is printed to indicate the end of the collection.

One thing to notice about Bags is that the contents of the collection are not necessarily in the same order as the order in which the elements are added. For instance, you might expect aBag to respond to the printOn message with the following output,

```
Bag('one' 'two' 'three')
```

but the odds are that this will not be the case. The order of elements in a Bag is determined by a hashing algorithm, which is implementation-dependent and undefined by the Smalltalk language itself. The hashing algorithm helps ensure that elements inside a collection are evenly distributed for the purpose of internal organization and fast lookup. Don't worry—you don't need to know anything about hashing to use collections.

All collections have certain distinguishing characteristics. One of the distinguishing characteristics of a Bag is that no special ordering of elements is guaranteed.

Sets are like Bags in that they do not guarantee the order of their elements. Figure 5-2 shows a Bag object containing six elements. Figure 5-3 shows a Set object also containing six elements, all Strings. Note that the order of elements is not even consistent between the Bag and Set collections. It is even possible that running either of these programs twice will produce a different order for the elements on the first evaluation than on the second.

Sets are different from Bags in that Sets automatically discard duplicated objects. That means no matter how many times you add the String 'three' to a Set, the Set will only contain one String object with a value of 'three'. Figure 5-4 shows what happens when three groups of duplicate Strings are added to a Set.

Bags, however, do not weed out duplicate elements. If you add the String 'one' three times to a Bag, the Bag will contain the String element 'one' in three different positions. Figure 5-5 shows a Bag that has the same three groups of duplicate Strings added to it.

Sets and Bags, like most collections, do not limit their elements to Strings. Figure 5-6 shows a Set that contains a String, a Point, and a Rectangle. A printout of the contents of this particular Set shows polymorphism at work.

Even though the elements of this set appear to have little in common, their polymorphism is established by the parent class they all share. Strings,

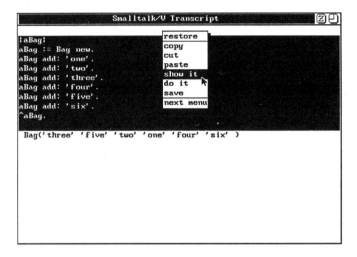

Figure 5-2.   Bags do not guarantee the order of their elements.

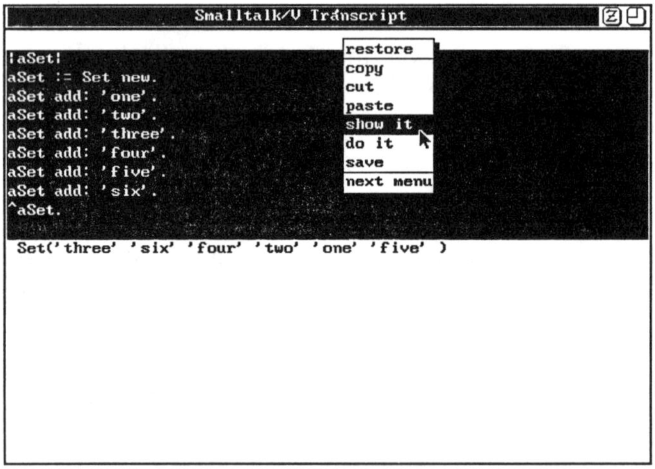

Figure 5-3.   Sets, like Bags, do not guarantee the order of their elements.

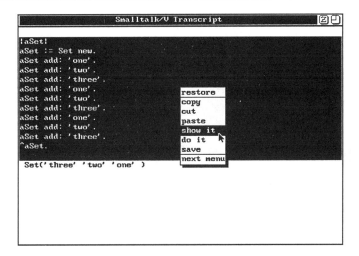

Figure 5-4.   Three groups of duplicate Strings added to a Set

Points, and Rectangles are all derived ultimately from the Object class. The Object class defines a common communication protocol dictating that, among other things, all objects respond to the printOn message. It is up to the derived class to override the printOn message defined for the Object class itself. Since the String, Point, and Rectangle classes all do override the printOn method, collection classes don't need to define any special code for printing out their contents.

When aSet receives the printOn message, it simply *iterates*, or loops over, each of its elements, passing the printOn message to each element in turn. You can even define a new class, create an object as an instance of that class, and then add the object to a collection. As long as you define the proper printOn method for the new class, the collection will automatically handle the printing of any elements. This works even though the printOn method for the collection class was implemented before the printOn method for your new class. This type of generalized iteration and response to common communication protocol would not be possible without polymorphism and dynamic binding. Some of the following examples will show other polymorphic messages, which can be sent to the elements of a collection using access objects called *iterators*.

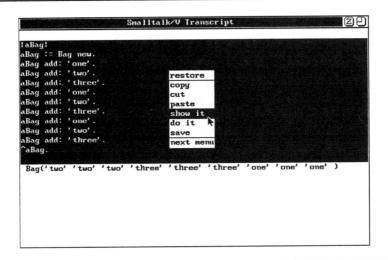

Figure 5-5.   Bags do not weed out duplicate elements.

When you invoke the "show it" command for the program shown in Figure 5-6, a number of things happen. First, a new Set is created, then the String, Point, and Rectangle are added to the Set. The last statement

```
^aSet.
```

returns a reference to aSet to the Smalltalk interpreter that was invoked by the "show it" command. The last thing that "show it" does is send the equivalent of a printOn message to the value returned by the program.

Rather than relying on "show it" to indirectly send the printOn message to a collection, you could explicitly send the printOn message to a collection. You might do this if you wanted to evaluate program source code in one window and send the output to another window.

You could explicitly send the printOn message to each element using an iterator. An iterator is a form of loop containing an object that is like a pointer. The pointer component of the iterator points to the current element in a collection and advances on each iteration to the next element in the collection. For instance, if you were designing the code for the "show

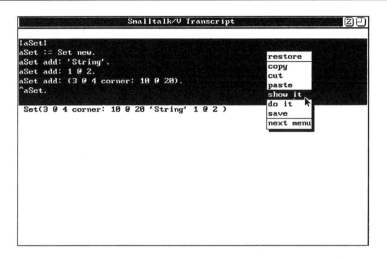

```
Smalltalk/V Transcript                    [Z][ ]
|aSet|
aSet := Set new.
aSet add: 'String'.               restore
aSet add: 1 @ 2.                  copy
aSet add: (3 @ 4 corner: 10 @ 20). cut
^aSet.                            paste
                                  show it
   Set(3 @ 4 corner: 10 @ 20 'String' 1 @ 2 )  do it
                                  save
                                  next menu
```

Figure 5-6.   Collections may contain polymorphic objects. This set contains a String, a Point, and a Rectangle.

it" command yourself, it might look something like Figure 5-7. The only new code in Figure 5-7 that you have not seen before is the code for the iterator itself.

```
.
.
.
aSet do: [:element |
        element printOn: Transcript.
        Transcript show: ' '.].
```

An iterator is invoked for a collection by sending the "do:" message to the collection object itself. In this case aSet receives the do: message. The do: message must be supplied with an argument, which is a *program block.* The program block is the code inside of and including the opening and closing square brackets.

```
["..."]
```

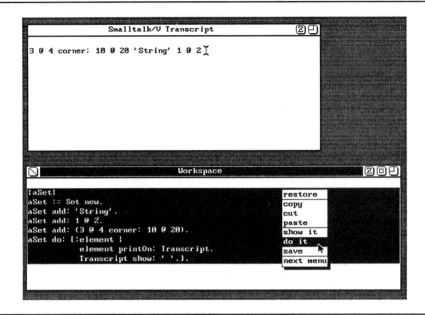

Figure 5-7.   Iterators such as do: can be used to print each of the elements of a
collection.

There is no exact equivalent of a program block in C, C++, or Pascal.
Though all these languages use the term *block* to signify a segment of code,
usually when discussing the scope of variables, there is a major difference
between program blocks in traditional structured languages and program
blocks in Smalltalk. In Smalltalk, a program block is an executable piece of
code that can be passed as an argument in the form of program text. It does
not necessarily exist as object code in memory. A program block in Smalltalk often does not occupy memory until it is evaluated. Program blocks are
discarded once they go out of scope and are no longer referenced. Program
blocks can be assigned to variables in Smalltalk. Variables that have been
assigned program blocks can then be evaluated. In this respect, program
blocks are more like data in a traditional language than like code.

    The closest thing to a Smalltalk program block in a traditional structured
language is a pointer to a function. But program blocks are much more
flexible. Both Actor and Smalltalk make extensive use of program blocks.

The details of memory management and evaluation of program blocks are unimportant at this point. However, since program blocks play such a critical role in both Smalltalk and Actor, it is important to be able to read them and grasp their meaning.

Arguments can be passed to program blocks. Any arguments must be declared at the beginning of the block, and the argument names must be preceded by a colon. Block arguments are separated from program text within the block by a vertical bar, ¦.

```
[:arg ¦ ... program text ...]
```

The program block in Figure 5-7 declares only one block argument.

```
[:element ¦ ...]
```

Blocks associated with iterators through the do: message must always declare exactly one *block argument*. This block argument is like a local variable, but the value of a block argument is passed to it from outside the block by the expression invoking the block. A block is like a function that has no name and can be moved anywhere in memory or discarded altogether when it is no longer needed.

The program block itself is also an argument for another expression. The block is an argument that is passed to the do: message, and it is the do: method that is responsible for supplying values to the block. The iterator variable inside the program block is "element". For each element in the collection, aSet, the do: method assigns the element to the block argument, element, and then invokes the code inside the block. This makes it possible to send the same message to each element of a collection or to perform a given operation using each of the collection elements.

For example, it might be useful to know the type or *species* of each of the elements of a collection when the collection is printed. You could do this by sending the message "species" to each of the objects in a collection. Smalltalk objects know their species because they retain information about their type after they are created, in contrast to C++, C, or Pascal, where the type information for an object is not available at run time. This is why, in a traditional compiled language, type information has to be specified at the point where variables are declared. The compiler, upon seeing the type of a variable object, sets aside enough memory for the object and then replaces all future references to the object with the address of the allocated memory.

Smalltalk variables or objects are more dynamic—they don't need to be declared with type information because the environment can always ask an object its type when a program is running.

The drawback of such dynamic objects is the extra memory required. Each object needs extra memory to retain type information, and the run-time environment needs extra memory to retain information about the entire type hierarchy for the class library. The advantage of dynamic typing is that you can always find the type of an object if you don't know what it is. For example, you could send the species message to the String 'Hello, world' as follows:

```
'Hello, world' species.
```

The result returned by evaluating this statement with "show it" would be

```
String
```

indicating that the object is a member of the String class. Similarly, sending the species message to the object (1@2) would produce the result Point.

It's often useful to find out the type of species of a complex object, such as the Transcript object, which is a TextEditor. Knowing this will help you explore other forms of documentation and use Smalltalk's class hierarchy browser to learn what you can do with the Transcript window. But for now, let's stick to iterators.

Figure 5-7 shows how you can use an iterator to format the output of each of the elements of a collection and send the result to the Transcript window. Now the elements are separated by a comma, a space, and a tab character making it easier to pick out the individual elements.

As suggested earlier, you may want to know the species of each of the elements of a collection when you print the collection. Figure 5-8 shows how the species of objects can be determined by sending them the species message. Figure 5-9 shows an iterator used to print each of the elements of a set to the Transcript window. The set has three elements, a String, a Point, and a Rectangle. You can use an iterator to print the species of each element of a collection to the Transcript window as well, followed by the elements themselves formatted with tabs and visual cues. Figure 5-10 shows a Smalltalk program that does this.

Smalltalk provides several different types of iterators. There are iterators to extract the members of a collection that meet a certain criterion; there are iterators that evaluate a block of code for each collection element and then

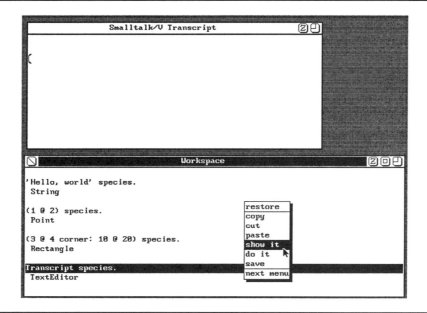

Figure 5-8.   The species message returns the class or type of an object.

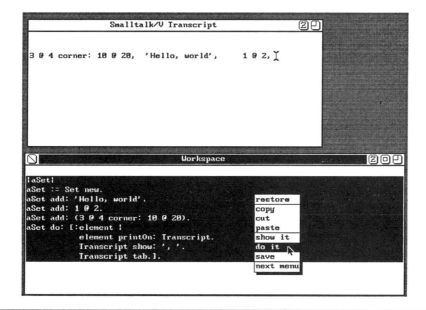

Figure 5-9.   Iterators are useful for controlling the output of collection elements.

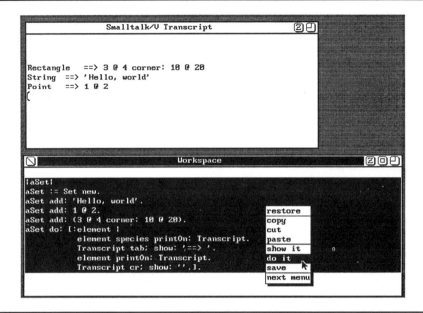

Figure 5-10.   Iterators can be used to extract and print information about the elements of a collection.

return a collection of results. It is primarily the general form of iterator, which is in the do: message, that you will see borrowed from Smalltalk by C++ and Pascal class libraries.

Dictionaries

You can see by looking at the Smalltalk class hierarchy at the beginning of the chapter that Dictionary is a subclass of Set. Dictionaries are useful for a number of applications, including phone or address databases, compiler symbol tables, or text replacement tables in a text editor or macro preprocessor.

It's pretty easy to guess how a Dictionary object works from its name. Like a standard dictionary, all entries are pairs of associations—that is, you have a word that you are looking up associated with the definition for that word. Smalltalk generalizes this concept and calls the elements of a Dictionary collection *key/value pairs.*

Another name for a key/value pair is an *association*. The key is like the word you are looking up. The value is like the definition. The difference is that neither the key nor the value need to be strings of text like you would find in a standard dictionary. The key could be a Number, a Point, a Window, or any other Smalltalk object—so could the value. The primary way that a Dictionary collection in Smalltalk differs from a standard dictionary is that every key must be unique. No duplicate keys are allowed. Recall that allowing no duplicate elements is a characteristic of a Set and that a Dictionary is a subclass of Set. It doesn't matter if the value associated with a duplicate key differs from the value of the original key/value pair. If you try to add an association to a Dictionary and the key is already used, the value associated with the original key is discarded and replaced by the new value. Let's see how this works.

This time, rather than creating and discarding the collection each time the program is run, a Dictionary will be created and made a permanent part of the Smalltalk environment. A global variable called NameDictionary is created by assigning a variable to reference a newly created object as follows:

```
NameDictionary := Dictionary new.
```

The Smalltalk interpreter doesn't have the symbol NameDictionary in its global symbol table so it assumes you want to add the name to the table and responds with a dialog window like that in Figure 5-11. If you had made a mistake and did not intend NameDictionary to become a permanent global variable, you would select the first menu choice.

```
'NameDictionary' is undefined
```

The interpreter would then generate an error dialog to let you know it cannot evaluate the expression.

If you select the second menu choice,

```
define 'NameDictionary' as global
```

the interpreter adds the symbol NameDictionary to the list of existing global symbols, and then creates a new Dictionary object and assigns Name-Dictionary to reference the object. If you are following along on your computer, select the second menu choice to make NameDictionary a global

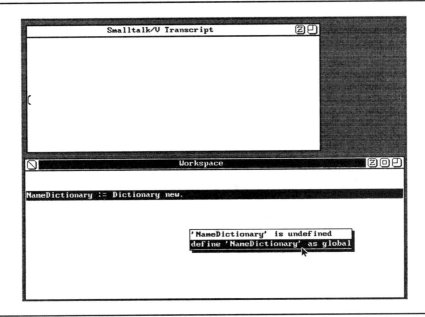

Figure 5-11.   Adding a new global variable to the Smalltalk programming
environment

variable. The NameDictionary will be a set of name pairs. The key will be
the last name, and the value will be the first name.

In Smalltalk, messages with one or more arguments are called *keyword
messages*. Because the elements of Dictionaries are associations and associations have two parts, a key and a value, Dictionaries provide a special
message with two keywords to add associations to a Dictionary. Instead of
using add: you can use the at:put: message, which consists of two keywords
and two arguments.

```
NameDictionary at: 'Armstrong' put: 'Louis'.
```

This would add one element to NameDictionary. The key for the association would be 'Armstrong' and the value associated with the key would be
'Louis'. After evaluating this expression you could print the contents of the
dictionary by highlighting the variable NameDictionary, and then selecting
"show it". Note that when you do this, as shown in Figure 5-12, only the
key is printed for the association, not the value.

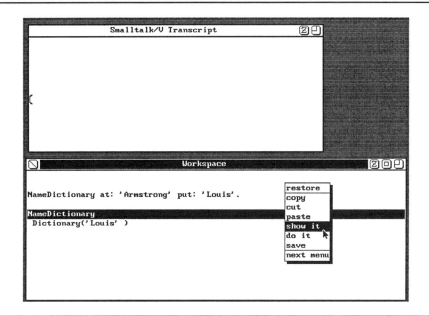

Figure 5-12.   Adding an association (key/value pair) to a Dictionary collection and printing the result

You could add several associations to a Dictionary in a single statement by cascading each of the at:put: messages sent to NameDictionary.

```
NameDictionary
    at: 'Armstrong' put: 'Louis';
    at: 'Steinbeck' put: 'John';
    at: 'Didion' put: 'Joan';
    at: 'Piaf' put: 'Edith'.
```

Then you could look up the value of any association by providing the key as an argument to the at: message and sending it to NameDictionary, as shown in Figure 5-13.

The at:put: message is really a shortcut. You could use the add: message to add elements to a Dictionary, but one of the characteristics of a Dictionary is that you can only add associations. You can create an association with 'Armstrong' as the key and 'Louis' as the value with the following statement:

```
Association key: 'Armstrong' value: 'Louis'.
```

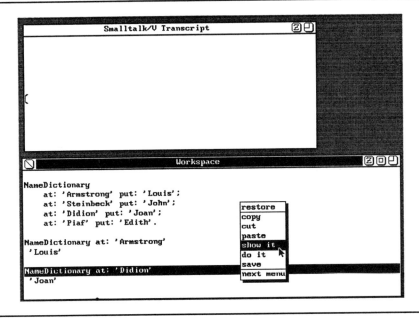

Figure 5-13.   Retrieving association values from a Dictionary collection by providing a key

You could use this code to create an association and then add the association to NameDictionary as follows.

```
NameDictionary add: (Association key: 'Armstrong' value: 'Louis').
```

Figure 5-14 shows the results of evaluating each of these three statements with "show it". Note that the result of evaluating the first and second expressions is the entire association,

```
'Armstrong' ==> 'Louis'
```

while the result of evaluating the third statement is the value of the association.

```
'Louis'
```

This is the primary difference between using add: and at:put:. The value returned by sending the add: message to a Dictionary object is an associa-

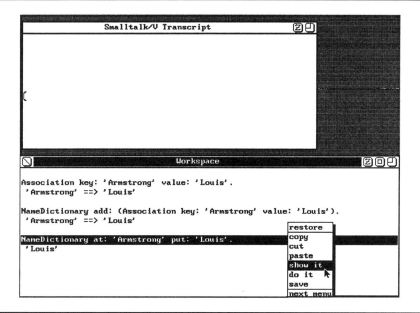

Figure 5-14.   Creating an association, then using add: is nearly equivalent to using at:put: with a key and a value.

tion. The value returned by at:put: is a value. In most cases it won't matter which technique you use because you don't often need the return value when adding an element to a collection.

Figure 5-15 illustrates how adding a new association to a Dictionary that already contains an association with the same key causes the value of the existing association to be replaced with the value of the new association. Figure 5-15 also shows that printing a Dictionary with "show it" causes the values rather than the keys to be printed. If you want, you can print the keys by evaluating the following expression with "show it".

```
NameDictionary keys
```

The result of evaluating this expression is a Set of keys in the dictionary.

You can send a similar message to create and print a collection of the values contained in the dictionary.

```
NameDictionary values.
```

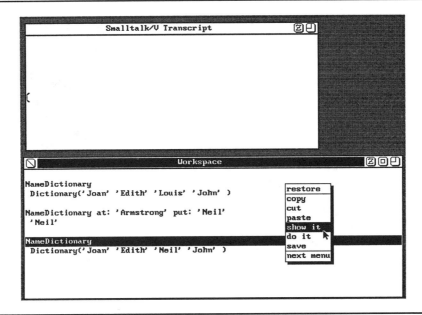

Figure 5-15.   Adding an association that duplicates an existing key causes the
new association to replace the old.

The result of evaluating this expression is a Bag. Remember that keys
cannot be duplicated. That is why the collection returned by the following
is a Set.

```
NameDictionary keys
```

There can, however, be duplicate values in a Dictionary, as shown in
Figure 5-16, where a second association with the value 'John' is added to
the dictionary.
    In addition to being able to retrieve a value associated with a key from a
dictionary,

```
NameDictionary at: 'Armstrong'.
```

you can also retrieve the entire association:

```
NameDictionary associationAt: 'Armstrong'.
```

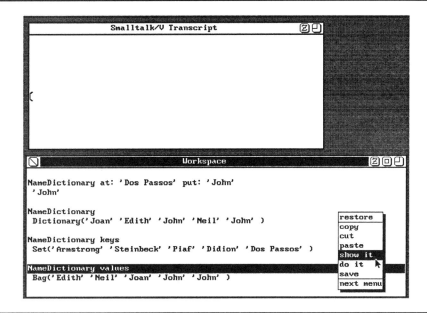

Figure 5-16. The keys message returns a Set when sent to a Dictionary object. The values message returns a Bag. Values may have duplicate elements, keys may not.

You can retrieve a key if you know the value of an association. For example:

```
NameDictionary keyAtValue: 'John'.
```

Note that this will only retrieve the key of the first association that matches the specified value.

Also, you can determine the number of elements in a collection like a Dictionary by sending the size message to the collection.

```
NameDictionary size .
```

Figure 5-17 shows the results of evaluating each of these expressions for a Dictionary containing five elements. The values and the keys for the dictionary are printed in the Transcript window. Note that the order of the

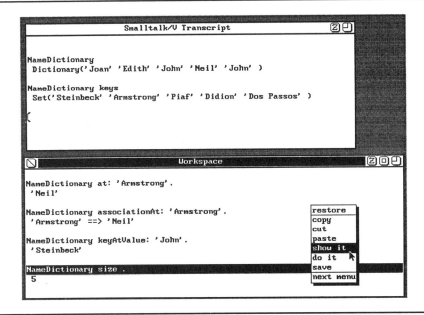

Figure 5-17. Different messages sent to Dictionaries produce different objects. Among other objects, dictionaries can return values (at:), associations (associationAt:), keys (keyAtValue:), and numbers (size:).

values in the Transcript window does not match the order of the keys. Dictionaries, like Bags and Sets, do not guarantee the order of their elements.

Dictionaries and Iterators

Iterators can be used on Dictionaries just like on Bags and Sets. When using the do: message to iterate over the elements of a Dictionary, the iterator is set to each of the values of the associations in the collection in turn, rather than being set to the associations themselves. Most often this is what you will want. Such an iterator can be used to print the values of the Dictionary associations to the Transcript window, as shown in Figure 5-18.

If, however, you need to perform an operation on each of the keys within the Dictionary rather than each of the values, you can use the keysDo: message to perform the iteration.

```
NameDictionary keysDo: [:element | ...]
```

The block that is evaluated for each member of the Dictionary with keysDo: is exactly the same as the block used with the do: message. Exactly one argument is expected followed by the program text for the block. Figure 5-19 shows how the keysDo: message can be used to print the Dictionary's keys in the Transcript window.

If you want to perform an operation on each of the associations within a Dictionary, you can send the Dictionary the associationsDo: message. This message takes a single block argument of exactly the same form as the blocks in the do: and keysDo: messages. Figure 5-20 shows how the associationsDo: message can be used to iterate over the elements of NameDictionary to print each of the associations in the Transcript window.

Dictionaries are used extensively in the Smalltalk programming environment. In fact, all global variables and classes are maintained in a dictionary. The dictionary itself is a global variable named "Smalltalk". The keys used to look up associations in the Smalltalk dictionary are *symbols* rather than strings. Symbols are exactly like strings except that only one copy of a

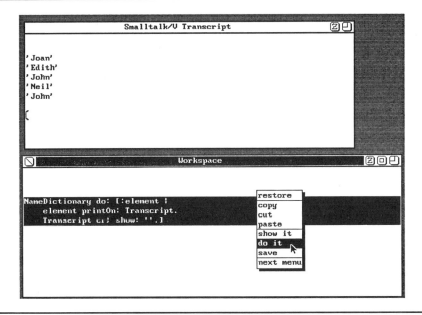

Figure 5-18.   Iterating with do: to print a Dictionary's values

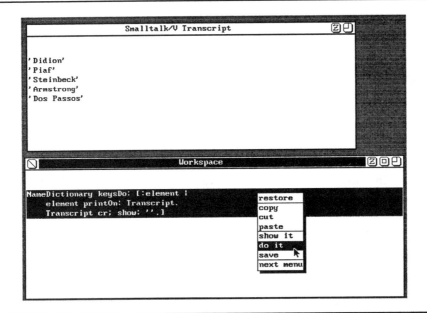

Figure 5-19.   Iterating with keysDo: to print associations

symbol is allowed to exist in the entire Smalltalk environment. There may be one or several copies of a String object. Rather than being surrounded by single quotes, Smalltalk Symbols are preceded by a pound sign, #. Thus, the symbol that could be used to look up the global variable NameDictionary in the Smalltalk dictionary would be

```
#NameDictionary
```

rather than

```
'NameDictionary'
```

Smalltalk also uses Dictionaries for each class in the system to keep the compiled method object code associated with the appropriate method name for a given class. Not surprisingly, these dictionaries are called *method dictionaries*. Other dictionaries keep track of global constants for printing special characters such as:

'Tab'
'Space'
'Cr' (carriage return)
'Ff' (form feed)

These constants are contained in a global dictionary called CharacterConstants.

Figure 5-21 shows that the Smalltalk global dictionary can be used just like NameDictionary except that Symbols are used to do the lookup instead of Strings. You can find the global variable NameDictionary, which was created in this chapter, in the Smalltalk dictionary by evaluating the following expression with "show it".

```
Smalltalk at: #NameDictionary
```

The Symbols #Transcript and #CharacterConstants can also be found in the Smalltalk dictionary using the at: message. CharacterConstant is itself a

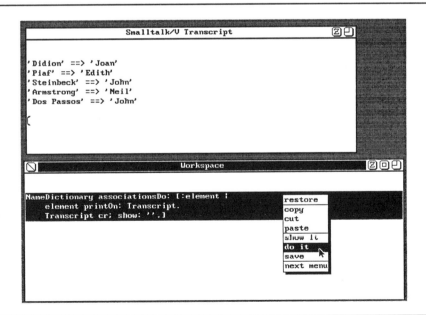

Figure 5-20.   Iterating with associationsDo: to print associations

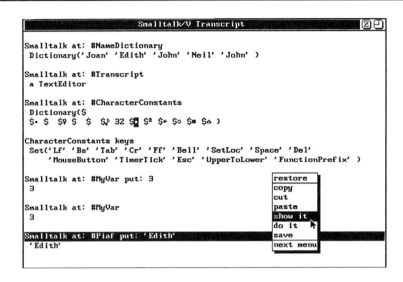

Figure 5-21.   Dictionaries are used extensively to implement the Smalltalk
                programming environment itself.

Dictionary containing String names for commonly used character constants
along with the associated ASCII value for the constant.

You can add associations to the Smalltalk dictionary with the at:put:
message just as you did with the NameDictionary. When you do this, the
new associations become a permanent part of the Smalltalk environment.

Smalltalk also provides special Dictionary *inspectors*, which allow you to
look at and edit the contents of a dictionary. For example, you could
inspect the NameDictionary created in this chapter by evaluating the following expression with "do it".

```
NameDictionary inspect
```

This will cause a new window to be opened, with the keys for Name-
Dictionary listed in the left pane of the window and the value for the
highlighted key in the right pane. Dictionary inspectors allow you to
remove, inspect, or add associations in the left pane, while you can edit

existing values in the right pane. Figure 5-22 shows two dictionary inspectors, one opened on NameDictionary, the other opened on CharacterConstants.

Ordered Collections

Bags, Sets, and Dictionaries are *unordered* collections. You cannot depend on the order of elements in any of these collections regardless of the order in which the elements are added. However, you frequently need to be able to count on the order of the elements in a collection to use the collection for a given task. Consider using some form of collection to represent a polygon. A polygon is a collection of points connected by lines in a specified order. When you create collections containing the points for drawing a polygon, you want the collection to keep the points in the same order in which they

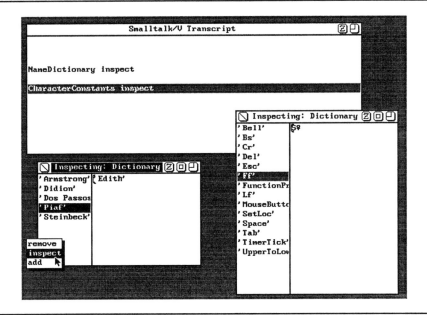

Figure 5-22.   Dictionary inspectors are windows that let you look at and modify the elements of Dictionary collections.

are added. Smalltalk provides a class, OrderedCollection, which does just this. An *ordered* collection is created just like a Bag or a Set—by sending the "new" message to the class.

```
OrderedCollection new
```

As with the example for NameDictionary it is desirable to create a global variable to represent the polygon and contain the collection of points. You could create a global variable called MyPolygon and make it an ordered collection by evaluating the following expression.

```
MyPolygon := OrderedCollection new.
```

This is the same technique that was used to create the global variable NameDictionary in the last section. Since MyPolygon does not yet exist in the Smalltalk dictionary, evaluating the above expression will open a dialog window asking if you want to make MyPolygon a global variable. If you select this option, MyPolygon is entered into the Smalltalk dictionary with the symbol #MyPolygon as the key and the newly created OrderedCollection as the value. You could now retrieve the value of MyPolygon by evaluating

```
Smalltalk at: #MyPolygon.
```

The result of evaluating this expression is an empty OrderedCollection, since this is the value in the Smalltalk dictionary associated with #MyPolygon. You would get exactly the same response by evaluating the following expression.

```
MyPolygon
```

The first thing the Smalltalk interpreter does when evaluating such an expression is look in the Smalltalk dictionary to see if a symbol exists that matches the highlighted identifier. If it does, the Smalltalk interpreter returns the value associated with the symbol used as a key. MyPolygon is now a permanent part of the Smalltalk programming environment. This makes it easier to add items to MyPolygon, to view the contents, and to test the use of iterators on MyPolygon.

If you use this technique frequently with many different variable names, you would eventually have many old and obsolete global variables lying around wasting memory and cluttering the environment. You need a way to remove a global variable from memory. The global variable MyPolygon can be removed from the Smalltalk Dictionary by evaluating the following expression.

```
Smalltalk removeKey: #MyPolygon.
```

Any association can be removed from any dictionary by sending the removeKey: message to the dictionary with the appropriate key for the association. The result of evaluating such an expression is to return the updated dictionary with the specified association removed. You can see the results of evaluating these four expressions with "show it" in Figure 5-23. Note that the object returned by sending removeKey: to the Smalltalk dictionary is a SystemDictionary containing all the Smalltalk classes and global variables. The result is printed on a single line, which is probably several thousand columns wide and extends far beyond the right edge of the Workspace window.

Since Smalltalk is a dictionary, you could also add a global variable like MyPolygon using the at:put: message.

```
Smalltalk at: #MyPolygon put: OrderedCollection new.
```

This expression has exactly the same effect as

```
MyPolygon := OrderedCollection new.
```

except that when you use the at:put: message, the interpreter assumes you know what you are doing and avoids the dialog box to confirm that you really do want to add a global variable to the system. Once you have created a global variable, MyPolygon, as an OrderedCollection, you can now add a set of points to the collection in the order you wish to connect bordering lines.

```
MyPolygon add: 10 @ 10.
MyPolygon add: 100 @ 10.
MyPolygon add: 100 @ 100.
```

```
MyPolygon add: 10 @ 100.
MyPolygon do: [:aPoint |
                aPoint printOn: Transcript.
                Transcript cr; show: ".].
```

You can then use an iterator to print the contents of MyPolygon to the Transcript window. Figure 5-24 shows the result of evaluating the code in the previous listing and printing the Point elements of MyPolygon to the Transcript window. Notice that the variable MyPolygon is returned and printed as a result of evaluating the highlighted program text, because that is the value returned by passing the do: iteration message to MyPolygon in the last program statement.

A program can now be written to draw lines between the points inside MyPolygon in the proper order. Program 5-1 uses a Pen object to draw lines between the points. Most Smalltalk systems provide a Pen class to draw graphic images. Anyone familiar with Turtle Graphics developed for Logo and used in many other graphics systems will know how Pens work. Pens use internal instance variables to remember their position, color, and

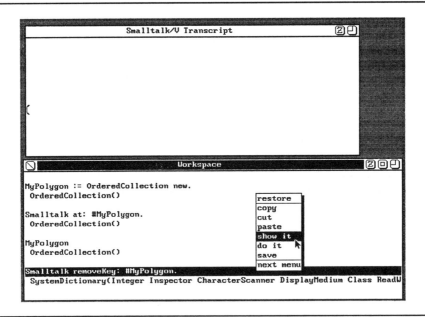

Figure 5-23.   Creating and removing a global variable, MyPolygon, from the Smalltalk dictionary

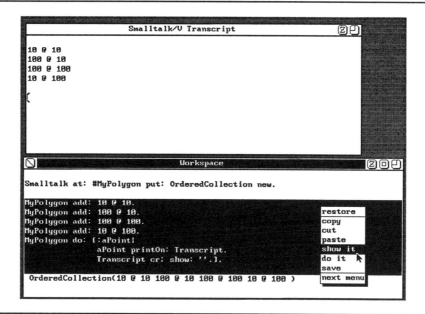

Figure 5-24.   Inserting MyPolygon into the Smalltalk dictionary, adding four
points to the OrderedCollection, and printing the collection in
the Transcript window with the do: iterator

whether they are in an up or down position. When a pen is in an up
position, you can move it anywhere on the screen without making any
marks. If the pen is down and you move it from its current position to a
new position, a line will be left on the screen connecting the old position to
the new.

You can send many different messages to Pen objects, but this program
only uses a few: up, down, and goto:. The goto: message takes a Point
object as an argument and moves the pen from its current position to a
new position indicated by the argument. When a new pen object is created,

```
pen := Pen new.
```

the pen is automatically initialized in the down position at the center of the
screen. If you want to move to a new starting position before drawing,
remember to lift the pen up.

```
pen up.
```

```
¦ pen ¦
Display white.
pen := Pen new.
pen up.
MyPolygon do: [:currentPoint ¦
               pen goto: currentPoint.
               pen down.].
Menu message: 'Press to continue'.
Scheduler systemDispatcher redraw.
```

Program 5-1.   A Pen object draws lines between points.

An iterator can then be used on the collection of points to connect the lines. For each point in the MyPolygon OrderedCollection, the pen is moved to the current point and put in the down position.

```
pen goto: currentPoint.
pen down.
```

Before any of this is done the Display is cleared to white. Display is a global object in the Smalltalk dictionary that is an instance of the Display-Screen class. Sending the message "white" to Display causes the screen to clear. After the screen is cleared and the iterator has drawn the connecting lines, a one-choice menu is invoked, stopping program execution until the user presses the left mouse button while pointing at the menu. This gives you a chance to see program output before the screen is cleared and the normal windows in the Smalltalk programming environment are redisplayed.

```
Menu message: 'Press to continue'
```

This statement sends the message "message:" to the Menu class with the string 'Press to continue' as an argument. After the user makes the selection with the mouse, program control passes to the last statement.

```
Scheduler systemDispatcher redraw
```

The Scheduler object is responsible for managing interaction between the user and the programming environment. The Scheduler is responsible for determining when windows should be redrawn and which windows and application programs (called *processes*) need to respond to keypresses and input from the mouse.

The statement in the previous listing forces all currently opened windows in the Smalltalk environment to be redrawn and then passes control to the active window. The screen that results from evaluating Program 5-1 is shown here.

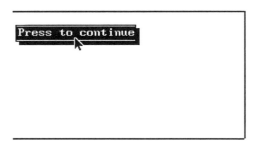

You will notice that the rectangle is not closed. In addition to iterating over each of the points in an OrderedCollection, you need to draw a line between the last point in the collection and the first point. Immediately after the iteration, the pen is positioned down. All you need is a statement to move the pen to the position of the first point in the collection. You can get the first point in the collection by using the at: message.

```
MyPolygon at: 1
```

Smalltalk collections are not 0-based like arrays in C and C++. As in Pascal, the first element in a collection or array is element number 1. Evaluating this expression would return the Point 10@10. Thus, if you put the following statement immediately after the do: iterator, you would see a complete box drawn with four sides.

```
pen goto: (MyPolygon at: 1)
```

The parentheses are necessary in the previous statement. Without them the interpreter would try to evaluate the expression from left to right and would think you were sending the pen object a message with two key-words, goto:at:. Since no such two-keyword message is defined for Pen objects, the system would generate an error dialog like this:

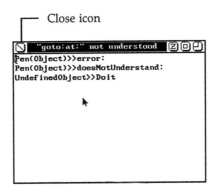

Close icon

```
"goto:at:" not understood
Pen(Object))>error:
Pen(Object))>doesNotUnderstand:
UndefinedObject>>DoIt
```

If such a dialog window ever does appear, you can get rid of it by closing the window. Simply press the left mouse button with the mouse pointer pointing to the close icon, which is the small box with a diagonal line through it just to the left of the highlighted title bar containing the string:

```
"goto:at:" not understood.
```

The parentheses around the argument for goto: force the following expression to be evaluated first.

```
(MyPolygon at: 1)
```

Using the resulting point as an argument, the goto: message is then sent to pen. The modified listing is included here for reference.

```
| pen |
Display white.
pen := Pen new.
pen up.
MyPolygon do: [:currentPoint |
                pen goto: currentPoint.
                pen down.].
pen goto: (MyPolygon at: 1).
Menu message: 'Press to continue'.
Scheduler systemDispatcher redraw.
```

Ordered Collections and Sorted Collections

Smalltalk provides a collection that guarantees all of its members will be sorted according to some form of comparison. The user can provide the sorting criteria for a SortedCollection in the form of a program block used to compare one element against another. The standard C library routine, qsort, provides a similar capability by requiring that the user specify the sort criteria in the form of a function. This function accepts two void pointers as arguments so that any two elements can be compared by the function. A pointer to this user-supplied function is then passed as one of the arguments to the qsort function. In Smalltalk, most objects from a given class have a method for comparing themselves to other objects from the same class. This default method is automatically used to order the elements of a given class inside a sorted collection. The class for creating sorted collection containers is SortedCollection. A new SortedCollection object is created as follows.

```
SortedCollection new.
```

SortedCollections are just as easy to use as OrderedCollections. In most cases you do not need to worry about supplying a program block to compare two objects. Simply create the collection and add elements. The elements are sorted as soon as they are added to the collection. Figure 5-25 shows the result of creating a SortedCollection as a temporary variable, adding two sets of duplicate strings to the collection, and printing the resulting collection. By default, the ordering for String objects follows standard lexicographical ordering as used in telephone books or spelling dictionaries.

Compare the order of the elements in the resulting SortedCollection to the ordering that results from adding the same elements in the same order to an OrderedCollection. Figure 5-26 shows the resulting OrderedCollection. As expected, the elements are retained in an OrderedCollection in the same order in which they are entered.

Arrays

Arrays are like OrderedCollections in that both classes are derived from IndexedCollections. The common property of IndexedCollections is that the

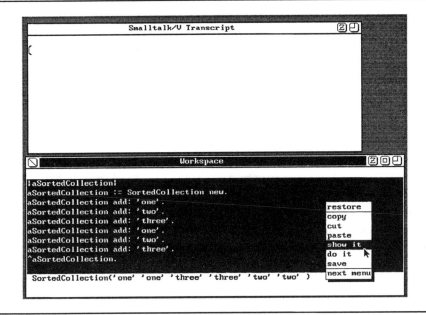

Figure 5-25.   A SortedCollection with duplicate entries

order of the elements is specified by the user and maintained by the collection automatically. Access to both Arrays and OrderedCollections is through an integer index. The main difference is that Arrays are fixed in size, while OrderedCollections can grow dynamically as more elements are added.

Array objects must be created in a slightly different manner than the collections covered so far. Sending the new message to Array creates an array of zero elements.

```
anArray := Array new.
```

Such an array would be useless since Array objects cannot grow dynamically, and it is an error to add an element outside the boundaries established when the array is created. You can create an Array object of a specified size by using the new: message along with an integer object.

```
anArray := Array new: 3.
```

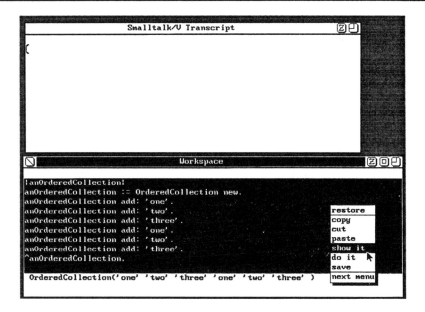

Figure 5-26.   An OrderedCollection with the same duplicate entries

The previous statement creates an array of three elements.

All the elements of the array are automatically initialized to "nil", the symbol Smalltalk uses to stand for an undefined object. There are definitely three elements in an array created with the previous statement; each object is undefined until something is put there. Printing such an array would produce the following:

```
(nil nil nil)
```

You could create an OrderedCollection, or any other collection that is not a FixedSizeCollection, using new: with an integer argument. The result, however, is meaningless since collections that are not fixed in size grow automatically to accommodate newly added elements. Further, nonfixed-size collections are not initialized to contain nil objects. While you could create an OrderedCollection large enough to contain three elements,

```
anOrderedCollection := OrderedCollection new: 3.
```

the resulting collection would be empty, rather than containing three undefined objects.

Figure 5-27 shows the results of creating four different collections. The first collection is an Array of zero elements, the second collection is an Array of three elements, and the third collection is an OrderedCollection of three elements. The output printed as a result of creating an OrderedCollection of a specified size, is simply an empty collection. If you were to add four elements to this ordered collection, the collection would grow to accommodate them, as shown in the fourth collection. There is really little use in specifying the size for such a collection when it is created.

You're probably used to arrays behaving in just this fashion if you're used to working in C or Pascal. In both these languages, arrays are fixed-

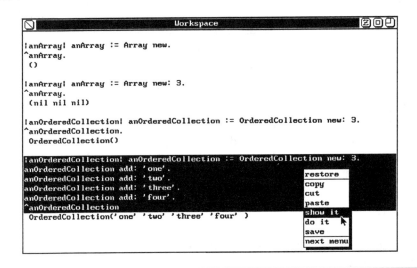

Figure 5-27.   Arrays are fixed-size collections whose elements are initialized to
nil. Non-fixed-size collections contain no elements when created,
even if a size is specified.

size objects. However, there is a difference between Smalltalk arrays and arrays from traditional structured languages—Smalltalk arrays are polymorphic. You can put any type of object inside a Smalltalk array without declaring the type of the array. You can also mix the types of elements contained inside of a single array.

You cannot send the add: message to Array objects. Trying to do so will bring up an error dialog window. Instead, insert elements into an array using the at:put: message with an integer index as an argument. The index must be greater than 0 and less than or equal to the size of the array. Besides Array, several other important classes are derived from Fixed-SizeCollection, notably, String, Symbol, and BitMap. BitMaps are fixed-sized collections of bits usually associated with a Rectangle to draw graphic images on the computer screen.

It is possible to create Array objects as literal expressions. Simply surround the array elements with parentheses and put a pound sign, #, before the opening parenthesis, like this:

```
#('one' 'two' 'three')
```

Evaluating the above expression creates an Array of three Strings.

You can send messages to Arrays created in this manner. For instance, to verify that the previous expression does in fact create an array, you could send it the species message.

```
#('one' 'two' 'three') species
```

Evaluating this expression with "show it" would produce Array as output.

Figure 5-28 shows the results of evaluating five short programs using arrays. The first program shows how to use at:put: to insert elements into an Array. The next three programs show how to create Array literals and send messages to the resulting literal objects. The last example shows that an Array literal can be assigned to a temporary variable and that the original elements of the array can be replaced with elements of different types. When this program is through evaluating, anArray contains an Integer, a Point, and a Rectangle.

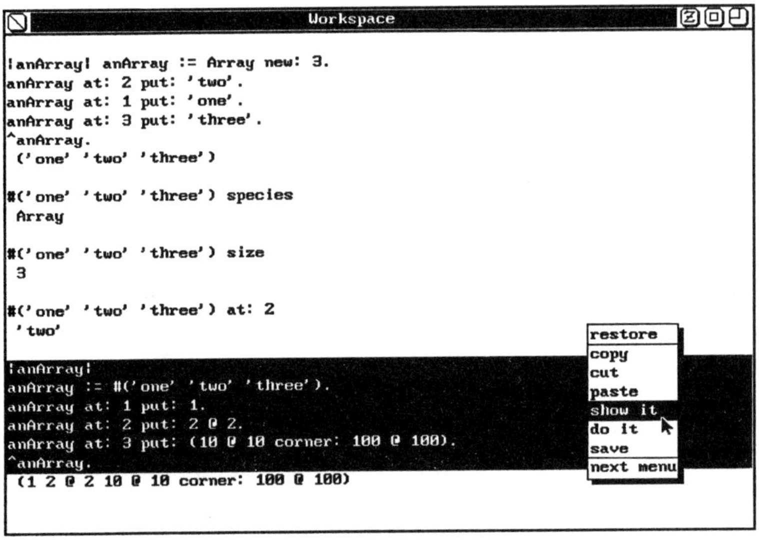

Figure 5-28.   Arrays are polymorphic: a single array can contain several different types of objects. Array literals are created by surrounding elements with parentheses preceded by a #.

CONVERTING COLLECTIONS

You can convert collections of one type to collections of another type. For instance, you can convert an OrderedCollection to a Bag, a Set, a Sorted-Collection, or an Array. Conversions result from sending one of the following messages to the collection to be converted.

```
asBag
asSet
asSortedCollection
asArray
```

Sending such a message to a collection does not actually convert the collection, but returns a new copy of the original collection that has the characteristics specified by the conversion message. To see conversions in action you could create an OrderedCollection as a global variable:

```
Smalltalk at: #MyOrderedCollection
        put: OrderedCollection new.
```

Next, add six elements, two sets of duplicate Strings:

```
aSortedCollection add: 'one'.
aSortedCollection add: 'two'.
aSortedCollection add: 'three'.
aSortedCollection add: 'one'.
aSortedCollection add: 'two'.
aSortedCollection add: 'three'.
```

You would then print the collection by evaluating

```
MyOrderedCollection.
```

Now, create and print a new Bag collection containing the same members as MyOrderedCollection by evaluating the following expression with "show it".

```
MyOrderedCollection asBag
```

Similarly, you could convert the collection to a Set with

```
MyOrderedCollection asSet
```

Figure 5-29 shows the results of converting MyOrderedCollection to a Bag, a Set, a SortedCollection, and an Array. In addition, Figure 5-29 shows that you can change the sorting order in a SortedCollection by providing a sort block:

```
[:a :b | a > b]
```

A *sort block* is a piece of program code that receives two arguments and returns either true or false. The two arguments represent two collection elements that are to be compared. The equivalent C++ code for the above sort block would be:

```
int sortBlock(ItemType *a, ItemType *b)
{
    if (*a > *b)
        return 1;
    else
        return 0;
}
```

The main difference is that the sort block in Smalltalk is type-indepen-
dent and has no identifier name. Sort blocks are nameless pieces of code
associated with specific instances of SortedCollections. SortedCollections
use their sort blocks to compare and order their elements. If no sort block is
supplied by the user, the following default sort block is supplied when a
SortedCollection is created.

```
[:a :b | a<=b]
```

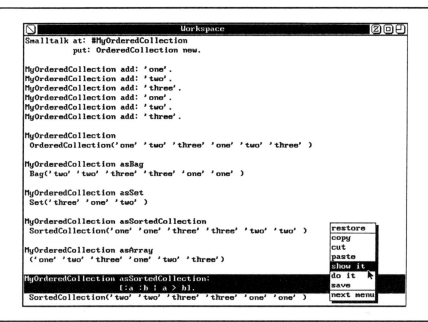

Figure 5-29.   Converting an OrderedCollection to a Bag, a Set, a Sorted
Collection, an Array, and a SortedCollection with elements
in reverse order

By supplying the sort block,

```
[:a :b | a > b]
```

you can reverse the order of a SortedCollection.

You can convert a collection and send the resulting collection another conversion. For example, recall that earlier in this chapter NameDictionary contained five associations with two duplicate first names as values.

```
NameDictionary
    Dictionary('Joan' 'Edith' 'John' 'Neil' 'John')
```

To get a sorted list of first names, you could first convert the values (a Bag) to a Set and then convert the Set to a SortedCollection.

```
NameDictionary values asSet asSortedCollection
```

Evaluating this expression would produce the following output with the "show it" command.

```
SortedCollection('Edith' 'Joan' 'John' 'Neil')
```

COUNTING AND SELECTING ELEMENTS OF A COLLECTION

One useful thing to do is count the number of elements in a collection. You do this by sending the message, occurrencesOf: to the collection. For instance, to count the number of times the name 'John' appears in the values of NameDictionary, you would evaluate the following expression.

```
NameDictionary values occurrencesOf: 'John'
```

The result would be 2.

Figure 5-30 shows the results of printing the values in NameDictionary as a sorted set and then counting the occurrences of three different values within the dictionary.

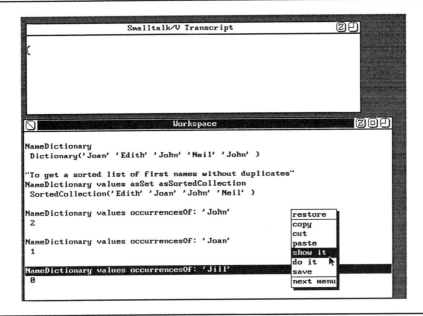

Figure 5-30.   Applying two conversions to the values in NameDictionary and counting occurrences of values

You can select out the members of a collection that meet a specified criterion and create a new collection consisting only of those members. To demonstrate, first add another name with a duplicate first name value to NameDictionary.

```
NameDictionary at: 'Bunker' put: 'Edith'
```

The NameDictionary now consists of the following six associations:

```
'Didion'     ==> 'Joan'
'Piaf'       ==> 'Edith'
'Bunker'     ==> 'Edith'
'Steinbeck'  ==> 'John'
'Armstrong'  ==> 'Neil'
'Dos Passos' ==> 'John'
```

You can select out duplicate values from NameDictionary by sending the select: message to the collection of values. The select: message is a form of iterator just as do: is. The select: message takes a single program block as an argument. The program block itself also expects one argument, which takes on the value of the next member of the collection for each iteration. The general format for select: when sent to a collection is

```
aCollection select: [:element | ...]
```

The result returned by this expression is a collection of the same type as aCollection containing only the members that evaluate to true when the code inside the block (indicated by ...) evaluates to true for the given member element.

For example, to create a collection of name values that occur more than once in NameDictionary, you could evaluate

```
NameDictionary  values select: [:element |
    (NameDictionary values occurrencesOf: element) > 1]
```

Of course, the resulting collection would contain duplicates. The select: iterator walks over each element in the Bag resulting from evaluating,

```
NameDictionary values
```

and sets the block variable argument, element, to the current element. The occurrencesOf: message is then sent to the NameDictionary values with element as an argument. If the current element occurs more than once in the Bag of values, it is added to the collection created by select. The resulting bag would therefore contain two copies of 'Edith' and two copies of 'John'.

You would probably want to weed out the duplicates of the resulting Bag by turning it into a Set. Figure 5-31 shows the results of doing this. Note that each of the five expressions evaluated in the Workspace window is accompanied by a comment. The second expression prints all the associations in NameDictionary to the Transcript window for reference. The next program shows how you can print only the associations that have duplicate values to the Transcript window.

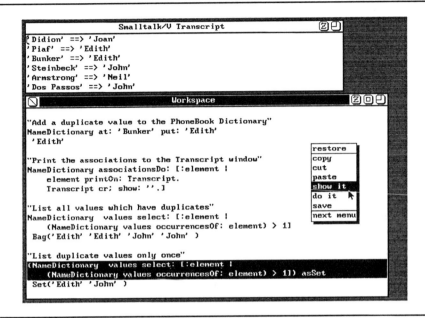

Figure 5-31.   Using the select: iterator to create collections of duplicate name
values from NameDictionary

Note: In Smalltalk, strings of characters surrounded by double quotes, ",
are interpreted as comments when evaluated. Comments are treated just
like white space and produce no effect.

```
| duplicates |
duplicates :=
NameDictionary  select: [ : element |
    (NameDictionary values occurrencesOf: element ) > 1].
duplicates associationsDo: [ : element |
    element printOn: Transcript.
    Transcript cr; show: ".].
^duplicates
```

First a new Dictionary is created by selecting out all associations that
duplicate name values. The resulting dictionary is assigned to the temporary variable "duplicates". The program then iterates over the duplicates
dictionary by sending it the associationsDo: message with a program block
that prints each association to the Transcript window.

COLLECTIONS CONTAINING COLLECTIONS

Collections can contain other collections. You've already seen an example of this in listings that use array literals. For example,

```
#('one' 'two' 'three')
```

is an Array of Strings, but Strings themselves are collections. For instance, you could send the at: message to a String with an integer index, and a character would be returned.

```
'one' at: 3
```

The result of evaluating this expression with "show it" would be

```
$e
```

Note: Smalltalk always precedes character objects with a dollar sign, $.

You can change the elements of String collections just like OrderedCollections and Arrays with the at:put: message. For instance, evaluating the following expression would correct an embarrassing mistake.

```
'Hello, wirld' at: 9 put: $o
```

This would change the ninth character in the string from an *i* to an *o*. When you have an array of Strings, you really have a collection of collections.

Figure 5-32 shows some things you can do with Strings and Arrays of Strings. Note that the extra parentheses are necessary around the at: message sent to the array:

```
(#('one' 'two' 'three') at: ?) ...
```

Without these parentheses the interpreter would think you were sending the message at:at: to an Array of Strings rather than sending an additional at: message to the String that results from evaluating this:

```
#('one' 'two' 'three') at: 2
```

Collections of collections are handy for building complex data structures. Suppose you wanted to build an address book as a database consisting of entries with three fields: last name, first name, and address. The logical choice would be to make the database a sorted collection and to specify sorting based on the last name. It would probably make sense to make each entry an array of strings. For instance, Babe Ruth's name might appear as

```
#('Ruth' 'Babe' '456 Mudville Flats')
```

You must create an address book collection before you add any entries. This might appear to be easy.

```
Smalltalk at: #AddressBook put: SortedCollection new.
```

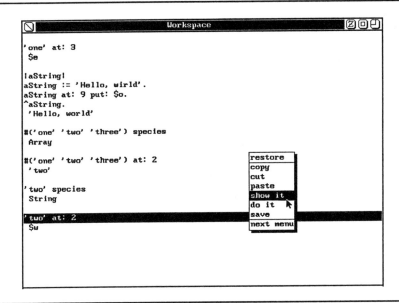

Figure 5-32.   Strings are collections. An Array of Strings is a collection of collections.

Evaluating this expression will create a SortedCollection called Address-Book in the Smalltalk dictionary, but there's a problem. As soon as you go to add an entry like the one above, the SortedCollection will signal an error to the Smalltalk environment. This would not have happened if Address-Book were created as a Set, a Bag, or an OrderedCollection. The problem is that the default sort block supplied when AddressBook was created,

```
[:a :b | a <= b]
```

won't work on Arrays of Strings. Arrays of Strings are not basic objects defined by Smalltalk, so no comparison methods for Arrays of Strings are defined. You could create a new class of objects called AddressBookEntry and define comparison operator methods, but there's an easier way.

When you create the AddressBook collection you can supply a sort block that tells the SortedCollection to sort by comparing the first element in the array of strings. This would be a String representing the last name. Since Smalltalk knows how to compare String objects, no programming other than supplying the sort block would be required. Here is a sort block that compares two objects assumed to be collections by comparing the first element of each of the collections:

```
[:a :b | (a at: 1) <= (b at: 1]
```

You can now create a SortedCollection using this sort block to compare elements.

```
Smalltalk at: #AddressBook
        put: (SortedCollection
                sortBlock: [:a :b | (a at: 1) <= (b at: 1)]).
```

The following listing shows how to add 26 entries to the address book in random order.

```
AddressBook
    add: #('Seuss'      'Doctor'       '18 Green Eggs Place');
    add: #('Lennon'     'John'         'Abbey Road');
    add: #('Bill'       'Buffalo'      '625 Western Drive');
    add: #('Tito'       'Josip Broz'   '305 Yugo Way');
    add: #('Knievel'    'Evel'         '202 Daredevil Drive');
    add: #('Genghis'    'Khan'         '806 Great Wall');
```

```
add: #('Xavier'        'Saint Francis'  '100 Church Street');
add: #('Hemingway'     'Ernest'         '66 Rue Street');
add: #('West'          'Mae'            'Upstairs');
add: #('Jefferson'     'Thomas'         '1 Independence Way');
add: #('Armstrong'     'Louis'          '91 Blueberry Hill');
add: #('Pocahontas'    'Princess'       '11 John Smith Way');
add: #('Zapata'        'Emiliano'       'Revolution Road');
add: #('Isabella'      'Queen'          '19 Aragon Boulevard');
add: #('Confucius'     'Fred'           '551 Wisdom Way');
add: #('Oakley'        'Annie'          'Bull"s Eye Boulevard');
add: #('Yogi'          'Bear'           'Jellystone Park');
add: #('Queequog'      'George'         'Spouter Inn');
add: #('Fuller'        'Buckminster'    '31 Critical Path');
add: #('Dickens'       'Charles'        '96 Pickwick Drive');
add: #('Ulysses'       'George'         'Odyssey Circle');
add: #('Ruth'          'Babe'           '456 Mudville Flats');
add: #('Einstein'      'Albert'         '112 Mercer Street');
add: #('Nefertiti'     'Queen'          '638 Nile Street');
add: #('Van Gogh'      'Vincent'        '976 Starry Street');
add: #('Mata'          'Hari'           '802 Spy Street').
```

The entries are automatically sorted according to the last name field for each entry as they are added. Once the entries have been added to AddressBook, you can print the contents of the collection to the Transcript window.

```
AddressBook do: [:entry |
                (entry at: 1) printOn: Transcript.
                (entry at: 1) size to: 15 do:
                              [:i | Transcript show: ' '].
                (entry at: 2) printOn: Transcript.
                (entry at: 2) size to: 15 do:
                              [:i | Transcript show: ' '].
                (entry at: 3) printOn: Transcript.
                Transcript cr; show: ".].
```

Evaluating this statement prints the 26 entries to the Transcript window in alphabetical order.

```
'Armstrong'   'Louis'         '91 Blueberry Hill'
'Bill'        'Buffalo'       '625 Western Drive'
'Confucius'   'Fred'          '551 Wisdom Way'
'Dickens'     'Charles'       '96 Pickwick Drive'
'Einstein'    'Albert'        '112 Mercer Street'
'Fuller'      'Buckminster'   '31 Critical Path'
'Genghis'     'Khan'          '806 Great Wall'
'Hemingway'   'Ernest'        '66 Rue Street'
'Isabella'    'Queen'         '19 Aragon Boulevard'
'Jefferson'   'Thomas'        '1 Independence Way'
```

```
'Knievel'        'Evel'            '202 Daredevil Drive'
'Lennon'         'John'            'Abbey Road'
'Mata'           'Hari'            '802 Spy Street'
'Nefertiti'      'Queen'           '638 Nile Street'
'Oakley'         'Annie'           'Bull"s Eye Boulevard'
'Pocahontas'     'Princess'        '11 John Smith Way'
'Queequog'       'George'          'Spouter Inn'
'Ruth'           'Babe'            '456 Mudville Flats'
'Seuss'          'Doctor'          '18 Green Eggs Place'
'Tito'           'Josip Broz'      '305 Yugo Way'
'Ulysses'        'George'          'Odyssey Circle'
'Van Gogh'       'Vincent'         '976 Starry Street'
'West'           'Mae'             'Upstairs'
'Xavier'         'Saint Francis'   '100 Church Street'
'Yogi'           'Bear'            'Jellystone Park'
'Zapata'         'Emiliano'        'Revolution Road'
```

The expression

```
(entry at: 1) size to: 15 do:
              [:i¦ Transcript show: ' '].
```

is used to pad the field with spaces for the String currently being printed so the entire field takes exactly 15 columns. The general form of this iterator is

```
startInteger to: stopInteger do:  [:count¦ ...]
```

This would be equivalent to

```
for count := startInteger to stopInteger do
    ...
```

in Pascal or

```
for (i=startInteger; i<= stopInteger; i++)
    ...
```

in C or C++.

To print the numbers 1 through 10 inclusive to the Transcript window you would evaluate the following expression.

```
1 to: 10 do: [:i ¦ i
              printOn: Transcript.
              Transcript show: ' '.].
```

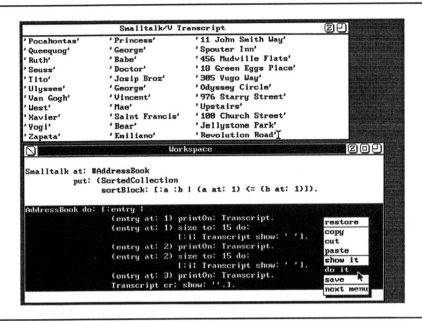

Figure 5-33. Printing the contents of AddressBook to the Transcript window

Figure 5-33 shows the result of evaluating the program in the Workspace window to print out the entire AddressBook. Even if you were to add more entries later, all entries in AddressBook would continue to be ordered according to the supplied sort block.

The final listing shows a program that can be used to print all the last names associated with duplicate first names for AddressBook.

```
"Print to Transcript window a sorted list of
 duplicate first names and the last names
 that share the common first name"

| firstNames duplicates |
firstNames := Bag new.
AddressBook do: [:entry | firstNames add: (entry at: 2)].
duplicates := firstNames select:
            [:name | (firstNames occurrencesOf: name) > 1].
```

```
duplicates := duplicates asSet asSortedCollection.
duplicates do: [:first |
              first printOn: Transcript.
              first size to: 15 do: [:i | Transcript show: ' '].
              Transcript show: '==>'.
              AddressBook do: [:entry |
                  (entry at: 2) = first ifTrue:
                      [Transcript show: ' '; tab.
                      (entry at: 1) printOn: Transcript]].
              Transcript cr; show: '.'].
```

Since AddressBook is a SortedCollection rather than a Dictionary like NameDictionary, you can add entries with duplicate last names as well. In the current example, there are no duplicate last names, but both the first names 'George' and 'Queen' appear twice.

Let's examine how this program works.

1. First it creates a new Bag and assigns it to the temporary variable firstNames.

2. Next, the program iterates over the AddressBook collection and adds each of the first names to the Bag.

3. Duplicate first names are selected from the firstNames Bag, and the resulting Bag of duplicates is assigned to a temporary variable called duplicates.

4. The duplicates Bag is then converted to a Set to weed out double entries of the duplicate names. The resulting Set is sorted and assigned as a SortedCollection back to the duplicates variable.

5. The last statement in the program is an iterator inside an iterator. This is like a loop inside of a loop in a traditional language. The outer iterator walks over the elements in the duplicates SortedCollection, which should contain two first names. On each iteration the first name is printed to the Transcript window and the spaces are printed to pad the field out to 15 columns.

6. Next, the string '= = >' is printed to separate the first name from the associated last names, which will be printed on the same line. Now for each first name in duplicates, another iteration occurs.

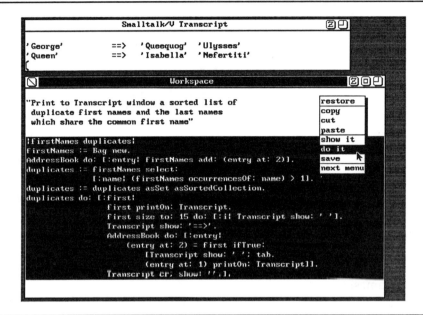

Figure 5-34. Iterators, Selectors, Bags, Sets, and SortedCollections can be used to extract and print information from the AddressBook database.

7. The program iterates over each entry in AddressBook and compares the first name for that entry against the current first name stored in the block argument variable first. If the first names match, the last name in the AddressBook entry is printed.

Figure 5-34 shows the results of evaluating this program text.

6

ENCAPSULATION, INHERITANCE, AND POLYMORPHISM IN ACTION

The example code used in this chapter is rather advanced. Don't let that scare you off. The intent is to show a representative program rather than a contrived one. It will help to know that you have already seen the code for the main part of this program in the rotate shapes example that was presented in Chapter 3, "Inheritance, Polymorphism, and Object-Oriented Programming".

The languages discussed in this book are not formally introduced until Part II, "Object-Oriented Programming Tools". Don't worry if you find the C++ code difficult to read at this point. You do not need to understand the fine points of the code in order to appreciate the flexibility demonstrated by using object-oriented programming techniques. If you already know C++, you'll benefit by seeing the language applied to a nontrivial problem. If you can't read C++ code, you may just want to skim this chapter for the main points until you've read Part II. The example is intended to provide motivation for working through the more simplistic programs used to introduce the languages in Part II. Variations of the rotate shapes program appear throughout the book and are presented at least once in each of the languages: C++, object-oriented Pascal, Actor, and Smalltalk.

MINIMIZING THE IMPACT OF CHANGE

Encapsulation protects users of classes from change. By providing an explicit specification for the use of an object of a certain type, class users and class implementors make an agreement that defines each one's responsibility. The user agrees to manipulate objects only in a way consistent with the interface specification. The builder guarantees that as long as the user only communicates with objects through the public interface, the objects will always produce the expected results. Some writers have even gone so far as to call this agreement a "contract", with the user referred to as the "client" or "buyer", and the builder referred to as the "seller" or "agent". This metaphor sheds a little light on the relationships established around building and using classes and objects. Regardless of the actual names used, the main thing to keep in mind is the reason for distinguishing between the role of the builder and the role of the user.

Encapsulation encourages a flexible separation of concerns between the builder and the user. The separation of concerns is made possible through a public interface to an object that can be enforced by a programming language. While it's nice that a user can count on a certain behavior based on a class specification, the builder is the one who acquires the most freedom from the relationship.

The notion of public access to functions as an interface to program modules is not unique to object-oriented programming. Data hiding and encapsulation through modules and separate source code files is practiced widely in C. In Pascal, nested functions and procedures also provide a form of data and function hiding. It's one thing to say on paper that a user should not access a global piece of data, but if the specification is not made clear or the implementation is not clean, there is too much temptation to cheat. Once users find out they can cheat and begin to write code that depends on the value of a global data structure that was theoretically supposed to be hidden, there is no going back. The relationships between the pieces of code grow in complexity as the number of pieces grows. As the interrelationships multiply, it becomes impossible to undo all the connections and go back to a cleaner design.

By agreeing on a specification at an early stage of design, a separation of concerns is established. Once an agreement is reached, the builder and the user can immediately go their separate ways and begin working on their own piece of the puzzle. As long as both stick to the agreement established in the class interface specification, neither needs to be concerned about what the other is doing. The user can build a dummy class that simulates the objects that the builder is working on. This allows the user to go ahead and actually compile, link, and run code that creates objects and sends messages to the objects that will eventually be implemented by the builder. The compiler verifies that the user has not violated any of the agreed upon message-passing protocol. The builder can go off and try many different implementations of a given class and perform experiments to see which implementations are most efficient in terms of space, speed, and ease of development. The agreement gives the builder the maximum flexibility possible to try alternative designs.

Let's see how this division of labor works in practice by analyzing the design of an abstract Screen class. The Screen class will provide graphics support for a Shape class hierarchy used to rotate shapes on the computer screen like Program 3-3 in Chapter 3. The goal is to run the rotate shapes program with as few modifications as possible in three different graphics environments: Borland's BGI (Borland Graphics Interface), Zortech's Flash Graphics library, and Microsoft Windows. The programming language will be C++.

DESIGNING AND IMPLEMENTING AN ABSTRACT SCREEN CLASS

The abstract Screen class provides a small number of functions or methods for manipulating a graphics screen. The purpose of the abstract Screen class is to provide the client or buyer with a portable way of specifying shapes to be drawn on a computer screen. The client would like to use the same coordinate system regardless of the coordinate system employed by the supporting graphics software and would like to port the abstract Shape class hierarchy to each of the target environments with the minimum number of modifications. It's up to the builder to implement a system and specify an interface that minimizes the number of changes in the client's code. It's up to the client to tell the builder exactly what functionality is required to support the client's application.

The screen is based on a virtual coordinate system, with the origin in the lower-left corner—x values increasing to the right and y values increasing as you move up the screen. Regardless of the actual hardware or software that implements the graphics system, the maximum x and y values for the virtual coordinate system are each 100. This means that the lower-left corner of the screen is the point 0,0, and the upper-right corner of the screen is 100,100. The screen uses an imaginary pen to draw lines. You can move the pen without leaving a mark, as well as draw a line to a new pen position. You can also draw circles. You can change and retrieve the background and foreground colors, and you can clear the screen. All graphics systems need to set up certain environmental conditions, which will be handled by a method (member function) called "initialize". Finally, many graphics systems need to do some housekeeping to shut down the environment, and these will be handled in a method called "cleanup".

The two preceding paragraphs amount to an informal specification for the public interface of the Screen class. Here's a first cut at a C++ implementation.

```
/////////////////////////////////////////////////////////
// class Screen (interface)
/////////////////////////////////////////////////////////
class Screen
{
public:
     void    initialize();
     void    cleanup();
     void    moveTo(Point p);
     void    lineTo(Point p);
     void    circle(Point p, int radius);
     void    background(int color);
     int     background();
     void    foreground(int color);
     int     foreground();
     void    clear();
};
```

With this much of an interface specified, the user and the builder can sit down and see if all the requirements have been met. Once it is agreed that all the requirements have been met, the user can go ahead and build the Shape class hierarchy based on the drawing functions provided in the Screen class interface.

The client can even go so far as to implement dummy code for each of the methods in the interface. The dummy methods (traditionally called *test stubs*) would do nothing, but it would at least allow the user to compile, link, and run the program. The stubs might simply do something like verify that the correct data has been passed to screen methods and print the results on a character-oriented output device. This allows the user to progress as far as possible without the involvement of the builder.

The Screen class will need a way to communicate color to the background and foreground methods. The user and builder can agree to a limited set of colors available in all three of the desired application environments. The following enumerated declaration of colors could be placed in the public section of the Screen class interface.

```
enum {  black,      blue,           green,       cyan,
        red,        magenta,        brown,       lightgray,
        darkgray,   lightblue,      lightgreen,  lightcyan,
        lightred,   lightmagenta,   yellow,      white
     };
```

Given a Screen object, screen, you could now specify a color by using the class name followed by :: followed by the name of the color. To indicate the color cyan, you would use the following expression:

```
Screen::cyan
```

To set the background color of the screen to cyan, you would use

```
screen.background(Screen::cyan);
```

Now it's up to the builder to decide the internal data variables that will be required to implement the Screen class. These variables will be declared in the private section of the interface. The builder needs to translate from the virtual coordinate system to the coordinate system used by the supporting graphics library. In order to do this, it's necessary for a Screen object to remember the maximum x and y values for the graphics library. This can be done with two private instance variables.

```
class Screen
{
    int      maxX;
    int      maxY;
    ...
};
```

In addition, functions are needed to translate the user's virtual coordinate system. The functions are declared in the private section of the interface because they are required by the builder and not by the user.

```
class Screen
{
    ...
    Point       translate(Point p);
    int         translateX(int x);
    int         translateY(int y);
    ...
};
```

That pretty much takes care of all the information that needs to be declared in the header file for the Screen class declaration. The entire file is included here for your reference.

```
file: screen1.h

#ifndef SCREEN_H
#define SCREEN_H

#include "point.h"
//////////////////////////////////////////////////////////////
// class Screen (interface)
//////////////////////////////////////////////////////////////
class Screen
{
    int         maxX;
    int         maxY;
    Point       translate(Point p);
    int         translateX(int x);
    int         translateY(int y);
public:
    enum {  black,      blue,           green,      cyan,
            red,        magenta,        brown,      lightgray,
            darkgray,   lightblue,      lightgreen, lightcyan,
            lightred,   lightmagenta,   yellow,     white
         };

    void        initialize();
    void        cleanup();
    void        moveTo(Point p);
    void        lineTo(Point p);
    void        circle(Point p, int radius);
    void        background(int color);
    int         background();
    void        foreground(int color);
    int         foreground();
    void        clear();
};
```

```
/////////////////////////////////////////////////////////////
// global screen object
// (only one instance of Screen allowed per program)
/////////////////////////////////////////////////////////////
extern Screen screen;

void far pascal rotateShapes();   // defined in rotate.cpp

#endif
```

There are a couple of fine points to note. The Screen class methods use
Point objects. Consequently, the line

```
#include "point.h"
```

must be included at the top of the file. The Point class was used in the
rotate shapes program in Chapter 3, but the code was not presented there.
All the code for the Point class is actually implemented in the header file
with all methods specified as inline method definitions. No .CPP file is
required.

```
file: point.h

#ifndef POINT_H
#define POINT_H

/////////////////////////////////////////////////////////////
// class Point (interface and implementation)
/////////////////////////////////////////////////////////////
class Point
{
    int xVal;
    int yVal;
public:
    Point() { xVal = 0; yVal = 0; }
    Point(int x, int y)  { xVal = x; yVal = y; }
    int x() { return xVal; }
    int y() { return yVal; }
    Point operator+(Point p)
        { return Point (xVal + p.x(), yVal + p.y()); }
    Point operator-(Point p)
        { return Point (xVal - p.x(), yVal - p.y()); }
    Point operator*(int i)
        { return Point (xVal * i, yVal * i); }
    Point operator/(int i)
        { return Point (xVal / i, yVal / i); }
};

#endif
```

This class provides methods for creating points, returning the x and y values of a given point, adding and subtracting one point with another, and multiplying or dividing one point by an integer scaler.

THE USER'S RESPONSIBILITY

The user is responsible for implementing an abstract class that defines the common properties of shapes. This was effectively done in Chapter 3. There will be a slight difference here. In an effort to isolate the parts of a program that are more likely to change from the parts of the program that are more likely to remain stable, the user can break the rotate shapes program up into three basic files or modules.

```
main.cpp
rotate.cpp
screen.cpp
```

The file ROTATE.CPP should be the most stable. In this file the user implements the classes Shape, Circle, Rectangle, and Triangle. Also in this file are two functions used to create three Shape objects and rotate them about the screen. The only function inside ROTATE.CPP that is exported and available to be called by routines outside of the file is rotateShapes. The function is exported by declaring it in the header file, SCREEN1.H, listed previously.

```
void far pascal rotateShapes();  // defined in rotate.cpp
```

Since this declaration is the only reference exported from ROTATE.CPP, rather than creating a header file, ROTATE.H, the declaration is placed in the same file that declares the Screen class. The code in MAIN.CPP is very short for the first two versions of the program. However, the third version is quite complicated because it needs to set up a number of functions required to run an application program under Microsoft Windows.

Since there will be three different versions of the rotate shapes program, there will be three different versions of several files.

```
BGI                    Flash Graphics          MS Windows

mainl.cpp              main2.cpp               main3
screenl.h              screen2.h               screen3.h
screenl.cpp            screen2.cpp             screen3.cpp
```

The files ROTATE.CPP and POINT.H are not changed. They retain the same names for each version of the program. The BGI version of the program is built with the Turbo C++ compiler. Both the Flash Graphics and Windows versions are built with the Zortech C++ compiler.

If you plan to follow along and actually build each of the three versions of the program, it's best to create two separate subdirectories to work in. One subdirectory should be created for working with the Borland compiler. The other subdirectory should be created for working with the Zortech compiler. You might want to call these subdirectories \ROTATE\TC and \ROTATE\ZTC. Separate make files will be specified to be placed in each of these subdirectories. For now, you are working on version 1, which means you should be logged into the directory \ROTATE\TC. Here's the main program for version 1 of rotate shapes:

```
file: mainl.cpp

#include "screenl.h"
#include <conio.h>

main()
{
    screen.initialize();
    screen.background(Screen::cyan);

    rotateShapes();

    getch();
    screen.cleanup();
}
```

The main thing that goes on here is the screen is initialized and the function rotateShapes is called. This is the exported function declared in SCREEN1.H and defined in ROTATE.CPP. This function draws a circle, a rectangle, and a triangle on the screen and rotates each of them about the origin eight times. The behavior is exactly the same as Program 3-3, whose output is the rotated shapes shown in Figure 3-19 (and in Figure 6-1, which you will see later). Then the program waits for the user to press a key. After this is done, any cleanup required by the Screen object is taken care of. Note that there is only one Screen object ever declared in a given program, as can be seen in the header file SCREEN1.H.

The only other thing that the user needs to take care of to make version 1 of rotate shapes work is to write a module to define, create, and use the desired shapes. This is ROTATE.CPP, which is exactly the same for all three versions of the program.

```
#if (defined VER1)
#include "screen1.h"
#elif (defined VER2)
#include "screen2.h"
#elif (defined VER3)
#include "screen3.h"
#else
#error("You must define one of: VER1, VER2, VER3");
#endif

//////////////////////////////////////////////////////////
// class Shape
//////////////////////////////////////////////////////////
class Shape
{
    Point center;
    int color;
    int angle;
    virtual void drawShape()=0;
public:
                Shape(Point p)              // constructor
                  : center(p),
                    color(screen.foreground()),
                    angle(0)     { }
    int         getColor()       { return color; }
    void        setColor(int c) { color = c; }
    int         getAngle()       { return angle; }
    void        setAngle(int a) { angle = a; }
    Point       position()       { return center; }
    void        moveTo(Point p) { center = p; }
    void        draw()   {
                    int saveColor = screen.foreground();
                    screen.foreground(getColor());
                    drawShape();
                    screen.foreground(saveColor);
                }
    void        rotate(int angle)
                    {
                    setAngle(getAngle()+angle);
                    draw();
                }
    void        hide()   {
                    int saveColor = screen.foreground();
                    screen.foreground(screen.background());
```

```
                    drawShape();
                    screen.foreground(saveColor);
                }
};


#include <math.h>   // required for rotations

#ifndef M_PI
#define M_PI PI     // Zortech uses PI
#endif

Point rotateAboutOrigin(Point p, int angle)
{
    double theta = angle * M_PI/180;
    double cos_theta = cos(theta);
    double sin_theta = sin(theta);
    int x = p.x()*cos_theta - p.y()*sin_theta;
    int y = p.x()*sin_theta + p.y()*cos_theta;
    return Point(x,y);
}

//////////////////////////////////////////////////////////
// class Circle
//////////////////////////////////////////////////////////
class Circle : public Shape
{
    int radius;
    virtual void drawShape()
    {
        Point ctr = rotateAboutOrigin(position(), getAngle());
        screen.circle(ctr, radius);
    }
public:
        Circle(Point p, int r)                // constructor
          : Shape(p), radius(r) {}
};

//////////////////////////////////////////////////////////
// class Rectangle
//////////////////////////////////////////////////////////
class Rectangle : public Shape
{
    virtual void drawShape()
    {
        Point a(position()-(extent/2));
        Point c(a+extent);
        Point b(c.x(), a.y());
        Point d(a.x(), c.y());

        a = rotateAboutOrigin(a, getAngle());
        b = rotateAboutOrigin(b, getAngle());
        c = rotateAboutOrigin(c, getAngle());
        d = rotateAboutOrigin(d, getAngle());

        screen.moveTo(a);
```

```
            screen.lineTo(b);
            screen.lineTo(c);
            screen.lineTo(d);
            screen.lineTo(a);
    }
protected:
    Point extent;
public:
        Rectangle(Point ctr, Point ext)      // constructor
            : Shape(ctr), extent(ext) {}
};

//////////////////////////////////////////////////////////////
// class Triangle
//////////////////////////////////////////////////////////////
class Triangle : public Rectangle
{
    virtual void drawShape()
    {
        int w2 = extent.x()/2;   // half the width
        int h2 = extent.y()/2;   // half the height
        Point a(position()+Point(  0,  h2));
        Point b(position()+Point( w2, -h2));
        Point c(position()+Point(-w2, -h2));

        a = rotateAboutOrigin(a, getAngle());
        b = rotateAboutOrigin(b, getAngle());
        c = rotateAboutOrigin(c, getAngle());

        screen.moveTo(a);
        screen.lineTo(b);
        screen.lineTo(c);
        screen.lineTo(a);
    }
public:
        Triangle(Point ctr, Point ext)       // constructor
            : Rectangle(ctr, ext) {}
};


//////////////////////////////////////////////////////////////
// main program
//////////////////////////////////////////////////////////////
typedef Shape *ShapePointer;

void rotateArray(ShapePointer array[], int size)
{
    for (int j=0; j<size; j++)
    {
        array[j]->draw();             // original position
        for (int i=0; i<8; i++)       // rotate shape 8 times,
        {                             // 10 degrees each rotation
            array[j]->rotate(10);     // rotate is relative to
        }                             // current angle setting
    }
}
```

```
void far pascal rotateShapes()
{
    ShapePointer shapeArray[10];
    int size=0;

    shapeArray[size++] = new Circle    (Point(60,6), 4);
    shapeArray[size++] = new Rectangle(Point(70,6), Point(8,8));
    shapeArray[size++] = new Triangle (Point(80,6), Point(8,8));

    rotateArray(shapeArray, size);
}
```

Nearly everything included in this file was already discussed in Chapter 3. The primary difference is that the methods implemented in the classes ROTATE.CPP need to use different versions of the abstract Screen. The interfaces for the three versions of the Screen class are declared in the files,

```
screen1.h
screen2.h
screen3.h
```

respectively. The different interfaces will be discussed as each version is presented.

The main thing to consider is the mechanism inside of ROTATE.CPP to determine which interface file is included when the program is compiled.

```
#if (defined VER1)
#include "screen1.h"
#elif (defined VER2)
#include "screen2.h"
#elif (defined VER3)
#include "screen3.h"
#else
#error("You must define one of: VER1, VER2, VER3");
#endif
```

This is a set of compiler directives—messages telling the compiler what to do rather than specifying statements to be carried out by the program.

You want your program to include only one of the files indicated by the three #include statements in the above listing. You can control which of the three #include statements the compiler will use by defining a macro. For version 1 of the program you would define the following macro:

```
#define VER1
```

For version 2 of rotate shapes you would define this macro:

```
#define VER2
```

Likewise for version 3 you would define this macro:

```
#define VER3
```

You could include one of these three #define directives before the set of #if...#elif...#endif directives. However, most compilers allow you to define macros either on the command line, when the compiler is invoked, or inside the integrated development environment. For example, both Turbo C++ and Zortech C++ command-line compilers allow you to define macros on the command line using the -D flag,

```
tcc -DVER1 rotate.cpp
```

to compile version 1 of ROTATE.CPP with Turbo C++ or,

```
ztc -DVER2 rotate.cpp
```

to compile version 2 with Zortech.

The only piece of code that remains to be discussed is the implementation of the Screen class for version 1 in SCREEN1.CPP. The implementation of this file is actually the concern of the builder. Consequently, the code for SCREEN1.CPP will be discussed in the following section. However, it is the responsibility of the user to specify how the three different modules making up the rotate shapes program should be compiled and linked together.

A Make File for Constructing the Rotate Shapes Programs

For programs built from several different source files, it's often best to automate the compilation and linking of separate program modules with a make file. A *make file* is a program used by the make utility. The make utility reads the make file and follows the instructions therein. The most common filename given to a make file is, not surprisingly, MAKEFILE. If you have such a file in your local directory then you can simply type

```
make
```

at the DOS prompt. The make program (both Turbo C++ and Zortech C++ provide a make utility) reads MAKEFILE and builds your program.

Here is the make file for the Turbo C++ BGI version of rotate shapes.

```
file: makefile

###########################################################
## makefile for Chapter 6, Encapsulation in Action
## rotate1.exe   TC++ version of rotate shapes
###########################################################


###### DEFAULT TARGET ####################################
rotate1.exe:
###########################################################


###########################################################
## rotate, version 1, Borland TC++ with BGI graphics
###########################################################
MODEL = s              # Turbo C++ small memory model
DEBUG = -v             # comment out if debugging not needed

CC = tcc
CFLAGS = -m$(MODEL) $(DEBUG)  -c
LFLAGS = -m$(MODEL) $(DEBUG)
LIBS = graphics.lib
###########################################################

ROTATE1_OBJS = main1.obj screen1.obj rotate1.obj

        ###################################################
        ## implicit rule for creating object files (.obj)
        ## from C++ files (.cpp)
        ###################################################
.cpp.obj:
    $(CC) $(CFLAGS) $<

        ###################################################
        ## BGI version of Screen class
        ###################################################
screen1.obj: screen1.cpp screen1.h point.h
        ###################################################
        ## All shape classes, and the rotateShapes function
        ## are unchanged but a different VERSION MACRO
        ## must be defined to include the proper version
        ## of screen.h (screen1.h).
        ###################################################
rotate1.obj : rotate.cpp screen1.h point.h
    $(CC) $(CFLAGS) -orotate1.obj -DVER1 rotate.cpp

        ###################################################
        ## standard Zortech C++ main function
        ## main calls rotateShapes
        ###################################################
main1.obj : main1.cpp screen1.h point.h
```

```
#################################################
## link object files to create executable
## uses tcc compiler to invoke tlink
## that way, you don't have to specify
## startup code and standard libraries
#################################################
rotate1.exe: $(ROTATE1_OBJS)
    echo LINKING rotate1.exe
    $(CC) $(LFLAGS) -erotate1 $(ROTATE1_OBJS) $(LIBS)
    echo to run under DOS type:    rotate1
#####################################################
```

Only the more general aspects of the operation of make will be covered here. Refer to your compiler documentation for details. The most important thing to know is that any line starting with a pound sign, #, is a comment, and text that occurs between the # character and the end of the line is ignored by the make utility. The comments are simply instructions to anyone trying to read and understand the make file. Make files specify rules and dependencies for building programs.

The general form of a make statement is

```
<target>:<dependency>
    <rule>
```

The targets are the names of files to be created by the make utility.

When make is given a target file, it looks for the file on the disk. If the file is not on the disk, or if the date of the file is older than the files on which it depends, make sees if it has enough information from the rules in the make file to figure out how to build the target. The previous make file includes four targets that have dependency lists:

```
screen1.obj:
rotate1.obj:
main1.obj:
rotate1.obj:
```

The dependency list for the second target above is specified after the colon. For example:

```
rotate1.obj : rotate.cpp screen1.h point.h
```

This dependency specification says that the target file ROTATE1.OBJ depends on the files ROTATE1.CPP, SCREEN1.H, and POINT.H.

If the current target file is ROTATE1.OBJ, make looks to see if it exists. If not, it executes the rule or rules underneath the dependency specification. The rule for building ROTATE1.OBJ is

```
$(CC) $(CFLAGS) -orotate1.obj -DVER1 rotate.cpp
```

The make utility will first expand any macros in the rule and then execute the rule as though it had been typed at the DOS command line. Any text in a make file that is surrounded by parentheses and preceded by a dollar sign, $,

```
$(CC)
```

is a macro. Macros are defined with an equal sign, =, for example:

```
CC = tcc
```

Any references to $(CC) that follow this macro definition will be substituted with the text *tcc*. Macros may include other macros. For example,

```
CFLAGS = -m$(MODEL) $(DEBUG)   -c
```

defines a macro, CFLAGS, which is defined in terms of two other macros, MODEL and DEBUG. If MODEL and DEBUG are defined as

```
MODEL = s           # Turbo C++ small memory model
DEBUG = -v          # comment out if debugging not needed
```

the make utility will substitute references to $(CFLAGS) with

```
-ms -v   -c
```

With full macro expansion, the rule

```
$(CC) $(CFLAGS) -orotate1.obj -DVER1 rotate.cpp
```

would be replaced with

```
tcc -ms -v   -c -orotate1.obj -DVER1 rotate.cpp
```

before it is executed as a DOS command. This line would invoke the Turbo C++ command-line compiler and create object code for a small memory model (-ms) including internal information for the debugger (-v), and only compile the program without linking (-c). The file to be compiled is the last item in the line:

```
rotate.cpp
```

By default, the compiler creates an object file with the same name as the source file by replacing the filename extension .CPP with .OBJ. The default name for compiling ROTATE.CPP would be ROTATE.OBJ. You can change the name of the output file with the -o flag. The *o* is immediately followed by the name of the desired output file. The flag -oROTATE1 would create an output filename ROTATE1.OBJ, keeping the numbering of all object files for a given version of the program consistent.

As mentioned earlier, -DVER1 is the equivalent of including the line

```
#define VER1
```

as the first line of the program file being compiled.

You can specify a target for make from the command line as follows.

```
make screen1.obj
```

However, it's usually more convenient to use a default target. The first target that appears in the make file becomes the default target. In the above make file, the default target is

```
rotate1.exe:
```

If make is invoked without a target on the command line,

```
make
```

ROTATE1.EXE becomes the target. Make now looks for the dependency list for ROTATE1.EXE.

```
rotate1.exe: $(ROTATE1_OBJS)
    echo LINKING rotate1.exe
    $(CC) $(LFLAGS) -erotate1 $(ROTATE1_OBJS) $(LIBS)
    echo to run under DOS type:    rotate1
```

The dependency list is specified by the macro $(ROTATE1_OBJS), which is defined earlier as

```
ROTATE1_OBJS = main1.obj screen1.obj rotate1.obj
```

You will notice that each of the files MAIN1.OBJ, SCREEN1.OBJ, and ROTATE1.OBJ are also targets. If these targets do not exist (or if the target files are older than their dependency files), these targets must be built before the rules for building ROTATE1.EXE can be executed.

It is possible to specify *implicit rules*. Implicit rules are based on the extension part of filenames. For example,

```
.cpp.obj:
```

announces an implicit rule to be applied to a .CPP file to produce an .OBJ file if no explict rule is given for a target.

The make file includes this implicit rule:

```
.cpp.obj:
    $(CC) $(CFLAGS) $<
```

This tells make that if it finds a target file with the extension .OBJ, it should look for a file with the same name ending in .CPP. It then executes the implicit rule and substitutes the filename with the .CPP extension for any references to the macro $<.

For example, the make file lists the following target dependency, which does not define any rules:

```
screen1.obj: screen1.cpp screen1.h point.h
```

Since no explicit rule is supplied, the following implicit rule is used:

```
    $(CC) $(CFLAGS) $<
```

The make utility first substitutes SCREEN1.CPP for $<, and the resulting command line executed by DOS is

```
tcc -ms -v  -c screen1.cpp
```

which creates the target SCREEN1.OBJ.

The net effect of executing make with this make file before any of the targets is built is to execute the following commands from the DOS command line.

```
tcc -ms -v -c screen1.cpp
tcc -ms -v -c -orotate1.obj -DVER1 rotate.cpp
tcc -ms -v -c main1.cpp
echo LINKING rotate1.exe
tcc -ms -v -erotate1 main1.obj screen1.obj rotate1.obj graphics.lib
echo to run under DOS type:     rotate1
```

Now if you change any of the files used to build the final target, only the commands necessary to build a new version of the program will be executed. Time is saved by omitting execution of unnecessary commands.

This should give you enough information about make to read subsequent make files listed in this book.

THE BUILDER'S RESPONSIBILITY

Everything covered up to this point has been the responsibility of the client or user. This includes the construction of the make file itself. Now it's interesting to turn things around and look at the implementation of the Shape class from the builder's point of view. The builder must build three versions of the Shape class. This implies responsibility for six files.

BGI	Flash Graphics	MS Windows
screen1.h	screen2.h	screen3.h
screen1.cpp	screen2.cpp	screen3.cpp

You already know what SCREEN1.H, which specifies the interface for the Screen class, looks like. The implementation is in SCREEN1.CPP.

```
file: screen1.cpp

#include <stdlib.h>
#include <stdio.h>
#include "screen1.h"
#include <graphics.h>

#define VIRTUAL_MAXX 100
#define VIRTUAL_MAXY 100
```

```
///////////////////////////////////////////////////////
// class Screen (implementation)
///////////////////////////////////////////////////////
Point Screen::translate(Point p)
{
    // coordinate range: 0,0 to maxX,maxY
    // maxX and maxY are device dependent
    // and set in Screen::initialize

    int x = translateX(p.x());
    int y = translateY(p.y());
    return Point(x,y);
}

int Screen::translateX(int x)
{
    return int(long(maxX) * long(x) / VIRTUAL_MAXX);
}

int Screen::translateY(int y)
{
    return maxY - int(long(maxY) * long(y) / VIRTUAL_MAXY);
}

void Screen::initialize()
{
    int gdriver = DETECT, gmode, errorcode;

    /////////////////////////////////////////////
    // last argument specifies directory
    // containing BGI drivers
    /////////////////////////////////////////////
    initgraph(&gdriver, &gmode, "\\tc\\bgi");

    errorcode = graphresult();
    if (errorcode != grOk)  // an error occurred
    {
        printf("Graphics error: %s\n", grapherrormsg(errorcode));
        exit(1); // terminate with an error code
    }
    maxX = getmaxx();
    maxY = getmaxy();
    foreground(Screen::white);
    background(Screen::blue);
}
void Screen::cleanup()
{
    closegraph();
}

void Screen::moveTo(Point p)
{
    p = translate(p);
    moveto(p.x(), p.y());
}
```

```
void Screen::lineTo(Point p)
{
    p = translate(p);
    lineto(p.x(), p.y());
}

void Screen::circle(Point p, int radius)
{
    p = translate(p);
    int xr = (long)maxX * (long)radius / VIRTUAL_MAXX;
    int yr = (long)maxY * (long)radius / VIRTUAL_MAXY;
    radius = (xr + yr) / 2;
    ::circle(p.x(), p.y(), radius);
}

void Screen::background(int color)
{
    setbkcolor(color);
}

int Screen::background()
{
    return getbkcolor();
}

void Screen::foreground(int color)
{
    setcolor(color);
}

int Screen::foreground()
{
    return getcolor();
}

void Screen::clear()
{
    cleardevice();
}

///////////////////////////////////////////////////////////
// global screen object
// (only one instance of Screen allowed per program)
///////////////////////////////////////////////////////////

Screen screen;
```

The first three methods are private and exist to translate the virtual coordinate system of the user to the internal coordinates used by Screen objects to communicate with the underlying graphics system. When a Screen object is initialized, the maximum x and y values of the graphics library being used are stored in maxX and maxY. Two of the translate utilities, translateX and translateY, take a single virtual coordinate and map it to an internal coordinate. These functions effectively carry out the following mapping, where 100 is the maximum possible value for the virtual coordinates x and y.

```
Xinternal = (maxX * Xvirtual) / 100
Yinternal = (maxY * Yvirtual) / 100
```

There's a slight twist, however, for the mapping of the y coordinate. In the virtual coordinate system specified by the user, the origin, Point (0,0), is at the lower-left corner of the screen. In the BGI, however, the origin is at the upper-left corner of the screen. In order to ensure the proper mapping, the y value needs to be subtracted from maxY. The actual mapping becomes

```
Yinternal = maxY - ((maxY * Yvirtual) / 100)
```

The main translate method then uses translateX and translateY so that the builder can do translation in terms of points rather than in terms of individual coordinates. The translate method takes a virtual point as an argument and returns a point mapped to the internal graphics system.

The most complicated method for Screen is initialize. This code first carries out the steps required to initialize the BGI. If the method is unable to initialize the BGI, which would happen if the proper BGI driver were not found in the directory specified by

```
initgraph(&gdriver, &gmode, "\\tc\\bgi");
```

an error message would be reported and the program would terminate. If initgraph is successful, the initialize method sets the maximum x and y values for the BGI internal coordinates.

```
maxX = getmaxx();
maxY = getmaxy();
```

Screen::initialize then calls two other Screen methods to set the foreground and background colors.

```
foreground(Screen::white);
background(Screen::blue);
```

Cleaning up the graphics environment when the program is through is straightforward. Screen::cleanup simply calls the BGI function

```
closegraph():
```

With the support of the private translate method, the public methods moveTo and lineTo are clean.

```
void Screen::moveTo(Point p)
{
    p = translate(p);
    moveto(p.x(), p.y());
}

void Screen::lineTo(Point p)
{
    p = translate(p);
    lineto(p.x(), p.y());
}
```

Note: The T in both method names, moveTo and lineTo, is uppercase, whereas the *t* in the BGI function names, moveto and lineto, is lowercase. If there were no difference in these names, both these methods would contain recursive calls to themselves and would never exit. A problem of this sort occurs with the method Screen::circle.

```
void Screen::circle(Point p, int radius)
{
    p = translate(p);
    int xr = (long)maxX * (long)radius / VIRTUAL_MAXX;
    int yr = (long)maxY * (long)radius / VIRTUAL_MAXY;
    radius = (xr + yr) / 2;
    ::circle(p.x(), p.y(), radius);
}
```

The method name, circle, is exactly the same as the BGI function name, circle. Inside the Screen class, specifying a call to circle would be taken to mean a call to Screen::circle. You can use the *scope resolution operator*, ::, to indicate that you want the reference to be made outside the scope of the current class. The call

```
::circle(p.x(), p.y(), radius);
```

invokes the BGI function, circle. If the :: were left out, this statement would recursively call Screen::circle and would never exit.

The rest of the methods are all direct calls to BGI functions. One new concept here is that of *function overloading*. You can have two or more functions with the same names, provided that the functions differ in either the number or the type of arguments passed to the function. The compiler can always tell which function you mean to call by looking at the arguments in the calling statement. For example, the call

```
screen.background(Screen::cyan);
```

would invoke the first definition of background in SCREEN1.CPP.

```
void Screen::background(int color)
{
    setbkcolor(color);
}
```

Whereas the call

```
int color = screen.background();
```

would invoke the second definition of background.

```
int Screen::background()
{
    return getbkcolor();
}
```

Note that you can't overload functions simply by specifying different return types.

```
Point Screen::translate(Point p)
...
int Screen::translate(Point p)      // error
...
```

The BGI functions used in the implementation of the Screen class are self-explanatory. But if you need more information on moveto, lineto, circle, setbkcolor, getbkcolor, setcolor, getcolor, or cleardevice, you can find detailed information in the Turbo C++ run-time library reference manual.

Finally, the last line in SCREEN1.CPP declares and sets aside storage for the single global instance of the Screen class.

```
Screen screen;
```

This creates a variable called screen, which is then used to invoke the methods inside the Screen class. The private instance variables inside screen are undefined until the statement

```
screen.initialize();
```

is called inside main. This completes the presentation of all code required to build ROTATE1.EXE.

ZORTECH FLASH GRAPHICS IMPLEMENTATION OF SCREEN

From the user's point of view, very little needs to be changed in order to use the Flash Graphics implementation of the Screen class. The files, POINT.H and ROTATE.CPP, are not changed at all. The builder needs to change the implementation in SCREEN2.CPP. A change in implementation usually results in slight modification to the header file, which specifies the public interface as well as the private instance variables used for Screen.

Even though the public interface to the Screen class is not changed, new private instance variables are required for the Screen class. The following three lines are added to the private section of the Screen class declaration in SCREEN2.H:

```
fg_color_t  drawColor;
fg_color_t  backgroundColor;
Point       penPos;
```

These private instance variables keep track of the foreground and background colors as well as the current pen position.

Unlike the BGI, the Flash Graphics library does not provide a pen that keeps track of its current color and position on the screen. To draw a line you must specify both the starting point and the ending point of the line as well as the color. You can mimic the behavior of the BGI by having the screen object keep track of and update the private instance variable, pen-Pos, every time a call is made to Screen::moveTo or Screen::lineTo. In addition, penPos must be initialized inside Screen::initialize.

```
penPos = Point(0,0);
```

A fourth line must also be added to SCREEN2.H:

```
#include <fg.h>
```

The file FG.H is the header file for the Flash Graphics library and declares the type fg_color_t, which is the type used for the instance variables, drawColor and backgroundColor.

These four lines constitute the only difference between SCREEN1.H and SCREEN2.H. SCREEN2.H is included here for reference.

```
file:screen2.h

#ifndef SCREEN_H
#define SCREEN_H

#include "point.h"
#include <fg.h>
//////////////////////////////////////////////////////////////
// class Screen (interface)
//////////////////////////////////////////////////////////////
class Screen
{
    fg_color_t  drawColor;
    fg_color_t  backgroundColor;
    Point       penPos;
    int         maxX;
    int         maxY;
    Point       translate(Point p);
    int         translateX(int x);
    int         translateY(int y);
public:
    enum { black,       blue,          green,       cyan,
           red,         magenta,       brown,       lightgray,
           darkgray,    lightblue,     lightgreen,  lightcyan,
           lightred,    lightmagenta,  yellow,      white
         };

    void    initialize();
    void    cleanup();
    void    moveTo(Point p);
```

```
    void    lineTo(Point p);
    void    circle(Point p, int radius);
    void    background(int color);
    int     background();
    void    foreground(int color);
    int     foreground();
    void    clear();
};

//////////////////////////////////////////////////////////////
// global screen object
// (only one instance of Screen allowed per program)
//////////////////////////////////////////////////////////////
extern Screen screen;

void far pascal rotateShapes();   // defined in rotate.cpp

#endif
```

MAIN2.CPP is virtually unchanged. The only difference is the inclusion of SCREEN2.H instead of SCREEN1.H at the top of the file.

```
#include "screen2.h"
#include <conio.h>

main()
{
    screen.initialize();
    screen.background(Screen::cyan);

    rotateShapes();

    getch();
    screen.cleanup();
}
```

So far the user has only had to change one line of code—if the name of the actual header file had not been changed, the user would not have been required to make any changes. The main work is done by the builder of the Screen class inside SCREEN2.CPP. The biggest difference between the Flash Graphics library and the BGI is that the origin for the Flash Graphics library is at the lower-left corner of the screen. Recall that the BGI's origin is the upper-left corner. The origin for the user's virtual coordinate system, like the origin for the Flash Graphics library, is at the lower-left corner. This means that the mapping used in the BGI system for the y coordinate has been changed from:

```
Yinternal = maxY - ((maxY * Yvirtual) / 100)
```

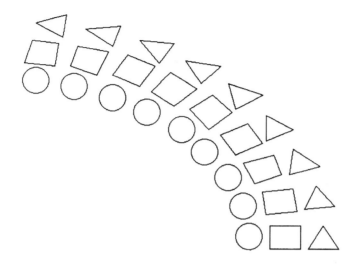

Figure 6-1.   Output from ROTATE2.EXE using Zortech's Flash Graphics library

to

```
Yinternal = (maxY * Yvirtual) / 100
```

Other than this, the modifications are pretty straightforward, with calls to the Flash Graphics library routine substituted for calls to the BGI functions. For details on the Flash Graphics functions, fg_init, fg_term, fg_drawline, fg_drawellipse, and fg_fillbox, refer to Zortech's C++ function reference manual.

Running ROTATE2.EXE produces output like that shown in Figure 6-1, which is identical to the output of ROTATE1.EXE. Here is a make file that will build ROTATE2.EXE using the Zortech C++ compiler.

```
FG_MODEL=s
FG_FLAGS= -v -a -b -c -u
FG_LFLAGS = /CO /MAP
FG_LIBS = fg.lib

ROTATE2_OBJS = main2.obj screen2.obj rotate2.obj

        #################################################
        ## Zortech Flash Graphics version of Screen class
        #################################################
screen2.obj: screen2.cpp screen2.h point.h
    ztc $(FG_FLAGS) $*

        #################################################
        ## All shape classes, and the rotateShapes function
        ## are unchanged but a different VERSION MACRO
        ## must be defined to include the proper version
        ## of screen.h (screen2.h).
        #################################################
rotate2.obj : rotate.cpp screen2.h point.h
    ztc $(FG_FLAGS) rotate.cpp -orotate2 -DVER2

        #################################################
        ## standard Zortech C++ main function
        ## main calls rotateShapes
        #################################################
main2.obj : main2.cpp screen2.h point.h
    ztc $(FG_FLAGS) $*

        #################################################
        ## link object files to create executable
        ## uses Zortech's BLINK
        #################################################
rotate2.exe: $(ROTATE2_OBJS)
    echo LINKING rotate2.exe
    blink $(FG_LFLAGS) $(ROTATE2_OBJS), rotate2,,$(FG_LIBS);
    echo to run under DOS type:    rotate2
#########################################################
```

MICROSOFT WINDOWS IMPLEMENTATION OF SCREEN

The Microsoft Windows implementation of rotate shapes (ROTATE3.EXE) is trickier than the BGI and Flash Graphics versions. It's not so much that SCREEN3.CPP is harder to implement than either SCREEN1.CPP or SCREEN2.CPP. It's more an issue of setting up the general program structure of a Microsoft Windows application. Before going into the differences in the implementation of the Screen class, it's nice to know that the code that makes up the application part of rotate shapes is entirely unchanged for Windows. That is, the files ROTATE.CPP and POINT.H are completely unchanged. The file MAIN.CPP is changed dramatically. This really isn't a surprise when you think about how typical C or C++ programs work.

Before the function main is entered, certain environmental conditions must be set up. In C there is a module, called the *startup module,* which has code that is executed before main is called. This code is usually completely invisible to the programmer. Under certain conditions you might need to modify the startup code if you need to operate the program in a nonstandard environment — for example, if you were developing a program to run on an 8086 computer that was operating as a controller for some hardware device in an embedded system. In such an environment you probably wouldn't have the support of DOS, so the startup code that initializes relevant DOS data structures would be removed. In this respect, the default startup code for both Turbo C++ and Zortech C++ programs sets up the environmental conditions that enable a C++ program to run under DOS.

In order for a program to run under Microsoft Windows, similar environmental conditions must be met. However, in the case of Windows, the programmer is responsible for more of the initialization code than for DOS programs. When you are running programs under Windows, you are really running under a different operating system. You need to adjust your programs to direct output through the Windows API (Application Program Interface). It is no longer valid to direct output to devices such as stdout, or stderr (cout and cerr in C++). Similarly, you cannot get input from stdin (cin in C++). These devices are part of the operating environment that is taken for granted for C and C++ programs whether the operating system is UNIX or MS-DOS. If you want to write Windows applications, you not only need to change the way you send output to the operating environment, you need to assist in setting up the output environment as well. To do this you need an understanding of the basic Windows operating environment.

MICROSOFT WINDOWS APPLICATIONS PROGRAMMING

Microsoft Windows allows you to run several instances of a given program at the same time. For this reason Windows makes a distinction between an *application* and an *instance* of a program. Regardless of how many instances of a program you have running, there is only one application running for a given program.

Consider a word processing program such as Microsoft Word for Windows. You might have one instance of Word running in which you are writing letters and correspondence; you might have another instance of Word running in which you are writing programs. The correspondence instance of Word would need to keep a local copy of the data required for your letters. The programming instance of Word would need an entirely different data area to maintain the source code files for the programs you are writing. However, there is no need to keep around a duplicate version of the code that Microsoft Word uses to carry out basic operations such as getting input from the keyboard, displaying text on the screen, loading and saving files, and formatting and printing text. All the code that can be shared across multiple instances of the Word program is kept in a single place in memory.

Windows Applications

The common code and data shared by instances is referred to as the *application*. There are certain data items that must be initialized for the application the first time it is run. The second time the program is run, there is no need to reinitialize this data. Initializations that must be handled only the first time a program is run are handled in a function usually called "InitApplication".

Windows Instances

Besides the internal data that a program operates on, such as the file being edited by a word processor, each application must keep data about the window in which it is being displayed. How big is the window? Where is it located on the screen? Is it shown in its icon form or in its full size as a window? This kind of data must be initialized for each instance of the application that runs in the Windows environment. Such initialization takes place in a function usually called "InitInstance".

The WinMain Function for Microsoft Windows Applications

Windows applications must provide a third function in addition to InitApplication and InitInstance. This third function is the equivalent to main in a standard C or C++ program and is called "WinMain". This function is always the first function to get control in a Windows application. First, it checks to see if any instances of the application are running. If not, it calls the InitApplication function. Next, the program initializes the current instance of the program by calling InitInstance. Finally, WinMain enters a message loop. Windows is an *event-driven* system. Events are usually some form of user input such as mouse movement, mouse button presses, or keyboard keypresses. Each time an event occurs, it gets put in a queue. The main event loop reads the next event in the queue and then dispatches the event to the appropriate Windows application. The pseudocode for the main event loop looks something like this:

```
while GetMessage
    DispatchMessage
```

Every Windows application has such an event loop. The application keeps running until it receives the WM_QUIT message, which usually happens when the user selects the Close entry in the system menu of the Window.

Message Handling

WinMain is responsible for message gathering and dispatching. The programmer must provide a fourth function, which actually handles the message dispatched by WinMain. This function can be called anything that you like; however, it is typically called "MainWndProc". MainWndProc is responsible for defining the messages that a given application will respond to. A function like MainWndProc is usually referred to as a *callback function*. This is because it is never called directly. The callback function for a given Windows application is specified in the function InitApplication. Once the callback function has been specified, it is invoked every time a message is sent to a given Windows application. Messages are sent to windows when input is focused on a particular window and the user causes an event to occur, such as a keypress or a mouse movement. The callback function for the application checks to see if it is supposed to respond to the specific message generated by the event. If it is, it handles the event by performing specified operations. Otherwise, it calls a default event handler, which checks to see if the event should be processed by other windows applications.

All callback routines respond to the WM_DESTROY message. This message is sent to a Windows application when the user selects the Close choice from the system menu associated with the window. Most callback functions handle this message by posting a quit message to the *window manager*.

Actually, there are several queues operating at a given time in the Windows environment. There's a System queue, which handles all input events for the entire system. The window manager checks the System queue for events, determines which application should handle a given event, and puts the event in a queue associated with the application. Each application instance also has its own event queue. For a given application instance, control is passed back and forth between the application queue and the callback function.

When the callback function receives the WM_DESTROY message, it typically executes the following statement:

```
PostQuitMessage(0);
```

This posts the message WM_QUIT to the application queue. The application queue, in turn, passes the WM_QUIT message back to the main event loop inside WinMain. Remember, WinMain is not the callback function; the callback function is typically called MainWndProc. MainWndProc handles the events sent to it through the window manager. WinMain, on the other hand, reads the next event from the application queue and dispatches it through the window manager to the callback function. When the callback function posts the WM_QUIT message to the window manager, this message is, in turn, passed back to the main event loop in WinMain. When this event loop receives the WM_QUIT message, the current instance of the application is terminated, and the window is closed.

All Windows applications must, therefore, provide at least four functions, as follows:

```
WinMain                    main entry point and event loop
InitApplication            initializes data shared by all instances
InitInstance               initializes data unique to each instance
MainWndProc                application event handler (callback function)
```

The name of MainWndProc can be changed and is specified by the user, but it's good to use the same name in each application program simply as a convention. All functions that communicate by message passing through the window manager must be declared by preceding them with the keyword *pascal*. This indicates that arguments passed to the function are to be placed on the stack in exactly the opposite order they would be for a standard C function. Of the four functions listed above, only WinMain and the callback function, MainWndProc, need to be declared as *pascal*. A header file for the third version of rotate called MAIN3.H declares the prototypes for all the global functions.

```
file: main3.h

#define IDM_ABOUT 100

int PASCAL WinMain(HANDLE, HANDLE, LPSTR, int);
BOOL InitApplication(HANDLE);
BOOL InitInstance(HANDLE, int);
long FAR PASCAL MainWndProc(HWND, unsigned, WORD, LONG);
BOOL FAR PASCAL About(HWND, unsigned, WORD, LONG);
void far pascal rotateShapes();
```

Two functions in addition to the four required to set up a Windows application appear here. We have seen rotateShapes before; formerly the declaration for rotateShapes appeared in SCREEN1.H and SCREEN2.H. Since all global functions are now being declared in MAIN3.H, it's better to include rotateShapes here.

The "Aboutfunction" is new. This function, also declared as *pascal*, invokes a dialog box in response to a menu selection provided in a menu inside the application. Dialog boxes are created with a *resource compiler*, which is unique to Microsoft Windows. The resource compiler handles a special form of program text, which is a convenient way of specifying application resources, such as menus and dialog boxes. The following resource file creates two resources: a menu and a dialog box.

```
file: rotate3.rc

#include "windows.h"
#include "main3.h"
```

```
RotateMenu MENU
BEGIN
    POPUP          "&Help"
    BEGIN
        MENUITEM "&About Rotate...", IDM_ABOUT
    END
END

AboutBox DIALOG 22, 17, 104, 75
STYLE DS_MODALFRAME | WS_CAPTION | WS_SYSMENU
CAPTION "About Rotate"
BEGIN
    CTEXT "Rotate Shapes"             -1,  0,  5, 104,  8
    CTEXT "Abstract Screen class"     -1,  0, 20, 104,  8
    CTEXT "adapted for"               -1,  0, 29, 104,  8
    CTEXT "Microsoft Windows"         -1,  0, 38, 104,  8
    DEFPUSHBUTTON "OK"               IDOK, 35, 55,  32, 14, WS_GROUP
END
```

The menu created by this resource file has one entry. The menu resource is called RotateMenu and is specified for the application inside the
setup function, InitApplication. The resource file indicates that the text
string that appears for this choice will be "About Rotate..." and indicates
that the IDM_ABOUT message should be sent to the application's callback
function (MainWndProc) if this choice is selected. The callback function is
then responsible for calling the dialog box function, AboutBox, which is
specified in the resource file. The menu generated by a RotateMenu has
only one entry, which, when selected, generates a message to invoke the
AboutBox dialog box. The About Rotate dialog box is invoked by calling the
function AboutBox. The menu generated by calling RotateMenu and the
dialog box generated by calling AboutBox are shown here:

The resource file, ROTATE 3.RC, is compiled with the command

```
rc -r rotate3.rc
```

which invokes the resource compiler and creates an output file named
ROTATE3.RES. The .RES file is later added into the executable program file
when the .EXE is created with the linker. The .RES file should have the
same filename as the .EXE file when the extensions are dropped. The file,
ROTATE3.RES, is added into the executable, ROTATE3.EXE, by invoking
the resource compiler with the following command:

```
rc rotate3.res
```

Typically, programmers use templates when programming Microsoft
Windows applications. All Windows applications have basically the same
form, and usually the main programming that needs to be done is specifying the messages that the callback routine (MainWndProc) will respond to.
In addition, the programmer must specify any routines that will be called
from MainWndProc. Here is the definition of MainWndProc found inside
the file MAIN3.CPP:

```
/////////////////////////////////////////////////////////////
// MainWndProc
/////////////////////////////////////////////////////////////
long FAR PASCAL MainWndProc(HWND hWnd,          // window handle
                            unsigned message,   // type of message
                            WORD wParam,
                            LONG lParam)
{
    switch (message) {
    case WM_COMMAND:                    // command command sent
                                        // from application menu
        if (wParam == IDM_ABOUT)
        {
            FARPROC lpProcAbout =
                MakeProcInstance(About,
                                 screen.instance());

            DialogBox(screen.instance(),    // current instance
                "AboutBox",                 // resource to use
                hWnd,                       // parent handle
                lpProcAbout);               // About() instance address

            FreeProcInstance(lpProcAbout);
            break;
        }
        else                                // let Windows process it
            return (DefWindowProc(hWnd, message, wParam, lParam));
```

```
    case WM_PAINT:
        {
            PAINTSTRUCT ps;
            HDC hDC = BeginPaint(hWnd, &ps);

            char szBuf[100];
            strcpy(szBuf, "Well-designed class interfaces");
            TextOut(hDC, 10,4, szBuf, strlen(szBuf));
            strcpy(szBuf, "produce modular objects and");
            TextOut(hDC, 10,20, szBuf, strlen(szBuf));
            strcpy(szBuf, "replaceable system components.");
            TextOut(hDC, 10,36, szBuf, strlen(szBuf));

            screen.initialize(hWnd, hDC);
            rotateShapes();
            screen.cleanup();

            EndPaint(hWnd, &ps);
        }
        break;

    case WM_DESTROY:              // message: destroy window
        PostQuitMessage(0);
        break;

    default:                      // Passes it on if unproccessed
        return (DefWindowProc(hWnd, message, wParam, lParam));
    }
    return (NULL);
}
```

Basically this boils down to a switch, which handles three messages.

```
switch (message) {
case WM_COMMAND:                  // command command sent
                                  // from application menu

    ...
    // invoke RotateMenu
    ...
case WM_PAINT:
    ...
    // set context for drawing graphics
    // write some text to the window
    // call rotateShapes
    ...
case WM_DESTROY:                  // message: destroy window
    ...
    // post WM_QUIT message to window manager
    ...

default:                          // Passes it on if unproccessed
    ...
    // call default event handler
    ...
}
...
}
```

The main item of concern here is the processing in response to the WM_PAINT message, which calls the rotateShapes function. In order to implement the Screen class, the builder needs to understand the concepts of handles and display contexts.

Window Handles and Instance Handles

Handles are used to retrieve data associated with a Window. Handles can provide information about a window's location, size, and *state* (whether it is shown in full or icon form). *Instance handles* give the programmer access to data associated with a given instance of a running program. You can actually get the window handle if you have the instance handle. Handles are a way of protecting sensitive data from accidental modification by the user.

Actually, handles implement a form of encapsulation. Remember that Microsoft Windows was originally intended to be programmed in C instead of C++. Since C does not provide the same form of encapsulation provided by C++ classes, handles were developed. When Windows programs are initialized, a copy of the instance handle associated with the program is usually saved in a global variable for later reference.

The actual *window handle* is usually passed as the first argument of most Microsoft Windows functions. In order to call a dialog box, the programmer must pass both the instance handle and the window handle to the dialog box function. Since so many Windows functions need both the instance handle and the window handle for a given application, the third implementation of the Screen class keeps track of both these pieces of data as private instance variables.

```
class Screen
{
    HWND        hWindow;          // window handle
    HANDLE      hCurrentInstance; // current window instance
    ...
};
```

In addition, two versions of the overloaded method, instance, are provided to set and retrieve the instance handle.

```
HANDLE instance()        { return hCurrentInstance; }
void   instance(HANDLE h) { hCurrentInstance = h; }
```

Now when the application is initialized (by calling InitInstance), the instance handle can be saved inside the global screen object.

```
BOOL InitInstance(HANDLE hInstance,       // current instance
                  int nCmdShow)           // for first call
                                          // to ShowWindow
{
    ////////////////////////////////////////////////////////
    // save window instance variable in global screen object
    ////////////////////////////////////////////////////////
    screen.instance(hInstance);
    ...
}
```

When calling the dialog box associated with ROTATE3.EXE, you can now use the Screen object to supply the instance handle, and you can get the window handle from the first argument of MainWndProc.

```
long FAR PASCAL MainWndProc(HWND hWnd,       // window handle
                            unsigned message,   // type of message
                            WORD wParam,
                            LONG lParam)
{
    ...
            DialogBox(screen.instance(),    // current instance
                "AboutBox",                 // resource to use
                hWnd,                       // window handle
                ...);
    ...
}
```

Display Context Handles

Before writing strings or drawing graphics inside a window, the *display context* for the window must be set. The display context automatically maps coordinates that are relative to the window origin to the appropriate global display coordinates. Other data retained by the display context includes the current text font, the color in which text is printed or the color used by a given pen, and the line style used for drawing lines. Whenever a function responds to the WM_PAINT message, it must create a new display context by calling the BeginPaint Windows function. The program may then output text or graphics to the specified window. When output operations have finished, the program must indicate so by calling the EndPaint Windows function. Both BeginPaint and EndPaint receive a window handle and a pointer to a paint data structure as arguments.

```
...
case WM_PAINT:
    {
        PAINTSTRUCT ps;
        HDC hDC = BeginPaint(hWnd, &ps);
        ...
        // output operations
        ...
        EndPaint(hWnd, &ps);
    }
    break;
```

Most Windows output operations require a display context, which is a specialized form of a device context. For example, to output the string "Hello, world" to the screen you would first set the device context and then execute the following statement:

```
TextOut(hDC, 10,4, "Hello, world", 12);
```

The first argument is the device context. The second and third arguments are the x and y values relative to the upper-left corner of the window output area where the string is to be displayed. The fourth argument is the string itself, and the fifth argument is the length of the string. You also need the device context to draw lines and circles. For this reason, the device context is also saved inside the global instance of the Screen class.

The Screen class now declares five private instance variables.

```
class Screen
{
    HWND        hWindow;            // window handle
    HDC         hDeviceContext;     // device context handle
    HANDLE      hCurrentInstance;   // current window instance
    int         maxX;
    int         maxY;
    ...
};
```

As mentioned earlier, two definitions of the overloaded method, instance, allow the programmer to set and retrieve the instance handle.

```
HANDLE instance()         { return hCurrentInstance; }
void   instance(HANDLE h) { hCurrentInstance = h; }
```

The user of the Screen class has always been required to call Screen::initialize before drawing on the screen and to call Screen::cleanup when finished drawing. Since all drawing functions require both a window handle and a device context, it makes sense to modify Screen::initialize to require arguments for these two pieces of data. This is really the only substantial change to the interface that affects the user's code. While the user is also expected to call Screen::instance to save the global instance handle for the application, this is really part of standard Windows application housekeeping. Finally, a constructor is provided, which initializes all the handles to NULL and sets the values of maxX and maxY to 0 whenever a Screen object is created.

```
Screen()                        // constructor
  : hWindow(NULL),
    hDeviceContext(NULL),
    hCurrentInstance(NULL),
    maxX(0),
    maxY(0)
  {}
```

The interfaces for the rest of the public methods are unchanged. The entire class declaration should be put in a file called SCREEN3.CPP. The complete file is listed here for your reference.

```
file: screen3.h

#ifndef SCREEN_H
#define SCREEN_H

#include "point.h"
#include "wintypes.h"

/////////////////////////////////////////////////////////////
// class Screen (interface)
/////////////////////////////////////////////////////////////
class Screen
{
    HWND        hWindow;            // window handle
    HDC         hDeviceContext;     // device context handle
    HANDLE      hCurrentInstance;   // current window instance
    int         maxX;
    int         maxY;
    Point       translate(Point p);
    int         translateX(int x);
    int         translateY(int y);
public:
    Screen()                        // constructor
```

```
        : hWindow(NULL),
          hDeviceContext(NULL),
          hCurrentInstance(NULL),
          maxX(0),
          maxY(0)
    {}
    HANDLE  instance()          { return hCurrentInstance; }
    void    instance(HANDLE h) { hCurrentInstance = h; }

    enum {  black,      blue,           green,       cyan,
            red,        magenta,        brown,       lightgray,
            darkgray,   lightblue,      lightgreen,  lightcyan,
            lightred,   lightmagenta,   yellow,      white
         };

    void    initialize(HWND hWnd, HDC hDC);
    void    cleanup();
    void    moveTo(Point p);
    void    lineTo(Point p);
    void    circle(Point p, int radius);
    void    background(int color);
    int     background();
    void    foreground(int color);
    int     foreground();
    void    clear();
};

/////////////////////////////////////////////////////////////
// global screen object
// (only one instance of Screen allowed per program)
/////////////////////////////////////////////////////////////
extern Screen screen;

#endif
```

The file SCREEN2.CPP included the line,

```
#include <fg.h>
```

which included the header file for the Zortech Flash Graphics library. This
line is replaced in SCREEN3.CPP with the line,

```
#include "wintypes.h"
```

which is a file that defines basic Microsoft Windows data types. Most
programs that use Windows functions include the following line:

```
#include <windows.h>
```

However, it is an error for a program to include this file more than once. Since Windows data types are required in the declaration for the Screen class, several files would be likely to contain both of the following lines:

```
#include "screen3.h"
#include <windows.h>
```

If SCREEN3.CPP also included the WINDOWS.H file, the compiler would generate an error when it encountered the previous code. Further, WINDOWS.H is a very large file requiring a great deal of memory and time to process. In order to minimize the resources required to compile the Screen class, a minimum number of Windows data types required by the class declaration are duplicated in the file WINTYPES.H.

```
file: wintypes.h

#ifndef WINTYPES_H
#define WINTYPES_H

/************************************************************
    In order to keep the Screen class as
    independent of windows as possible
    windows.h is not included. Only
    the necessary data types for the
    private instance variables are
    redefined here.

    These typedefs must be kept consistent
    with those in windows.h for subsequent
    releases of MS-Windows.
************************************************************/
#ifndef WORD
typedef unsigned int        WORD;
#endif

#ifndef HANDLE
typedef WORD                HANDLE;
#endif

#ifndef HWND
typedef HANDLE              HWND;
#endif

#ifndef HDC
typedef HANDLE              HDC;
#endif

#ifndef NULL
#define NULL        0
#endif

#endif /* WINTYPES_H */
```

This file also has the advantage that if it is included twice, the surrounding #ifndef...#endif compiler directives prevent the macros from being defined twice.

```
#ifndef WINTYPES_H
#define WINTYPES_H
...
#endif
```

In fact, this technique can also be used to guarantee that WINDOWS.H is never included more than once during a given compilation. First, create a file MSW.H as follows:

```
file: msw.h

#ifndef MSW_H
#define MSW_H

#ifdef NULL
#undef NULL
#endif

extern "C" {
#include "windows.h"
}

#endif  /* MSW_H */
```

You should then keep this file in the directory in which you're building your Microsoft Windows application and use #include "msw.h" instead of #include <windows.h>.

You're now ready to look at the Windows implementation of the Screen class.

```
file: screen3.cpp

#include <stdlib.h>
#include <stdio.h>
#include "screen3.h"
#include "msw.h"

#define VIRTUAL_MAXX 100
#define VIRTUAL_MAXY 100

//////////////////////////////////////////////////////////
// class Screen (implementation)
//////////////////////////////////////////////////////////
Point Screen::translate(Point p)
{
```

```
    // coordinate range: 0,0 to maxX,maxY
    // maxX and maxY are device dependent
    // and set in Screen::initialize

    int x = translateX(p.x());
    int y = translateY(p.y());
    return Point(x,y);
}

int Screen::translateX(int x)
{
    return int(long(maxX) * long(x) / VIRTUAL_MAXX);
}

int Screen::translateY(int y)
{
    return maxY - int(long(maxY) * long(y) / VIRTUAL_MAXY);
}

void Screen::initialize(HWND hWnd, HDC hDC)
{
    hWindow=hWnd;
    hDeviceContext=hDC;
    RECT  aRect;
    GetClientRect(hWnd, &aRect);
    maxX = aRect.right;
    maxY = aRect.bottom;
}

void Screen::cleanup()
{
    hWindow=hDeviceContext=NULL;
    maxX = maxY = 0;
}

void Screen::moveTo(Point p)
{
    if (hWindow==NULL)  // error, screen not initialized
        return;
    p = translate(p);
    MoveTo(hDeviceContext, p.x(), p.y());
}

void Screen::lineTo(Point p)
{
    if (hWindow==NULL)  // error, screen not initialized
        return;
    p = translate(p);
    LineTo(hDeviceContext, p.x(), p.y());
}

void Screen::circle(Point p, int radius)
{
    if (hWindow==NULL)  // error, screen not initialized
        return;
    p = translate(p);
```

```
        int xr = (long)maxX * (long)radius / VIRTUAL_MAXX;
        int yr = (long)maxY * (long)radius / VIRTUAL_MAXY;
        radius = (xr + yr) / 2;
        Ellipse(hDeviceContext, p.x()-radius, p.y()-radius,
                                p.x()+radius, p.y()+radius);
}

void Screen::background(int color)
{
}

int Screen::background()
{
}

void Screen::foreground(int color)
{
}

int Screen::foreground()
{
}

void Screen::clear()
{
}

////////////////////////////////////////////////////////////
// global screen object
// (only one instance of Screen allowed per program)
////////////////////////////////////////////////////////////

Screen screen;
```

The coordinate system of Microsoft Windows is like the BGI in that the origin is in the upper-left corner. In order to properly translate from the user's coordinate system to the Windows coordinate system, translateY must subtract the internal y coordinate from maxY.

```
Yinternal = maxY - ((maxY * Yvirtual) / 100)
```

Recall that Screen::initialize now receives two arguments: the window handle and the device context handle. A copy of these handles is saved inside the internal instance variables. A Windows rectangle object (type RECT) called aRect is created. The coordinates of the rectangle bounding box for a window can be retrieved inside a RECT data structure with the following call,

```
GetClientRect(hWnd, &aRect);
```

where the first argument is the window handle and the second argument is a pointer to a RECT structure. The values for maxX and maxY can then be retrieved from the structure. The user should not try to draw anything in the window area until Screen::initialize is called. When the Screen object is created the internal instance variable hWindow is set to NULL. Each of the routines that draws to the screen checks to make sure that hWindow is not set to NULL before performing output. If hWindow is set to NULL, then Screen::initialize has not been called and the functions return without performing any output.

```
...
if (hWindow==NULL)  // error, screen not initialized
    return;
...
```

To ensure that the screen is never written to after cleanup, the method Screen::cleanup sets hWindow back to NULL. It does the same for hDevice-Context, and, at the same time, sets maxX and maxY to 0.

```
void Screen::cleanup()
{
    hWindow=hDeviceContext=NULL;
    maxX = maxY = 0;
}
```

There are only three other lines in SCREEN3.CPP that you have not seen before. These are used to move the drawing pen, draw a line from the current pen position to a new pen position, and to draw an ellipse inside the box specified by the last four arguments to Ellipse.

```
MoveTo(hDeviceContext, p.x(), p.y());
...
LineTo(hDeviceContext, p.x(), p.y());
...
Ellipse(hDeviceContext, p.x()-radius, p.y()-radius,
                        p.x()+radius, p.y()+radius);
```

Each of these Windows output functions requires a device context as its first argument.

Finally you're ready to look at the complete definition for handling the WM_PAINT message inside the callback function, MainWndProc.

```
long FAR PASCAL MainWndProc(HWND hWnd,              // window handle
                           unsigned message,        // type of message
                           WORD wParam,
                           LONG lParam)
{
    switch (message) {
    case WM_COMMAND:                       // command command sent
        ...
    case WM_PAINT:
        {
            PAINTSTRUCT ps;
            HDC hDC = BeginPaint(hWnd, &ps);

            char szBuf[100];
            strcpy(szBuf, "Well-designed class interfaces");
            TextOut(hDC, 10,4, szBuf, strlen(szBuf));
            strcpy(szBuf, "produce modular objects and");
            TextOut(hDC, 10,20, szBuf, strlen(szBuf));
            strcpy(szBuf, "replaceable system components.");
            TextOut(hDC, 10,36, szBuf, strlen(szBuf));

            screen.initialize(hWnd, hDC);
            rotateShapes();
            screen.cleanup();

            EndPaint(hWnd, &ps);
        }
        break;

    case WM_DESTROY:                  // message: destroy window
        ...

    default:                         // Passes it on if unproccessed
        return (DefWindowProc(hWnd, message, wParam, lParam));
    }
    return (NULL);
}
```

The code inside this case statement creates a paint structure and then
creates and initializes a handle for the display or device context. Three
strings are then output to the window using the device context handle.
Next, the global screen object is initialized using the window handle and
the device context handle. The function rotateShapes is then called. This
function is still defined in ROTATE.CPP. None of the code in this file has
been changed. Next Screen::cleanup is called to reset the instance variables
for screen. Finally, the display context is released with a call to the Windows EndPaint function.

The MainWndProc can be found in its entirety in the file MAIN3.CPP,
which is included here for your reference.

file: main3.cpp

```
/////////////////////////////////////////////////////////////
// PROGRAM: rotate3.exe
// FILE:    main3.cpp
//
// PURPOSE: template for C++ Windows applications
//
// FUNCTIONS:
//     WinMain          initialization, processes message loop
//     InitApplication  initializes window data and registers window
//     InitInstance     saves instance handle and creates main window
//     MainWndProc      processes messages
//     About            processes messages for "About" dialog box
/////////////////////////////////////////////////////////////
#include <string.h>
#include "msw.h"          // ms-windows prototypes for Zortech C++
#include "main3.h"        // specific to this file
#include "screen3.h"      // abstract screen class

/////////////////////////////////////////////////////////////
// WinMain
/////////////////////////////////////////////////////////////
int PASCAL WinMain(HANDLE hInstance,        // current instance
                   HANDLE hPrevInstance,    // previous instance
                   LPSTR lpCmdLine,         // command line
                   int nCmdShow)            // show as (open/icon)
{
    /////////////////////////////////////////////////////////
    // Application-specific initialization
    /////////////////////////////////////////////////////////
    if (!hPrevInstance)                      // other instances running
        if (!InitApplication(hInstance))     // Initialize shared data
            return (FALSE);                  // exit--can't initialize

    /////////////////////////////////////////////////////////
    // Instance-specific initializations
    /////////////////////////////////////////////////////////
    if (!InitInstance(hInstance, nCmdShow))
        return (FALSE);

    /////////////////////////////////////////////////////////
    // Main dispatch loop
    // Get and Dispatch messages
    // until WM_QUIT received
    /////////////////////////////////////////////////////////
    MSG msg;                    // message
    while (GetMessage(&msg,     // message structure
        NULL,                   // handle of window receiving the message
        NULL,                   // lowest message to examine
        NULL))                  // highest message to examine
    {
        TranslateMessage(&msg); // Translates virtual key codes
        DispatchMessage(&msg);  // Dispatches message to window
    }
    return (msg.wParam);        // Returns value from PostQuitMessage
}
```

```
////////////////////////////////////////////////////////////
// InitApplication
////////////////////////////////////////////////////////////
BOOL InitApplication(HANDLE hInstance) // current instance
{

    ////////////////////////////////////////////////////////////
    // initialize window class structure for  main window
    ////////////////////////////////////////////////////////////
    WNDCLASS  wc;
    wc.style = NULL;                    // class style(s)
    wc.lpfnWndProc = MainWndProc;       // callback function handles
                                        // messages for this window
                                        // class
    wc.cbClsExtra = 0;                  // no per-class extra data
    wc.cbWndExtra = 0;                  // no per-window extra data
    wc.hInstance = hInstance;           // application that owns class
    wc.hIcon=LoadIcon(NULL,
                   IDI_APPLICATION);
    wc.hCursor=LoadCursor(NULL,
                       IDC_ARROW);
    wc.hbrBackground=
        GetStockObject(WHITE_BRUSH);
    wc.lpszMenuName = "RotateMenu";     // name of menu in RC file
    wc.lpszClassName = "RotateWClass";  // used in call to CreateWindow

    ////////////////////////////////////////////////////////////
    // register the window class and return status
    ////////////////////////////////////////////////////////////
    return (RegisterClass(&wc));
}

////////////////////////////////////////////////////////////
// InitInstance
////////////////////////////////////////////////////////////
BOOL InitInstance(HANDLE hInstance,    // current instance
              int nCmdShow)            // for first call
                                       // to ShowWindow
{
    ////////////////////////////////////////////////////////////
    // save window instance variable in global screen object
    ////////////////////////////////////////////////////////////
    screen.instance(hInstance);

    HWND hWnd = CreateWindow(           // create main window
        "RotateWClass",                 // see RegisterClass call
        "C++ MS Windows Rotate Shapes",
                                        // text for window title bar
        WS_OVERLAPPEDWINDOW,            // window style
        CW_USEDEFAULT,                  // default horizontal position
        CW_USEDEFAULT,                  // default vertical position
        CW_USEDEFAULT,                  // default width
        CW_USEDEFAULT,                  // default height
        NULL,                           // no parent for overlapped
        NULL,                           // use the window class menu
        hInstance,                      // instance owning this window
        NULL                            // pointer not needed
    );
```

```
/////////////////////////////////////////////////////////
// window could not be created, return failure
/////////////////////////////////////////////////////////
if (!hWnd)
    return (FALSE);

/////////////////////////////////////////////////////////
// display window, return success
/////////////////////////////////////////////////////////
ShowWindow(hWnd, nCmdShow);          // show the window
UpdateWindow(hWnd);                  // sends WM_PAINT message
InvalidateRect(hWnd, NULL, TRUE);    // forces window redraw
return (TRUE);                       // returns value from
                                     // PostQuitMessage
}

/////////////////////////////////////////////////////////
// MainWndProc
/////////////////////////////////////////////////////////
long FAR PASCAL MainWndProc(HWND hWnd,         // window handle
                        unsigned message,      // type of message
                        WORD wParam,
                        LONG lParam)
{
    switch (message) {
    case WM_COMMAND:                  // command command sent
                                      // from application menu
        if (wParam == IDM_ABOUT)
        {
            FARPROC lpProcAbout =
                MakeProcInstance(About,
                                screen.instance());

            DialogBox(screen.instance(),   // current instance
                "AboutBox",                // resource to use
                hWnd,                      // parent handle
                lpProcAbout);              // About() instance address

            FreeProcInstance(lpProcAbout);
            break;
        }
        else                              // let Windows process it
            return (DefWindowProc(hWnd, message, wParam, lParam));
    case WM_PAINT:
        {
            PAINTSTRUCT ps;
            HDC hDC = BeginPaint(hWnd, &ps);

            char szBuf[100];
            strcpy(szBuf, "Well-designed class interfaces");
            TextOut(hDC, 10,4, szBuf, strlen(szBuf));
            strcpy(szBuf, "produce modular objects and");
            TextOut(hDC, 10,20, szBuf, strlen(szBuf));
            strcpy(szBuf, "replaceable system components.");
            TextOut(hDC, 10,36, szBuf, strlen(szBuf));
```

```
                    screen.initialize(hWnd, hDC);
                    rotateShapes();
                    screen.cleanup();

                    EndPaint(hWnd, &ps);
              }
              break;

        case WM_DESTROY:              // message: destroy window
              PostQuitMessage(0);
              break;

        default:                      // Passes it on if unproccessed
              return (DefWindowProc(hWnd, message, wParam, lParam));
        }
        return (NULL);
}

//////////////////////////////////////////////////////////////
// About
//////////////////////////////////////////////////////////////
BOOL FAR PASCAL About(HWND hDlg,           // window handle for dialog box
                      unsigned message,    // type of message
                      WORD wParam,          // message-specific information
                      LONG lParam)
{
    switch (message) {
    case WM_INITDIALOG:                    // initialize dialog box
        return (TRUE);

    case WM_COMMAND:                       // received command
        //////////////////////////////////////////////////////////
        // if "OK" box selected
        // or system menu close command
        // exit  dialog box
        //////////////////////////////////////////////////////////
        if (wParam == IDOK || wParam == IDCANCEL)
        {
            EndDialog(hDlg, TRUE);
            return (TRUE);
        }
        break;
    }
    return (FALSE);                        // message not processed
}
```

You will need a make file to construct ROTATE3.EXE. The rules for building ROTATE3.EXE can be added to the same make file that was used to build ROTATE2.EXE. Both ROTATE2.EXE and ROTATE3.EXE use the Zortech compiler, so a single make file can build both targets. You should create all the files for versions 2 and 3 of rotate shapes in the subdirectory \ROTATE\ZTC. The make file will build both versions by default. If you only want version 2, for example, you could type:

```
make rotate2.exe
```

instead of

```
make
```

The file MAKEFILE is included here for your reference.

```
file: makefile

###########################################################
## Windows makefile for Zortech C++ compiler
## Adapted from GENERIC makefile from Windows SDK
###########################################################

###### DEFAULT TARGET #####################################
all: rotate2.exe rotate3.exe
##rotate2.exe:
##rotate3.exe:
###########################################################


###########################################################
## rotate, version 3, Microsoft Windows, Zortech C++
###########################################################
MODEL=1
CFLAGS= -v -a -b -c -u
LFLAGS =    /NOE /CO /MAP
LIBS = libw $(MODEL)libcew

ROTATE3_OBJS = main3.obj screen3.obj rotate3.obj

        ###################################################
        ## implicit rule for creating object files (.obj)
        ## from C++ files (.cpp)
        ###################################################
.cpp.obj:
    ztc $(CFLAGS) -m$(MODEL)  $*
        ###################################################
        ## update the resource
        ###################################################
rotate3.res: rotate3.rc main3.h
    rc -r rotate3.rc

        ###################################################
        ## update Screen class
        ###################################################
screen3.obj: screen3.cpp screen3.h

        ###################################################
        ## All shape classes, and the rotateShapes function
        ## are unchanged but a different VERSION MACRO
```

```
        ## must be defined to include the proper version
        ## of screen.h (screen2.h).
        ##################################################
rotate3.obj: rotate.cpp
    ztc $(CFLAGS) -m$(MODEL) rotate.cpp -orotate3 \
                        -DVER3


        ##################################################
        ## MS Windows program template
        ##
        ## WinMain      sets up Windows environment and
        ##              sets callback routine, MainWndProc
        ## MainWndProc  roughly equivalent to main
        ##              in a standard C or C++ program
        ## MainWndProc  calls rotateShapes
        ##
        ##################################################
main3.obj: main3.cpp main3.h


        ##################################################
        ## link exe and add in resources
        ## uses Microsoft's LINK
        ##################################################
rotate3.exe: $(ROTATE3_OBJS) rotate3.def rotate3.res
    echo now LINK her up: rotate3.exe
    link $(LFLAGS) $(ROTATE3_OBJS), rotate3,,    \
                                    $(LIBS),     \
                                    rotate3.def
    echo adding in resources
    rc rotate3.res
    echo to run under Windows type:    win rotate3
##########################################################



##########################################################
## rotate, version 2, flash Zortech Flash Graphics, C++
##########################################################
FG_MODEL=s
FG_FLAGS= -v -a -b -c -u
FG_LFLAGS =  /CO /MAP
FG_LIBS = fg.lib

ROTATE2_OBJS = main2.obj screen2.obj rotate2.obj

        ##################################################
        ## Zortech Flash Graphics version of Screen class
        ##################################################
screen2.obj: screen2.cpp screen2.h point.h
    ztc $(FG_FLAGS) $*

        ##################################################
        ## All shape classes, and the rotateShapes function
        ## are unchanged but a different VERSION MACRO
        ## must be defined to include the proper version
        ## of screen.h (screen2.h).
```

```
        ##################################################
rotate2.obj : rotate.cpp screen2.h point.h
    ztc $(FG_FLAGS) rotate.cpp -orotate2 -DVER2

        ##################################################
        ## standard Zortech C++ main function
        ## main calls rotateShapes
        ##################################################
main2.obj : main2.cpp screen2.h point.h
    ztc $(FG_FLAGS) $*

        ##################################################
        ## link object files to create executable
        ## uses Zortech's BLINK
        ##################################################
rotate2.exe: $(ROTATE2_OBJS)
    echo LINKING rotate2.exe
    blink $(FG_LFLAGS) $(ROTATE2_OBJS), rotate2,,$(FG_LIBS);
    echo to run under DOS type:    rotate2
##########################################################
```

Running ROTATE3.EXE will produce output like that in Figure 6-2. Note that this figure shows the About dialog box as well as the window with the rotated shapes when opened at its default size. When you change the size of the window, the shapes are automatically scaled to fit into the resized window. Note in Figure 6-3 that while the shape sizes change, the size of the text in the window does not change.

CHAPTER HIGHLIGHTS

By properly specifying the interface to an abstract Screen class, which restricts methods to the minimum set required by a user, you can ease the burden of porting software to different operating environments. This chapter has shown the interface for an abstract Screen class used to draw and rotate shapes about the origin of a virtual coordinate system.

Three different implementations of the Screen class were shown. The first version was for Borland Turbo C++'s BGI library. The second version was implemented for Zortech's Flash Graphics library. The third version was built using Zortech's C++ compiler to implement the Screen class to run under Microsoft Windows.

The fact that the two files, ROTATE.CPP and POINT.H, were completely unchanged shows that good design and use of encapsulation can truly minimize the impact of change when replacing modular components within a software system based on classes and objects.

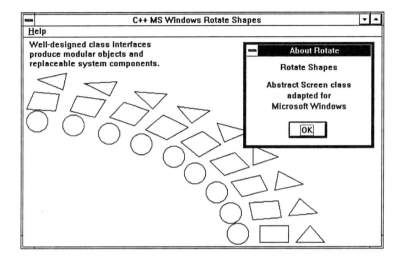

Figure 6-2.   Output from ROTATE3.EXE using Microsoft Windows. The actual Shape classes, which draw the shapes and perform the rotations, require no modification from the Zortech Flash Graphics implementation.

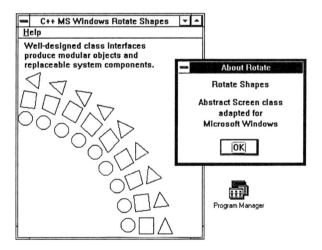

Figure 6-3.   The window associated with ROTATE3.EXE is resized. All shapes in the window are automatically rescaled to fit in the window. The About Rotate dialog box is invoked by selecting the first entry in ROTATE3's Help menu.

II

OBJECT-ORIENTED
PROGRAMMING TOOLS

7

LANGUAGE SUPPORT FOR
USER-DEFINED TYPES

Many different programming techniques are practiced today. *Structured* programming introduced language features known as control structures to support conditional execution (if, if/else, and case constructs) and iteration (for and while constructs).

Procedural programming (*procedure-based* programming) advocates program organization based on abstract procedures, which bundle many small actions into a larger action and hide the implementation details of procedures from users of procedures. Like objects, procedures have an *interface*. The interface to a procedure is the set of arguments that the procedure receives and returns with respect to the calling statement.

Rule-based programming is frequently used in artificial intelligence and is commonly associated with the construction of knowledge-based systems. Rule-based programming is beyond the scope of this book, but is mentioned to illustrate the point that many different programming methodologies are available and that different methodologies are appropriate for solving different kinds of problems. It's important to be familiar with a variety of programming methodologies and the problems they are intended to address.

Data abstraction (*object-based* programming) balances out procedure-based programming by placing equal emphasis on actions and data. Object-based programming groups relate data and procedures together into newly defined types and allow objects to be created and manipulated as instances of these user-defined types. The implementation details of actions as well as data are hidden from users of abstract data types. Object-oriented programming adds the specification of hierarchy and inheritance to object-based programming.

Most programmers now take structured programming and procedural programming for granted. Object-based programming and object-oriented programming are becoming popular because they impose manageable and comprehensible structure on complex systems. The appeal of object-oriented programming is that it is applicable to the solution of a wide variety of programming problems. Object-oriented programming is not so much different from other programming techniques as it is more comprehensive. Object-oriented programming embraces data abstraction (object-based programming), as well as structured programming and procedure-based programming.

WHAT MAKES A PROGRAMMING LANGUAGE OBJECT-ORIENTED?

Several features are required for languages to claim that they are object-oriented. Before explaining specific language features, it's important to understand the general programming techniques language features are designed to support.

Figure 7-1 shows the outstanding characteristics that distinguish object-based and object-oriented programming techniques, as well as the language features required to support those techniques.

Consider more carefully, the key concepts that distinguish object-based programming and object-oriented programming: data abstraction and hierarchical classification of objects.

Data Abstraction

Data abstraction provides a way for the user to define new data types that integrate well into the built-in system of types provided by the language.

Programming Method:	Object-Based Programming
Characterized by:	• Data abstraction (programming with user-defined types)
Ideal language features supporting object-based programming:	• Bundling data and operations in new types defined by user • Data hiding and access mechanisms • Automatic initialization of objects • Automatic cleanup of objects • Operator overloading

Programming Method:	Object-Oriented Programming
Characterized by:	• Object-based programming *plus:* • Hierarchical organization of classes and objects • Polymorphic communication through message passing
Ideal language features supporting object-oriented programming:	• Inheritance • Dynamic binding (virtual functions)

Figure 7-1.   Hierarchical organization and polymorphic communication are the essence of object-oriented programming.

Data types are abstractions, and the process of building new types by bundling data and operations to create new kinds of objects is called *data abstraction.* Newly defined data types are often called *abstract data types* or *user-defined data types.*

Data abstraction encompasses data hiding (encapsulation) and bundling of data and procedures into modular units (objects). Programming languages that support programming with objects that are extended data types built by users are said to support *object-based programming.*

Hierarchical Classification of Objects

Hierarchical classification of objects provides the means to organize object types (classes) into a hierarchy expressing relationships and common properties of objects. Polymorphism has no meaning until a hierarchy of classes exists. Recall that polymorphism involves sending messages to objects of unknown type that share a common interface or communication protocol. The explicit specification of common properties and communication protocol defined in interfaces to objects makes possible polymorphic communication based on message passing. Sending the same message to objects of similar, but slightly different types and eliciting a different response from each object, based on its exact type, is the essence of object-oriented programming.

This chapter explores the extent to which popular programming languages support programming with user-defined types—that is, data abstraction. The languages discussed include C++, Smalltalk, Actor, and object-oriented Pascal. These languages will be considered to the extent that they support definition of new types, data hiding and data access mechanisms in newly defined types, automatic initialization and cleanup of objects, and operator overloading, to allow user-defined types to behave like built-in types of the language.

The following chapter will discuss the extent to which C++, Smalltalk, Actor, and object-oriented Pascal support object-oriented programming.

USER-DEFINED TYPES IN C++ AND OBJECT-ORIENTED PASCAL

All modern procedural languages have built-in types. C has chars, ints, floats, and doubles. Pascal has Integers, Reals, and Strings. In addition, most procedural languages have *aggregate* types—types built from basic types. For instance both C and Pascal allow you to declare and use arrays. You can build arrays of integers, arrays of characters (this is what C uses to simulate String types), or arrays of floating point numbers. Further, most procedural languages allow you to create structures or records. C *structs* and Pascal *records* are literally new types that can be defined by the user.

Yet arrays, structs, and records are not user-defined types in the exact sense. To understand why, let's look more closely at built-in data types so you can contrast them with types defined by the user.

Built-in Types

Types are abstractions. They are convenient ways of thinking about and manipulating a group of bits. It's a lot easier to think about a group of 8 bits as a character, or a group of 16 bits as an integer. Computer languages provide a uniform interface to the underlying hardware so that manipulating basic types is easy and consistent from machine to machine, whether the underlying hardware is an 80386-based PC, a 68000-based workstation, or an expensive supercomputer like a Cray. As long as C or Pascal is available on the computer you are working on, the computer knows exactly what to do when you instruct it to execute a statement like this:

```
x2 := maxX - (maxX * x / virtualMaxX);
```

The type system of a computer language allows you to work with data abstractions, rather than having to work in the machine language of the host computer.

The language is doing a lot of work here that most programmers take for granted. For example, assuming that all the types in the previous statement are integers, the compiler will parse the statement and turn it into a series of calls to lower-level functions, possibly declaring temporary variables to keep track of intermediate results:

```
temp1 := integerMultiply(maxX, x);
temp2 := integerDivide(temp1, virtualMaxX);
x2    := integerSubtract(maxX, temp2);
```

Even the assignment operator is a form of abstraction, which makes convenient notation and expression of solutions possible. Ultimately, assignment is performed by a low-level routine. If the basic data types are integers, the assignment might be performed by a single machine-language instruction that takes the result of an operation from a register or from the stack and moves it into a memory location associated with a variable. For example:

```
mov x2, ax
```

However, if the basic data types were floating point numbers represented by four bytes or eight bytes, assignment would become a sequence of machine instructions, which would be more conveniently represented as a procedural abstraction.

```
floatAssign(destination, source);
```

The amount of work done by the compiler to assign a floating point representation of a number to a floating point variable is quite complex. For example, look at the following C statement:

```
float pi = 3.14159;
```

This statement effects some complex processing:

1. Determine that 3.14159 is a floating point number — that is, determine the type of the object 3.14159.

2. Create enough temporary storage to hold an object of type float.

3. Construct a 32-bit representation of the number 3.14159.

4. Copy this representation into the temporary storage.

5. Create permanent storage for the floating point variable, pi. (Again, the type of the object or number is required to create the storage.)

6. Assign the value of the number in temporary storage to the permanent storage created for and referred to by the variable pi.

7. Release or destroy the storage used for the temporary representation of the number 3.14159.

An *interpreted* language would have to perform all of these steps after the user enters the C expression before it can produce the desired result. A *compiled* language will perform as many of the steps as possible when the program is compiled. The remaining steps are carried out when the program is run. That's the basic advantage of a compiler over an interpreter: as much work as possible is accomplished before the program is run, allowing the program to run faster when it is executed.

It would be very inconvenient if programmers had to specify all the low-level procedures and data representations in order to evaluate a sequence of expressions such as

```
pi     := 4*arctan(1);
radius := diameter / 2;
area   := square(radius) * pi;
```

The complication is even greater than it appears at first because the statements contain mixed types. For example, 4 and 2 are integer types, typically represented by 16 bits, where pi, radius, and area are floating point numbers typically represented by 32 or 64 bits—possibly more. The compiler knows that if it is going to multiply an integer type by a floating point type, it must first convert the integer to a floating point number before performing the multiplication. Further, the program must maintain different routines to perform floating point multiplication than for integer multiplication.

In this respect, the basic type system for numbers and algebraic expressions supported by most modern languages is polymorphic. That means different number objects respond to the same message requests (multiplication, division, addition, subtraction) in different ways, depending upon their exact type.

User-Defined Types (Data Abstraction)

As mentioned earlier, most procedural languages allow you to build abstract aggregate types using arrays, structures, and records. The question is, how well do these user-defined types integrate into the built-in system of types provided by the language?

For example, most languages allow programmers to specify a data structure to represent complex numbers containing real and imaginary components, as shown here:

```
/* C */

struct Complex
{
  float : re;
  float : im;
};

struct Complex pl;

{ Pascal }

type Complex = record
  re : Real;
  im : Real;
end;

var cl : Complex;
```

Or languages allow programmers to specify a structure representing a point as a pair of x and y coordinates, as shown here:

```
/* C */

struct Point
{
  int x;
  int y;
};

{ Pascal }

type Point = record
  x : Integer;
  y : Integer;
end;
```

Points are easily created and assigned values.

```
/* C */

struct Point p1;

p1.x = 10;
p1.y = 20;
```

Most languages even allow one structure to be copied to another through simple assignment statements:

```
/* C */

struct Point p2;

p2 = p1;
```

Again, the real issue is how well the user-defined types integrate with the existing types of the language. Can you add two complex numbers together or subtract one point from another with the same ease that you can add and subtract floating point numbers or integers?

Shortcomings of C and Pascal

Standard C and Pascal don't let you treat user-defined types like built-in types. You cannot do the following:

```
/* C */

struct Point p1, p2, p3;

p1.x = 10;
p1.y = 2;

p2.x = 70;
p2.y = 20;

p3 = p2 - p1;    /* error */

{ Pascal }

var p1, p2, p3 : Point;

p1.x := 10;
p1.y := 2;

p2.x := 70;
p2.y := 20;

p3 := p2 - p1;    { error }
```

First of all, no routine has been defined for subtracting one point from another. This would be easy enough to do in C.

```
/* C */

#include <stdio.h>

struct Point
{
    int x;
    int y;
};

struct Point subtractPoint(struct Point a, struct Point b)
{
    struct Point c;
    c.x = a.x - b.x;
    c.y = a.y - b.y;
    return c;
}

main()
{
    struct Point p1, p2, p3;

    p1.x = 10;
    p1.y = 2;

    p2.x = 70;
    p2.y = 20;
```

```
    p3 = subtractPoint(p2, p1);          /* p3 = p2 - p1; */
    printf("p3==>%d, %d\n", p3.x, p3.y);
    return 0;
}
```

The Pascal solution is a little more complicated because Pascal functions cannot return records. Return types for functions must be either the built-in types for the Pascal language (Integer, Char, String, Word, LongInt, Byte, Boolean) or pointers. Having a function return a pointer to a TPoint object is an awkward solution because it would force users of the class to be aware of creating and destroying TPoint objects on the heap. Ideally, you want the subtractPoint method to return an object of type TPoint. Pascal won't allow functions to return TPoints because they are user-defined records (that is, objects). You can, however, return user-defined types in variable arguments passed to procedures. In the case of subtractPoint, you can specify a third argument to the subtractPoint procedure, which is a variable used for the return value (see Program 7-1).

In the end, both C and Pascal support the definition of user-defined types, but usage of the newly defined types is awkward and not well integrated into the languages. As types get extremely complex, objects such as Windows, Dictionaries, Stacks, and Queues require more and more knowledge on the part of the programmer using extended types supplied by libraries. However, a principle of data hiding says that well-designed programming modules hide as much implementation detail as possible from the users of those modules. A good indicator of the success in data hiding achieved by the built-in types real and float is that most programmers have no idea what kinds of data representations underlie the use of floating point numbers or the routines activated to perform operations on floating point objects. Programmers only see the interface for floating point data types, which is basically the algebraic expression of formulas.

How C++ and Object-Oriented Pascal Support User-Defined Types

One of the goals of data abstraction is to achieve the same level of data hiding accomplished with built-in types. C++ achieves the goal of good programming through data abstraction by allowing newly defined types to hide data and by allowing operations to be performed on user-defined types with the same syntax that can be applied to built-in types, as shown in Program 7-2.

PROGRAM 7-1.PAS

```pascal
{ Pascal }

program struct3;

type Point = record
    x : Integer;
    y : Integer;
end;

(**************************************************************
 * Illegal declaration in Pascal:
 * functions can't return records,
 * only pointers to records.
 *
 * function subtractPoint(a, b : Point) : Point;
 * begin
 *    subtractPoint.x := a.x - b.x;
 *    subtractPoint.y := a.y - b.y;
 * end;
 **************************************************************)

procedure subtractPoint(a, b : Point; var c : Point);
begin
  c.x := a.x - b.x;
  c.y := a.y - b.y;
end;

var p1, p2, p3 : Point;

begin
  p1.x := 10;
  p1.y := 2;

  p2.x := 70;
  p2.y := 20;

  subtractPoint(p2, p1, p3);            { p3 := p2 - p1; }

  writeln('p3==>', p3.x, ', ', p3.y);
end.
```

Program 7-1.   Subtracting one point from another in Pascal is complicated, since Pascal functions can't return user-defined types.

The C++ code in Program 7-2 demonstrates strong support for user-defined types. You can see examples of data hiding, automatic initialization of objects, and operator overloading. All three features are necessary to make user-defined types behave like built-in types.

```
PROGRAM 7-2.CPP

// C++

#include <stdio.h>

class Point
{
    int xVal;
    int yVal;
public:
    Point()                    { xVal=0; yVal=0; }
    Point(int x, int y)        { xVal=x; yVal=y; }
    int x()                    { return  xVal;   }
    int y()                    { return  yVal;   }
    Point operator-(Point p)
    {
        return Point(xVal-p.x(), yVal-p.y());
    }

};

main()
{
    Point p1, p2, p3;

    p1 = Point(10,2);
    p2 = Point(70,20);

    p3 = p2 - p1;              // calls user-defined method:
                               // Point::operator-

    printf("p3==>%d, %d\n", p3.x(), p3.y());
}
```

Program 7-2.   C++ allows user-defined types to hide data and respond to the same syntax as built-in types.

Object-oriented Turbo Pascal provides some features that make user-defined types easier to use than standard Pascal. However, as Program 7-3 shows, object-oriented Pascal does not go quite as far as C++.

Object-oriented Pascal provides data hiding. Automatic initialization of objects is supported as a programming convention, but the language only makes initialization convenient; it does not guarantee initialization. Operator overloading is not supported by object-oriented Pascal.

As mentioned earlier, there are several specific language features required to support convenient use of data abstraction or user-defined types:

- Data hiding

- Automatic initialization (constructors)

- Automatic cleanup (destructors)
- Operator overloading

PROGRAM 7-3.PAS

```
{ Pascal }

program dataAbstraction1;

type
  Point = object
    constructor init(x, y : Integer);
    function getX : Integer;
    function getY : Integer;
    procedure subtract(p : Point; var result : Point);
  private
    xVal : Integer;
    yVal : Integer;
  end;

constructor Point.init(x, y : Integer);
begin
  xVal := x;
  yVal := y;
end;

function Point.getX : Integer;
begin
  getX := xVal;
end;

function Point.getY : Integer;
begin
  getY := yVal;
end;

procedure Point.subtract(p : Point; var result : Point);
begin
  result.init(xVal - p.getX, yVal - p.getY);
end;

var
  p1, p2, p3 : Point;

begin
  p1.init(10,2);
  p2.init(70,20);
  p2.subtract(p1, p3);                      { p3 := p2 - p1; }

  writeln('p3==>', p3.getX, ', ', p3.getY);
end.
```

Program 7-3.   Although object-oriented Pascal provides data hiding, it doesn't guarantee initialization of objects, and it doesn't support operator overloading.

Let's look at each of these features in turn and see how C++ and object-oriented Pascal support these features.

Data Hiding

Data hiding refers to the ability of a programming language to hide implementation details of structures from users of those structures. The more a language supports data hiding, the easier it is to isolate the work of implementors of objects from users of objects. Data hiding is provided by standard C and Pascal in the form of programming modules. C programs can be broken up into a set of files. Header files are used to declare the interface to routines defined in modules. Many Pascal implementations provide a similar form of modular data hiding with *units*. Units are files that have an interface section and an implementation section. Users of modules only need the interface (header file) and not the source code for the implementation of the module. Only the library or compiled unit file (having the .LIB or .TPU extension) is required to link programs that make use of units. Data hiding through modular structure of source code files is standard practice in procedural programming.

Object-based or object-oriented programming extends the concept of data hiding used in file modules to data structures. The first step is to bundle all data and related routines allowed to manipulate that data into a single structure. Both C++ and object-oriented Pascal do this by extending the basic struct and record declarations. In C++, the keyword *class* is introduced as a special kind of struct.

```
/* C */

struct Point
{
    int x;
    int y;
};

// C++

class Point
{
    int x;
    int y;
};
```

At this level, the word *class* has little to do with classification. It is merely a synonym for a struct that is a template from which an object can be created. Object-oriented Pascal extends the basic record type in the same way. Instead of the keyword *class*, Pascal uses the word *object.*

```
{ Standard Pascal }

type
    Point = record
        x : Integer;
        y : Integer;
    end;

{ Object-Oriented Pascal }

type
    Point = object
        x : Integer;
        y : Integer;
    end;
```

The issue of data hiding now becomes one of access. What kind of access does a programming language allow for objects? Another way of putting the question is, what kinds of restrictions does a programming language provide to ensure that the elements of an object are not accidentally modified? This sort of protection, is after all, the end goal of data hiding.

Public and Private Sections in C++ and Object-Oriented Pascal

Both C++ and Pascal provide a mechanism for making certain elements of an object inaccessible. Objects can be divided up into public and private sections. The public section is the interface to the object. The private sections of the object constitute the implementation. Users have no need to know about the implementation or private sections of objects in order to use them. A design goal for a user-defined type (an object template) should be to make the interface as simple as possible, which means make as much of the object private as possible without making the object difficult to use.

   C and C++ allow unrestricted access to any member element of a data structure.

```
/* C or C++ */

struct Point
{
    int x;
    int y;
};
```

```
...
main()
{
    Point p1;
    int a, b;

    p1.x = 1;
    p2.y = 2;

    a = p1.x;
    b = p1.y;
    ...
}
```

However, each of the four assignment statements in the previous listing is illegal in C++ if the keyword *class* is substituted for the keyword *struct*.

```
// C++

class Point
{
    int x;
    int y;
};

...
main()
{
    Point p1;
    int a, b;

    p1.x = 1;    // error: x is a private member of Point
    p2.y = 2;    // error: y is a private member of Point

    a = p1.x;    // error: x is a private member of Point
    b = p1.y;    // error: y is a private member of Point
    ...
}
```

C++ provides a mechanism whereby an object template can be divided into private and public sections. By default, the first section in a class declaration is private. This can be changed by inserting the keyword *public* followed by a colon before any parts of the class you want to make public.

```
// C++

class Point
{
public:
    int x;
```

```
    int y;
};

...
main()
{
    Point pl;
    int a, b;

    pl.x = 1;    // ok: x is a public member of Point
    p2.y = 2;    // ok: y is a public member of Point

    a = pl.x;    // ok: x is a public member of Point
    b = pl.y;    // ok: y is a public member of Point
    ...
}
```

In fact, a struct in C++ is exactly the same as a class in which all sections are public. The following code,

```
// C++

class Point
{
public:
    int x;
    int y;
};
```

has exactly the same meaning as

```
/* C or C++ */

struct Point
{
    int x;
    int y;
};
```

Turbo Pascal 5.5 does not have the equivalent of a private section of an object template. However, Turbo Pascal 6.0 introduces the keyword *private*, which can be used to restrict access to elements of an object.

```
{ Pascal }

type Point = object
        { public member elements }
    private
        xVal : Integer;
        yVal : Integer;
    end;
```

The mechanism is a little different in Turbo Pascal than in C++. First of all, only the last part of an object can be private. C++ provides two keywords, *public* and *private*. You can have several public and several private sections within a C++ object.

```
class Point
{
    // private data and methods
    ...
public:
    // public data and methods
    ...
private:
    // private data and methods
    ...
public:
    // public data and methods
    ...
}
```

Turbo Pascal objects, on the other hand, have only one public section, which must come first, and one private section, which must be last and follow the keyword *private*. Turbo Pascal does not provide the equivalent of the *public* keyword available in C++.

Further, the restricted access to the private elements of Turbo Pascal is not enforced in the same file that declares the object. The restriction is enforced, however, when references are made to the private elements of objects whose templates are defined outside the file where the reference is made.

```
{ Pascal }

{ File 1 }

type Point = object
        { public member elements }
    private
        x : Integer;
        y: Integer;
    end;
  .
  .
  .
procedure file1Procedure
var p1 : Point1;
    a, b : Integer;
begin
    p1.x := 1;    // ok: x is public in file 1
    p1.y := 2;    // ok: y is public in file 1
```

```
    a := p1.x;    // ok: x is public in file 1
    b := p2.y;    // ok: y is public in file 1
end;
.
.
.

{ File 2 }

.
.
.
procedure file2Procedure
var p1 : Point1;
    a, b : Integer;
begin
    p1.x := 1;    // illegal: x is private in file 2
    p1.y := 2;    // illegal: y is private in file 2

    a := p1.x;    // illegal: x is private in file 2
    b := p2.y;    // illegal: y is private in file 2
end;
.
.
.
```

This kind of enforcement works pretty well since object types are usually defined in separate unit modules. Since units are predefined libraries existing in files separate from the source files for the main program, the restricted access to private variables is enforced for programmers who use units developed by others.

Automatic Initialization of Objects (Constructors)

Sometimes it's important to guarantee that objects are initialized when they are created. Both C++ and object-oriented Pascal allow the programmer to specify special routines called *constructors*, which are called when objects are created.

Constructors guarantee that objects are initialized to contain proper values. In C++, constructor functions are called automatically when an object is created. In object-oriented Pascal, the programmer must explicitly call the constructor. In C++, the constructor is a member method with the same name as the object's type or class. For example, the constructor for a Point class would be called Point::Point and might be defined as follows:

```
class Point
{
```

```
    int x, y;
public:
    Point()  { x=0; y=0; }
    .
    .
    .
};
```

With such a constructor, it is guaranteed that when a new Point object is created with a declaration such as,

```
Point p1;
```

the initial values of x and y for the object are set to 0.

Because C++ allows function overloading, you may declare more than one constructor for a type.

```
// C++

class Point
{
    int xVal, yVal;
public:
    Point()                { xVal=0; yVal=0; }
    Point(int x, int y)    { xval=x; yVal=y; }
    Point(Point p)         { xVal=p.x(); yVal=p.y(); }
    int x()                { return xVal; }
    int y()                { return yVal; }
    .
    .
    .
};
```

This listing declares three constructors for a Point object. The first constructor receives no arguments; the second receives two integer arguments; the third receives one Point object as an argument.

The compiler can determine which version of constructor to call depending on the number and types of the arguments supplied when a Point object is declared. For example, the following declaration

```
Point p1;
```

would automatically invoke the first constructor, setting both the x and y values of p1 to 0. The statement

```
Point p2(10,20);
```

would invoke the second constructor and set the initial value of Point p2 to 10@20. The declaration

```
Point p3(p2);
```

would invoke the third constructor and set p3 to the same x and y values as p2.

Turbo Pascal Constructors

Turbo Pascal supports the definition and use of constructors to initialize objects. However, Turbo Pascal constructors are *not* called automatically; the programmer must include an explicit call to the constructor.

```
{ Pascal }

type Point = object
        constructor init(x, y : Integer);
        ...
     private
       xVal, yVal : Integer;
     end;

constructor Point.init(x, y : Integer);
begin
    xVal := x;
    yVal := y
end;
.
.
.
{ main program }
begin
  pl.init(10,20)    { Call Point.init constructor }
                    { to initialize Point pl.     }
.
.
.
end.
```

In Turbo Pascal, there is nothing in the language that forces the programmer to call a constructor to initialize an object. Further, a Turbo Pascal programmer can give any name desired to a constructor. The name "init" is used by convention, but there is nothing to keep constructors for the Point class from being called "create", "assign", or "initialize". In fact, since Turbo Pascal does not support function overloading (giving the same name to different functions that can be distinguished by the number and types of

their arguments), you must give different names to constructors if you want
to provide more than one way to initialize an object.

```
{ Pascal }

type Point = object
        constructor init;
        constructor initXY(x, y : Integer);
        constructor initPoint(p : Point);
     private
        xVal, yVal : Integer;
     end;
```

Of course, the danger in naming constructors anything you please is
that you can easily forget what they are called. You simply have to remember the names of the constructors associated with the types of arguments
you want to specify.

What, then, are the advantages of constructors in object-oriented Pascal?
Why can you not simply call a procedure that is a member method having
the name init?

First of all, constructors build virtual method tables for virtual methods
defined for a class when they are called. An object cannot invoke a virtual
method for its class until the object's constructor has been called. (Virtual
methods and support for dynamic binding are covered under the topic of
object-oriented programming and will be discussed in Chapter 8, "Language Support for Object-Oriented Programming".)

There is another reason for defining initialization procedures as constructors in Turbo Pascal. New objects can be created either on the stack or
on the heap. The heap is a more versatile storage area than the program
stack. Objects in both standard Pascal and object-oriented Pascal are created
on the heap with the new operator. Given a pointer to a real number, p, a
real number can be created on the heap as follows:

```
{ Pascal }

type PReal = ^Real

var p : PReal

begin

    p := new(PReal);
    .
    .
    .
```

Similarly, if p were declared as a pointer to a Point object, a Point could be created on the heap.

```
{ Pascal }

type PPoint = ^Point

var p : PPoint

p := new(PPoint);
```

The variable p now points to a Point object. Such an object is referenced by appending the caret, ^, to p:

```
p^
```

You could use such a reference to call the constructor for Point,

```
p^.init(10,20);
```

or to reference any other method defined for the Point class.

```
a := p^.getX;
b := p^.getY;
.
.
.
writeln('p^==>', p^.getX, ' @ ', p^.getY);
.
.
.
```

Since it makes sense to create and initialize an object at the same time, Turbo Pascal extends the standard Pascal syntax for creating objects on the heap with new. In Turbo Pascal with object-oriented extensions, new takes an optional second argument, which must be defined as a constructor for the object type given as the first argument.

```
p := new(PPoint, init(10,20));
```

The first argument to new must be a pointer for the desired type of object. The extended syntax of new makes it easier to remember to invoke constructors at the time the objects are created.

C++ borrows from Pascal by providing a new operator for creating objects on the heap. For example, given a pointer to a Point object, p, you could create a Point object, initialize it with the Point constructor expecting two integer arguments, and assign p to point to the resulting object in a single C++ statement.

```
// C++

Point *p = new Point(10,20);
```

In C++, as in C, pointers are dereferenced using the -> operator.

```
// C++

int a = p->x();
int b = p->y();
```

Once a Point object created on the heap is no longer needed, it can be deleted, and the memory it once occupied can be returned to the free-storage pool.

```
// C++

delete p;
p = NULL;
```

This only works as long as p points to a legitimate object on the heap. It's always best to immediately set a pointer to point to either a new object or to NULL once the object it was pointing to has been destroyed. This practice allows conditional testing to ensure that objects are not destroyed twice.

```
// C++

if (p != NULL)
{
    delete p;
    p = NULL;
}
```

The equivalent of "delete" in Pascal is "dispose".

```
{ Pascal }

dispose(p);
p := nil;
```

or

```
{ Pascal }

if p <> nil then
begin
    dispose(p);
    p := nil;
end;
```

Automatic Cleanup of Objects (Destructors)

If automatic initialization of objects helps relieve the programmer of some of the housekeeping associated with creating and using objects, automated cleanup is equally important. *Destructors* are used for this purpose. Destructors are usually only necessary to undo some sort of initialization that is performed by a constructor. For instance, a window object may create temporary storage for a buffer containing text displayed in the window.

```
// C++

class Window
{
    char *pBuffer;
public:
    Window(Point origin, Point extent);
};

Window::Window(Point origin, Point extent)
{
    int width = extent.x();
    int height = extent.y();
    int bufSiz = 2*(width*height);    // Leave enough room
                                      // for text character
                                      // and attribute byte
                                      // for IBM PC screen.
    pBuffer = new char[bufSiz];
    .
    .
    .
}
```

The pointer pBuffer is automatically set to point to a buffer of the appropriate size when a Window object is created.

```
Window w1(Point(10,2), Point(40,10));
```

The constructor will automatically create on the heap a text buffer large enough to contain 40 * 10 character-attribute pairs on an IBM PC screen.

When the object is destroyed, the buffer is no longer needed. In C++, an object created on the stack is destroyed automatically at the end of the function that creates the object. An object created on the heap, however, must be explicitly destroyed.

C++ destructors have the same name as the class for which they are defined. Destructors are preceded by a tilde, ~, to distinguish them from constructors. For example, a destructor for a Window object would be called ~Window and might be defined as follows:

```
class Window
{
    char *pBuffer;
    .
    .
    .
public:
    // Constructor
    Window(Point origin, Point extent);
    // Destructor
    ~Window();

};
    .
    .
    .
Window::~Window()
{
    if ()
    {
        delete pBuffer;
        pBuffer = NULL;
    }
}
    .
    .
    .
```

Destructors nearly always have some kind of mirror relationship with their constructor counterparts.

Turbo Pascal Destructors

Turbo Pascal destructors can be given any name desired. By convention, the name given to a destructor is "done". The keyword *destructor* is substituted for the keyword *procedure* for a destructor in a Turbo Pascal object declaration.

```
type
  PWindow = ^Window
  Window = object
    constructor init(origin, extent : Point);
    destructor done;
    procedure display;
    .
    .
    .
  end;
```

Just as Turbo Pascal extends the syntax for new to support calls to constructors, Turbo Pascal also extends the syntax of dispose to call destructors, as in:

```
var
    p : PWindow;

{ main program }
begin
    p := new(PWindow, init(Point(10,2), Point(40,10)));
    p^.display;
    ...
    dispose(p, done);
end;
```

Note that extended syntax allows dispose to accept either one or two arguments. If two arguments are provided, the second argument must be a destructor for the class of object referenced by the first argument. Program 7-4 shows a complete Turbo Pascal program in which Point objects are created on the heap with new and removed from the heap with dispose. Note the use of both standard and extended syntax for new and dispose.

As you can see in this program, there is nothing preventing the programmer from calling dispose without providing a destructor, even when one is defined. Even though this is legal, it does not release the storage originally created for the object pointed to by pWindow. This storage is now lost until the program terminates. There is no way to return allocated storage back to the free-storage pool if you don't have a pointer to it.

```
PROGRAM 7-4.PAS

{ Pascal }

program newAndDispose;

type
  Point = object
    constructor init(x, y : Integer);
    destructor   done;

    function getX : Integer;
    function getY : Integer;
  private
    xVal : Integer;
    yVal : Integer;
  end;
  PPoint = ^Point; {------------------------}
                   { new and dispose require }
                   { a pointer for the       }
                   { proper type of object   }
                   { to be created on the    }
                   { heap.                   }
                   {------------------------}

{-------------------------------------------}
{ constructor                               }
{                                           }
{ In addition to initializing private       }
{ instance variables of objects,            }
{ constructors frequently allocate          }
{ memory required to construct objects.     }
{-------------------------------------------}
constructor Point.init(x, y : Integer);
begin
  xVal := x;
  yVal := y;
end;

{-------------------------------------------}
{ destructor                                }
{                                           }
{ Normally destructors are used to free     }
{ any memory that is allocated for an       }
{ object by its constructor.                }
{-------------------------------------------}
destructor Point.done;
begin
  writeln('returning memory for Point object to heap');
end;
```

Program 7-4.   The "new" and "dispose" routines used in standard and extended syntax in Turbo Pascal

```
function Point.getX : Integer;
begin
  getX := xVal;
end;

function Point.getY : Integer;
begin
  getY := yVal;
end;


var
  ptr : PPoint;

begin

  ptr := new(PPoint);                      {------------------}
                                           { Create object on }
                                           { heap without     }
                                           { calling          }
                                           { constructor.     }
                                           {------------------}

  dispose(ptr);                            {------------------}
                                           { Return memory to }
                                           { heap without     }
                                           { calling          }
                                           { destructor.      }
                                           {------------------}

  ptr := new(PPoint, init(1,2));           {------------------}
                                           { Create object on }
                                           { heap and call    }
                                           { constructor in   }
                                           { single statement.}
                                           {------------------}

  writeln('ptr^==>', ptr^.getX,            {------------------}
          ',  '    , ptr^.getY);           { Access object on }
                                           { heap: apply ^ to }
                                           { dereference      }
                                           { pointer.         }
                                           {------------------}

  dispose(ptr, done);                      {------------------}
                                           { Call destructor  }
                                           { and return memory}
                                           { to heap in single}
                                           { statement.       }
                                           {------------------}
end.
```

Program 7-4.   *Continued*

Consider the following program fragment showing the constructor and the destructor for a Window object.

```pascal
{ Pascal }

type

  Point = object
    constructor initXY(x, y : Integer);
    constructor init;
    constructor initPoint(p : Point);
    function getX : Integer;
    function getY : Integer;
    procedure subtract(p : Point; var result : Point);
  private
    xVal : Integer;
    yVal : Integer;
  end;

  Window = object
      constructor init(origin, extent : Point);
      destructor  done;
  private
      pBuffer : Pointer;
      bufSiz  : Integer;
      _origin : Point;
      _extent : Point;
  end;

constructor Window.init(origin, extent : Point);
var
    width, height : Integer;
begin
    _origin.initPoint(origin);
    _extent.initPoint(extent);

    width  := extent.getX;
    height := extent.getY;
    bufSiz := 2*width*height;
    GetMem(pBuffer, bufSiz);
    {---------------------------------------------------------}
    { GetMem is a standard Turbo Pascal procedure which       }
    { allocates a block of memory on the heap. The size       }
    { of the block is specified as the second argument to     }
    { GetMem. The first argument is a variable pointer        }
    { which is set to point to the newly allocated block.     }
    { GetMem is similar to new except that memory blocks      }
    { allocated with GetMem should be returned to the free    }
    { storage pool (the heap) with FreeMem.                   }
    {---------------------------------------------------------}
end;

destructor Window.done;
begin
    if pBuffer <> nil then
    begin
```

```
        FreeMem(pBuffer, bufSiz);      {-----------------}
                                       { blocks that are }
                                       { allocated with  }
                                       { GetMem should be }
                                       { disposed with   }
                                       { FreeMem.        }
                                       {-----------------}
        pBuffer := nil;
        bufSiz := 0;
    end;
end;
    .
    .
    .
```

Creating a new Window object and including a call to the constructor causes memory to be allocated on the heap to hold a buffer used inside the Window object. Note that memory for this buffer is allocated on the heap regardless of whether the Window object itself is allocated on the heap,

```
var p : PWindow;  { pointer to window object }

begin
    p := new(PWindow, init(Point(10,2), Point(40,10)));
```

or on the stack:

```
var w Window;      { variable for window object }
begin
    w.init(init(Point(10,2), Point(40,10)));
```

In either case, forgetting to call the destructor, done, when the object is no longer needed causes unnecessary loss of heap memory. For example, if the variable or pointer for the window is local to a subroutine, it will go out of scope when the subroutine ends, and the memory cannot be reclaimed until the program terminates. To prevent such memory loss, be sure to call the destructor when an object that uses heap memory is no longer needed.

For an object created on the heap, include the call to destructor when the object is "disposed".

```
dispose(p, done);
```

For a variable object created on the stack, simply call the destructor directly.

```
w.done;
```

In Turbo Pascal it is up to the user of a class to balance calls to constructors with calls to destructors if destructors are provided.

Operator Overloading

You already have a clue as to the meaning of operator overloading. In Program 7-2, earlier in this chapter, you saw that defining a member function in the Point class called Point::operator- made it possible to subtract Point objects from one another using the same syntax that you would apply to integers or to floating point numbers.

```
...
Point pl, p2, p3;

pl = Point(10,2);
p2 = Point(70,20);

p3 = p2 - pl;          // calls user-defined method:
                       // Point::operator-
...
```

You have also seen that C++ allows you to define more than one constructor for a given class. Since, by definition, C++ constructors for a given class must all have the same name, constructors can be overloaded. In fact, with the proper definition, any function in C++ can be overloaded, including the built-in operators of the C++ language itself.

Before exploring operator overloading, consider the more general case of function overloading.

Function Overloading

Turbo Pascal does not support function overloading, so the examples in this section will be confined to C++.

Function overloading is a form of polymorphism. It's convenient to only have to remember the name of one single operation even though it might be possible to perform that operation on many different types of objects. For instance, you might want to define a max function to return the greater of two integers:

```
int   max(int a, int b)
{
    return (a>b) ? a : b;
}
```

Then you discover that you also need to calculate the maximum of two floating point values declared as doubles.

In C, you would have to define a function with a different name to handle the doubles.

```
double maxDouble(double a, double b)
{
    return (a>b) ? a : b;
}
```

C++ provides *function overloading*, which allows two or more functions to have exactly the same name as long as they differ in either the number or the type of their arguments. Thus, both functions defined above could be called "max" in a C++ program. You might want to declare another max function that accepts two Points as arguments or returns the maximum of three integer arguments. You could even declare a max function that accepts a pointer to an array of integers and returns the largest element in the array. The following listing declares six different max functions, all of which could be used legally in the same program.

```
int    max(int    a, int    b);
int    max(int    a, int    b, int    c);
double max(double a, double b);
double max(double a, double b, double c);
Point  max(Point  a, Point  b);
Point  max(Point  a, Point  b, Point  c);
```

The compiler can tell from a statement that calls max, which version of max should be used by looking at the number and type of arguments in the calling statement. For instance, the following statement would invoke the first version of max,

```
int x = max(1,2);
```

while the next statement would invoke the second version:

```
int x = max(1,2, 3);
```

This statement would invoke the last version of max:

```
Point p = max(Point(1,2),
              Point(3,4),
              Point(5,6));
```

If function overloading were not supported, you would have to come up with a unique name for each version of max.

```
/* C */

int    max2ints   (int    a, int    b);
int    max3ints   (int    a, int    b,  int   c);
double max2doubles(double a, double b);
double max3doubles(double a, double b,  double c);
Point  max2Points (Point  a, Point  b);
Point  max3Points (Point  a, Point  b,  Point c);
```

This is a lot of extra information to remember for an operation that is really the same, regardless of the types of objects on which the operation is being performed. This is why function overloading and operator overloading support polymorphism: you can use a single common protocol to communicate with objects sharing common properties.

Operator Overloading Versus Function Overloading

C++ not only allows you to overload functions; you can overload built-in operators of the language as well. You saw an example of this when an operation for subtracting Point objects from one another was defined.

```
class Point
{
    int xVal;
    int yVal;
public:
    Point()                    { xVal=0; yVal=0; }
    Point(int x, int y)        { xVal=x; yVal=y; }
    int x()                    { return  xVal;   }
    int y()                    { return  yVal;   }
    Point operator-(Point p)
    {
        return Point(xVal-p.x(), yVal-p.y());
    }
}
```

The syntax for declaring a method or function that overloads a built-in operator in C++ is to precede the symbol for the operator (− in this case) with the keyword operator. When you overload a built-in operator of the language, you need to give it exactly the same number of arguments that it expects in normal use. For instance, +, −, *, and / are all *binary operators*, meaning they expect two arguments. When you override an operator as a class method, you specify one argument fewer inside the argument list for the operator's definition. The first argument is the object to which the operator message is sent. This becomes clear when you realize that operator functions can be expressed in either *infix* or *functional* notation. With infix notation, for example, a binary operator appears between the two objects on which it operates:

```
int a = 12 - 11;
```

Here, the operator, −, operates on the two integers, 12 and 11. With the class definition for Point, infix notation can be applied to Point objects:

```
Point b = Point(79,24);
Point a = b - Point(10,12);
```

The Point:operator- member function determines the precise meaning of this expression.

Subtraction can be expressed in functional notation as well.

```
Point b = Point(79,24);
Point a = b.operator-(Point(10,12));
```

The two listings have exactly the same meaning in C++. Now you can see why the member method inside the Point class only has one argument. The first argument is implicitly the first Point object in an expression like the following:

```
point1 - point2
```

Operator Overloading and User-Defined Types

Function overloading is merely a convenience. Operator overloading, on the other hand, is required to make user-defined types behave like built-in types. You can see the difference between implementations of a Point class in C++ and a Point class in Turbo Pascal. In C++ it is possible to manipulate points, complex numbers, or any user-defined type with built-in operators like $+$, $-$, $*$, $/$, $<<$, and $>>$. It's very natural to think of adding or subtracting points when manipulating objects on the screen.

```
Point extent = window.corner() - window.origin();
```

With Turbo Pascal, you have to settle for making calls to functions or procedures and remember a different syntax than you have already embedded in your mind from high school algebra.

```
var
    window : Window;
    extent : Point;
begin
    window.init(Point(10,2), Point(40,20));
    subtractPoint(window.getCorner, window.getOrigin, extent);
```

You have to think more carefully to follow the exact meaning of the Pascal example. The advantage of using infix notation for math operations on new types of objects is that everyone already knows the meaning of the syntax for built-in operators. Because no standard practice is established for using the functional notation for performing subtraction and assignment operations required by Pascal, it's easy to forget whether the variable argument to subtractPoint comes first or last. If you get the order backward, you can easily destroy the value of objects unintentionally.

How Well Do C++ and Object-Oriented Pascal Support Programming with User-Defined Types?

Both C++ and object-oriented Pascal supply the basic language features required to program in an object-based style. Both permit the programmer to define new types or classes of objects and to create instances of objects from those classes. Both C++ and Pascal support the bundling or encapsulation of data and procedures inside of objects.

C++ is a little better than Pascal at hiding the data from users of classes. In Apple's Object Pascal, there is no *private* keyword to keep users from directly accessing the elements of an object, which is basically record structure extended to contain procedures and functions, as well as data. Quick-Pascal and Turbo Pascal 5.5 follow Apple in this regard: no mechanism is provided to restrict access to private data elements inside an object. Turbo Pascal 6.0, on the other hand, extends the basic syntax of Object Pascal to include the *private* keyword. The Turbo Pascal compiler only prohibits access to private components of objects for objects that are used in a different unit or file from the class definition.

In C++, it is never possible to access private members of an object except in class methods for the specific object type. C++ goes a step further and provides the keyword *protected*, which determines the access privileges of descendant classes. The concept of protected data elements will be covered in the next chapter.

Both C++ and Pascal provide constructors and destructors to help automate the initialization and cleanup of newly created objects. In C++, constructors are called automatically when objects are created, and destructors are called automatically when objects go out of scope or are explicitly destroyed by the programmer. C++ can force users of classes to properly initialize objects. Pascal does not force the initialization or cleanup of objects. Using an object before it is properly initialized in Pascal can cause the program to crash. To avoid such problems, the programmer must remember to explicitly call constructors and destructors. Turbo Pascal extends the syntax of new to allow an optional second argument that invokes a constructor compatible with the type of object being created. Similarly, Turbo Pascal extends the syntax of dispose to accept a call to a destructor as an optional second argument. Even with the extended syntax of new and delete, the programmer must still remember to explicitly call constructors and destructors.

While C++ supports both function and operator overloading, Pascal permits neither. Function overloading is a convenience; it really has little to do with integrating user-defined types into the existing types of the language. On the other hand, *operator overloading*—a specialized form of function overloading—is important in object-based programming and programming with user-defined types. Overloading operators can make programs easier to read and allow programmers to treat newly defined types using the same syntax they are accustomed to using with built-in types.

Object-oriented Pascal is said to provide a more gentle transition from a procedural style of programming to an object-oriented style. It allows programmers to experiment with new object-oriented features without forcing them to immediately give up old habits, such as direct access to data elements inside objects. In object-oriented Pascal, restricted access to data elements of an object is recommended, but not strictly enforced by the compiler.

For large and complex projects involving more than a few people, C++ enforcement of restricted access to objects and guaranteed initialization and cleanup of objects means safety and convenience, as well as power and flexibility. The cost, however, is a steeper learning curve. Of course you can always use C++ as a C compiler with stricter type checking, in which case very little learning is involved. You can think of C++ as a C compiler that allows you to overload functions and replace error-prone macro definitions with type-secure inline functions. In addition, C++ provides type-safe linkage. Since C++ program modules can link to C program modules, C programmers can continue to program in the familiar procedural manner and grow into object-oriented programming at a gradual pace. In addition, C++'s ability to include C source code and to link to C program libraries is attractive to companies that have a substantial investment in existing C code.

Both C++ and object-oriented Pascal are good choices for learning object-oriented programming on PCs or the Macintosh.

USER-DEFINED TYPES IN SMALLTALK
AND ACTOR

Smalltalk and Actor give new meaning to the concept of types, particularly to programmers who are familiar with compiled languages. Recall that to support object-oriented programming, compiled languages usually build on structures or records to give the programmer a way to define object templates (types), from which object instances are created. In compiled languages, the record templates or type definitions exist only in the source code: they are not entities that exist in the program when the program is run.

In Smalltalk and Actor, types (or classes) are objects—that is, classes are special kinds of objects that know how to create instances of themselves. Classes are real objects that exist in the environment when the program is developed *and* when the program is run. In Actor and Smalltalk, the distinction between the programming environment and the run-time environment is blurred.

Both Smalltalk and Actor take the concept of the object to its logical conclusion: Every entity within each of these systems is an object. There are no global functions. All functions are methods that *must* be associated with an object from a given class. All processing is initiated by sending messages to the various objects in the system. Even the interpretation for source code and the compilation of methods is carried out by objects in the system — the interpreter is an object and so is the method compiler. This forces you to think about types in an entirely different manner. Since every entity in the system is an object, every object knows its own type. Every object maintains a pointer to its class. That means that every object has a pointer to the object from which it was created. At any time you can ask an object about its type, and the object will query its creator, which will return a string object indicating the name of the class or type.

In compiled languages, type checking is almost always *static*. That means the compiler checks arguments passed to and from functions or assignments to variables, and signals an error when the type used in a statement does not match the type indicated in a declaration. Smalltalk and Actor do not support static type checking. When variables are declared, their type is not specified. That's because, during its lifetime, a variable can hold a variety of different types of objects. For example, a variable might be initially set to nil:

```
MyVariable := nil;
```

Later it might be changed to hold a string:

```
MyVariable := "Hello, world";
```

Still later the same variable might hold an array of strings,

```
MyVariable := #("one" "two" "three" "four");
```

or a window object:

```
MyVariable := defaultNew(Window, "A Sample Window");
```

This kind of type mixing is *dynamic*, that is, the type of a variable can change while a program is running. For this reason the static type checking that programmers of compiled languages are accustomed to cannot be applied to Smalltalk and Actor. Instead, type checking is done at the time that messages are sent to objects. When a message is sent to an object, the object looks to its class object to find a list of methods defined for the class. If the object can find a method to match the message it has received, it executes the method. If not, the object continues the search for a matching method in its parent class. This goes on until the highest level object in the system is reached—Object.

All classes ultimately descend from the class called Object in both Smalltalk and Actor. If a matching method is not found by the time the class Object is reached, an error is signaled, and a debugger window pops up allowing the programmer to explore all the methods that were activated in the process of generating the error. This is how type mismatches are found. Of course, other kinds of errors besides type mismatching can generate error dialogs, but the main point is that the matching of types is done dynamically (at run time) rather than statically (at compile time) in Smalltalk and Actor.

Built-in Types

In some ways it makes little sense to talk about support for user-defined types in Smalltalk and Actor. Both Smalltalk and Actor embody the ideals and standards of object-oriented programming by which other languages measure themselves. In both Smalltalk and Actor, every component within the programming environment is an object. Both languages support definition of new types in such a manner that it is impossible to tell the difference between built-in types provided by the language and additional types defined by the programmer.

Figures 7-2 and 7-3 show the built-in type hierarchies provided by Smalltalk and Actor. Each of the items listed in these hierarchies is a class or a type. Note the similarity of the names and structures of the two hierarchies. The influence of Smalltalk on Actor is evident from the common names and structures used for built-in types.

You can see from the class hierarchies that both Smalltalk and Actor provide an elaborate set of built-in types. Both provide points, rectangles, and windows (Smalltalk calls them panes), which would have to be defined by programmers in C++ or object-oriented Pascal. Smalltalk and Actor provide most of the support to write the user interface to their programming environment. This is not said lightly, because Smalltalk's original graphical user interface was the inspiration for the design of the user

Smalltalk
Class Hierarchy
(Built-in Types)

Object	**Inspector**
Behavior	Debugger
Class	DictionaryInspector
MetaClass	**Magnitude**
Boolean	Association
False	Character
True	Date
ClassHierarchyBrowser	Number
Collection	Float
Bag	Fraction
IndexedCollection	Integer
FixedSizeCollection	Time
Array	**Menu**
CompiledMethod	**Message**
Bitmap	**Pane**
ByteArray	SubPane
FileHandle	GraphPane
Interval	ListPane
String	TextPane
Symbol	TopPane
OrderedCollection	**Point**
SortedCollection	**Rectangle**
Set	**Stream**
Dictionary	ReadStream
IdentityDictionary	WriteStream
MethodDictionary	ReadWriteStream
SystemDictionary	FileStream
SymbolSet	TerminalStream
Compiler	**StringModel**
DiskBrowser	**UndefinedObject**
DisplayObject	
DisplayMedium	
Form	

Figure 7-2. A subset of the built-in types provided by Smalltalk. Indentation represents inheritance. A listing of types organized by inheritance is called a class hierarchy.

interface for Apple's Macintosh and, more recently, for Microsoft Windows and OS/2 Presentation Manager.

Actor
Class Hierarchy
(Built-in Types)

Object
  Association
  Debugger
  ErrorBox
  Menu
  MenuItem
  NilObject
  Point
  Primitive
  StopWatch
  System
  Application
   ActorApp
  Behavior
   Meta
  Collection
   Bag
   IndexedCollection
    ByteCollection
    String
     Symbol
    Struct
     GraphicsObject
      Rect
       WinEllipse
      WinPolygon
    Interval
    Array
     Function
     OrderedCollection
      SortedCollection
      TextCollection
    KeyedCollection
    Dictionary
     MethodDictionary
     IdentityDictionary
   Set
    SymbolTable

File
  TextFile
   SourceFile
Stream
Magnitude
  Char
  Number
   Int
   Long
    Date
    Time
   Real
WindowsObject
  Control
   Edit
   Button
   ListBox
   ScrollBar
  Dialog
   ClassDialog
   DebugDialog
   FileDialog
   PrintDialog
   InputDialog
    ReplaceDialog

Figure 7-3. A subset of the built-in types provided in Actor's class hierarchy. Note that many class names are borrowed directly from Smalltalk.

The entire set of container classes provided by Smalltalk (covered in Chapter 5, "Class Libraries") is reproduced almost exactly in Actor, and most container class libraries provided for C++ and object-oriented Pascal show strong influence from the bags, sets, ordered collections, arrays, associations, and dictionaries originally designed for Smalltalk. All these classes are considered built-in types in Smalltalk and Actor.

Most of the built-in types provided by Smalltalk and Actor would be considered as a set of several different add-on class libraries in C++ or object-oriented Pascal. The support of the Smalltalk and Actor class libraries for building applications is so powerful that traditional languages allowing the use of class libraries for user-interface design give these add-on libraries a special name: *application frameworks*. The third part of this book is devoted to application frameworks. It's hard to believe that in Smalltalk and Actor most of the classes required for the construction of sophisticated applications and graphical user interfaces are simply built-in types.

User-Defined Types (Data Abstraction)

Because every element in the environment of both Smalltalk and Actor is an object, newly created classes and objects are indistinguishable from the built-in types provided by the language. Both Smalltalk and Actor provide a rich set of types and predefined global objects. One of the biggest advantages of programming in Smalltalk and Actor is the power made available by these predefined classes to the programmer.

Both Smalltalk and Actor provide Points and Rectangles as built-in types. Recall that these types had to be created by the programmer for programs in C++ and object-oriented Pascal. For the sake of comparison let's look at the process involved in creating a Point class in Smalltalk and then in Actor. To keep the name of the new class from conflicting with the built-in Point class, the new class will be called "TPoint" in both Smalltalk and Actor.

In Smalltalk and Actor the first step of programming is to create classes required by the application. That involves defining the instance variables and the public methods that make up the interface to instances of the class. Normally, the creation of classes and the definition of methods is done inside special windows called *browsers*.

Note: With browsers you typically only see source code for one method at a time. Source code listings often show all method definitions for a given class. You should get used to seeing source code presented in browsers as well as in listings.

New classes in Smalltalk and Actor are defined with class browsers. Normally the Smalltalk or Actor programmer does not see source code presented the way it is in this chapter. Eventually programmers do need to learn how to read the source code for Smalltalk and Actor classes without the benefit of a browser. You already know how to do this from looking at class definitions for C++ and Pascal. The main difference is that Smalltalk and Actor do not provide distinct interfaces and implementations in the source code files that define classes because the browser provides an overview of the class. When you look at a class object with a browser, at first you don't see any method definitions at all—all you see is the class name highlighted from a list of classes at the left and the list of methods available for the class in the pane at the right.

Smalltalk Code for a TPoint Class

Figure 7-4 shows a browser's view of the final version of the Smalltalk TPoint class. Here's what the Smalltalk source code for the TPoint class looks like:

```
File: TPOINT.CLS

"Smalltalk"

Object subclass: #TPoint
  instanceVariableNames:
    'xVal yVal '
  classVariableNames: ''
  poolDictionaries: '' !

!TPoint class methods !
new
        "Don't allow the creation of TPoint
         objects that are not supplied with
         initial x and y values."

    ^self error:
        'Use newWithX:andY: to initialize TPoint objects '!

newWithX: x andY: y
        "create new object and initialize
         with specified x and y values."
    | newObject |
    newObject := super new.
    newObject x: x.
    newObject y: y.
    ^newObject.! !
```

```
!TPoint methods !

initialize
        "Default initialization"
    xVal := 0.
    yVal := 0.!

x
        "Return x value of point"
    ^xVal.!

x: anInteger
        "Set x value of point"
    xVal := anInteger.!

y
        "Return y value of point"
    ^yVal.!

y: anInteger
        "Set y value of point"
    yVal := anInteger.! !
```

Several methods that appear in the source file are not listed in the class browser window. These are class methods. Figure 7-5 shows that by select-

Figure 7-4.   Smalltalk browser showing class definition and instance method names for TPoint class

ing the *class* keyword below the pane that shows the list of methods, the browser displays a different set of methods. Class methods are methods that can be invoked by sending a message directly to the class, rather than to an instance of the class. Such methods are typically used to perform special kinds of initialization when instances are created. Class methods in Smalltalk provide the equivalent of constructors in C++ and object-oriented Pascal. The definition and use of class methods will be explained in the sections on automatic initialization and cleanup of objects later in this chapter.

The source code file for the TPoint class can be read directly by the Smalltalk interpreter. Reading class files directly into Smalltalk provides an alternative to using the class browser to define new classes. This file is called TPOINT.CLS and would be read into the Smalltalk environment by evaluating the following expression in the Transcript or the Workspace window:

```
(File pathName: 'tpoint.cls') fileIn
```

Exclamation points (! and !!), sometimes called *chunk marks,* are used to break up the source code into sections or chunks. Chunk marks signal to

Figure 7-5.   Smalltalk browser showing class methods for TPoint

the compiler that the end of a section of code has been reached. For instance, the definition for the class is considered one section. This includes a declaration of the class name, the parent class, and the private instance variables inside objects created from the class template.

```
Object subclass: #TPoint
  instanceVariableNames:
    'xVal yVal '
  classVariableNames: ''
  poolDictionaries: '' !
```

Another section of code surrounded by chunk marks announces the beginning of definitions for class methods:

```
!TPoint class methods !
      .
      .
      .
!
```

Finally, the instance methods for the class are announced:

```
!TPoint methods !

initialize
      ...!

x
      ...!

x: anInteger
      ...!

y
      ...!

y: anInteger
      ... !
!
```

Actor Code for a TPoint Class

Actor code also makes use of chunk marks. The Actor code for a TPoint class follows. Note that the names given to methods are not identical to those used for Smalltalk. In fact, the TPoint implementation in Actor varies in other subtle ways, partly because Actor does not support the overloading of method names in the way that Smalltalk does, and partly to highlight different features between the two languages.

```
File: TPOINT.CLS

/* Actor */

/* A user-defined Point class for Actor */!!

inherit(Object, #TPoint, #(xVal yVal), 2, nil)!!

now(class(TPoint))!!

/* alternate way to create
 * new TPoint objects without
 * supplying arguments
 */
Def defaultNew(self)
{
  ^init(new(self:ancestor), 0, 0);
}
!!

/* Force user to supply two arguments
 * when creating a new TPoint object
 */
Def new(self, x, y)
{
  ^init(new(self:ancestor), x, y);
}
!!

now(TPoint)!!

/* Subtract self from aPoint using - operator
 */
Def -(self, aPoint | resultPoint)
{
  resultPoint := new(TPoint,
                     x(aPoint) - xVal,
                     y(aPoint) - yVal);
  ^resultPoint;
}
!!

/* Print a point to the system window */
Def print(self)
{
  print(xVal);
  print("@");
  print(yVal);
}
!!
```

```
/* Return y value of point */
Def y(self)
{
  ^yVal;
}
!!

/* Return x value of point */
Def x(self)
{
  ^xVal;
}
!!

/* Initialize point instance variables */
Def init(self, x, y)
{
  xVal := x;
  yVal := y;
}
!!
```

Figure 7-6 shows an Actor browser listing the instance methods for TPoint, and Figure 7-7 shows an Actor browser listing the class methods for TPoint.

Rather than explaining the details of the implementations of TPoint, development of the TPoint class will be presented incrementally in both

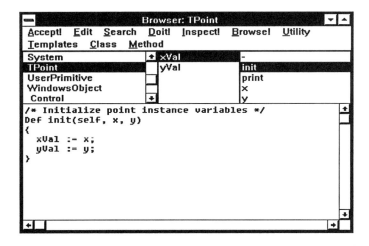

Figure 7-6.   Actor browser showing instance methods for TPoint

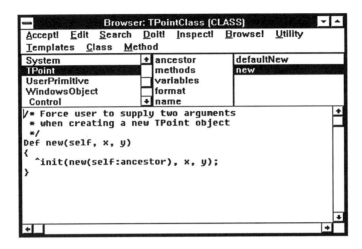

Figure 7-7.   Actor browser showing class methods for TPoint

Smalltalk and Actor. This will provide a chance to consider the Smalltalk and Actor features supporting definition and use of new types: data hiding, automatic initialization of objects, automatic destruction of objects through a process called *garbage collection,* and the unique ways in which Smalltalk and Actor support operator overloading to allow algebraic operators to be defined for newly created types.

Data Hiding

First consider a very simple definition for a TPoint class in Smalltalk:

```
"Smalltalk"

Object subclass: #TPoint
  instanceVariableNames:
    'xVal yVal '
  classVariableNames: ''
  poolDictionaries: '' !

!TPoint class methods !!

!TPoint methods !

x
      "Return x value of point"
    ^xVal.!
```

```
x: anInteger
        "Set x value of point"
    xVal := anInteger.!

y
        "Return y value of point"
    ^yVal.!

y: anInteger
        "Set y value of point"
    yVal := anInteger.! !
```

This file defines four public methods and two private variables for a Smalltalk TPoint class. The private variables represent the x and y coordinate values of a point: xVal and yVal. Two methods are provided for setting the value of a new TPoint object: x: and y:. Each of these methods expects to receive an integer argument, which is used to set the corresponding instance variable inside a TPoint object. The colon appended to the method name indicates that an argument is expected for the method.

Smalltalk can distinguish between methods with the same name if each method having the same name declares a different number of expected arguments. Two overloaded methods are provided to retrieve the instance variable values of a TPoint object: x and y. These methods expect no arguments, indicated by the fact that they do not have colons appended to their names. An uninitialized TPoint object would be created by sending the new message to the TPoint class:

```
MyPoint := TPoint new.
```

Recall that TPoint is itself an object in the Smalltalk system. When the Smalltalk interpreter encountered the declaration for the TPoint class,

```
Object subclass: #TPoint
  instanceVariableNames:
    'xVal yVal '
  classVariableNames: "
  poolDictionaries: " !
```

it created a global object called TPoint.

All class objects know how to create instances of themselves when they receive the new message. Evaluating the following expression,

```
MyPoint := TPoint new.
```

creates a global object in the Smalltalk dictionary called MyPoint. This is an uninitialized TPoint object, meaning its instance variables, xVal and yVal, are both set to nil. You can verify this by inspecting the MyPoint object. Evaluate the following expression,

```
MyPoint inspect.
```

and the inspector shown here will appear.

Inspectors allow you to look inside objects. By clicking the mouse on the appropriate instance variable, you can see its value. For instance, the Smalltalk inspector pictured here shows that uninitialized instance variables inside newly created objects are set to nil. Note that Smalltalk support for data hiding is 100 percent. Given an object, there is no way to get at the values inside. You can look at them with an inspector, but there is no syntax in the Smalltalk language (like the dot notation in C++ and Pascal) for gaining access to elements of an object. The only way to view or manipulate the values of instance variables through the Smalltalk language is to define public methods in the object interface.

Data Hiding in Actor

Actor's approach to data hiding is a little more flexible. Actor does allow the use of dot notation to look at instance variables from language constructs. However, it only allows this for debugging purposes and frowns upon the use of dot notation in method definitions. Actor is like object-oriented Pascal in this respect—it encourages encapsulation and data hiding, but does not enforce it. It's less tempting to "cheat" in Actor than in Pascal, because object-oriented principles are learned from the beginning when programming in Actor. You don't have people learning Actor who are making the transition from procedural to object-oriented programming in a language that is already familiar. There are no old habits to break.

Here's the definition of a simple TPoint object in Actor:

```
/* Actor */

/* A user-defined Point class for Actor */!!

inherit(Object, #TPoint, #(xVal yVal), 2, nil)!!

now(class(TPoint))!!

now(TPoint)!!

/* print a point to the system window */
Def print(self)
{
  print(xVal);
  print("@");
  print(yVal);
}
!!

/* return y value of point */
Def y(self)
{
  ^yVal;
}
!!

/* return x value of point */
Def x(self)
{
  ^xVal;
}
!!

/* initialize instance variables */
Def init(self, x, y)
{
  xVal := x;
  yVal := y;
}
!!
```

The first thing the previous code does is define a new class, which has the class Object as its parent. Objects from this class will have two instance variables, xVal and yVal. All this information is declared in the single line:

```
inherit(Object, #TPoint, #(xVal yVal), 2, nil)!!
```

In addition, four public methods are declared for TPoint objects: x, y, init, and print. A new TPoint object is created by evaluating the following code in the Actor Workspace window:

```
MyPoint := new(TPoint);
```

You'll notice that Actor syntax is inverted from Smalltalk. The previous statement sends the message new to the class object TPoint and assigns the resulting object to the global variable MyPoint. Programmers who are accustomed to procedural languages are tempted to see the statement as a call to the global function new. But remember, there are no global functions in Actor or Smalltalk. The last statement is exactly equivalent to the following Smalltalk statement,

```
MyPoint := TPoint new;
```

which makes the message-passing syntax more clear: The new message is being sent to the TPoint class object to create an instance of TPoint.

For the definition of TPoint in Actor, new instances of TPoint are not initialized—in other words, the instance variables xVal and yVal are set to nil. You could use the init method defined in Actor to specify the initial values of MyPoint:

```
init(MyPoint, 1, 4);
```

This sends the init message to the MyPoint object and sets xVal to 1 and yVal to 4.

Actor also allows you to inspect objects. To invoke an inspector for MyPoint, evaluate the following expression:

```
inspect(MyPoint)
```

The resulting Actor inspector is shown in Figure 7-8.

The methods x and y could be used to retrieve the values of the instance variables. Sending the x message to MyPoint

```
x(MyPoint)
```

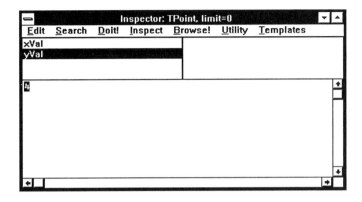

Figure 7-8.   An Actor inspector shows the value of a TPoint object after it is initialized.

returns a value of 1. Sending the y message to MyPoint

```
y(MyPoint)
```

returns a value of 4.

Most objects in Actor know how to print themselves. You can send the print message to an integer or a string and the result will be printed to the System window. For example, the statement

```
print("Hello, world")
```

will print the String object "Hello, world" in the system window.

You can use the ability of strings and integers to print themselves and define a print method for TPoint. The definition for TPoint.print is shown in the Actor class definition file: TPOINT.CLS. Evaluating the following expression will print the string "1@4" in the System window.

```
print(TPoint);
```

This is the typical form used for printing the built-in Point types provided by Smalltalk and Actor.

Automatic Initialization of Objects

It's often important to guarantee that newly created objects are initialized to predetermined values. This was done in C++ and object-oriented Pascal with constructors. In Smalltalk and Actor, this sort of initialization is accomplished with a combination of class methods and instance methods. Suppose, for example, that you want to ensure that all new TPoint objects are automatically initialized to set xVal and yVal to 0. In Smalltalk, you would first define a regular method for default initialization. By Smalltalk convention, such a method is given the name "initialize".

```
"Smalltalk"

!TPoint methods !

initialize
        "Default initialization"
    xVal := 0.
    yVal := 0.!
```

After adding an initialize method to TPoint, you can always remember to send an initialize message to a newly created object to make sure its instance variables are not nil:

```
"Smalltalk"

MyPoint := TPoint new.

MyPoint initialize.

MyPoint inspect.
```

Rather than explicitly sending the initialize message to the newly created TPoint object, you need to ensure that initialize is called automatically when a new TPoint object is created. This is done by overriding the class method new, which TPoint formerly inherited from its parent class, Object. Such a definition might look like this:

```
"Smalltalk"

new
        "create new object and initialize."
    | newObject |
    newObject := super new.
    newObject initialize.
    ^newObject.
```

All class objects inherit a basic definition of the new method from a common base class. All objects in Smalltalk eventually trace their ancestry back to the class called Object. Since all class objects inherit a basic form of new, you don't need to define a new method when you create a class object unless you want it to do something special. Initializing instance variables is a special case. If you want the class method new to call the object method initialize, you have to write a new method. Typically, such a method will pass the new message onto its parent class to create the actual object in object memory, and then use the pointer returned by the parent to call an initialize method for the object.

```
    | newObject |
    newObject := super new.
```

The keyword *super* tells the method that rather than binding the new message to its own new method, the parent class's new method should be used instead—Object:new in this case.

With this definition for TPoint.new, all point objects will be automatically initialized when created.

```
MyPoint := TPoint new.

MyPoint inspect.
```

Inspecting the newly created MyPoint object will reveal that its instance variables, xVal and yVal, are set to 0 automatically.

Of course, the class new method can be simplified. There really is no need to use a temporary variable in the method definition. The method is currently defined with a temporary variable declaration and three statements:

```
¦ newObject ¦
newObject := super new.
newObject initialize.
^newObject.
```

The first statement assigns the temporary variable, newObject, to refer to a new object created by sending the "new" message to the superclass of TPoint. The superclass of TPoint is Object. TPoint can't simply send the new message to itself; if it did, TPoint.new would be invoked recursively and would never exit.

The second statement initializes the new object by calling TPoint:initialize. The third and final statement returns a pointer to the newly created object. Returning a pointer is mandatory if new is to be used consistently. Whenever new is sent to any Class object in the Smalltalk environment, the return value is expected to be a pointer to an object. This pointer is then typically assigned to a variable.

```
MyPoint := TPoint new.
MyRectangle := Rectangle new.
MyWindow := Pane new.
```

If new does not return a pointer, assignment of newly created objects to variables is not possible.

As long as you remember to return a pointer to the newly created object, you can abbreviate the definition for TPoint:new.

```
new
        "create new object and initialize"
    ^super new initialize.
```

This definition is more compact and more readable if you know how to follow the syntax. This is also typical of the type of definition of new you will find for many Smalltalk classes.

First, the message new is sent to the super class of the receiver object. The receiver object here is the TPoint object in the expression

```
MyPoint := TPoint new.
```

The result of evaluating the subexpression

```
super new
```

is to return a new object, which in turn is sent the message initialize. The initialize method for TPoint is invoked, returning a TPoint object. By default, all methods return the object on which they operate when invoked. You can change this default return value by using the caret, ˆ, followed by the expression or object you want to return. By Smalltalk convention, initialize is a method that is called by new, which is expected to return the receiver object on which it operates. For this reason you should not have initialize return anything other than the receiver object.

The result of evaluating the following expression (note that the caret is missing) is to return the newly created object after it is initialized.

```
super new initialize
```

However, the method will not return this newly created object by default. By default, the original object receiving the new message (TPoint) is returned. You want to return the newly created instance, not the class object. The class object, TPoint, is a global symbol in the Smalltalk environment. If you did not put a caret in front of the subexpression listed above, you would return the class rather than the instance. In order to return the instance, put the caret before the subexpression:

```
^super new initialize.
```

This returns the newly created and initialized object, which can now be assigned to a variable.

```
MyPoint := TPoint new.
```

Constructors with Arguments and Multiple Constructors

You might want to force users of a class to supply initial values for an object, or you might want to provide several different ways of initializing objects.

First, consider providing several class methods for creating new TPoint objects. The TPoint class method definition for newWithX:andY: is as follows:

```
newWithX: x andY: y
        "create new object and initialize
        with specified x and y values."
```

```
| newObject |
newObject := super new.
newObject x: x.
newObject y: y.
^newObject.
```

Now you can specify the values to be contained by TPoints at the same time that TPoints are created, thus combining creation and initialization.

```
MyPoint := TPoint newWithX: 10 andY: 20

MyPoint inspect
```

The second step is to prohibit TPoints from being initialized without supplying initial values. It might seem logical that simply deleting the TPoint:new method would do the job, but it won't. If you delete the TPoint new and then try to evaluate the following statement,

```
MyPoint := TPoint new.
```

MyPoint will simply contain an uninitialized TPoint. What you need to do is redefine TPoint:new so that an error is generated if it is invoked. The error should give useful information because a debugger dialog will be invoked when the error message is encountered.

The Boolean class in Smalltalk provides an example of how to handle such a situation. The following definition of TPoint:new is exactly the same as Boolean:new.

```
new
        "Don't allow the creation of TPoint
        objects that are not supplied with
        initial x and y values."

    ^self invalidMessage
```

With this definition of new, an error dialog is initiated when the following expression is evaluated:

```
MyPoint := TPoint new.
```

The debug window will contain a string like "inappropriate message for this object". The user can then invoke the debugger through the local menu for the error dialog window.

You might want to provide the user with a hint by creating a different string for the title of the error window. You can do this by sending an error to the object invoking new. Since all classes ultimately trace their heritage back to the Object class, the error message eventually is handled by the method Object:error.

The modified definition of TPoint:new is as follows:

```
new
        "Don't allow the creation of TPoint
         objects that are not supplied with
         initial x and y values."

     ^self error:
         'Use newWithX:andY: to initialize TPoint objects '
```

Now when you evaluate this statement,

```
MyPoint := TPoint new.
```

you'll see the error dialog illustrated here:

Users are now forced to initialize TPoint objects when they are created with the TPoint >> newWithX:andY: class method.

Automatic Initialization in Actor

Automatic initialization in Actor is nearly identical to that in Smalltalk. Different naming conventions are used; for example, initialization methods are named init rather than initialize. This is a conventional practice rather than a requirement. Since method names cannot be overloaded in Actor, different names are given to different class methods provided as alternative ways to initialize objects of a given class. Consider first the Actor definition of a TPoint class, which does not automatically initialize new instances:

```
/* A user-defined Point class for Actor */!!

inherit(Object, #TPoint, #(xVal yVal), 2, nil)!!

now(class(TPoint))!!

now(TPoint)!!

/* print a point to the system window */
Def print(self)
{
  print(xVal);
  print("@");
  print(yVal);
}
!!

/* return y value of point */
Def y(self)
{
  ^yVal;
}
!!

/* return x value of point */
Def x(self)
{
  ^xVal;
}
!!

/* initialize instance variables */
Def init(self, x, y)
{
  xVal := x;
  yVal := y;
}
!!
```

An init method is provided but must be called explicitly after a TPoint object is created.

```
MyPoint := new(TPoint);
init(MyPoint,1,4);

inspect(MyPoint);
```

Inspecting MyPoint reveals that xVal is set to 1 and yVal is set to 4. Had the init message not been sent, the value of both these instance variables would be nil.

The next step is to define a class method, called new, for TPoint.

```
/* force user to supply two arguments
 *when creating a new TPoint object
 */
Def new(self, x, y)
{
  ^init(new(self:ancestor), x, y);
}
```

Recall that class methods allow messages to be sent to the global class objects like TPoint. By default, TPoint inherits a class method, new, from Object. Object's version of new accepts no arguments. TPoint can change this by overriding its parent's definition of new.

In the previous definition, Object's version of new is called first by the expression:

```
new(self:ancestor)
```

The object returned by this expression is sent the init message. Since this object is a TPoint, the new message binds with the init method definition for TPoint, which expects two arguments.

```
/* initialize instance variables */
Def init(self, x, y)
{
  xVal := x;
  yVal := y;
}
```

TPoint.new simply passes the arguments it receives for x and y onto init. Finally, the caret is used so that TPoint.new returns the newly created object rather than returning the TPoint global class object. Now TPoint objects can be initialized automatically when they are created.

```
MyPoint := new(Point, 3,4);
```

The previous statement creates a new TPoint object on the heap and sets the global variable, MyPoint, to point to the object. The TPoint object is automatically initialized to the value 3@4. By defining the class method TPoint:new in Actor, which accepts two arguments, you force users to supply two arguments when instances are created. This is not true in Smalltalk, which will still allow users to use the Object:new method that TPoint automatically inherits. In Smalltalk it is necessary to override the inherited new method to make it generate an error dialog. Actor will generate an error dialog automatically if you try to create a new TPoint object without supplying arguments for x and y. This is because Actor does not allow the overloading of method names, as does Smalltalk, for methods that can be distinguished by the number of arguments passed to them.

Automatic Cleanup of Objects

Though Smalltalk and Actor provide constructors, they do not provide destructors. All objects in Smalltalk and Actor are created on a heap-like storage pool. Objects in C++ and object-oriented Pascal can be created on the heap, but by default they are created on the stack. Only objects created on the heap need to be explicitly destroyed by the programmer. Constructors are handy for this. In fact, the main purpose for constructors in C++ and Pascal is to return storage to the heap. Since Smalltalk and Actor create all their objects on the heap, constructors do not need to explicitly request a specific amount of storage. Further, Smalltalk and Actor automatically keep track of all references to objects. An object is deleted automatically when all references to it have been eliminated. This automatic management of memory provided by Smalltalk and Actor is called *garbage collection.*

Every time you create an object in Smalltalk and Actor, even a literal value or a temporary variable, memory is allocated for the object in a place called *object memory* (usually a heap) and an entry for the object is made in an object table. The entry in the object table keeps track of the number of references to the object. For instance, evaluating the following code fragment would cause one TPoint object to be created. One entry for the object would be maintained in the object table and the reference counter in the entry would be set to 2.

```
"Smalltalk"

| a |
  a := TPoint new.
  GlobalVariable := a.
```

As long as either of the variables, a or GlobalVariable, continues to point to the TPoint object, the reference counter in the object table will not be set to 0. When the method containing the previous code fragment terminates, the variable, a, will be destroyed, but GlobalVariable will continue to point to the TPoint object. The reference counter in the object table will be decremented, but is still not 0. If GlobalVariable were set to contain another value,

```
GlobalVariable := 10@20.
```

the reference counter in the object table for the original TPoint object would again be decremented—only this time it would be set to 0.

Objects with reference counts of 0 are eligible for garbage collection. The automatic garbage collection facility of Smalltalk or Actor is invoked whenever available memory drops below a certain threshold. Alternatively, the user can explicitly indicate that memory should be cleaned and compacted by selecting a menu command or sending a special message to the system. When garbage collection is invoked and no references are left in the memory management system to an object, the memory manager automatically reclaims the storage for the object and removes the entry for the object from the object table.

Method Name and Operator Overloading in Smalltalk and Actor

As mentioned in the section on automatic initialization, Actor method names cannot be overloaded at all. Smalltalk allows two or more methods to have the same name as long as each has a different number of arguments.

For example, TPoints have an x method that accepts no argument, as well as an x method that accepts a single argument.

```
"Smalltalk"

x
        "Return x value of point"
    ^xVal.!

x: anInteger
        "Set x value of point"
    xVal := anInteger.!
```

Note: The colon at the end of a method name (x:) indicates that the method expects an argument.

Smalltalk can decide what to do with x messages sent to TPoint objects by looking to see whether or not an argument is supplied.

```
"Smalltalk"
¦ aPoint a ¦
  aPoint := TPoint newWithX: 1 andY: 2.

  "set a to 1"
  a := aPoint x.

  "set the x value of aPoint to 3"
  aPoint x: 3.
```

Actor does not allow the overloading of names based on the number of arguments received. You might want to provide several ways to create a new TPoint object in Actor. The only way to do this is to provide two different names for the class methods. By convention, objects that normally require arguments to be passed to new often use the method name default-New to provide an additional constructor that sets objects to a predetermined value. The TPoint class might define defaultNew to set the initial xVal and yVal instance variables of TPoint objects to 0.

```
/* Actor */

/* alternate way to create
 * new TPoint objects without
 * supplying arguments
 */
Def defaultNew(self)
{
  ^init(new(self:ancestor), 0, 0);
}
```

Now you have two choices when creating TPoint objects in Actor.

```
MyPoint := defaultNew(TPoint);
print(MyPoint);
MyPoint := new(TPoint, 10, 20);
print(MyPoint);
```

This set of statements will print "0@0" followed by "10@20" in the Actor system window.

Operator Overloading

Actor appears to support operator overloading, but technically it does not. As mentioned in the previous section, Actor cannot overload method names at all. The operator overloading that allows the use of $+$, $-$, $*$, and $/$ operators for points, complex numbers, and other types of objects in Smalltalk and Actor is enabled by treating these operators as messages sent to number objects. Smalltalk and Actor represent every element in the system as an object. This includes integers and floating point numbers. The built-in types of C++ and object-oriented Pascal are technically not objects: they cannot receive and respond to messages. Operator overloading in traditional languages allows the user to redefine the behavior of operators, but there really are no operators in Smalltalk or Actor—only messages. The following expression,

```
2 - 1
```

is interpreted as sending the $-$ message to the integer 2 with an argument of 1. Integers, as well as floating point numbers, know how to respond to the messages $+$, $-$, $*$, and $/$, as well as other arithmetic symbols.

Both Smalltalk and Actor allow certain messages to be expressed in infix notation. Messages that are intended to be expressed in infix notation can be placed in a special infix operation table allowing syntactical expression of these messages to appear like algebraic expressions. This is already done for the basic arithmetic symbols, but you can define your own messages to be expressed in infix form as well.

The upshot is that operator overloading is not required to create methods that allow TPoints to be added or subtracted from one another. Here's the definition of $-$ for the TPoint class in Actor:

```
/* Subtract self from aPoint using - operator
 */
Def -(self, aPoint | resultPoint)
{
  resultPoint := new(TPoint,
                     x(aPoint) - xVal,
                     y(aPoint) - yVal);
  ^resultPoint;
}
```

Argument order is inverted inside the Actor definition from what might be expected. The inversion of infix arguments when converting expressions from infix to functional form must be taken into account. In Actor, the following infix expression

```
p1 - p2
```

is interpreted as

```
-(p2, p1)
```

in standard Actor syntax. The variable p2 is bound to self in the method definition. The variable p1 is the argument to the message and is bound to aPoint inside the method definition. The logic seems counterintuitive, but makes sense from the standpoint of Actor's parsing mechanism. The main thing is that the infix form of expression makes sense to users of TPoint. You only need to remember to invert the argument order when defining methods for infix expressions.

You can now create, initialize, subtract, and print the resulting value of TPoints in a single Actor expression.

```
print(new(TPoint, 30, 4) - new(TPoint, 10, 2))
```

The same result could be achieved by evaluating a block expression in which a, b, and c are declared as temporary variables.

```
eval({using( | a b c)
  a := new(TPoint, 30, 4);
  b := new(TPoint, 10, 1);
  c := a - b;

  print(c);
});
```

The same technique is used to create infix math operations for user-defined types in Smalltalk.

How Well Do Smalltalk and Actor Support Programming with User-Defined Types?

The support for user-defined types in Smalltalk and Actor surpasses C++ and object-oriented Pascal. There is no distinction between the types defined by the user and the types provided by the programming environment. This makes extension of the programming environment possible. In fact, programming is viewed as extending the programming environment until it achieves a desired state. Then the environment is sealed off and delivered as a final application.

The only problem with the homogeneous type system provided with Smalltalk and Actor is the integration of existing code in C, Pascal, or FORTRAN. Older code from traditional languages does not represent internal objects in a compatible fashion. It is possible to link C code to Actor and user-defined C and assembly language subroutines to Smalltalk, but very strict rules for passing and returning arguments must be followed. Integration with the large body of existing code is the only downside to using Smalltalk and Actor.

This problem can often be rendered transparent by having Actor or Smalltalk call programs on disk that were compiled with a traditional compiler and transferring data back and forth in files. Other solutions to integration of different languages are possible, such as building class libraries in C++ on top of database engines, file servers, or remote terminals, and then having Actor or Smalltalk act as the user interface by controlling I/O through serial ports, networks, or special operating systems. Yet another possibility is to develop prototypes for applications taking advantage of advanced interface features and interactive development in Smalltalk and Actor, then use a compatible application-framework class library to deliver the final application in object-oriented Pascal or C++.

CHAPTER HIGHLIGHTS

User-defined types are the key to data abstraction. Data abstraction allows complex systems to be broken down into active processing components, which hide implementation detail and minimize connections between each other. Connections are minimized in a complex system by defining restrictive interfaces for components in order to ensure that the implementation of one component never relies on the internal representation of another component.

Allowing users to define new types of objects to create sophisticated components and treating instances of those types as objects to be manipulated through message passing is called *object-based* programming. User-defined types are the key language feature required to support object-based programming.

Still another tool is required for *object-oriented* programming. Object-oriented programming gives further organizational structure to complex systems by identifying the common features in a set of objects and allowing this commonality to be expressed in a programming language.

Commonality of object types is achieved by grouping classes into a hierarchy and classifying types according to the shared properties.

Hierarchical programming, inheritance of common features, and language support for object-oriented programming are discussed in the following chapter.

## 8

LANGUAGE SUPPORT FOR OBJECT-ORIENTED PROGRAMMING

Polymorphic objects are objects that have features in common yet differ in some fundamental way. For convenience, polymorphic objects are frequently put into an array or a collection. Iterators are then used on the collection to manipulate the elements. The problem is that once objects are put in a collection, their exact type is not immediately visible. If, however, you only put a certain class of objects, such as Shape objects, into a collection, you can safely manipulate each of the elements in the collection by using an iterator to send any one of the messages defined in the public interface for Shape.

The Circle, Rectangle, and Triangle objects introduced in Chapter 3, "Inheritance, Polymorphism, and Object-Oriented Programming", are polymorphic because they share properties: a center point, a color, and an angle of rotation. More importantly, each of these shapes responds to the same messages: position, moveTo, getColor, setColor, getAngle, setAngle, draw, hide, and rotate. The common implementation components and method names for Circles, Rectangles, and Triangles are specified in the abstract parent class called Shape. All classes that inherit from Shape class will respond to the set of messages defined in the public interface for Shape. These methods are considered *polymorphic messages* because the result of sending a polymorphic message to an object that inherits properties from

Shape will be different depending on the exact type of Shape that receives the message. Sending a draw message to a Circle will evoke a different response than sending a draw message to a Rectangle or a Triangle.

Object-oriented programming means sending polymorphic messages to different types of objects. Even though polymorphic objects have different types, they must share common properties. At the very least they share a common set of method names. If objects of different types did not share at least a subset of their method names, polymorphism would not be possible because the objects would not respond to the same messages. You would not be able to simplify communication by sending the same message to evoke different responses in different objects. Chapter 3 introduces the technique of object-oriented programming from the standpoint of *using* objects. This chapter discusses object-oriented programming from the standpoint of *defining* objects and classes of objects.

Two special language features are required to support polymorphic message passing. First you need a way of classifying objects according to shared properties. Second, you need a mechanism that binds function calls (messages) to object code for function definitions (methods) at run time. At the time the program is run, the dispatching mechanism must use the type of the object receiving a message to determine which method should be invoked.

OBJECT-BASED PROGRAMMING VERSUS OBJECT-ORIENTED PROGRAMMING

You can use a language that is object-oriented and not take advantage of the object-oriented features of the language. Simply defining and using new types of objects is not object-oriented programming. A higher level of organization is imposed on object-oriented programs. The purpose of a higher degree of organization is to simplify the management of complexity and detail. This is accomplished by identifying similarities in the way that objects are manipulated and classifying objects according to the properties they have in common.

The classification of objects by shared properties is referred to as *inheritance*. Binding, based on object type, of messages to methods is called *dynamic binding* and requires the support of virtual functions. This chapter examines the goals of classification and polymorphism and shows how inheritance and dynamic binding are specified in object-oriented languages.

OBJECT-ORIENTED PROGRAMMING TECHNIQUES

First of all, object-oriented programming requires the support of user-defined types (discussed in Chapter 7). User-defined types are characterized by the way they can be manipulated. This requires that methods for manipulating user-defined types be bundled together with the data that implements them. From the standpoint of data abstraction, you should only be concerned with the methods of a type and not with its representation. You will notice after building many different types of objects that not only do many objects use the same method names to identify common forms of manipulation, but also that many of these methods are implemented using exactly the same code. If the methods for moving a Circle and moving a Rectangle are implemented using exactly the same code, duplicating the code in two different places is wasteful.

```
class Circle
{
    Point center;
    int radius;
    int angle;
public:
    ...
    void  moveTo(Point p)    { center = p; }
    ...
};

class Rectangle
{
    Point center;
    Point extent;
    int angle;
public:
    ...
    void  moveTo(Point p)    { center = p; }
    ...
};
```

Not only is extra memory occupied by duplicated code, but maintenance efforts are increased if you decide to change the internal representation of objects. What happens, for example, if you decide you don't want to use points in the shape objects you want to rotate on the screen. You decide to use x and y values to represent coordinates instead. You have to change the moveTo method for each type of shape, for example:

```
class Circle
{
    int centerX;
    int centerY;
    int radius;
    int angle;
public:
    ...
    void  moveTo(x, y)    { centerX = x; centerY = Y; }
    ...
};

class Rectangle
{
    int centerX;
    int centerY;
    int extentX;
    int extentY;
    int angle;
public:
    ...
    void  moveTo(x, y)    { centerX = x; centerY = Y; }
    ...
};
```

Typically, method definitions are more complicated than moveTo. Since you are likely to include many different types of shapes in a typical program, maintenance and modification will depend on your ability to keep track of relationships among the implementation of these types. That's a lot of detail. The detail that you are forced to remember is structural:

- What are the relationships that all shapes share?

- How many different shapes share exactly the same code for a given method?

Typically, without language support for specifying relationships among types, organization goes undocumented, and much time is spent trying to recall the structural intentions of the designer.

Hierarchical organization of types lets you specify structural relationships explicitly in a programming language. The code itself documents the relationships; the result is that others can read the hierarchical structure from the code. Also, programming tools like debuggers and browsers can use the hierarchical specification to help programmers navigate through complex type hierarchies to find the appropriate code to study or modify. The compiler or interpreter can also catch overlooked code in derived classes that is affected by a change in hierarchy or protocol at a higher level.

Hierarchical Classification of Objects

Inheritance allows you to look at two or more types of objects and to specify the features they have in common:

```
class Shape
{
    Point center;
    int angle;
public:
    ...
    void  moveTo(Point p)    { center = p; }
    ...
};

class Circle : public Shape
{
    int radius;
public:
    .
    .
    .
};

class Rectangle : public Shape
{
    Point extent;
public:
    .
    .
    .
};
```

The instance variables "center" and "angle" are both inherited by Circle and Rectangle objects. So is the moveTo method. Now if you want to change the representation of Shape objects, most of your changes are isolated inside the abstract base class called Shape.

```
class Shape
{
    int centerX;
    int centerY;
    ...
public:
    ...
    void  moveTo(x, y)   { centerX = x; centerY = Y; }
    ...
};
class Circle : public Shape
{
    // unchanged
};

class Rectangle : public Shape
{
    int extentX;
    int extentY;
public:
    // unchanged
};
```

If you were developing a computer-aided design program, you would
need many different types of shapes besides rectangles and circles. If you
had 20 different types of shapes, you would have to change 20 different
moveTo methods when most of them probably would have exactly the
same definition. Typically, more than one method will share exactly the
same implementation among a given set of related objects.

```
////////////////////////////////////////////////////////////////
// class Circle
////////////////////////////////////////////////////////////////
class Circle
{
    Point center;
    int radius;
    int angle;
public:
        Circle(Point p, int r)              // constructor
          : center(p), radius(r), angle(0) {}

    int   getAngle()        { return angle; }
    void  setAngle(int a)   { angle = a; }
    Point position()        { return center; }
    void  moveTo(Point p)   { center = p; }
    void  rotate(int angle) { setAngle(getAngle()+angle); }
    void  draw()            { ... }
    void  hide()            { ... }
};
```

```
/////////////////////////////////////////////////////////
// class Rectangle
/////////////////////////////////////////////////////////
class Rectangle
{
    Point center;
    Point extent;
    int angle;
public:
        Rectangle(Point ctr, Point ext)      // constructor
            : center(ctr), extent(ext), angle(0) {}

    int    getAngle()          { return angle; }
    void   setAngle(int a)     { angle = a; }
    Point  position()          { return center; }
    void   moveTo(Point p)     { center = p; }
    void   rotate(int angle) { setAngle(getAngle()+angle); }
    void   draw()              { ... }
    void   hide()              { ... }
};
```

In this listing, the data elements center and angle are shared. In addition, the methods getAngle, setAngle, position, moveTo, and rotate all have exactly the same implementation. Only the draw and hide methods are different for circles and triangles.

Object-oriented programming languages allow you to specify common data and methods of objects through inheritance.

```
/////////////////////////////////////////////////////////
// abstract base class: Shape
//
// expresses data and methods common
// to all objects which can be classified
// as Shapes
/////////////////////////////////////////////////////////
class Shape
{
    Point center;
    int angle;
public:
        Shape(Point p, int r)                    // constructor
            : center(p), radius(r), angle(0) {}

    int    getAngle()          { return angle; }
    void   setAngle(int a)     { angle = a; }
    Point  position()          { return center; }
    void   moveTo(Point p)     { center = p; }
    void   rotate(int angle) { setAngle(getAngle()+angle); }
};
```

```
/////////////////////////////////////////////////////////
// derived class Circle (inherits from Shape)
/////////////////////////////////////////////////////////
```

```
class Circle : public Shape
{
    Point center;
public:
        Circle(Point p, int r)                 // constructor
            : center(p), radius(r), angle(0) {}

    void  draw()            { /* code to draw circles */ }
    void  hide()            { /* code to hide circles */ }
};

///////////////////////////////////////////////////////////
// derived class Rectangle (inherits from Shape)
///////////////////////////////////////////////////////////
class Rectangle : public Shape
{
    Point extent;
public:
        Rectangle(Point ctr, Point ext)     // constructor
            : center(ctr), extent(ext), angle(0) {}

    void  draw()            { /* code to draw rectangles */ }
    void  hide()            { /* code to hide rectangles */ }
};
```

Classes Are Types

Templates for creating types in object-oriented programming languages are called *classes*. The word *class* is used instead of the word *type* to indicate that types can be organized into hierarchies. Properties defined for a given type of object can be inherited by other types derived from it. A class of objects shares a common type definition somewhere in its ancestry.

Polymorphic Message Passing

Hierarchical organization based on common method definitions alone is not enough to support object-oriented programming. Note that the preceding implementation of the Shape class hierarchy does not define hide and draw in the class definition for Shape. It is possible to send a draw message or a hide message to a Circle or a Rectangle, but not to a Shape.

```
main()
{
    Shape *p;  // pointer to a shape.

    Circle aCircle(Point(60,6), 4);
    Rectangle aRectangle(Point(70,6), Point(8,8));
```

```
    p = &aCircle;   set p to point to circle
    p->rotate(45);   // legal: calls Shape::rotate
    p->moveTo(50,50);// legal: calls Shape::moveTo
    p->draw();       // illegal: draw defined for Circle
                     //          but not for Shape

    p = &aRectangle; set p to point to rectangle
    p->rotate(30);   // legal: calls Shape::rotate
    p->moveTo(10,80);// legal: calls Shape::moveTo
    p->draw();       // illegal: draw defined for Rectangle
                     //          but not for Shape
    .
    .
    .
}
```

If you have a pointer to any object derived from Shape, you can rotate the object or move it to a new location, but you can't draw or hide it. In order to do this, you need to specify that draw and hide are part of the protocol to which all Shape objects should respond. In C++, you would do this by providing *do-nothing* definitions of draw and hide in the declaration for Shape, as in the following listing:

```
/////////////////////////////////////////////////////////////
// abstract base class: Shape
//
// expresses data and methods common
// to all objects which can be classified
// as Shapes
/////////////////////////////////////////////////////////////
class Shape
{
    Point center;
    int angle;
public:
        Shape(Point p, int r)              // constructor
          : center(p), radius(r), angle(0) {}

    int   getAngle()        { return angle; }
    void  setAngle(int a)   { angle = a; }
    Point position()        { return center; }
    void  moveTo(Point p)   { center = p; }
    void  rotate(int angle) { setAngle(getAngle()+angle); }
    void  draw()            { }  // do nothing
    void  hide()            { }  // do nothing
};
    .
    .
    .
```

Now it's legal to send the draw or hide message to any object, even if you only have a pointer to the object.

```
main()
{
    Shape *p;  // pointer to a shape.

    Circle aCircle(Point(60,6), 4);
    Rectangle aRectangle(Point(70,6), Point(8,8));
    p = &aCircle;   set p to point to circle
    p->rotate(45);    // legal: calls Shape::rotate
    p->moveTo(50,50);// legal: calls Shape::moveTo
    p->draw();        // legal: calls Shape::draw

    p = &aRectangle;   set p to point to rectangle
    p->rotate(30);    // legal: calls Shape::rotate
    p->moveTo(10,80);// legal: calls Shape::moveTo
    p->draw();        // legal: calls Shape::draw
    .
    .
    .
}
```

However, nothing will happen when you run this program in C++ or the
equivalent in object-oriented Pascal because when the compiler looks at the
statement,

```
p->draw();
```

it knows that p points to a Shape object, so it binds the above call to the
method for Shape::draw, which does nothing. What you want is for the last
statement to invoke Circle::draw, if p points to a circle, and to invoke
Rectangle::draw, if p points to a rectangle. However, the decision about
matching the above call to the appropriate version of draw cannot be made
at compile time — the decision must be deferred until the program is run.

Object-oriented programming languages, even compiled languages,
support this sort of deferred decision by maintaining dispatch tables and
type information for objects requiring polymorphic dispatch and binding.
These tables are called *virtual function dispatch tables*, and they do take up
extra room in memory. For the sake of efficiency, data types in C++ and
object-oriented Pascal that do not need support for polymorphism and
dynamic binding do not create virtual function tables and do not maintain
type information at run time. However, if polymorphism is desired, it can
be specified for some or all of the methods defined in a base class of a class
hierarchy. In C++, this is done by putting the word *virtual* before the
declaration of a method requiring polymorphic dispatch.

```
class Shape
{
    ...
public:
    ...
    virtual void  draw()  { }  // specify dynamic binding
    virtual void  hide()  { }  // specify dynamic binding
};
.
.
.
```

For the Shape class, there's no sense in specifying dynamic binding for the methods setAngle, getAngle, position, moveTo, or rotate. These methods carry out exactly the same action regardless of the type of object. However, by specifying that draw and hide are virtual, the following statement,

```
p->draw();
```

will now draw a circle, if p points to a circle, or a rectangle if p points to a rectangle. Now any shape object can be put in the same array and manipulated at run time without the programmer needing to maintain switches based on object type to call the appropriate methods. This leads to code that looks like this:

```
typedef Shape *ShapePointer;

main()
{
    ShapePointer shapeArray[10];
    int size=0;

    shapeArray[size++] = new Circle    (Point(60,6), 4);
    shapeArray[size++] = new Rectangle(Point(70,6), Point(8,8));
    shapeArray[size++] = new Triangle (Point(80,6), Point(8,8));

    for (int i=0; i<8; i++)         // rotate shape 8 times
    {
        for (int j=0; j<size; j++)
        {
            shapeArray[j]->draw();
            pause();
            shapeArray[j]->hide();
            shapeArray[j]->rotate(10);
            shapeArray[j]->draw();
        }
    }

}
```

Being able to use the same message protocol simplifies program construction, and makes the program more readable and easier to maintain. But is dynamic binding really that big a deal? After all, you don't have to use a polymorphic array—you could create a variable for each object you want to manipulate. Typically such an array might have 100 objects falling into perhaps 20 different type categories. There's no point in you keeping track of object types if the compiler will do it for you. The overhead cost in terms of run time is minimal, and you'd be hard pressed to tell the difference in execution speed of a program that uses dynamic binding and one that doesn't. Furthermore, why would you want to send such a message to a shape? After all, don't you always know by context whether you are dealing with circles or rectangles?

The answer to the question is a question. Why should you have to worry about the type of an object if the computer can take care of the details for you? Consider how a CAD program might allow users to define shapes for a drawing.

An Example of Common Method Definitions in a CAD Program

Users of a CAD program do not typically interact with a programming language when they draw lines, circles, ellipses, triangles, and other complex shapes that are standard parts of a drawing library. For instance, most drawing packages allow circles to be drawn by first clicking the mouse pointer on a circle icon. Next, the user moves the mouse pointer to the desired location on the screen and presses the mouse button again to indicate the location of the center point. Finally, the user drags the mouse away from the center point and clicks again to indicate the radius of the circle, which is immediately drawn.

The program can't know ahead of time whether the user is going to draw a circle, a rectangle, or a line. Further, a typical drawing of an electric circuit board of a machine part will include hundreds of lines, circles, and shading specifications, as well as complex shapes represented as compound objects. The CAD package receives instructions from the user in the form of mouse input to create a circle of a given size at a given location. The program then adds the newly specified shape to a polymorphic collection of objects. In fact, CAD packages typically have many different collections of shape objects representing the different layers of a drawing to simulate transparent overlays used to classify different subsystems in complex drawings.

One command frequently used while drawing is "zoom". You might zoom in or zoom out and scale the drawing, depending on the level of detail you want to see, or you might want to change the rotation of a given set of objects. If a programmer has set up all shapes to respond to a scale method or a rotate method, the problem is easily solved: simply send the same sequence of messages to each of the objects in the appropriate collection. First tell each object in the collection to hide itself, then send the scale message to each object in the collection. Finally, tell each object to redraw itself. If polymorphic dispatch at run time is supported, the programmer doesn't need to worry about maintaining information about the type of each shape object that needs to be manipulated. The compiler or interpreter will see to it that a different routine is invoked for drawing circles than for drawing rectangles.

Maintaining a set of objects in a polymorphic collection and defining a common protocol for all members of the collection simplifies program construction and maintenance. It's a lot easier to remember and specify one name that can be performed on any shape object for each operation than it is to remember 20 different names for the same operation.

Let's look a little more closely at inheritance and dynamic binding to see how a programmer can use these language features to simplify program organization and communication.

OBJECT-ORIENTED LANGUAGE FEATURES

C++, object-oriented Pascal, Smalltalk, and Actor all support specification of inheritance in the building of class hierarchies. Further, these languages all facilitate polymorphic dispatch of messages to objects from such a hierarchy to invoke the appropriate methods at run time. In all cases, the binding of messages to methods is based on object type. As mentioned in the previous chapter, two language features are required in addition to user-defined types in order to program in an object-oriented style:

- Inheritance and classification of objects

- Dynamic binding and virtual functions

Inheritance Specifies Hierarchy

In languages that support inheritance, a new class can inherit the properties of an existing class. This means that the instance variables and methods
defined in the parent class are available to the child class. Different languages impose different sorts of restrictions on access to inherited object
components. For example, C++ does not allow inherited classes to access
the private elements of a parent class.

There are ways around this. In Smalltalk, all derived classes have access
to the instance variables of all their ancestor classes without restriction.
Some languages, including C++, allow new classes to be derived from more
than one parent. Such languages are said to support *multiple inheritance.*
Multiple inheritance can be useful, but is rarely required. In most cases,
multiple inheritance needlessly complicates programs. However, it can be
convenient if two existing classes together can provide a complete implementation for a new type.

Many classes can be derived from a single class. Descendant or child
classes can in turn be the parents of other classes. You can build complex
hierarchies of types by specifying a chain of inheritance for a given set of
classes. In fact, such a hierarchy must exist in order to make polymorphic
message passing possible.

Dynamic Binding Enables Polymorphism

Each of the languages covered in this book differs in the way it supports
dynamic binding. By default, all messages are dynamically bound to methods in both Smalltalk and Actor. In C++ and object-oriented Turbo Pascal,
static binding—where messages and methods are bound at compile time—is
used by default for all methods. This is understandable, since C++ and
object-oriented Pascal build new features on top of the base languages, C
and Pascal, in order to support dynamic binding. For the sake of efficiency
and compatibility with existing C and Pascal code, the default binding
mechanism is static. The programmer can change the default binding for
methods from static to dynamic by using the keyword *virtual* in both C++
and object-oriented Pascal. (Microsoft's QuickPascal and Apple's Object
Pascal allow only dynamic binding.)

Together, inheritance and dynamic binding let you build polymorphic class hierarchies in which all objects respond to a common set of messages known as the *protocol* for the hierarchy. The remainder of this chapter will show specific examples that use inheritance and dynamic binding in C++, object-oriented Pascal, Smalltalk, and Actor.

CLASSIFYING WITH INHERITANCE

Object-oriented programming is frequently presented as programming by specialization. You start out with a general definition for a class of objects, for example, a Shape class. Then you define subclasses by specifying the special-case properties of descendant classes. You define Shapes as objects that have a center point and an angle of rotation, and that can be drawn, moved to a new position, or have their angle of rotation changed. For example:

- Circles are Shapes that require users to specify radius in addition to a center point and angle of rotation.

- Rectangles are Shapes that require users to specify *extent* (height and width) in addition to a center point and angle of rotation.

- Triangles are like Rectangles in that they can be specified by a center point, an angle of rotation, and an extent.

The extent for a triangle represents a box circumscribing an upward-pointing triangle when the degree of rotation is 0. Such a triangle defines width as the distance along its horizontal base and height as the vertical distance between the base and the top of the triangle. Even though the interface for creating Rectangles and Triangles is the same, a different interpretation of extent is required, and a different implementation of draw is required to ensure that Triangles are drawn differently from Circles.

Such a definition of the relationship among Shapes, Circles, Rectangles, and Triangles leads to the following hierarchy:

```
Shape
  Circle
  Rectangle
    Triangle
```

The more general the class, the closer it appears to the left margin. New classes are defined as specializations of existing classes and appear below and indented to the right of their immediate ancestor.

Note: This classification is based on generalizing a communication protocol, not on specifying the geometric properties that the shapes have in common.

Look for Shared Properties

Geometry has little to do with this scheme of classification. If it were important to lay down the hierarchy according to the classifications used in geometry, you would start with polygons as the most general case and then proceed down the line of descendants. A triangle is a polygon with three sides. A rectangle is a polygon with four sides. A circle is a polygon with an infinite number of sides. Although this is a useful way of classifying properties of shapes when teaching geometry, it is of little use in programming.

When programming examples present inheritance with complete examples of class hierarchies, the implication is that definition of a type hierarchy is the first thing a programmer does in object-oriented programming. This perspective leads to thinking that whenever possible, new classes should always be based on existing classes. Programmers new to object-oriented programming are tempted to draw erroneous conclusions from this perspective. For example, many people new to object-oriented programming will see the definition of a point and conclude that a rectangle is the next logical progression of type definition—a rectangle is like a point, except that it specifies an additional point.

Evolution Versus Design

In reality, class hierarchies evolve; they rarely take the form originally imagined. Typically, a programmer will define many different types of objects in the system, use them for a while, and then begin to see the properties shared in common by different objects. The objects are then grouped together, and an explicit expression of their shared properties is made through inheritance. Class declarations in object-oriented languages provide for the specification of inheritance.

The idea of starting by designing a class hierarchy is a simplification of the way object-oriented programming works in practice. The implication of such a design is that you already know the common properties of a set of objects when you start. But in practice, when designing a class hierarchy, you will frequently start out with a set of objects that appear at first to have no relationship. Then you will find that you need to do the same things with different types of objects. You need, for example, to move icons about the screen as well as windows.

When you buy an existing class library, what you don't see is that when many of the types were first designed, their place in the class hierarchy probably was not known, or that a first guess at where they belonged was actually wrong. However, as you use objects, you begin to see their similarities and can then begin to classify them. In practice, classification is often performed as a second step rather than a first step in object-oriented programming.

Start with Objects, Not Hierarchies

The "moral" of all this is don't start with hierarchies. Use them, but don't start with them when building your own set of types. Suppose you need an object that will do serial communication, so you build a user-defined type called SerialPort. Later, you find common properties required to communicate with TTY output devices, such as a screen or a printer. You can select the common communication protocol for all TTY devices and put them in a TTYdevice class. Serial ports, mouse drivers, screens, and printers then become specialized subclasses of TTYdevice. Hierarchies are often very specific to an application. You often can't see the shared properties of a given set of objects until you have defined and used them.

Communication Protocol Defines Shared Properties

From a purely logical standpoint, it seems to make sense to derive a rectangle class from a point class and to derive a window class from a rectangle. More careful analysis, however, reveals that a rectangle *is* not a point—rather, it *has* two points. Further, a window *is* not a rectangle—it is defined by a rectangle. A window therefore *has* or contains a rectangle. You do not move rectangles about the screen, you move icons and windows about the screen. Icons and windows have more in common than windows and rectangles. The verb *is* implies inheritance: a circle is a shape. The verb *has* implies assembly structure of internal components: a rectangle has two points.

The mistaken idea of inheriting rectangles from points and windows from rectangles comes from a misplaced emphasis on implementation rather than on interface. You should classify objects according to how they are manipulated or how you communicate with them, rather than by how they are implemented.

User-defined types are characterized by the operations that can be performed on them, not by their implementations. Another way of saying this is that the most important design decision regarding objects is selection of a set of methods for the protocol used to manipulate them.

You don't care how floating point numbers are represented when you use them. The odds are that you'll rarely, if ever, need to examine them at the bit level. You're interested in the messages that can be sent to floating point numbers. You might not think of it that way; you might think of it as being interested in the operations or the protocol defined for floating point numbers. Floating point numbers can respond to messages for addition, subtraction, division, multiplication, and assignment.

Floating point objects actually have a rather limited protocol, but that's not the point. The point is that the class of all numbers, including floating point numbers, responds to a certain protocol—this is what is meant when it is said that an abstract data type is characterized by its protocol. When designing a class hierarchy, think of how objects are going to look on the outside. How will these objects appear to users? This is the primary perspective required when designing class hierarchies. It's easy to get lost inside the bits when you're allowed to see inside. Resist the temptation.

Classify by Interface, Not Implementation

Ask yourself these questions when designing a set of objects:

- Are there certain objects that would make the user's life easier if they could be treated with the same protocol (like integers and floating point numbers)?

- What do you want to do to points?

- Do you want to do the same thing to points that you want to do to rectangles?

- Do you want to do to windows the same thing that you want to do to rectangles?

For points, you want to add points to points; subtract points from points; multiply and divide points by constants; and test to see if one point is less than, equal to, or greater than another point.

Most of these operations either don't apply to rectangles, or the meaning is so different for a rectangle it's hard to figure out the meaning of the message. Inheriting the interface and communication protocol applied to points makes little sense for rectangles. What would be the object that results from adding a point to a rectangle? The only real shared operation common to points and rectangles is moving them to a new location. Closer analysis reveals that a different protocol is used for manipulating rectangles. In addition to defining and moving rectangles, you will want to resize them by changing the width or the height. A point is useful for changing the width and height of a rectangle simultaneously as well as for specifying a new position for rectangle's origin, corner, or center point. You might want to ask a rectangle if it contains a point or to return a given corner as a point. Points are useful for implementing rectangles, especially if a rich protocol is provided for manipulating points. However, because you do not want to communicate with a point in the same way you want to communicate with a rectangle, it makes little sense for a rectangle to inherit the properties of a point. There is not really enough of a shared protocol to justify classifying rectangles as descendants of points.

Specifying Inheritance

In the example programs that implement the rotateShapes program in each of the four languages, slight variations occur to accommodate the features provided by a specific language. For instance, C++ uses protected inheritance when specifying the inheritance of class Rectangle from which class Triangle is derived. The Rectangle class is a built-in type for Smalltalk, so the name of the class used in the example is changed to TRectangle, following an object-oriented Pascal convention of preceding all type or class names with the letter *T*. Actor calls the rectangle class "Rect", but to avoid name conflicts in general, all the types in the rotate shapes example programs for both Smalltalk and Actor have a *T* in front of them: TShape, TCircle, TRectangle, TTriangle.

First, let's look at how each of the languages specifies a class that involves no inheritance: Shape or TShape.

Specifying the Abstract Base Class, Shape

Before you can see how inheritance is specified in any language, you need a base class from which newly defined classes can be derived. The Shape class introduced in Chapter 3 is such a base class. Consider how this class would be declared in each language.

You've already seen how the abstract base class Shape is declared in C++.

```
// C++

//////////////////////////////////////////////////////////////
// class Shape
//////////////////////////////////////////////////////////////
class Shape
{
    Point center;
    int color;
    int angle;
    virtual void drawShape()=0;
public:
                    Shape(Point p)                  // constructor
                      : center(p),
                        color(screen.foreground()),
                        angle(0)     { }
    int         getColor()      { return color; }
    void        setColor(int c) { color = c; }
    int         getAngle()      { return angle; }
    void        setAngle(int a) { angle = a; }
    Point       position()      { return center; }
    void        moveTo(Point p) { center = p; }

    void        draw()  {
                        int saveColor = screen.foreground();
                        screen.foreground(getColor());
                        drawShape();
                        screen.foreground(saveColor);
                    }
    void        rotate(int angle)
                    {
                        setAngle(getAngle()+angle);
```

```
                            draw();
                        }
    void        hide()  {
                            int saveColor = screen.foreground();
                            screen.foreground(screen.background());
                            drawShape();
                            screen.foreground(saveColor);
                        }
};
```

Because all methods are defined inline in the C++ declaration, the previous code serves as both a declaration and a definition.

Object-oriented Pascal does not allow inline definitions. Therefore, the definition (implementation) of class methods is separated from the declaration (interface). At this point, the emphasis is on the interface declaration because the interface specifies the communication protocol for a class.

```
{ Pascal }

type

  {-----------------------------------------------------------}
  { TShape class (interface)                                  }
  {-----------------------------------------------------------}
  PShape = ^TShape;
  TShape = object
    constructor init(p: TPoint);
    procedure   setAngle(a: Integer);
    function    getAngle : Integer;
    procedure   position(var p : TPoint);
    procedure   moveTo(p : TPoint);
    procedure   draw; virtual;
    procedure   rotate(a : Integer);
    procedure   print; virtual;
  private
    center : TPoint;
    color  : Integer;
    angle  : Integer;
  end;
```

You have already seen this declaration, too.

Smalltalk and Actor declare classes in a slightly different manner. You won't see source code for classes divided into an interface and an implementation in Smalltalk and Actor. The interface and the implementation are fused into a single definition for the class. The reason for this is the close tie between the programming environment and the programming language

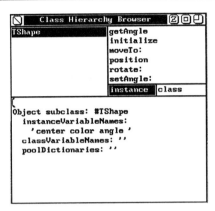

Figure 8-1.   A Smalltalk browser shows the interface for the TShape class. When no methods are selected in the right pane, the class definition is displayed in the bottom pane.

for both Actor and Smalltalk. The most common way to program in these languages is with a *class browser*. Class browsers make it easy to overview class definitions.

Figure 8-1 shows a browser for Smalltalk presenting the view you would see of a TShape class containing a comparable set of instance variables and method definitions as those defined for C++ and object-oriented Pascal. In Figure 8-1 no methods are selected for viewing, so the class definition is displayed. Figure 8-2 shows the same browser after selecting the initialize method for viewing. The bottom pane in the browser is an edit window, which provides the primary means of creating and editing source code for Smalltalk classes.

To understand the implementation of a class, the main thing to consider when looking at the browser is to look at the class declaration:

```
"Smalltalk"

Object subclass: #TShape
  instanceVariableNames:
    'center color angle '
  classVariableNames: ''
  poolDictionaries: '' !
```

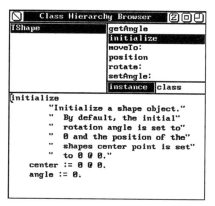

Figure 8-2.   The same Smalltalk browser with the initialize method selected in the right pane. The source code for initialize is shown in the bottom pane.

This code declares a new class called TShape, which is inherited from the superclass called Object. TShape declares three private instance variables: center, color, and angle.

You can see the names of the methods defined for TShape objects in the list in the upper-right corner of the class browser. You don't have to use a browser to program in Smalltalk or Actor, but the convenience provided by browsers is substantial. Compiling of methods is incremental—that is, each new method is checked for syntax and compiled as you create it, helping you catch mistakes immediately, rather than waiting until you have completed an entire class definition before compiling and testing your work. When you are through defining a class, you *file out* the class, meaning you create a source code file for it that reflects the definition you have specified using the browser. The file for the TShape class in Smalltalk looks like this:

```
"Smalltalk"

Object subclass: #TShape
  instanceVariableNames:
    'center color angle '
  classVariableNames: ''
  poolDictionaries: '' !

!TShape class methods !

center: aPoint
```

```
        "set new center point"
   ^self new initialize;
          moveTo: aPoint.!

new
        "create new object, initialize variables"
     ^super new initialize! !

!TShape methods !

getAngle
        "returns integer between 0 and 360"
     ^angle!

initialize
        "Initialize a shape object."
        "  By default, the initial"
        "  rotation angle is set to"
        "  0 and the position of the"
        "  shapes center point is set"
        "  to 0 @ 0."
     center := 0 @ 0.
     angle := 0.!

moveTo: aPoint
        "Move center of shape to"
        "point indicated by argument."
     center := aPoint.!

position
        "Return center point of shape."
     ^center.!

rotate: anInteger
        "Rotate a TShape object by
          anInteger degrees."
     ^angle := angle + anInteger.!

setAngle: anInteger
        "set rotation angle"
        " argument is an integer"
        " between 0 and 360 representing"
        " number of degrees of rotation"
     angle := anInteger! !
```

When you want to load the TShape class, you simply *file in* the previous file, and the TShape class is added to the Smalltalk programming environment. You could have created the previous file with a standard text editor and then filed it in.

More typically when working in Smalltalk and Actor, rather than file classes in and out, you save a single image of the system before exiting the environment. This will save all the classes that you have added to the programming environment with the browser. Normally, you would use a different system image for each project you are working on.

Figure 8-3 shows an Actor browser opened on the TShape class.

Here's the code Actor uses to specify a new TShape class derived from the Object class:

```
/* Actor */

/* TShape class */!!

inherit(Object, #TShape, #(center color angle), 2, nil)!!
```

The # in #TShape indicates that TShape is a symbol. This syntax is borrowed from Smalltalk. Symbols are like strings except that only one symbol in the entire programming environment can exist for a given name. The statement sends the inherit message to Object, the first argument of the expression. The new subclass of Object is the second argument. The third

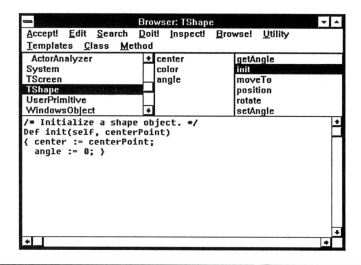

Figure 8-3.   The TShape class shown with a browser in Actor. The Actor browser provides an additional pane in the center that always shows instance variables.

argument is an array. Literal arrays are declared in Actor (as in Smalltalk) by surrounding the array elements with parentheses and preceding the entire expression with a pound sign: #(...).

The fourth argument is a value describing the format of objects made by the class: 0 = byte, 1 = word, 2 = pointer, nil = use the ancestor's format. The final argument determines whether or not the newly created class has indexed objects. This argument is ignored if it is nil. For the most part, you don't need to worry about the last two arguments.

As in Smalltalk, a TShape class built with a browser can be filed out. Here's the filed-out Actor source code for the entire TShape class definition:

```
/* Actor */

/* TShape class */!!

inherit(Object, #TShape, #(center color angle), 2, nil)!!

setClassVars(TShape, #(ShapeScreen))!!

now(class(TShape))!!

/* create new object, initialize variables */
Def new(self, centerPoint)
{ ^init(new(self:ancestor), centerPoint); }
!!

now(TShape)!!

/*
 * Increase rotation angle by
 * anInteger degrees.
 */
Def rotate(self anInteger)
{
  angle := angle + anInteger;
}
!!

/* Initialize a shape object. */
Def init(self, centerPoint)
{ center := centerPoint;
  angle := 0; }
!!

/* Move center of shape to
 * point indicated by argument.
 */
Def moveTo(self, aPoint)
{ ^center := aPoint; }
!!
```

```
/* Return center point of shape. */
Def position(self)
{ ^center; }
!!

/* Return rotation angle of shape. */
Def getAngle(self)
{ ^angle; }
!!

/*
 * set rotation angle
 * argument is an integer
 * between 0 and 360 representing
 * number of degrees of rotation
 */
Def setAngle(self, newAngle)
{ ^angle := newAngle; }
!!
```

Specifying the Derived Class, Circle

Now look at how each language specifies inheritance. The Circle (TCircle) class is derived from Shape in each of the languages. A Circle object is a Shape object that adds radius as a private instance variable and adds methods for setting and retrieving the radius of an object. Each of the languages except Pascal forces the user to properly initialize newly created Circles. Pascal provides a constructor that hints that an init method should be called as soon as an instance of Circle is created, but the Pascal compiler does not force you to call the constructor.

First C++:

```
// C++

//////////////////////////////////////////////////////////////
// class Circle
//////////////////////////////////////////////////////////////
class Circle : public Shape
{
    int radius;
    virtual void drawShape()
    {
        Point ctr = rotateAboutOrigin(position(), getAngle());
        screen.circle(ctr, radius);
    }
public:
        Circle(Point p, int r)                  // constructor
           : Shape(p), radius(r) {}
};
```

C++ inserts the inheritance specification immediately after the declaration of the class name and just before the opening curly brace of the class declaration.

```
class Circle : public Shape
{
    ...
}
```

C++ allows two types of inheritance, public and private. The keyword *public* in the code above could be exchanged for *private*.

```
class Circle : private Shape
```

If the keyword is left out, private inheritance is assumed by default.

```
class Circle : Shape  // defaults to private inheritance
```

C++ is the only language presented in this book that provides private as well as public inheritance. If private inheritance is specified, the public members of the base class become private members of the derived class. Private members of the parent class are not accessible to methods of the derived class. In public inheritance, private members of the parent are inherited as private members of the derived class. Public members of the parent class become public members of the derived class. C++ also provides the keyword *protected*, which is used inside a class declaration. The Triangle class includes such a declaration.

```
class Rectangle : public Shape
{
    virtual void drawShape();       // private method
protected:
    Point extent;                    // protected data
public:
    Rectangle(Point ctr, Point ext); // public method
    ...
};
```

The keyword *protected* is used typically for data that would normally be private. However, if a derived class needs to reference a private variable of the parent, the parent must declare the variable as protected. In the previous example, the Triangle class derived from Rectangle needs to reference the instance variable, extent, so extent is declared as protected. If extent were private and a method declared in Triangle tried to reference extent, a compiler error would be generated. If public inheritance is specified for a derived class, protected members of the parent class become private members of the derived class. If private inheritance is specified, protected members of the parent are not accessible in the derived class.

Here's how object-oriented Pascal specifies a TCircle class inherited from TShape:

```
{ Pascal }

  {-----------------------------------------------------------}
  { TCircle class (interface)                                 }
  {-----------------------------------------------------------}
  PCircle = ^TCircle;
  TCircle = object(TShape)
    constructor init(p : TPoint; r : Integer);
    procedure   setRadius(r : Integer);
    function    getRadius : Integer;
    procedure   draw; virtual;
    procedure   print; virtual;
  private
    radius : Integer;
  end;
```

Inheritance is specified by putting the parent class in parentheses after the keyword *object*.

```
TCircle = object(TShape)
   .
   .
   .
```

Compare this with TShape, which does not specify inheritance.

```
TShape = object
   .
   .
   .
```

Notice that all object-oriented Pascal class declarations also include the declaration of a type for pointing to the class:

```
PCircle = ^TCircle;
```

This is because in Pascal, the global function New, which is used to create objects on the heap, requires pointers to objects. In C++ and object-oriented Pascal, polymorphism is always achieved with pointers to objects. However, the C++ new operator accepts any type of object as an argument, not only pointers, so C++ does not force you to declare a pointer to an object in order to take advantage of polymorphism.

Smalltalk declares a TCircle class derived from TShape as follows:

```
"Smalltalk"

TShape subclass: #TCircle
  instanceVariableNames:
    'radius '
  classVariableNames: "
  poolDictionaries: " !
```

When the Smalltalk interpreter evaluates the preceding code it actually creates a new object in the system called TCircle. TCircle is a class object from which instances can be created. Newly created classes automatically inherit the "new" method that is used to create instances. Instances of TCircle are useless unless you define methods for TCircle objects.

The following listing is the entire Smalltalk definition for TCircle.

```
"Smalltalk"

TShape subclass: #TCircle
  instanceVariableNames:
    'radius '
  classVariableNames: "
  poolDictionaries: " !

!TCircle class methods !

center: aPoint radius: anInteger
      "Set center point and radius."
    ^(super center: aPoint)
        radius: anInteger.! !

!TCircle methods !

draw
        "Draw a circle using the
        current position and radius
        values of the receiver."

    | newPosition |
    newPosition := Screen rotateAboutOrigin: self position
                                angle: self getAngle.
```

```
        Screen circle: newPosition
              radius: self radius.!
radius
        "Return an integer representing
         the radius of the receiver."
    ^radius.!

radius: anInteger
        "Set radius of receiver
         circle to anInteger."
    radius := anInteger.! !
```

The Actor declaration for a TCircle class derived from TShape looks like this:

```
/* Actor */

/* TCircle class */!!

inherit(TShape, #TCircle, #(radius), 2, nil)!!
```

Like Smalltalk, Actor immediately creates a TCircle object when it encounters this code. TCircle is a class object, as opposed to an object like aCircle, which would be an instance of TCircle. Here's the entire Actor definition for TCircle and its object methods:

```
/* Actor */

/* TCircle class */!!

inherit(TShape, #TCircle, #(radius), 2, nil)!!

now(class(TCircle))!!

/*
 * Create new Circle object and
 * initialize center point and radius.
 */
Def new(self, centerPoint, initRadius)
{ ^init(new(self:Behavior), centerPoint, initRadius); }

!!

now(TCircle)!!

/*
 * Draw a circle using the
 * current position and radius
 * values of the receiver.
```

```
*/
Def draw(self ¦ newCenter)
{
  newCenter := rotateAboutOrigin(Screen,
                                 position(self),
                                 getAngle(self));
  circle(Screen, newCenter, getRadius(self));
}
!!

/*
 * Initialize instance variables.
 * Called by new to
 * set center point and radius.
 */
Def init(self, centerPoint, initRadius)
{ init(self:ancestor, centerPoint);
  radius := initRadius; }
!!

/*
 * Set radius of receiver
 * circle to newRadius."
 */
Def setRadius(self, newRadius)
{ ^radius := newRadius; }
!!

/*
 * Return an integer representing
 * the radius of the receiver.
 */
Def getRadius(self)
{ ^radius; }
!!
```

Specifying the Derived Class, Rectangle

The Rectangle (TRectangle) class is very similar to Circle (TCircle), in that it is inherited from Shape. However, rectangles are created by specifying an extent (width and height) rather than a radius.

Here's the C++ declaration for Rectangle:

```
/////////////////////////////////////////////////////////////
// class Rectangle
/////////////////////////////////////////////////////////////
class Rectangle : public Shape
{
    virtual void drawShape()
    {
        Point a(position()-(extent/2));
        Point c(a+extent);
```

```
        Point b(c.x(), a.y());
        Point d(a.x(), c.y());

        a = rotateAboutOrigin(a, getAngle());
        b = rotateAboutOrigin(b, getAngle());
        c = rotateAboutOrigin(c, getAngle());
        d = rotateAboutOrigin(d, getAngle());

        screen.moveTo(a);
        screen.lineTo(b);
        screen.lineTo(c);
        screen.lineTo(d);
        screen.lineTo(a);
    }
protected:
    Point extent;
public:
        Rectangle(Point ctr, Point ext)      // constructor
            : Shape(ctr), extent(ext) {}
};
```

The Pascal declaration for TRectangle is straightforward:

```
{ Pascal }

  {----------------------------------------------------------}
  { TRectangle class (interface)                             }
  {----------------------------------------------------------}
  PRectangle = ^TRectangle;
  TRectangle = object(TShape)
    constructor init(ctr : TPoint; ext : TPoint);
    procedure   setExtent(ext : TPoint);
    procedure   getExtent(var ext : TPoint);
    procedure   draw; virtual;
    procedure   print; virtual;
  private
    extent : TPoint;
  end;
```

Only the declaration is included here, since Pascal forces the separation of interface and implementation. The interface is the only concern when designing type hierarchies. For the complete implementation of the rotate shapes program in C++, object-oriented Pascal, Smalltalk, and Actor, see Appendix A, "Rotate Shapes in Pascal, Smalltalk, and Actor". Instructions for compiling and running the program in each language are included.

By now, you should be accustomed to reading Smalltalk code. If you're not, keep looking for similar method implementations in C++ or object-oriented Pascal.

```
"Smalltalk"

TShape subclass: #TRectangle
  instanceVariableNames:
    'extent '
  classVariableNames: "
  poolDictionaries: " !

!TRectangle class methods !

center: centerPoint extent: extentPoint
      "comment"
    ^(super center: centerPoint)
        extent: extentPoint.! !

!TRectangle methods !

draw
      "Draw a rectangle using the
       current position and radius
       values of the receiver."
  ¦ a b c d aa bb cc dd ¦

  a := self position -
        (self extent // 2).
  c := a + self extent.
  b := (c x) @ (a y).
  d := (a x) @ (c y).
  aa := Screen rotateAboutOrigin: a
                        angle: self getAngle.
  bb := Screen rotateAboutOrigin: b
                        angle: self getAngle.
  cc := Screen rotateAboutOrigin: c
                        angle: self getAngle.
  dd := Screen rotateAboutOrigin: d
                        angle: self getAngle.
  Screen moveTo: aa.
  Screen lineTo: bb;
         lineTo: cc;
         lineTo: dd;
         lineTo: aa.!

extent
      "Return a point representing
       the height and width of the
       receiver rectangle."
    ^extent.!

extent: aPoint
      "Set extent (width and height)
       of receiver rectangle to
       x and y values of aPoint."
    extent := aPoint.! !
```

The Actor implementation of TRectangle is very similar to Smalltalk:

```
/* Actor */

/* TRectangle class  */!!

inherit(TShape, #TRectangle, #(extent), 2, nil)!!

now(class(TRectangle))!!

/*
 * Create new TRectangle.
 * (new is statically bound to Behavior:new.)
 * Call init to set init to initialize
 * instance variables.
 */
Def new(self, centerPoint, extentPoint)
{ ^init(new(self:Behavior), centerPoint, extentPoint); }
!!

now(TRectangle)!!

/*
 * Draw a rectangle using the
 * current position and radius
 * values of the receiver.
 */
Def draw(self ¦ a b c d aa bb cc dd)
{
  a := point(x(center) - (x(extent)/2),      /* left    bottom */
             y(center) - (y(extent)/2));
  c := point(x(a) + x(extent),               /* right   top */
             y(a) + y(extent));
  b := point(x(a), y(c));                     /* left    top */
  d := point(x(c), y(a));                     /* right   bottom */

  aa := rotateAboutOrigin(Screen, a, getAngle(self));
  bb := rotateAboutOrigin(Screen, b, getAngle(self));
  cc := rotateAboutOrigin(Screen, c, getAngle(self));
  dd := rotateAboutOrigin(Screen, d, getAngle(self));

  moveTo(Screen, aa);
  lineTo(Screen, bb);
  lineTo(Screen, cc);
  lineTo(Screen, dd);
  lineTo(Screen, aa);
}
!!

/*
 * Return a point representing
 * the height and width of the
 * receiver rectangle.
 */
Def getExtent(self)
{ ^extent; }
!!

/*
```

```
 * Set extent (width and height)
 * of receiver rectangle to
 * x and y values of aPoint.
 */
Def setExtent(self, extentPoint)
{ ^extent := extentPoint; }
!!

/*
 * Initialize instance variables.
 * Called by new. new forces
 * users to specify center point
 * and extent when creating
 * TRectangles.
 */
Def init(self, centerPoint, extentPoint)
{ init(self:ancestor, centerPoint);
  extent := extentPoint; }
!!
```

You might notice certain conventions as you see more code. Smalltalk, by convention, uses the name initialize to set default values for newly created objects. C++ uses constructors with the same name as the class. Object-oriented Pascal uses the name init for constructors. Actor, by convention, uses init as the name of the initialization method for a class. Neither Smalltalk nor Actor guarantees the call of initialize or init. Instead, the class method for creating new instances must explicitly call the initializer. Typically, the name of this class method is new, but this also is a convention.

Specifying the Derived Class, Triangle

Finally, let's look at the Triangle (TTriangle) class. Triangles use exactly the same internal representation and initialization as Rectangles. The data is interpreted differently, however, when it's time to draw a triangle. This relationship can be specified by deriving Triangle from Rectangle and then overriding the definition for the draw method.

The Triangle class in C++ inherits the protected instance variable extent from its parent, TRectangle.

```
/////////////////////////////////////////////////////////
// class Triangle
/////////////////////////////////////////////////////////
class Triangle : public Rectangle
{
    virtual void drawShape()
```

```
    {
        int w2 = extent.x()/2;   // half the width
        int h2 = extent.y()/2;   // half the height
        Point a(position()+Point( 0,  h2));
        Point b(position()+Point( w2, -h2));
        Point c(position()+Point(-w2, -h2));

        a = rotateAboutOrigin(a, getAngle());
        b = rotateAboutOrigin(b, getAngle());
        c = rotateAboutOrigin(c, getAngle());

        screen.moveTo(a);
        screen.lineTo(b);
        screen.lineTo(c);
        screen.lineTo(a);
    }
public:
        Triangle(Point ctr, Point ext)       // constructor
          : Rectangle(ctr, ext) {}
};
```

Only the draw method is reimplemented in the object-oriented Pascal declaration for TTriangle.

```
{ Pascal }

  {---------------------------------------------------------}
  { TTriangle class (interface)                             }
  {---------------------------------------------------------}
  PTriangle = ^TTriangle;
  TTriangle = object(TRectangle)
    procedure   draw; virtual;
  end;
```

Likewise, Smalltalk and Actor only reimplement the draw method for TTriangles. You'll notice that fewer definitions require overriding as you move downward in a class hierarchy. That's the nature of specialization and a sign that the right features were abstracted for the set of classes and defined in the base class.

```
"Smalltalk"

TRectangle subclass: #TTriangle
  instanceVariableNames: "
  classVariableNames: "
  poolDictionaries: " !

!TTriangle class methods ! !

!TTriangle methods !
```

```
draw
        "Draw a triangle using the
         current position and radius
         values of the receiver."
     ¦ a b c w2 h2 aa bb cc ¦

    w2 := self extent x // 2.
    h2 := self extent y // 2.
    a := self position + (  0 @ h2).
    b := self position + (  w2 @ h2 negated).
    c := self position + (w2 negated @ h2 negated).
    aa := Screen rotateAboutOrigin: a
                                angle: self getAngle.
    bb := Screen rotateAboutOrigin: b
                                angle: self getAngle.
    cc := Screen rotateAboutOrigin: c
                                angle: self getAngle.

    Screen moveTo: aa;
           lineTo: bb;
           lineTo: cc;
           lineTo: aa.! !
```

As usual, the Actor code for TTriangle is almost exactly like Smalltalk.

```
/* Actor */

/* TTriangle class */!!

inherit(TRectangle, #TTriangle, nil, 2, nil)!!

now(class(TTriangle))!!

now(TTriangle)!!

/*
 * Draw a triangle at using the
 * current position and radius
 * values of the receiver.
 */
Def draw(self ¦ a b c w2 h2 aa bb cc)
{
  w2 := x(extent) / 2;
  h2 := y(extent) / 2;
  a  := position(self) + point(      0,         h2);
  b  := position(self) + point(      w2, negate(h2));
  c  := position(self) + point(negate(w2), negate(h2));

  aa := rotateAboutOrigin(Screen, a, getAngle(self));
  bb := rotateAboutOrigin(Screen, b, getAngle(self));
  cc := rotateAboutOrigin(Screen, c, getAngle(self));

  moveTo(Screen, aa);
```

```
    lineTo(Screen, bb);
    lineTo(Screen, cc);
    lineTo(Screen, aa);
}
!!
```

PROGRAMMING WITH POLYMORPHISM

Now you can see how class hierarchies and polymorphism combine to manipulate collections of objects. Typically, a collection is declared as an array of elements having the type of the base class for the hierarchy. In C++ and Pascal this is done with pointers. It's also possible to use more generalized collections if you have a container class library for C++ or Pascal. Smalltalk and Actor also use pointers to objects in polymorphic collections, but the dereferencing of these pointers is automatic and therefore transparent. Users of collections treat the elements like normal objects in Smalltalk and Actor.

Specifying Dynamic Binding

By default, all messages are dynamically bound to methods in Smalltalk and Actor. Smalltalk provides a way to alter the dynamic binding mechanism so that in specified classes the search for a method to match the received message begins in the superclass of the object receiving the message. Actor provides a similar feature and also allows the specification of the exact class method that should be bound to a given message call. In other words, it is possible to specify static binding in Actor, even though dynamic binding is the default message dispatching mechanism.

In C++ and object-oriented Pascal, all methods are statically bound by default. If you want methods to be dynamically bound, you need to specify the appropriate methods as virtual in the appropriate base class methods.

```
/////////////////////////////////////////////////////////
// class Shape
/////////////////////////////////////////////////////////
class Shape
{
```

```
    ...
    virtual void drawShape()=0;
    ...
};


{ Pascal }

type

  {-----------------------------------------------------------}
  { TShape class (interface)                                  }
  {-----------------------------------------------------------}
  PShape = ^TShape;
  TShape = object
    ...
    procedure   draw;  virtual;
    ...
  end;
```

Polymorphic Collections Respond to Polymorphic Messages

All the rotate shape programs assume the presence of a global variable, Screen, which is an abstract Screen class. Screen has a coordinate system that ranges from 0@0 to 100@100 with the origin in the lower-left corner, as used in mathematics. The Screen object knows how to draw lines and circles and not much else. Complete implementation of the Screen class is shown for each of the four languages covered in this book in Appendix A.

You've already seen how to rotate a polymorphic array of shapes in C++.

```
// C++
////////////////////////////////////////////////////////////
// main program
////////////////////////////////////////////////////////////
typedef Shape *ShapePointer;

void rotateArray(ShapePointer array[], int size)
{
    for (int j=0; j<size; j++)
    {
        array[j]->draw();              // original position
        for (int i=0; i<8; i++)        // rotate shape 8 times,
        {                              // 10 degrees each rotation
            array[j]->rotate(10);      // rotate is relative to
                                       // current angle setting
        }
```

```
        }
}

void main()
{
    ShapePointer shapeArray[10];
    int size=0;

    shapeArray[size++] = new Circle    (Point(60,6), 4);
    shapeArray[size++] = new Rectangle(Point(70,6), Point(8,8));
    shapeArray[size++] = new Triangle (Point(80,6), Point(8,8));

    rotateArray(shapeArray, size);

}
```

The Pascal version appears a little more complicated because it uses pointers.

```
{ Pascal }
program RotateShapes;

{$N+}
{$E+}

uses Crt, Point, Shapes, Screen;

procedure wait;
var
  junk : Char;
begin
  junk := ReadKey;
end;

var
  p1, p2     : TPoint;
  i, j       : Integer;
  shapeArray : Array[0..9] of PShape;
  size       : Integer;

begin

  Display.initialize;

  {---------------------------------------------------------}
  { POLYMORPHISM                                            }
  {   Rotate and display an array of shapes                 }
  {---------------------------------------------------------}
                                        { First create an   }
                                        { array of TShape   }
                                        { objects.          }
                                        {                   }
                                        { These objects have}
```

```
                                        { no names because  }
                                        { they are created  }
                                        { with New which    }
                                        { returns a pointer.}
                                        {                    }
                                        { Therefore,         }
                                        { shapeArray is an  }
                                        { array of pointers }
                                        { to TShape objects.}
                                        {-------------------}

   size := 0;                           { size keeps track
                                          of the number of
                                          items in array.
                                          Increment size
                                          each time a new
                                          shape is added to
                                          the array.        }

   {-------------------------------------------------------}
   { Create the array                                      }
   {-------------------------------------------------------}
   p1.init(60, 6);
   shapeArray[size] := New(PCircle, init(p1, 4));
   inc(size);

   p1.init(70, 6);
   p2.init(8,8);
   shapeArray[size] := New(PRectangle, init(p1, p2));
   inc(size);

   p1.init(80, 6);
   p2.init(8,8);
   shapeArray[size] := New(PTriangle, init(p1, p2));
   inc(size);

   {-------------------------------------------------------}
   { Draw and rotate the shape array 9 times               }
   {-------------------------------------------------------}
   for i := 0 to 8 do
   begin
     for j := 0 to size-1 do
     begin
       shapeArray[j]^.draw;
       shapeArray[j]^.rotate(10);
     end;
   end;

   wait;
   Display.cleanup;
end.
```

Since there are no global functions in either Smalltalk or Actor, special Demo classes must be created to implement the code to rotate the shapes.

Alternatively, the statements to create and rotate a collection of shapes can be evaluated interactively in a Workspace window.

The method demoRotateShapes is defined in the Smalltalk class TScreen, declared as follows:

```
"Smalltalk"

Object subclass: #TScreen
  instanceVariableNames:
    'maxX maxY virtualMaxX virtualMaxY pen sinTable
  classVariableNames: "
  poolDictionaries: " !
```

Complete implementation of TScreen is described in Appendix A. For now, all you need to know is that the draw methods of TCircle, TRectangle, and TTriangle refer to a global instance of TScreen called Screen. Only the demoRotateShapes method of TScreen is listed here, to demonstrate polymorphism in Smalltalk.

```
"Smalltalk"
"demoRotateShapes method defined for TScreen class"

demoRotateShapes
      "Demonstration program to rotate objects of class
       TShape about the origin of the virtual screen."

  | shapeArray |
  shapeArray := OrderedCollection new.
  shapeArray add:
      (TCircle center: 60 @ 6
              radius: 4).
  shapeArray add:
      (TRectangle center: 70 @ 6
                extent:  8 @ 8).
  shapeArray add:
      (TTriangle center: 80 @ 6
                extent:  8 @ 8).
  self clear.
  shapeArray do: [ :shape | shape draw.].
  1 to: 8 do: [ :i |
     shapeArray do: [ :shape | shape rotate: 10.
                               shape draw.].].
  self cleanup.!
```

Two messages are sent to the Screen object to clear the display and to wait for a user to press a mouse button before clearing the screen and returning to the Smalltalk programming environment.

The messages are

```
self clear
```

and

```
self cleanup
```

Without this delay, the screen would be cleared, and the Smalltalk programming environment and windows would be redisplayed before you had a chance to see the rotated shapes.

In Actor, the method that rotates and displays the shape array is found in the class TDemoWindow. A global instance of this object, called DemoWindow, is created. TDemoWindow is derived from the Actor Window class, which means TDemoWindow automatically responds to standard Microsoft Windows messages like "paint", which is sent whenever an exposure event occurs affecting a given rectangular region on the screen. If you define a paint method for a class derived from Window, the method is invoked automatically when the window is displayed or uncovered. Simply sending the show message to DemoWindow enables DemoWindow:paint to respond to the paint message.

```
/* Actor */

/* TDemoWindow class */!!

inherit(Window, #TDemoWindow, nil, 2, nil)!!

now(class(TDemoWindow))!!

now(TDemoWindow)!!

/* The paint method is invoked automatically
 * for all subclasses of Window whenever
 * MS-Windows sends an exposure event to
 * the displayed window.
 */
Def paint(self, hDC | shapeArray)
{
  init(Screen, self, hDC);
  if isInitialized(Screen)
  then
    /* Create and draw shapes */
    shapeArray := new(OrderedCollection, 10);
    add(shapeArray, new(TCircle, 60@6, 4));
    add(shapeArray, new(TRectangle, 70@6, 8@8));
```

```
      add(shapeArray, new(TTriangle, 80@6, 8@8));
      do(shapeArray, {using(shape) draw(shape); });
      do(over(0,9), {using(i)
         do(shapeArray, {using(shape)
            rotate(shape,10);
            draw(shape);
         });
      });
   endif;
   cleanup(Screen);
}
!!
```

CHAPTER HIGHLIGHTS

- In addition to abstract data types, object-oriented programming requires the ability to organize objects into classes according to shared properties and communication protocol.

- Polymorphic communication is possible if a base class common to all classes in the hierarchy defines the basic communication protocol by declaring a set of common methods as virtual methods.

- Language features required to support classification and polymorphic communication are inheritance and dynamic binding. C++, object-oriented Pascal, Smalltalk, and Actor all support inheritance and dynamic binding.

- In Smalltalk and Actor, all methods are virtual (dynamic) by default. In C++ and Pascal, methods are static by default.

- Dynamic binding of messages to methods can be specified by declaring methods as virtual in the base classes defining the communication protocol in both C++ and object-oriented Pascal.

- Object-oriented programming usually involves collections of objects from a given class such as windows, shapes, controls, streams, or files.

- Powerful windowing systems depend heavily on inheritance and polymorphic message passing to simplifying the programming interface.

- The main difference between class libraries for object-oriented programming and traditional libraries provided by C and Pascal is that object-oriented class libraries support polymorphic message passing and allow the user to build new special-case classes based on the classes provided in the class library.

- Access to the source code for the library is not important because dynamic binding in a well-designed library gives the user complete control over the degree of specialization required for new types of objects.

The power of polymorphic class libraries will become apparent when you read Part III of this book on application frameworks. Application frameworks are special types of polymorphic class libraries used to build programming interfaces for application programs. Application frameworks evolved from object-oriented programming environments and class libraries in general. In particular, the programming environments of Smalltalk and Actor are important because they inspired the idea of application frameworks now being adapted to C++ and object-oriented Pascal.

III

CLASS LIBRARIES AND
APPLICATION FRAMEWORKS

Janie Wooldridge

9

GENERAL CHARACTERISTICS
OF AN APPLICATION
FRAMEWORK

Application frameworks are special types of object-oriented class libraries that take much of the drudgery out of programming applications that require sophisticated user interfaces. Strictly speaking, application frameworks provide run-time support for applications. However, they accomplish far more than typical window libraries for standard C and Pascal. Application frameworks are designed to generalize the handling of program input and output. By generalizing and managing mouse and keyboard input and providing output support for a variety of types of windows, application frameworks allow programmers to concentrate on what is unique to an application program.

This chapter introduces the general characteristics of application frameworks and shows how application frameworks provide components that can generally be classified as views, controllers, or models. *Views* include the visible interface to the application program and are sometimes called windows. The term *view* is more general. *Controllers* include visible and invisible objects that handle user input and translate the input into program actions by sending messages to the appropriate model components. *Model* is a fancy name for an application program or subroutine. Models usually manipulate data when directed to do so by controllers. Each model component of a program typically has a view associated with it. The view uses the model's data to display information for the user to see.

Models are the parts of the application framework that must be provided by the programmer. In addition to providing the basic models for a program, the programmer must assemble the proper views and controls for the models and connect each of the components so that proper communication is assured. This chapter shows examples of text views and graphic views. The controllers discussed include buttons, scrollbars, list selectors, and text editors. Event-driven control is introduced, and example programs that use application frameworks are presented in C++ and object-oriented Pascal.

Application frameworks automate the process of communicating with the user by making it easy to build windows, menus, and dialog boxes. Application frameworks also generalize the manner in which program control is handled. This frees the programmer from explicitly having to define how components of a software system need to monitor and respond to mouse and keyboard input. Instead, application frameworks implement a generalized control mechanism whereby all input is routed to a central dispatcher. All input, whether from the keyboard, mouse, serial port, disk drive, or other I/O device, is classified as an *event*. The general dispatcher automatically monitors all events.

Program control is handled very differently in an event-driven system. Instead of specifying and directing a sequence of steps for the program to follow from beginning to end, the programmer specifies what types of events the program will respond to. The portion of the program that you write only becomes active when the proper event occurs. The event dispatcher passes only events of the specified type on to the program as they occur. It's up to the programmer to implement methods that respond to, or *handle*, the events.

APPLICATION FRAMEWORKS ARE CLASS LIBRARIES

Most application frameworks provide general container classes for handling polymorphic objects. These containers include lists, sets, dictionaries, stacks, queues, strings, and file streams. Not all application frameworks will include each of these different types of containers. But most application frameworks include at least a subset of these generic container classes. In addition, most application frameworks include classes that support window-oriented display of data. Some application frameworks support character-oriented window systems (COWS). Others support graphical user interfaces (GUIs). This almost always implies support for creating and manipulating point and rectangle objects.

Although seldom described this way, Microsoft Windows itself can be classified as an application framework. Microsoft Windows applications rely on a polymorphic message-passing scheme: messages are sent to objects without knowing the exact type of the recipient, and the recipient is expected to respond appropriately to the messages. Since Microsoft Windows is implemented in C, it is not truly object-oriented, but instead uses some tricks to behave in a manner that is compatible with object-oriented programming. It is possible to wrap a shell around Microsoft Windows that will allow you to program Windows applications in a completely object-oriented manner. Class libraries for C++ and object-oriented Pascal that simplify the interface to Microsoft Windows functions and dramatically ease the construction of Windows application programs are available.

Common characteristics of application frameworks include object-oriented program structure and polymorphic command dispatch. Application frameworks are class libraries designed specifically to ease the creation and maintenance of application programs. Consequently, application framework class libraries consist of templates for building the objects most commonly used in window-oriented application programs. An *application framework* is exactly what its name suggests. It is a framework providing the scaffolding into which an application can be fitted.

Typically, application frameworks provide support for building user interfaces that look like today's professional application programs, such as the Turbo languages' integrated development environments or sophisticated spreadsheet, word processing, and database programs. Often these programs have a main menu bar at the top of the screen and a status bar at the bottom of the screen. The main menu bar across the top of the screen contains words associated with pull-down menus. When you click the mouse on a word in the menu bar, a pull-down menu appears. You can then select among the choices on the menu to invoke certain actions in the program. Usually, these pull-down menus can also be activated by pressing special hot-key combinations, such as ALT-F to invoke a file menu, or ALT-H to invoke a help menu. Such hot-key support is usually indicated by underlining or otherwise highlighting one of the letters in the words contained in the menu bar. Similar hot-key protocols can also be specified in the menu entries themselves. Anyone who has used modern programming environments is probably already familiar with menus and protocol for activating menus and selecting menu choices.

Dialog boxes are also becoming more popular as a form of communicating input and output activities to a user. Most application frameworks provide support for building complex dialog boxes. Further, they supply support for getting data into and out of dialog boxes, as well as automating control mechanisms required to modify data inside of them.

PROGRAM = APPLICATION = MODEL

In the context of an application framework, the word *program* carries special meaning. The terms *program*, *application*, and *model* are used interchangeably in this context. The specific meaning of these terms will become more clear as you read on. In traditional structured programming, the term *program* usually refers to the entire executable piece of software that is run on a computer.

In order to facilitate code reuse and minimize the impact of change on software, object-oriented programming takes a program and breaks it up into several major conceptual pieces. There is the piece of the program that maintains and manipulates data, such as the text being edited by a word processor. There is the piece that presents the data to the user in a meaningful format, such as a text display window. There is the piece that interacts with the user by accepting commands from a keyboard or mouse and then passes those commands to the application program.

The piece of the software system that maintains and manipulates data is called the *model*. Sometimes this piece is also called the *application*—and though it can be confusing, sometimes this piece is called the *program*.

The piece of the software system that presents the data to the user is often called a *view*. A window is the most typical form of view. However, the practice of structuring a piece of software into separate modules or components, where one component is the data model and another component is the view, can even be used where the only form of output is a TTY output device.

The piece of the software system that interacts with the user, gathering commands from the keyboard, mouse, and other input devices, and dispatching those commands to the program is called the *controller*. Actually, a typical piece of software contains many controller components. Buttons, scrollbars, and mouse pointers are all such components. Control and management of all these controller components is typically handled by a centralized control gathering and dispatching mechanism. The word *controller* generally refers to this central dispatch mechanism and the module of the software system that implements the individual control components.

Model-View-Controller Program Components

Model   Maintains and manipulates data unique to application
View   Presents data to user; windows are views
Controller   Gets commands from user and dispatches them to application
             program

Other organizations are possible, but the *model-view-controller* organization in object-oriented software systems is typical. The most difficult task in developing programs that take advantage of today's advanced graphical display devices is building the user interface. Some experts estimate that as much as 80 percent of the code in a typical application goes into the user interface. The user interface includes the components of the application that present the data to the user and manage and dispatch commands from the user (generated by keyboard and mouse input). In other words, the user interface consists of the view and controller components of software.

Fortunately, these components are the easiest to generalize, and that is what an application framework does. It generalizes the view and controller components of software and packages those components into reusable class libraries. These class libraries are often portable across operating systems and display devices. If 80 percent of programming effort goes into building user interfaces, using application frameworks can dramatically cut workload and development time for application programs.

The downside of application frameworks is the time required to learn how to use them. At first, they can appear quite complex. However, like any well-designed tool, once you learn how to use application frameworks, you will wonder how you ever got along without them. The time invested in learning an application framework is time well spent. The major problem in programming then becomes the selection of the appropriate application framework for the application at hand. The remainder of this book is devoted to application frameworks in general, and discusses four specific application frameworks:

Turbo Vision
C++ Views
Smalltalk and Actor
ObjectWindows

Turbo Vision is Borland's character-oriented application framework for MS-DOS. Though it works with both C++ and Pascal, the discussion in this book will focus on use of Turbo Vision with Pascal. C++ Views is an application framework using a model-view-controller structure developed by CNS, Inc. C++ Views is a powerful application framework for writing C++ programs that operate under Microsoft Windows. Smalltalk and Actor are also discussed as application frameworks. In addition to being programming environments and programming languages, both Smalltalk and Actor are application frameworks, due to the sophisticated class libraries provided by both systems. ObjectWindows is Borland's answer to C++ Views. The ObjectWindows application framework operates under Microsoft Windows and uses a class hierarchy similar to that found in Turbo Vision. In addition to working with Turbo Pascal and Borland C++, ObjectWindows works with Actor.

Most model-view-controller application frameworks are inspired by the Smalltalk design. Actor is nearly identical to Smalltalk in both its programming environment and its class library. The major difference between Smalltalk and Actor is in language syntax. In addition, Smalltalk defines its own graphical user interface, while Actor operates under Microsoft Windows. Recently, Smalltalk has been released to operate under Windows and under the OS/2 Presentation Manager, further blurring the distinction between Smalltalk and Actor. It is highly recommended that you experiment with either Smalltalk or Actor. Which system you select depends on whether or not you require support for Microsoft Windows programming. There is no easier way to program Windows applications than with Actor. Even if you are developing programs for Windows with stand-alone C, C++, or Pascal compilers, Actor is highly recommended. The interactive command execution and program development environment of Actor can't be beat for quickly learning the basic concepts of Windows applications programming. If you do not require support for Microsoft Windows, Smalltalk is recommended because it is cheaper and runs on a wider variety of hardware.

PROGRAM COMPONENTS

The basic program components provided by application frameworks are views. Views are display objects used to convey information to the user on the display screen. The most common forms of views include windows, control views, and data views. Windows are the most general form of display object. They can simply define static rectangular regions on the screen for displaying text or graphics, or they can be movable objects with borders, scrollbars, and icons to close, move, and resize the window frame. Windows typically display text, but they often contain other types of views, such as pushbuttons. Pushbuttons are a type of *control view*. You cannot move control views; they are usually fixed permanently to a specified location inside a movable window. Another type of view is a specialized *data view* used to display common data structures such as lists. Examples of each of these types of views appear throughout this chapter. Views are the basic components of application frameworks.

Windows and Views

All display objects in application frameworks are views. The most common type of view is a window. The following illustration shows a typical character-oriented window:

```
┌─[■]─────── D:\TP\DOCDEMOS\P11-2.PAS ───────[↑]─┐
│var                                             █
│  MyApp: TMyApp;                                █
│                                                █
│begin                                           █
│  MyApp.Init;                                   █
│  ReportDialog('Hello, world');                 █
│  MyApp.Run;                                     █
│  MyApp.Done;                                   █
│end.                                            █
└─◆── 27:1 ════◄□▒▒▒▒▒▒▒▒▒▒▒▒▒▒▒▒▒▒▒▒▒▒▒▒▒▒▒▒▒► ┘
```

The next illustration shows a graphics window from a Microsoft Windows application. Most windows can be moved, resized, or closed, and they display some form of data—such as a message to the user—or data to be manipulated by the user, such as a text edit buffer or an input line.

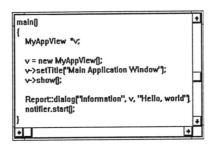

```
main()
{
    MyAppView *v;

    v = new MyAppView();
    v->setTitle("Main Application Window");
    v->show();

    Report::dialog("Information", v, "Hello, world");
    notifier.start();
}
```

It is not required that all views be windows of this type. Most application frameworks use a top-level view, which is usually referred to as the
display or the *desktop*. Figure 9-1 shows a typical desktop containing a
menu bar, a status line, and a text window. A view may contain any
number of *subviews*. The desktop shown in Figure 9-1 contains three
subviews: the menu bar, the status bar, and the edit window are all views in
themselves. The *hot spots* within the menu bar at the top of the screen and
in the status bar at the bottom of the screen are also views. In fact, every
button or control device on the screen is a view. This includes the OK, Yes,
No, and Cancel buttons found in dialog boxes as well as control icons
found in text windows, such as scrollbars, resize handles, and the close,
zoom, minimize, and maximize icons found in most windows.

Menus

Everyone is familiar with menus. Menus are a special form of view for
displaying lists of menu items. Menu items contain other objects as subcomponents. Typically, menu objects contain a string, a hot-key specification,
and an action that is to be invoked. Some systems use a pointer to a
function, stored in the menu-item object. Other systems embed a unique
integer associated with a command in the menu object. When the menu
item is selected, this unique integer command is passed to the central
dispatch mechanism, which, in turn, passes it to the application program.

The program should then define methods for handling the specified
command. The program also has the option of doing nothing on receipt of

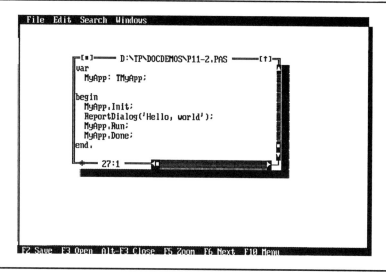

Figure 9-1.   Turbo Vision desktop with three subviews: a menu bar, a status line, and a text window

a command dispatched in such a manner. This makes it possible to design and implement a complete menu without having to define the actions that will take place until you are satisfied that the menu is working properly. This is just another example of the separation of functions typical of application frameworks that makes it easier to build application programs. The following illustration shows two views of a typical menu.

Dialog Boxes

Dialog boxes provide an easy way to specify user-controlled parameters for an application program. Such parameters might include the name of a file to be edited, the type of display to be used for output, the position of tab stops in an editor, or the communications parameters to be used by a modem program. Dialog boxes have become very popular devices for getting input from users and displaying the values of user-controlled operating parameters. Dialog boxes typically consist of a movable window view. This window usually contains one or more pushbutton objects. Pushbuttons labeled OK and Cancel are used most often to accept or reject modifications made to the operating parameters controlled by a dialog box. Other types of objects found inside dialog boxes include check boxes for turning on and off binary switches, and radio buttons for selecting one of a mutually exclusive set of options. Other view objects found in dialog boxes include text labels and text input fields. This illustration shows a typical dialog box:

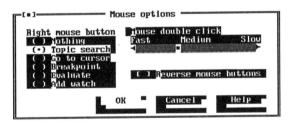

Text Views

Text views are character-oriented output rectangles on the display screen. They are used to display the contents of large data structures such as text editing buffers, long text display messages, text input fields in dialog boxes, and list selection boxes for displaying lists of strings. The following illustration shows a text view with two pane subviews:

Graphics Views

Graphics views are not available in text-oriented window systems. Only graphical user interfaces allow the display of graphics, such as bitmapped graphics icons, lines, circles, and other geometric shapes. Graphical user interfaces allow graphics and text to be displayed in the same window. Graphics views are constructed by using pens, palettes, and paintbrush objects. The details of using such objects are beyond the scope of this book. However, many application frameworks provide shortcuts for creating more common shapes and drawing lines. In fact, the text that is displayed in a graphics window is simulated using graphic representation of characters. This is what makes it possible to display different types of fonts on the computer screen to match the output you will get when printing to a laser printer for WYSIWYG word processors and desktop publishing programs. The following illustration shows a graphics view in which text and graphics output are displayed simultaneously:

Control Views

Control views are special views that respond to user input. For example, buttons can be selected by the user by pointing the mouse at them and pressing the left mouse button. The difference between control views and normal views, which strictly display data, is that control views, when activated, send control messages to the event manager. Control views seem confusing because they are both views and controllers. In order for the user to activate control views, they must be visible on the screen. Therefore, control views share common characteristics of view objects and control objects.

A text editing window or a text input field is classified as a control view rather than a data view because it responds to user input. A text editing window or a text input field must respond to events such as keypresses. For a typical edit view, each keypress causes a character to be displayed in the view. Usually, the character is also appended to a data buffer maintained by the underlying application model. This means that edit views must monitor and respond to user events. This is distinct from a view that exists strictly to display text, such as a file or data buffer viewer. For such views, keypresses do not cause any action to take place—data display views ignore input events except those required to close, move, or resize the view. Consequently, views that exist simply to display data are not classified as control views.

The major control views provided by application frameworks are buttons and button groups, scrollbars, list selectors, and text editors. Text editors are actually a very broad group. They encompass single-line input fields, such as those found in a dialog box, as well as sophisticated control objects that can edit large data buffers and disk files. Some of the more complicated editors include sub-objects to handle searching and replacing of text and include default menus for invoking common editor actions.

Buttons and Button Groups

There are three types of buttons: pushbuttons, check boxes, and radio buttons. *Pushbuttons* are used to activate directly executable commands, for example, the OK and Cancel buttons. *Check boxes* allow the users to turn on or off parameters that have binary values. *Radio buttons* represent a way of specifying one choice out of a mutually exclusive set of choices—they almost always come in groups. The following illustration shows a modem parameter dialog box containing each of these various types of control buttons. Any set of buttons may be bundled together into a group.

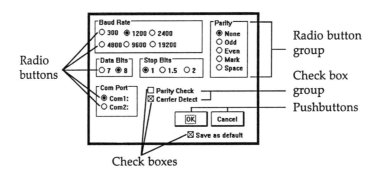

Bundling buttons into a group under a heading, such as "Baud Rate" or "Parity", has the effect of causing control to pass to the entire group when TAB or SHIFT-TAB is pressed. The TAB or SHIFT-TAB key is used to indicate that the user wants to move control to the next field in a dialog box. If there are many check boxes or radio buttons in a dialog box, consolidating them into a group makes it easier to move among the control views in the dialog box.

Scrollbars

Both vertical and horizontal scrollbars are used to specify values that are a percentage of some given range of potential values. For instance, you might want to indicate that you would like a window to position itself to view halfway into a data buffer. You would do this by moving the vertical scrollbar at the right of the window so that the thumb tab is halfway between the up-arrow button at the top of the controller and the down-arrow button at the bottom of the controller. Horizontal scrollbar controllers work in a similar fashion.

Scrollbars can also be used to control volume in a program that generates sound, or to control screen intensity or mouse sensitivity for programs that give users control over such parameters. Vertical scrollbars are frequently used to scroll through long lists of strings in selector boxes. This next illustration shows a view with both horizontal and vertical scrollbars. Note that the file list box, which is activated, uses a vertical scrollbar to scroll among filename strings.

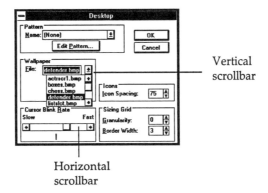

Vertical scrollbar

Horizontal scrollbar

List Selectors

List selectors are seen most frequently in the dialog boxes used to open files. List selectors allow users to select from a long list of strings associated with given objects. For instance, every file in a given disk directory is associated with a string. The user can indicate which file should be opened by pointing at one of the strings, highlighting it, and pressing an OK button. Alternatively, the user can double-click the mouse button on the string. For long lists, the desired string may not appear in the list window. In this case, a vertical scrollbar will appear at the right of the list box and can be used to scroll through the list. A typical list selector box can be seen here:

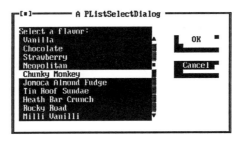

Text Views and Text Editors

Text views and text editors can be used to display and edit text. These are actually forms of controllers, since they're designed to respond to input from the user. These usually have vertical and horizontal scrollbars and have the usual icons for closing, moving, zooming, and resizing the view. Text views also have methods for getting data in and out of the view. Typically, text views work on String objects. String objects can be quite large. String objects can occupy all available program memory, if allowed. Some virtual String objects are sophisticated enough to spool themselves onto and off of a disk, keeping in memory only the portions of the string that are necessary for immediate access. In this respect, Strings are very similar to random-access data files. In fact, in C++ Views, File objects are a subclass of Streams, which are, in turn, a subclass of Strings. This powerful representation of large String objects, and the ability of a text editor to operate on any string, makes it very easy to implement sophisticated text editors in application frameworks. Figure 9-2 shows a text editor view.

```
 File  Edit  Search  Windows
┌[■]══════════════ D:\TP\DOCDEMOS\P11-1.PAS ═══════════════[↕]┐
│program p11_1;                                                │
│                                                             │
│uses App;                                                    │
│                                                             │
│type                                                         │
│  TMyApp = object(TApplication)                              │
│  end;                                                       │
│                                                             │
│var                                                          │
│  MyApp: TMyApp;                                             │
│                                                             │
│begin                                                        │
│  MyApp.Init;                                                │
│  MyApp.Run;                                                 │
│  MyApp.Done;                                                │
│end.                                                         │
│                                                             │
│                                                             │
│┌══ 17:1 ══◄■                                           ►┘
 F2 Save  F3 Open  Alt-F3 Close  F5 Zoom  F6 Next  F10 Menu
```

Figure 9-2.   A text editor view created with Turbo Vision

Special forms of text editors are available to edit single lines of input. These single-line editors are typically used in dialog boxes. The following illustration shows a single-line text editor used as an input field in a dialog box.

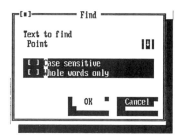

Data Views

Data views exist as a means of displaying different kinds of data that the user is likely to need in a typical application. In a sense, it makes little difference to distinguish between data views and normal windows. However, data views are used primarily to *display* data rather than to *manipulate* it. For example, given a very simple window object, it's easy to create a data-display view for dumping the contents of a file or displaying the contents of a dictionary. Message boxes and dialog boxes that require no input from the user might be considered data-display views. Existing data-view classes provide a quick-and-dirty means for a programmer to get data from an application model and display it for the user. Though dialog boxes consist of control views, dialog boxes themselves are considered data or application views because, technically, it is not the dialog box that responds to user input events, but the control views *built into* a dialog box. The distinction may seem a little arbitrary, but it will become more clear as you gain an understanding of how events are processed by an application program.

PROGRAM STRUCTURE AND ORGANIZATION

As mentioned earlier, application frameworks typically break programs up into three different components: a model, a view, and a controller.

Separation of Application from Views and Controls

Although the model, the view, and the controller constitute the major subdivisions of a program, further subdivisions are necessary. Views contain subviews and controllers contain subcontrollers. Models may contain subcomponents as well. Models are usually simpler than views and controllers, so it is not uncommon for a model to have no subcomponents. Views and controllers, on the other hand, always have subcomponents. For this reason, a hierarchy of views and controllers is established. There is always one main view and one main controller for a program. The main view is called the *top-level view* and the main controller is called the main program event manager or the *main event loop*.

Model-View-Controller

The main reason for separation of the components of a program is to minimize the effects of change on a program. The idea is to make the model as independent as possible of the view and the controller. For this reason, programs are structured so that views know about models, but models know nothing about views. Another way of saying this is that a view maintains a connection or a pointer to the model. The view needs to know about the kinds of information contained inside the model. It is therefore responsible for reading data from the model and writing data to the model when appropriate. Data would be written to the model of a text file, for example, in response to keys typed by the user.

The view must also know about controls used by a program. For this reason, the top-level view maintains a connection to the top-level controller as well. The controller, in turn, must know about the view. The controller needs to pass event messages generated by the user on to the view, and the view decides what to do with the event messages. Sometimes the event messages passed to the view will cause the view to be updated without changing the programming model. For instance, selecting a menu item might cause the top-level view to display an information dialog box as a subview. Display of the dialog box might have no effect on the underlying program model.

Figure 9-3 diagrams the connections between the top-level components of a software structure based on model-view-controller. The data or model component is the most independent; it maintains no connections to the other components. Therefore, any change in either the view or the controller will have no impact on the model.

The view is the central component. It is, therefore, the most volatile and the most sensitive to change. It maintains connections to both the model and the controller. The user does not interact directly with the view; the view merely presents data to the user that it gets from the model, and responds to events generated by the controller.

On the other hand, the user interacts directly with the controller— actually, with subcomponents of the controller. These subcomponents, called *control views*, were discussed earlier. Control views are programmed to generate certain types of messages or commands when they are activated. They can be activated directly by pointing to them with the mouse or clicking a mouse button. Control views can also be activated directly with *hot keys*, which tie keyboard events directly to control subcomponents. The top-level controller always exists. However, the top-level view and subviews create new controllers that are appropriate to the views currently being displayed. For example, when a user opens a new edit view, the edit view automatically creates scrollbar controllers and window icon controllers for moving, resizing, and closing the window. In addition, a typical view

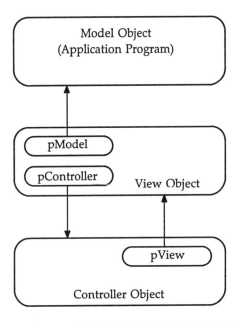

Figure 9-3.   Many application frameworks use model-view-controller objects as major functional program divisions, making the model or underlying application as independent as possible from the operating system and window system used to display data.

will create and add menus to the top-level menu bar. Menus are technically a form of controller that have a view associated with them.

Control Mechanisms Versus Control Components

It's often confusing to make the distinction between the top-level controller and the control components in a program. The top-level controller is a loop that reads all input events and dispatches the events to the top-level view. The top-level view decides what to do with the events. If a programmer wants a program to respond to keypresses or mouse movement events within a window, for example, event handlers need to be encoded in the top-level view for the application. Event gathering and dispatch at the highest level are therefore controlled by the main event loop.

The main event loop is the primary control mechanism for the program. However, the programmer needs to provide control components in the form of control views in order for a user to indicate that a certain type of action is desired. Providing a menu, a pushbutton, or a check box within a view automatically enables event generation if a user activates the control view. However, simply because a control view generates an event does not mean that the program will respond to it. To complete the control cycle, the programmer needs to create both control components to allow the user to generate events and to define event handlers within views and subviews, which respond to the events. The event handlers may simply update views, close views, or create new subviews. In addition, event handlers may change data in the underlying model, or the views may update themselves by reading new data from the model. In order to have a complete under-standing of the model-view-controller structure, you need to understand the event gathering and dispatching mechanism of the top-level controller.

EVENT-DRIVEN CONTROL

Event-driven control is a natural consequence of a program organization based on model-view-controller. Rather than have each and every subrou-tine of a program be responsible for monitoring the various hardware devices for potential input activity, the central control mechanism monitors all hardware devices for input. The central control mechanism or event manager then passes all events on to the top-level view, which has been programmed to handle the events and dispatch them to the appropriate subviews. The subviews, in turn, may pass the events on to other subviews or they may consume the events. Any subview may directly manipulate the model or submodel to which it is attached.

Gathering Events

Each time a key is pressed, a character arrives at a serial port, the mouse pointer is moved, or a button on the mouse is pressed, the event is noted and placed in an event queue by the event manager. Each event is placed on one end of this first-in first-out queue. Program control at the highest level is implemented as a loop, which reads the next event from the event queue and then dispatches the event to the top-level view. The top-level view, in turn, passes the event on to the appropriate subview.

Main Event Loop

All events in a program based on model-view-controller at the highest level pass through the main event. The main event loop is sometimes referred to as the *top-level controller* and maintains a direct connection to the top-level view. The top-level view, in turn, maintains a direct connection to the main event loop. The main event loop is responsible for reading events placed in the event queue by the event manager.

The main event loop is actually one of the easiest program structures to understand in a typical application framework. The pseudocode for the main event loop looks like this:

```
forever
    e = readNextEvent
    dispatchEvent(e)
```

The code that implements this main event loop is something that you will never see, unless you implement your own application framework. This code exists inside the application framework class library and is really of little interest other than to understand how events work. More important is knowing how to activate the event read/dispatch mechanism. This is typically done with a single call. Before this call can be made, however, certain classes must be defined, certain objects must be created, and certain initializations must occur. For example, in Turbo Vision, an application class must be created by deriving the new class from the existing class, called TApplication. The following code creates such a class template in Turbo Pascal:

```
type
  TMyApp = object(TApplication)
end;
```

This code defines a new class template for creating objects. The new class is called TMyApp. Next, the program needs to create an instance of this main application object, which is a form of view.

A new object called MyApp can be created from TMyApp with the following variable declaration in Turbo Pascal:

```
var
  MyApp: TMyApp;
```

Finally, the main program consists of only three statements:

```
begin
  MyApp.Init;
  MyApp.Run;
  MyApp.Done;
end.
```

The first statement, MyApp.Init, performs all the initialization required by the application object. The second statement, MyApp.Run, activates the event read/dispatch mechanism. (Sometimes this mechanism is simply referred to as the *event dispatcher* or the *main event loop*.) This mechanism remains active until the user indicates that the program should be terminated. This is usually done by selecting an exit command from a menu or status bar line at the bottom of the screen. When the exit command is given, the main event loop is deactivated, and the program control loop passes to the last statement, MyApp.Done. At this point, any cleanup necessary for the application takes place, and the program terminates.

Setting up a C++ Views application program is equally simple. Here is the entire main program for a typical C++ application:

```
main()
{
    MyAppView  *v;

    v = new MyAppView();
    v->show();
    notifier.start();
}
```

The main event loop for C++ Views is encapsulated inside the Notifier class. A global instance of this class, called notifier, is generated automatically by all applications. All the programmer has to do is create an application view:

```
v = new MyAppView();
```

Next, the view must be displayed on the screen. This does not happen automatically when the view is created, so the following call is necessary to force display of the new view objects:

```
v->show();
```

Finally, the main event loop is activated.

```
notifier.start();
```

That is all the programming necessary to get a simple application up and running in C++ Views. Normally, applications are slightly more complicated. Programmers typically must create a model and attach that model to the top-level view. It is then the user's responsibility to dispose of the model object when the event loop terminates.

Dispatching Events

Dispatching of events at the top level is handled automatically by the program. If only the top-level view needs to respond to dispatching events, the programmer need not worry about handling events at all. However, if the programmer creates subviews or adds control events to views to do special processing, event handlers in the top-level view can be programmed to be dispatched to subviews or to parent views.

Handling Events

Neither of the previous programs actually implements event handlers. There are generic event handlers built into both application frameworks so that a program template can be created and tested with minimal effort. Of course, these programs don't do anything interesting. In order for programs to do anything beyond even the most basic display of the desktop and application framework exit commands, event handlers must be defined.

Hello Again, World

In application frameworks that provide multiple resizeable windows, you cannot simply write text anywhere on the screen as you would with C's printf or Pascal's writeln routines. You must first open a window and then write the strings to the window in a special manner. Actually, you must provide a method that writes the desired string to the window every time it is necessary to update the window contents. The window contents would automatically be updated, for example, if a second window were moved to cover it, and then the second window were closed or moved away. Such an occurrence is called an *exposure event*. Exposure events automatically send messages to all windows on the desktop, along with a rectangle parameter indicating the region that has been exposed. The window can then see if it needs to redraw any portion of itself and does so by calling the view's draw method in Turbo Vision or the view's paint or show method in C++ Views.

Report Dialogs

Shortcuts exist in both frameworks to create simple dialog box windows that display string messages. The programmer simply calls a dialog box routine and passes arguments, including the string to be printed. These types of dialogs are called *report dialogs*. The report dialog opens on the screen, displays the string, and waits for the user to either activate the OK pushbutton or to close the window through the control icon at the upper-left corner of the screen.

Two complete example programs are provided here to show how to print "Hello, world" in dialog boxes. The first version is for Turbo Vision.

```
uses App Objects, MsgBox;

type
  TMyApp = object(TApplication)
  end;

procedure ReportDialog(S: String);
var
  R: TRect;
  C: Word;
begin
  R.Assign(25,5,55,12);
  C := MessageBoxRect(R, S, nil, mfInformation + mfOkButton);
end;

var
  MyApp: TMyApp;

begin
  MyApp.Init;
  ReportDialog('Hello, world');
  MyApp.Run;
  MyApp.Done;
end.
```

The only difference between this Turbo Vision program and the previous Turbo Vision program is the definition and call to the new procedure, ReportDialog. The ReportDialog procedure accepts a string as an argument. It then creates a rectangle object and assigns its dimensions on the desktop.

Next, the procedure MessageBoxRect is called, with the rectangle as the first parameter and the string as the second parameter. The third argument, nil, is a pointer to a list of parameters. The string variable, S, which is passed to MessageBoxRect, is actually a format string very similar to the first argument passed to C's printf library routine. Together, the second and third arguments of MessageBoxRect provide the same powerful formatting capabilities of printf. Formatting is not used here since it is only necessary to print a simple string variable. (For more information on how to use formatted output strings, see the FormatStr procedure documented in Turbo Pascal's *Turbo Vision Guide*.) The example programs in Chapter 14, "ObjectWindows: A Language-Independent Application Framework", show how this formatting is done with ObjectWindows.

The fourth and final argument to MessageBoxRect contains several bit fields to specify dialog box options. Bit-field arguments are added together using the + operator. The bit-field arguments specify the type of window (mfInformation) and any control-view buttons that should be included in the window (mfOkButton, mfCancelButton, mfYesButton, mfNoButton). You may include one, two, three, or all four buttons in the message dialog box by simply adding together the desired buttons. The dialog box will automatically be resized to accommodate all the buttons.

The MessageBoxRect function is defined in the Turbo Pascal unit Msg-Box (found in the file MSGBOX.PAS). In order to use this function you must specify the unit in the "uses" clause declared at the top of the program. In order to create and use rectangle objects defined by TRect, you must also include the Objects unit. Finally, all Turbo Vision applications must include the App unit so the uses line now has two more elements than the Turbo Vision program shown in Figure 9-2.

```
uses App, Objects, MsgBox;
```

When this program is run, the resulting screen will appear like that in Figure 9-4.

The C++ Views example "Hello, world" dialog closely parallels the Turbo Vision implementation.

```
#include "notifier.h"
#include "appview.h"
#include "report.h"

char *CTWindow = __FILE__;
```

```
class MyAppView : public AppView
{
public:
    MyAppView()      {}            // constructor
    ~MyAppView()     {}            // destructor
    boolean free() { delete this; return TRUE; }
    Class   *iam();
};

defineClass(MyAppView,AppView)  // defines iam method

main()
{
    MyAppView  *v;

    v = new MyAppView();
    v->setTitle("Main Application Window");
    v->show();

    Report::dialog("Information", v, "Hello, world");
    notifier.start();
}
```

It is not necessary to define a separate routine ReportDialog because the Report class provided by C++ Views does the work for you. The dialog method within report is static, making it possible to invoke the method

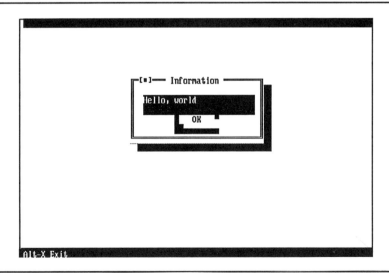

Figure 9-4.   Desktop and dialog box resulting from Turbo Vision "Hello, world" program

without creating an object of type Report as long as the call to the method is preceded by the Report:: scope specifier. In order to use this method, you must include the header file REPORT.H before reference to the method is made. The first argument to the report method is the title to be displayed in the dialog window. The second argument is a pointer to the window which is the parent of the dialog window. In this case, the parent window is the main application window. The third argument is again a format string like that accepted by the standard printf library routine. If format specifiers such as %s or %d were included in the format string, additional arguments of the appropriate type would then be appended to the argument list. Running the previous C++ program produces the screen shown in Figure 9-5.

CHAPTER HIGHLIGHTS

Application frameworks are class libraries that provide the basic structure and user interface components for application programs. Components of application frameworks are broken up into three functional categories: models, views, and controllers.

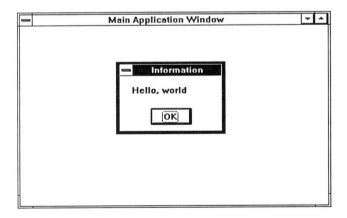

Figure 9-5.   Desktop and dialog box resulting from C++ Views "Hello, world" program

- *Models* manipulate data and are often the only part of a program that must be built by a programmer.

- *Views* are windows used to display data from the model.

- *Controllers* accept input from the user and translate input events into messages sent to other objects in the application.

Application frameworks do most of the work of managing output to windows and getting input from the keyboard and mouse. A window manager and an event manager take the place of control constructs and sequences of statements specified by the programmer in typical structured programs. Programming an event-driven system requires that you think in terms of events you want your program to react to or handle rather than thinking in terms of the sequence of statements the program will follow from beginning to end.

Keep in mind that Smalltalk and Actor *are* application frameworks, even though they are not usually called application frameworks. The class libraries for Smalltalk and Actor provide most of the interface components and event-management objects required by an application. As C and Pascal have been extended to support object-oriented programming, many designers have seen the leverage made available to the programmer by these class libraries and have sought to bring some of that power to class libraries for C++ and object-oriented Pascal.

While this chapter has covered the basic characteristics of application frameworks, the remaining chapters will show specific examples of application frameworks for C++ and object-oriented Pascal, including Turbo Vision, C++ Views, and ObjectWindows.

10

TURBO VISION: CONSTRUCTING MENUS FOR A CHARACTER-ORIENTED APPLICATION FRAMEWORK

The previous chapter introduced the general characteristics of an application framework. The model-view-controller components of a typical application framework were presented along with automated window and event management. This chapter and those that follow show specific application frameworks solving common programming problems.

This chapter uses Turbo Vision to show how to construct menus and menu command handlers. Menus are specific types of controller objects within an application framework. As you'll see, there's more to a menu than what it looks like on the screen. Application frameworks make it easy to specify command events to be generated when a user selects a specific menu entry. All you need to do to complete the picture is build event-handler methods to respond to each menu command event you've specified for the menu.

The advantage of using event-driven command dispatch is that you can test the look and feel of your menus before you build any event-handler methods. Using such an incremental development strategy, you can prototype and test the user interface for an entire application in less than a day.

When programming with Turbo Vision, you will create many different types of views. The two most common types of views that nearly every program requires are menus and dialog boxes. If you're reading carefully, you'll notice that the above paragraphs refer to a menu as both a view and a controller. Recall that a controller receives input from the user and translates the input into messages, which are sent to the appropriate objects. A view is a window used to display graphics or text. A menu is both a view and a controller because it is a visible window, and it receives input from the user and dispatches messages. A menu is a special form of controller that is visible. *Visible controllers* are necessary to guide the user when directing commands at visible objects on the display screen. Other examples of visible controllers include pushbuttons, radio buttons, check boxes, and text edit fields found in dialog boxes. Scrollbars are another type of visible controller. Contrast these types of controllers with the event manager, which is not visible anywhere on the screen. Visible controllers are often called *control views*, which are the primary components you'll use to build interfaces for your programs when working with an application framework.

Without an application framework, most programming effort usually goes into the construction and maintenance of user-interface components. Turbo Vision makes it extremely easy to build menus and dialog boxes. Chapter 9 showed the basic structure of the most simple Turbo Vision program. This chapter starts with that same example and shows how to build more complex and realistic application programs. Here, again, is the simplest possible Turbo Vision program:

```
program template;

uses App;

type
  TMyApp = object(TApplication)
  end;

var
  MyApp: TMyApp;

begin
  MyApp.Init;
  MyApp.Run;
  MyApp.Done;
end.
```

When run, this program simply creates and displays the desktop, including a menu bar at the top of the screen and a status bar at the bottom of the screen. However, no other views are displayed. The only thing you can do with this program is exit from it by clicking on the Alt-X control-view icon in the status bar at the bottom of the screen. Alternatively, the ALT-X key combination can be pressed as a shortcut.

CREATING A SIMPLE MENU

The first thing you need to do to make any application useful is to add menus to the menu bar at the top of the screen. Menu controls can be added to a program automatically by specifying a special method in the main user-defined application class, in this case TMyApp. The method is called InitMenuBar and is declared inside TMyApp.

```
type
  TMyApp = object(TApplication)
    procedure InitMenuBar; virtual;
  end;
```

In addition to the declaration, the actual method must be defined.

```
procedure TMyApp.InitMenuBar;
var
  R: TRect;
begin
  GetExtent(R);
  R.B.Y := R.A.Y + 1;
  MenuBar := New(PMenuBar, Init(R, NewMenu(
    NewSubMenu('Menu 1', hcNoContext,
      NewMenu(
        NewItem('Choice 1', '', 0, 100, hcNoContext,
        nil)                    { 1 ) for each NewItem }
      ),
      nil )                     { 1 ) for each NewMenu }
    )));
end;
```

This procedure creates a new menu bar and then adds one submenu to it.

Figure 10-1 shows the screen when this submenu is active. The main menu bar has no label associated with it. However, each submenu that appears as a control view on the menu bar has a string label. This string label is specified as the first argument to the NewSubMenu function for each submenu added to the top-level menu bar. For instance, the following expression,

```
NewSubMenu('Menu 1', hcNoContext, NewMenu(...), nil)
```

creates a single submenu with the label "Menu 1". This is the string that will appear as a control view in the menu bar at the top of the screen.

You can chain together a number of these submenus. In the previous statement the last argument is nil, indicating that this menu is the last in a sequence of menus within the top menu bar. However, the last argument could also be another NewSubMenu, in which case, there would be at least a second submenu appearing in the top menu bar. Submenus within the top submenu bar are maintained as a linked list, with each submenu maintaining a pointer to the next submenu. If a submenu's pointer has a value of nil, it means that submenu is the last in the list.

The choice items within a submenu are also maintained as a linked list. The InitMenuBar procedure adds only one choice item to the Menu 1 submenu.

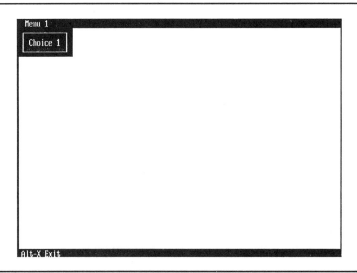

Figure 10-1.   Menu bar initialized with one menu. The menu is active and contains one choice item.

```
NewItem('Choice 1', '', 0, 100, hcNoContext, nil)
```

The first argument to NewItem is the string that appears in the menu. The last argument is a pointer to the next choice item in the menu. If the last argument is nil, this menu item is the last in the list of choices for the given menu. This is all the code that is necessary to create and activate a simple menu.

Program 10-1 shows a complete program using the InitMenuBar method defined above.

```
Program 10_1;

uses App, Objects, Menus, Views;

type
  TMyApp = object(TApplication)
    procedure InitMenuBar; virtual;
  end;

procedure TMyApp.InitMenuBar;
var
  R: TRect;
begin
  GetExtent(R);
  R.B.Y := R.A.Y + 1;
  MenuBar := New(PMenuBar, Init(R, NewMenu(
    NewSubMenu('Menu 1', hcNoContext,
      NewMenu(
        NewItem('Choice 1', '', 0, 100, hcNoContext,
        nil)                        { 1 ) for each NewItem }
      ),
      nil )                         { 1 ) for each NewMenu }
    )));
end;

var
  MyApp: TMyApp;

begin
  MyApp.Init;
  MyApp.Run;
  MyApp.Done;
end.
```

Program 10-1.   InitMenuBar method is used here to create a simple menu bar.

Notice that InitMenuBar is defined as a virtual procedure.

```
type
  TMyApp = object(TApplication)
    procedure InitMenuBar; virtual;
  end;
```

Recall the discussion of virtual functions and dynamic binding from Chapter 3, "Inheritance, Polymorphism, and Object-Oriented Programming". Through the polymorphism provided by deriving TMyApp from TApplication, the procedure TMyApp.InitMenuBar; is invoked automatically in Program 10-1 even though no direct call to the TMyApp.Init-MenuBar is specified. TMyApp inherits a number of methods from TApplication, including Init, Run, and Done. TApplication, in turn, inherits most of its methods from TProgram.

The following listing diagrams the inheritance tree for the three classes in question, where TMyApp is a new class defined by the programmer.

```
TProgram
  TApplication
    TMyApp
```

The constructor for TApplication does a number of things, the last of which is to call TProgram.Init.

```
constructor TApplication.Init
begin
  .
  .
  .
  TProgram.Init;
end;
```

The TProgram class also defines the virtual methods InitDeskTop, Init-MenuBar, and InitStatusLine. The last thing that TProgram.Init does is call each of these virtual methods.

```
constructor TProgram.Init
begin
  .
  .
  .
  InitDeskTop;
  InitStatusLine;
  InitMenuBar;
end;
```

Because these methods are virtual, calls to them are directed to the appropriate subclass methods, which override the default base class definitions. TProgram defines default methods for InitDeskTop, InitStatusLine, and InitMenuBar. If the programmer does not override these base class methods, they are invoked automatically through the call:

```
MyApp.Init;
```

The default method TProgram.InitMenuBar creates a menu bar at the top of the screen with no entries in it. If you want entries to appear in the menu, all you need to do is override TProgram.InitMenuBar by defining TMyApp.InitMenuBar. There is, however, no need to call TMyApp.InitMenuBar directly from your program. Because this method is defined as virtual, the call MyApp.Init invokes TMyApp.InitMenuBar automatically through the object-oriented dynamic binding mechanism provided by Turbo Pascal. Figure 10-2 diagrams the manner in which dynamic binding invokes TMyApp.InitMenuBar indirectly through TProgram.Init.

MULTIPLE MENUS WITH MULTIPLE CHOICES

Most programs provide more than one menu and most menus provide more than one choice item. The following fragment modifies TMyApp.InitBar to add two submenus to the top-level menu bar.

```
procedure TMyApp.InitMenuBar;
var
  R: TRect;
begin
  GetExtent(R);
  R.B.Y := R.A.Y + 1;
  MenuBar := New(PMenuBar, Init(R, NewMenu(
    NewSubMenu('Menu 1  ', hcNoContext,
      NewMenu(
        NewItem('Choice 101', '', 0, 101, hcNoContext,
        NewItem('Choice 102', '', 0, 102, hcNoContext,
        NewItem('Choice 103', '', 0, 103, hcNoContext,
        nil )))                 { 1 ) for each NewItem }
      ),
    NewSubMenu('Menu 2  ', hcNoContext,
      NewMenu(
        NewItem('Choice 201', '', 0, 201, hcNoContext,
```

```
    NewItem('Choice 202', '', 0, 202, hcNoContext,
    NewItem('Choice 203', '', 0, 203, hcNoContext,
    nil )))                { l ) for each NewItem }
  ),
 nil ))                    { l ) for each NewSubMenu }
 )));
end;
```

What this method effectively does is create a list with two submenus.

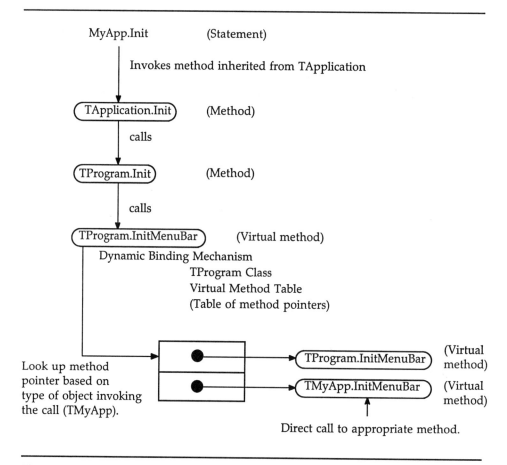

Figure 10-2.   Dynamic binding mechanism used to call InitMenuBar

The following illustration shows the two menus that result from initializing the menu bar with the previous method.

```
┌─────────────────────┐        ┌─────────────────────┐
│ Menu 1    Menu 2    │        │ Menu 1    Menu 2    │
│ ┌─────────────┐     │        │      ┌─────────────┐│
│ │ Choice 101  │     │        │      │ Choice 201  ││
│ │ Choice 102  │     │        │      │ Choice 202  ││
│ │ Choice 103  │     │        │      │ Choice 203  ││
│ └─────────────┘     │        │      └─────────────┘│
└─────────────────────┘        └─────────────────────┘
```

Submenus are linked together by replacing nil as the last argument

```
NewSubMenu('Menu 1 ', ... nil)
```

with yet another nested call to NewSubMenu.

```
NewSubMenu('Menu 1 ', ... NewSubMenu(...))
```

Lists of menu items work the same way. For menu-item lists containing more than one choice, the last argument, nil, to the function NewItem

```
NewItem('Choice 101', ... nil)
```

is replaced with:

```
NewItem('Choice 101', ... NewItem(...))
```

Figure 10-3 diagrams the tree structure created by these nested sub-menu and choice-item lists.

Program 10-2 includes the modified TMyApp.InitMenuBar method.

The application shown in Program 10-2 currently does nothing when any of the menu items is selected. You need a way to invoke specific procedures or methods when menu items are selected. In a way, it's nice that you don't have to specify the procedures that react to menu-item selection in order to build and test menus. To get your application to do anything useful, however, you need to build a dispatch mechanism to handle events generated by selecting menu items.

MENUS AND EVENTS

Menu items are selected either by pressing the left mouse button while-pointing at a menu-item choice string, or by moving the menu highlight bar

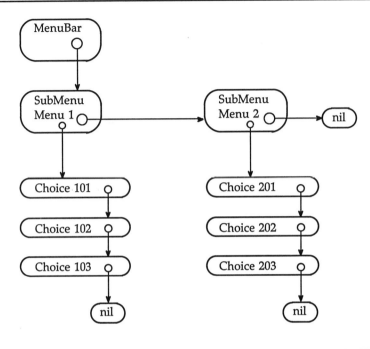

Figure 10-3.   Menu bar objects and links created by TMyApp.InitMenuBar

to the desired menu choice with the keyboard arrow keys and pressing RETURN (ENTER). When a menu item is selected, Turbo Vision automatically generates an event. Turbo Vision generates and handles many different types of events. The type of event generated by selecting a menu item is called a *command event*. Though it was not explicitly pointed out, the previous definition of TMyApp.InitMenuBar did indicate the command events to be dispatched when the user selected any of the specified menu choice items. You need to distinguish between *dispatching* events and *handling* events. You specify the events that you want dispatched in the menu items themselves. The Turbo Vision main event loop then dispatches these events automatically, based on input from the user. It's up to the programmer, however, to specify how these events are to be handled. Let's look more closely at how events are dispatched.

```
Program 10_2;

uses App, Objects, Menus, Views;

type
  TMyApp = object(TApplication)
    procedure InitMenuBar; virtual;
  end;

procedure TMyApp.InitMenuBar;
var
  R: TRect;
begin
  GetExtent(R);
  R.B.Y := R.A.Y + 1;
  MenuBar := New(PMenuBar, Init(R, NewMenu(
    NewSubMenu('Menu 1  ', hcNoContext,
      NewMenu(
        NewItem('Choice 101', '', 0, 101, hcNoContext,
        NewItem('Choice 102', '', 0, 102, hcNoContext,
        NewItem('Choice 103', '', 0, 103, hcNoContext,
        nil )))              { 1 ) for each NewItem }
      ),
    NewSubMenu('Menu 2  ', hcNoContext,
      NewMenu(
        NewItem('Choice 201', '', 0, 201, hcNoContext,
        NewItem('Choice 202', '', 0, 202, hcNoContext,
        NewItem('Choice 203', '', 0, 203, hcNoContext,
        nil )))              { 1 ) for each NewItem }
      ),
    nil ))                   { 1 ) for each NewSubMenu }
  )));
end;

var
  MyApp: TMyApp;

begin
  MyApp.Init;
  MyApp.Run;
  MyApp.Done;
end.
```

Program 10-2.   TMyApp.InitMenuBar method modified to create two menus with three choices each

Dispatching Events

First of all, the menus must be set up in such a way that each menu item specifies a unique command-event message. Command events are represented by a unique integer and are specified as the fourth argument in a call to the procedure NewItem.

```
NewSubMenu('Menu 1  ', hcNoContext,
  NewMenu(
    NewItem('Choice 101', '', 0, 101, hcNoContext,
    NewItem('Choice 102', '', 0, 102, hcNoContext,
    NewItem('Choice 103', '', 0, 103, hcNoContext,
    nil )))                 { 1 ) for each NewItem }
```

For example, the above code fragment specifies three new menu items for a menu. The integer command codes for the respective menu items are 101, 102, and 103. The second menu added to Program 10-2 specifies the additional command-event integers 201, 202, and 203:

```
NewSubMenu('Menu 2  ', hcNoContext,
  NewMenu(
    NewItem('Choice 201', '', 0, 201, hcNoContext,
    NewItem('Choice 202', '', 0, 202, hcNoContext,
    NewItem('Choice 203', '', 0, 203, hcNoContext,
    nil )))                 { 1 ) for each NewItem }
  ),
```

Handling Events

For every unique command code specified in the application menu tree, there is usually a corresponding case switch in an event handler that is defined as a member method of the user-defined application class.

```
procedure TMyApp.HandleEvent(var Event: TEvent);
begin
  TApplication.HandleEvent(Event);
  if Event.What = evCommand then
  begin
    case Event.Command of
      101: ReportDialog('Execute command 101');
      102: ReportDialog('Execute command 102');
      103: ReportDialog('Execute command 103');
      201: ReportDialog('Execute command 201');
      202: ReportDialog('Execute command 202');
      203: ReportDialog('Execute command 203');
    else
      Exit;
    end;
    ClearEvent(Event);
  end;
end;
```

This event-handler method is called every time a menu choice item is selected from one of the menus within a Turbo Vision application. If you want nothing to happen when a particular menu item is selected, simply leave the command integer and associated statement out of the case statement in the event handler. Each of the commands in the preceding event handler calls the global procedure ReportDialog with a string uniquely identifying the invoking command. This technique provides a quick way to see that the event handler is properly dispatching calls for each of the menu items you have specified. The ReportDialog procedure was introduced in Chapter 9 and is shown again here for reference.

```
procedure ReportDialog(S: String);
var
  R: TRect;
  C: Word;
begin
  R.Assign(25,5,55,12);
  C := MessageBoxRect(R, s, nil, mfInformation + mfOkButton);
end;
```

In order to define the TMyApp.HandleEvent method, it must first be declared as a member of TMyApp at the top of the program file:

```
type
  TMyApp = object(TApplication)
    procedure InitMenuBar; virtual;
    procedure HandleEvent(var Event: TEvent); virtual;
  end;
```

Program 10-3 shows a complete program that creates two menus with three choices in each menu. The command-event handler provides a case switch for each menu item.

The following illustration shows the dialog box generated by selecting the third menu choice item from the second menu bar submenu.

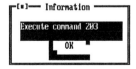

```
Program 10_3;

uses App, Objects, MsgBox,
     Menus, Views, Drivers;

type
  TMyApp = object(TApplication)
    procedure InitMenuBar; virtual;
    procedure HandleEvent(var Event: TEvent); virtual;
  end;

procedure ReportDialog(S: String);
var
  R: TRect;
  C: Word;
begin
  R.Assign(25,5,55,12);
  C := MessageBoxRect(R, s, nil, mfInformation + mfOkButton);
end;

procedure TMyApp.InitMenuBar;
var
  R: TRect;
begin
  GetExtent(R);
  R.B.Y := R.A.Y + 1;
  MenuBar := New(PMenuBar, Init(R, NewMenu(
    NewSubMenu('Menu 1  ', hcNoContext,
      NewMenu(
        NewItem('Choice 101', '', 0, 101, hcNoContext,
        NewItem('Choice 102', '', 0, 102, hcNoContext,
        NewItem('Choice 103', '', 0, 103, hcNoContext,
        nil )))              { 1 ) for each NewItem }
      ),
    NewSubMenu('Menu 2  ', hcNoContext,
      NewMenu(
        NewItem('Choice 201', '', 0, 201, hcNoContext,
        NewItem('Choice 202', '', 0, 202, hcNoContext,
        NewItem('Choice 203', '', 0, 203, hcNoContext,
        nil )))              { 1 ) for each NewItem }
      ),
    nil ))                   { 1 ) for each NewSubMenu }
  )));
end;

procedure TMyApp.HandleEvent(var Event: TEvent);
begin
  TApplication.HandleEvent(Event);
  if Event.What = evCommand then
  begin
```

Program 10-3.   Application with two menus, three choices each, and command-event handler that provides a case switch for each choice

```
   case Event.Command of
     101: ReportDialog('Execute command 101');
     102: ReportDialog('Execute command 102');
     103: ReportDialog('Execute command 103');
     201: ReportDialog('Execute command 201');
     202: ReportDialog('Execute command 202');
     203: ReportDialog('Execute command 203');
   else
     Exit;
   end;
   ClearEvent(Event);
  end;
end;

var
  MyApp: TMyApp;

begin
  MyApp.Init;
  MyApp.Run;
  MyApp.Done;
end.
```

Program 10-3.   *Continued*

SPECIAL MENU FEATURES

Using Turbo Vision menus is straightforward. You activate a submenu in the top-level menu bar by pointing at the menu's name with a mouse pointer and pressing the left mouse button. The menu view then appears, displaying all the choice items. The menu is now active, and you can select a choice item from the menu by pointing at the item with the mouse and pressing the left mouse button.

Some users prefer to use keystrokes to activate menu items. Either a mouse is not available, or fast interaction with the program is desired. In such a case, pressing F10 causes the top-level menu bar to become active. A highlight bar appears over the name of the first submenu when the menu bar is activated. The LEFT ARROW and RIGHT ARROW keys can be used to move the highlight in the menu bar to various submenu names. With the highlight on the desired menu, press RETURN to activate the associated menu. The

UP ARROW and DOWN ARROW keys can be used to move the item selector highlight bar among the menu items in the active menu. Pressing RETURN with one of these menu items highlighted causes the command event associated with that menu item to be generated.

Shortcut Keys

Once you become familiar with an application, the method of invoking menu-item commands begins to feel awkward. Most users are familiar with shortcut keystrokes provided by program development environments and other application programs with pull-down menus. For instance, if a menu bar at the top of the screen contains submenus with the names "File" and "Search", the File menu can usually be activated by pressing ALT-F. This is indicated by displaying the letter *F* underlined, highlighted, or in a different color from the rest of the menu name string. In addition, the choices that appear in a normal File menu also provide similarly highlighted letters to invoke menu items, once the File menu has been activated. Figure 10-4 shows the File menu inside the Turbo Pascal integrated development environment. After pressing ALT-F to activate this menu, you can now press N to activate the New command, O to activate the Open command, S to activate the Save command, and so forth.

Turbo Vision provides a number of ways to specify shortcut or accelerator keys for quickly invoking menu-item commands from the keyboard. Going back to Program 10-2 you can specify shortcut keys similar to those discussed for the File menu by surrounding the appropriate letters of the submenu and menu-item name strings with the ~ (tilde) character.

```
MenuBar := New(PMenuBar, Init(R, NewMenu(
  NewSubMenu('Menu ~1~ ', hcNoContext,
    NewMenu(
      NewItem('Choice 10~1~', '', 0, 101, hcNoContext,
      NewItem('Choice 10~2~', '', 0, 102, hcNoContext,
      NewItem('Choice 10~3~', '', 0, 103, hcNoContext,
      nil )))              { 1 ) for each NewItem }
    ),
  NewSubMenu('Menu ~2~ ', hcNoContext,
    NewMenu(
      NewItem('Choice 20~1~', '', 0, 201, hcNoContext,
      NewItem('Choice 20~2~', '', 0, 202, hcNoContext,
      NewItem('Choice 20~3~', '', 0, 203, hcNoContext,
      nil)))               { 1 ) for each NewItem }
    ),
```

```
   nil ))                        { 1 } for each NewSubMenu }
 )));
```

The characters surrounded by the tildes (for example, the *1* in ~1~) in the name strings will appear either in a different color than the rest of the string on a color monitor or in inverse video on a monochrome monitor.

If no menus are currently active when the program is run with this modification, pressing ALT-1 will cause Menu 1 to be activated. Subsequently, pressing 2 will generate the command event associated with the second choice in that menu. Alternatively, you can activate the third choice in the second menu by pressing ALT-2, 3.

Accelerator Keys

Sometimes commands are invoked so frequently that even more direct command dispatch from the keyboard is desired. For example, files are opened and saved so frequently that many applications provide single

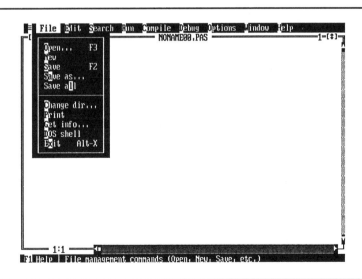

Figure 10-4.   File menu found in Turbo Pascal integrated development environment

keystrokes to evoke the Open and Save commands found in a typical File menu. Pressing F3 in the Turbo Pascal integrated development environment automatically invokes the Open File dialog box without ever causing the File menu itself to appear. Similarly, pressing F2 causes the file in the currently active edit window to be saved to disk. The third argument to NewItem lets you specify a single keyboard *accelerator key*, which will directly generate the associated command event without activating the menu in which the menu-item choice is defined. For example, the following code assigns the function keys F1, F2, and F3 to directly generate the command events 101, 102, and 103.

```
NewMenu(
    NewItem('Choice 10~1~', '', kbF1, 101, hcNoContext,
    NewItem('Choice 10~2~', '', kbF2, 102, hcNoContext,
    NewItem('Choice 10~3~', '', kbF3, 103, hcNoContext,
    nil )))                { 1 ) for each NewItem }
  ),
```

Pressing F2 will now cause the command event 102 to be generated.

You cannot use the same keys in the second menu or a conflict will occur. For this reason you might want to use a parallel set of keys, such as ALT-F1, ALT-F2, and ALT-F3 to invoke the commands in the second menu.

```
NewMenu(
    NewItem('Choice 20~1~', '', kbAltF1, 201, hcNoContext,
    NewItem('Choice 20~2~', '', kbAltF2, 202, hcNoContext,
    NewItem('Choice 20~3~', '', kbAltF3, 203, hcNoContext,
    nil)))                 { 1 ) for each NewItem }
  ),
```

Turbo Vision defines a number of extended keyboard key combinations that can be used for accelerator key specifications. A list of these keys can be found in the DRIVERS.INT file found in the DOC subdirectory. A list is also included in the appendix of the *Turbo Vision Guide.*

Accelerator Key String Names

The second argument to NewItem allows you to specify a second string that will appear in the menu entry. The second string appears to the left of the first string in the menu entry. The second string is used to remind the user that an accelerator combination key exists as a means of activating the associated command event. Typically, several of the items within a menu will contain accelerator key strings. These strings are all printed in the same column. The position of the column is adjusted automatically to accommodate the largest menu-entry string (the first argument to NewItem), which appears to the left of the accelerator key strings. The following listing shows how to create a submenu that specifies such accelerator key strings.

```
NewSubMenu('Menu ˜1˜  ', hcNoContext,
   NewMenu(
     NewItem('Choice 10˜1˜', 'F1', kbF1, 101, hcNoContext,
     NewItem('Choice 10˜2˜', 'F2', kbF2, 102, hcNoContext,
     NewItem('Choice 10˜3˜', 'F3', kbF3, 103, hcNoContext,
     nil )))                { 1 ) for each NewItem }
   ),
   NewSubMenu('Menu ˜2˜  ', hcNoContext,
   NewMenu(
     NewItem('Choice 20˜1˜', 'Alt-F1', kbAltF1, 201, hcNoContext,
     NewItem('Choice 20˜2˜', 'Alt-F2', kbAltF2, 202, hcNoContext,
     NewItem('Choice 20˜3˜', 'Alt-F3', kbAltF3, 203, hcNoContext,
     nil)))                 { 1 ) for each NewItem }
   ),
   nil ))                    { 1 ) for each NewSubMenu }
```

This illustration shows both of the new menus resulting from this specification.

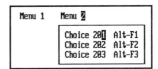

Using Symbolic Constants for Command Events

Other features you will want to use in creating menus include horizontal *bar separators* and user-defined *symbolic constants* to help keep track of a large number of command-event integers. To complete the menu example and show these features, three new items will be added to Menu 1: a newline separator; an About command, invoked by the ALT-A accelerator key; and an Exit command, invoked by the ALT-X accelerator key. To implement these changes, the single line in the last listing:

```
nil )))                    { 1 ) for each NewItem }
```

is replaced by the following:

```
NewLine(
  NewItem('~A~bout',  'Alt-A', kbAltA,  cmAbout, hcNoContext,
  NewItem('E~x~it',   'Alt-X', kbAltX,  cmQuit, hcNoContext,
  nil ))))))                 { 1 ) for each NewItem }
```

The NewLine function inserts a horizontal spacing bar, which is useful for grouping sets of menu items within a menu. Also, two symbolic constants, cmAbout and cmQuit, are used in place of integers for the command events. Some other predefined command constants include cmError, cm-Menu, cmClose, cmZoom, cmResize, cmOK, cmCancel, cmYes, and cmNo. The constant cmAbout is predefined by Turbo Vision. Turbo Vision reserves the integers 0 through 99 and 256 through 999 for its own use. Programmers can use the integers 100 through 255 and 1000 through 65535 to define constants unique to their applications. The constant cmAbout is defined at the top of the program:

```
const
  cmAbout = 104;
```

The event handler can now use this symbolic name, making the case statement easier to read.

```
procedure TMyApp.HandleEvent(var Event: TEvent);
begin
  TApplication.HandleEvent(Event);
  if Event.What = evCommand then
  begin
    case Event.Command of
      101:      ReportDialog('Execute command 101');
      102:      ReportDialog('Execute command 102');
      103:      ReportDialog('Execute command 103');
      cmAbout:  ReportDialog('Invoke About Dialog');
      201:      ReportDialog('Execute command 201');
      202:      ReportDialog('Execute command 202');
      203:      ReportDialog('Execute command 203');
    else
      Exit;
    end;
    ClearEvent(Event);
  end;
end;
```

The entire definition for TMyApp.InitMenuBar now looks like this:

```
procedure TMyApp.InitMenuBar;
var
  R: TRect;
begin
  GetExtent(R);
  R.B.Y := R.A.Y + 1;
  MenuBar := New(PMenuBar, Init(R, NewMenu(
    NewSubMenu('Menu ˜1˜ ', hcNoContext,
      NewMenu(
        NewItem('Choice 10˜1˜', 'F1', kbF1, 101, hcNoContext,
        NewItem('Choice 10˜2˜', 'F2', kbF2, 102, hcNoContext,
        NewItem('Choice 10˜3˜', 'F3', kbF3, 103, hcNoContext,
        NewLine(
        NewItem('˜A˜bout', 'Alt-A', kbAltA,  cmAbout, hcNoContext,
        NewItem('E˜x˜it',  'Alt-X', kbAltX,  cmQuit, hcNoContext,
        nil ))))))             { 1 ) for each NewItem }
      ),
    NewSubMenu('Menu ˜2˜ ', hcNoContext,
      NewMenu(
        NewItem('Choice 20˜1˜', 'Alt-F1', kbAltF1, 201, hcNoContext,
        NewItem('Choice 20˜2˜', 'Alt-F2', kbAltF2, 202, hcNoContext,
        NewItem('Choice 20˜3˜', 'Alt-F3', kbAltF3, 203, hcNoContext,
        nil)))                 { 1 ) for each NewItem }
      ),
    nil ))                     { 1 ) for each NewSubMenu }
  )));
end;
```

The following illustration shows the menu created by this definition.

Normally, all of your command events will be specified by symbolic constants rather than by numbers. Program 10-4 shows the entire modified program, included here for reference.

```
Program 10_4;

uses App, Objects, MsgBox,
     Menus, Views, Drivers;

const
  cmAbout = 104;

type
  TMyApp = object(TApplication)
    procedure InitMenuBar; virtual;
    procedure HandleEvent(var Event: TEvent); virtual;
  end;

procedure ReportDialog(S: String);
var
  R: TRect;
  C: Word;
begin
  R.Assign(25,5,55,12);
  C := MessageBoxRect(R, s, nil, mfInformation + mfOkButton);
end;

procedure TMyApp.InitMenuBar;
var
  R: TRect;
begin
  GetExtent(R);
  R.B.Y := R.A.Y + 1;
  MenuBar := New(PMenuBar, Init(R, NewMenu(
    NewSubMenu('Menu ~1~ ', hcNoContext,
      NewMenu(
        NewItem('Choice 10~1~', 'F1', kbF1, 101, hcNoContext,
        NewItem('Choice 10~2~', 'F2', kbF2, 102, hcNoContext,
        NewItem('Choice 10~3~', 'F3', kbF3, 103, hcNoContext,
        NewLine(
        NewItem('~A~bout', 'Alt-A', kbAltA,  cmAbout, hcNoContext,
        NewItem('E~x~it',  'Alt-X', kbAltX,  cmQuit, hcNoContext,
        nil ))))))            { 1 ) for each NewItem }
      ),
    NewSubMenu('Menu ~2~ ', hcNoContext,
      NewMenu(
        NewItem('Choice 20~1~', 'Alt-F1', kbAltF1, 201, hcNoContext,
        NewItem('Choice 20~2~', 'Alt-F2', kbAltF2, 202, hcNoContext,
        NewItem('Choice 20~3~', 'Alt-F3', kbAltF3, 203, hcNoContext,
        nil)))               { 1 ) for each NewItem }
      ),
    nil ))                    { 1 ) for each NewSubMenu }
  )));
end;
```

Program 10-4.   The entire modified menu program

```
procedure TMyApp.HandleEvent(var Event: TEvent);
begin
  TApplication.HandleEvent(Event);
  if Event.What = evCommand then
  begin
    case Event.Command of
      101:       ReportDialog('Execute command 101');
      102:       ReportDialog('Execute command 102');
      103:       ReportDialog('Execute command 103');
      cmAbout:   ReportDialog('Invoke About Dialog');
      201:       ReportDialog('Execute command 201');
      202:       ReportDialog('Execute command 202');
      203:       ReportDialog('Execute command 203');
    else
      Exit;
    end;
    ClearEvent(Event);
  end;
end;

var
  MyApp: TMyApp;

begin
  MyApp.Init;
  MyApp.Run;
  MyApp.Done;
end.
```

Program 10-4. *Continued*

CHAPTER HIGHLIGHTS

- All good application frameworks make it easy to build menus and to handle commands generated by selecting menu choices.

  Some systems require that you specify the method to be called at the point where you define the corresponding menu item. More general menu systems, like that in Turbo Vision, generate *command events*, usually encoded as numbers or symbolic constants.

- Using command messages makes it easier to prototype a user interface without having to define test stubs for each menu item as you go.

- Keyboard accelerators are another important feature for making programs easy to use.

You'll be surprised how similar programs look when written for several different application frameworks, even when written in different programming languages. Turbo Vision programs can be written in either C++ or object-oriented Pascal. The same is true for ObjectWindows. ObjectWindows programs can even be written in Actor.

The following chapter shows how the menus and command events presented here can be implemented in C++ using the C++ Views application framework. Dialog boxes play as important a role as menus in window-oriented programs. After you get a feel for menus and dialog boxes using C++ Views, you can see how the same problems are handled in ObjectWindows using both C++ and object-oriented Pascal.

11

C++ VIEWS: MENUS AND COMMAND EVENTS

Chapter 10 introduced the Turbo Vision application and showed how to construct menus and handle command events generated by menus. This chapter discusses similar menus and event handling for the C++ Views application framework. C++ Views applications run under Microsoft Windows and are compiled using either Zortech C++ or Borland C++. C++ Views is not provided with either compiler—you must purchase it separately from CNS, Inc. or from a distributor.

Programming with C++ Views, like programming with Turbo Vision, involves the creation and use of many different types of views and windows. C++ Views provides the two most commonly used views also found in Turbo Vision—menus and dialog boxes. It also provides elaborate support for various types of windows, all under the Microsoft Windows operating environment. C++ Views has an extremely rich class library, particularly in the area of construction and maintenance of user-interface components. This chapter focuses on the construction of menus and discusses event commands generated by menu selections. Several complete programs are presented, showing menus and event handling methods that you'll find at the core of all applications developed with C++ Views.

BUILDING A MENU FRAMEWORK

Before you can get going with a C++Views program to implement and test menus, you need to build the basic scaffolding for creating an executable program file. In reference to the model-view-controller application program structure discussed in Chapter 9, this particular program doesn't use a model. No model is necessary, since the program only provides a framework for testing menus and invoking dialog boxes. No real processing is done. The control mechanism is, for the most part, already built into the C++Views class library. All you need to do is concentrate on developing the view. You can use the C++Views program presented at the end of Chapter 9 as a starting point for a framework program to implement and test menus.

```
#include "notifier.h"
#include "appview.h"
#include "report.h"

char *CTWindow = __FILE__;

class MyAppView : public AppView
{
public:
    MyAppView()     {}              // constructor
    ~MyAppView()    {}              // destructor
    boolean free() { delete this; return TRUE; }
    Class   *iam();
};

defineClass(MyAppView,AppView)   // defines iam method

main()
{
    MyAppView  *v;

    v = new MyAppView();
    v->setTitle("Main Application Window");
    v->show();

    Report::dialog("Information", v, "Hello, world");
    notifier.start();
}
```

The source code for both the main function and the MyAppView class are included in the same file, in this case MYAPP.CPP. Normally, however, this code would be broken up into two separate files. For this chapter, only the main program function will be implemented in MYAPP.CPP:

```
FILE: MYAPP.CPP

#include "notifier.h"
#include "myappvw.h"

char *CTWindow = __FILE__;

main()
{
    MyAppView *v = new MyAppView();
    v->show();
    notifier.start();
}
```

The header file declaring the class interface for MyAppView is moved to the file MYAPPVW.H:

```
FILE: MYAPPVW.H

#ifndef MYAPPVW_H
#define MYAPPVW_H

#include "appview.h"
#include "popupmen.h"

class MyAppView : public AppView
{
public:
    MyAppView();
    ~MyAppView();
    boolean free();
    Class   *iam();
};

extern Class *MyAppViewCls;
#endif
```

The methods are now defined in a separate file, instead of being defined inline in the declaration of MyAppView. The file MYAPPVW.CPP implements the methods for MyAppView:

```
FILE: MYAPPVW.CPP

#include "myappvw.h"
#include <stdio.h>
#include <string.h>

#include "report.h"
#include "menuitem.h"

defineClass(MyAppView,AppView)
```

```
static char *WindowTitle="C++ Views Menus for MS-Windows";

MyAppView::MyAppView()      // constructor
{
   setTitle(WindowTitle);
}

MyAppView::~MyAppView()     // destructor
{
}

boolean MyAppView::free()
{
    delete this;
    return TRUE;
}
```

You now need a make file, a linker response file (.LNK), and a Microsoft Windows module definition file (.DEF) to put the program together and build the executable file, MYAPP.EXE.

```
FILE: MAKEFILE

CFLAGS = -a -p -u -W -c -ml -br -DARCHIVER -DZORTECH -DMSDOS \
                            -DMS_WINDOWS -DFAR_OBJECT
OBJECTS = myappvw.obj
CC = ztc

myapp.exe: myapp.obj $(OBJECTS)
    link   @myapp.lnk
    rc     myapp.exe

.cpp.obj:
        $(CC) $(CFLAGS) $*

myappvw.obj:    myappvw.cpp   myappvw.h    appview.h   view.h        \
                window.h      display.h    object.h    class.h       \
                defs.h        wintypes.h   ordcllct.h  collectn.h    \
                containr.h    object.h     menu.h      window.h      \
                object.h      dlgmodel.h   object.h    Str.h         \
                dictinry.h    set.h        collectn.h  assoc.h       \
                object.h      str.h        containr.h  str.h         \
                input.h       dialog.h     poppwndw.h  view.h        \
                popupmen.h    menu.h       str.h       brchrtvw.h    \
                view.h        report.h     dialog.h
```

This make file specifies an unusually large number of dependencies for the MYAPPVW.OBJ target. Don't let this intimidate you. The make file is generated automatically when you work with the C++ Views Browser. The long list of header files includes all the interface specifications for the classes provided by C++Views. Scanning this list will give you an idea of the types of objects supported by C++Views: views, windows, menus, dialogs, containers, collections, dictionaries, sets, and strings.

The C++Views Browser is like an integrated development environment, which, itself, runs under the Microsoft Windows operating environment. The C++Views Browser works almost exactly like a Smalltalk Browser. It lets you quickly navigate through the classes used in a C++Views application program. The Browser allows easy maintenance of specific projects by bundling associated files together into a single archive. It then allows you to delete or insert classes in the class hierarchy that specifically support the current project. The Browser also lets you quickly find methods in a class and add, edit, or delete methods. A complete text editor is provided. As mentioned earlier, the Browser automatically generates a make file based on the class hierarchy associated with a given project. In addition to maintaining all the .CPP and .H files for a given application program, the Browser automatically generates a linker response file (.LNK) and a Microsoft Windows module definition file (.DEF) specific to the project. The linker response file and Windows module definition file generated for MYAPP are included here for reference. Again, you would not normally need to worry about these files because they are generated automatically— they are included here in case you are not working directly inside the C++Views Browser.

The linker response file looks like this:

```
FILE: MYAPP.LNK

myapp+
myappvw+
/align:16/packc:8192
myapp.exe
myapp.map
cppview+llibcew+libw /NOD /NOE
myapp.def
```

The module definition file looks like this:

```
FILE: MYAPP.DEF

NAME            myapp
DESCRIPTION     'C++ 2.0 Skeleton for MS Windows Programming'
EXETYPE         WINDOWS
STUB            'WINSTUB.EXE'
```

```
CODE            MOVEABLE
DATA            FIXED MULTIPLE
HEAPSIZE        22000
STACKSIZE       8192
EXPORTS CTalkWndProc
```

With this scaffolding in place, you can now confine all modifications to
the files MYAPPVW.H and MYAPPVW.CPP because the only class that
needs to be modified to implement and test menus is MyAppView.

CREATING A SIMPLE MENU

The first thing that you'll want to do is add a new method to the application view called initMenuBar. While you're at it, you may as well add the
event-handler method that is called when a specific menu choice is selected. Add the following two declarations to the header file, MYAPPVW.H:

```
void      initMenuBar();
boolean   testChoice1(MenuItem*);
```

With a comment thrown in for readability, the entire header file now
looks like this:

```
#ifndef MYAPPVW_H
#define MYAPPVW_H

#include "appview.h"
#include "popupmen.h"

class MyAppView : public AppView
{
public:
    MyAppView();
    ~MyAppView();
    Class     *iam();
    boolean   free();
    void      initMenuBar();

    //////////////////////////////////////////////////
    // menu demo methods
    //////////////////////////////////////////////////
    boolean testChoice1(MenuItem*);
};
```

```
extern Class *MyAppViewCls;
#endif
```

At this point, you need to have the constructor call initMenuBar. The definition of the constructor inside of MYAPPVW.CPP should now look like this:

```
MyAppView::MyAppView()
{
    setTitle(WindowTitle);
    initMenuBar();
}
```

The constructor above is invoked automatically when the program is first run. Entering the main function causes an instance of MyAppView to be created. This is the only instance of MyAppView ever created. This instance becomes the top-level view for the program. When the view is created, the above constructor is called automatically. The window title is set and the menu bar is initialized before the view is displayed.

Next, you need to define initMenuBar. To add a pop-up menu requires the creation of at least two objects, a Menu object and one or more MenuItem objects. The Menu object can be created with a statement like the following:

```
PopupMenu *MENU1pop = new PopupMenu("Menu 1   ");
```

This creates a pointer to a menu object called MENU1pop. The string that will appear in the menu bar used to activate this menu is "Menu 1". Extra spaces are left at the end of the string so that when additional menus are added to the menu bar, they will not butt up too closely against one another.

Once created, the menu must then be added to the top-level view. Remember that MyAppView is the top-level view derived from the class AppView. The following call inserts the pop-up menu into the top-level view by calling the inherited method AppView::addPopup.

```
addPopup(MENU1pop);
```

This method takes a pointer to a pop-up menu as an argument, not an actual menu object. The menu currently has no choice items in it. The second type of item you must create for a menu to work is an instance of MenuItem. The following statement creates a menu item with a choice string of "Choice 1", which calls MyAppView::testChoice1 when selected.

```
id menuItem = new MenuItem("Choice 1",
                            this,
                            methodOf(MyAppView,testChoice1));
```

The first argument to the menu-item constructor is the string that will appear in the menu-item entry. The second argument is a pointer to the window that owns the menu. In this case, the single instance of MyApp-View created when the program runs becomes the parent of this menu item. The third argument is a pointer to a method. A macro called method-Of is used to generate this pointer. Remember that the new operator returns a *pointer* to an object and not an object. The identifier, "id", in the above statement is type-compatible with pointers. Any C++ Views object can be pointed to by an instance of id. In this case, menuItem is assigned to point to the newly created menu item. This pointer can then be used to add the new item to the pop-up menu, MENU1pop:

```
MENU1pop->addItem(menuItem);
```

The entire definition for MyAppView::initMenuBar looks like this:

```
void MyAppView::initMenuBar()
{
        /////////////////////////////////////////////
        // create MENU1 and add to menu bar
        /////////////////////////////////////////////
        PopupMenu *MENU1pop = new PopupMenu("Menu 1   ");
        id menuItem = new MenuItem("Choice 1",
                            this,
                            methodOf(MyAppView,testChoice1));
        addPopup(MENU1pop);
        MENU1pop->addItem(menuItem);
}
```

The last thing you have to do is define the testChoice1 method called when the menu item is selected.

```
boolean MyAppView::testChoice1(MenuItem*)
{
    Report::dialog("Test Stub", this, "Choice 1 selected");
}
```

In C++ Views, all methods that can be called from a MenuItem object must accept exactly one argument. This argument is a pointer to the MenuItem object that invoked the call. The method, testChoice1, is really a command event handler. There is no central command handler associated with a given menu in C++ Views to parallel the TMyApp.HandleEvent method required in a Turbo Vision application. Recall that in Chapter 10, this method contained a case statement with switches for each possible command that could be generated from a menu. These commands were unique integer identifiers in Turbo Vision. For menus, C++ Views does away with integer command identifiers and the general event-handler/dispatcher method (for example, TMyApp.HandleEvent, found in Chapter 10) by having each menu item directly specify a pointer to the method to be invoked when the menu item is selected.

In order for this to work, the handler method must be a member of the view to which the menu item belongs. That is why testChoice1 is a member of the MyAppView class and why it must have exactly one argument, which is a pointer to a MenuItem. In practice, the pointer argument is rarely used by the command event handlers associated with a particular menu item. However, the pointer is always available if access to the selected MenuItem is required.

MYAPPVW.CPP is presented below and includes definitions for all methods in the MyAppView class required to build and test a single pop-up menu with a single menu-item entry.

```
#include "myappvw.h"
#include <stdio.h>
#include <string.h>

#include "report.h"
#include "menuitem.h"

defineClass(MyAppView,AppView)
static char *WindowTitle="C++ Views Menus for MS-Windows";

MyAppView::MyAppView()
{
    setTitle(WindowTitle);
    initMenuBar();
}
```

```
MyAppView::~MyAppView()
{
}

boolean MyAppView::free()
{
    delete this;
    return TRUE;
}

void MyAppView::initMenuBar()
{
        /////////////////////////////////////////////
        // create MENU1 and add to menu bar
        /////////////////////////////////////////////
        PopupMenu *MENU1pop = new PopupMenu("Menu 1   ");
        id menuItem = new MenuItem("Choice 1",
                                    this,
                                    methodOf(MyAppView,testChoice1));
        addPopup(MENU1pop);
        MENU1pop->addItem(menuItem);
}

boolean MyAppView::testChoice1(MenuItem*)
{
    Report::dialog("Test Stub", this, "Choice 1 selected");
}
```

Figure 11-1 shows the menu and the dialog generated when this menu item is selected. The dialog box is used as a *test stub* to identify menu selections. To exit the program, you must use the Close selection in the system control menu found in all Microsoft Windows application programs.

Realistically, a menu will have more than one entry. To test out two additional menu entries, you can add two new methods to the MyAppView class. The following declarations must go in the header file:

```
    boolean testChoice2(MenuItem*);
    boolean testChoice3(MenuItem*);
```

The definitions should be added to the end of MYAPPVW.CPP.

```
boolean MyAppView::testChoice2(MenuItem*)
{
    Report::dialog("Test Stub", this, "Choice 2 selected");
}

boolean MyAppView::testChoice3(MenuItem*)
{
```

```
        Report::dialog("Test Stub", this, "Choice 3 selected");
}
```

Now, only the initMenuBar method needs modification. It's really not necessary to declare an id object to point to a newly created menu item. A new menu item can be created and added to the pop-up menu in a single statement. For example, you can replace the following two statements inside of MyAppView::initMenuBar

```
        id menuItem = new MenuItem("Choice 1",
                                   this,
                                   methodOf(MyAppView,testChoice1));
        MENU1pop->addItem(menuItem);
```

with a single statement:

```
        MENU1pop->addItem(new MenuItem("Choice 1",
                                        this,
                                        methodOf(MyAppView,testChoice1)));
```

The program is now ready to run. Figure 11-2 shows the menu and dialog box generated by selecting the second menu item.

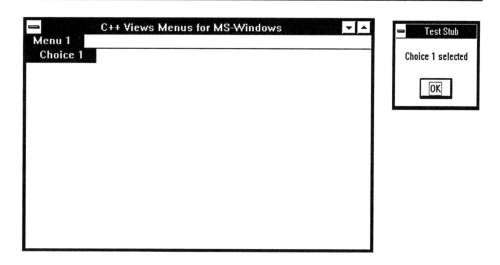

Figure 11-1.   C++ Views menu with a single menu-item selection and the dialog box generated when this menu item is selected

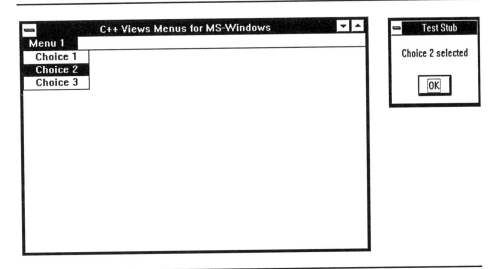

Figure 11-2.   Menu with three menu item selections and the dialog box
generated by selecting the second menu item

C++ Views provides a shortcut technique for constructing menus. You
can construct a static array of character strings to be used for the choice
items.

```
static char *MENUlnames[] =
{
    "Choice 1",
    "Choice 2",
    "Choice 3",
    0
};
```

The array of strings is terminated by a null string to indicate the last
definition.
A parallel array of method pointers can also be defined as a static array.

```
static method MENUlnameMthds[] =
{
    defMethod(MyAppView,testChoicel),
    defMethod(MyAppView,testChoice2),
    defMethod(MyAppView,testChoice3),
};
```

Now, instead of having to add each item individually to the pop-up menu inside MyAppView::initMenuBar, you can add all the items at once.

```
MENU1pop->addItems(MENU1names,
                   MENU1nameMthds,
                   this);
```

The first argument is the array of names. The second argument is an array of method pointers. The third argument is a pointer to the window that owns the menu and the menu items. The entire definition for init-MenuBar is really very simple:

```
void MyAppView::initMenuBar()
{
        /////////////////////////////////////////////
        // create MENU1 and add to menu bar
        /////////////////////////////////////////////
        PopupMenu *MENU1pop = new PopupMenu("Menu 1   ");
        addPopup(MENU1pop);
        MENU1pop->addItems(MENU1names,
                           MENU1nameMthds,
                           this);
}
```

This technique of using arrays to specify menus makes the going a little bit easier when your application requires a set of complex menus.

MULTIPLE MENUS WITH MULTIPLE CHOICES

You'll probably want more than one menu in your program. As with the Turbo Vision example in Chapter 10, you could add a second menu, which has three menu choices. First, declare the menu command handlers in the header file MYAPPVW.H. While you're at it, it's probably wise to rename the existing handlers, so it's easy to tell the choices in the second menu from the choices in the first menu. The following listing shows all six handlers after renaming the original three:

```
#ifndef MYAPPVW_H
#define MYAPPVW_H

#include "appview.h"
```

```
#include "popupmen.h"

class MyAppView : public AppView
{
public:
    MyAppView();
    ~MyAppView();
    Class    *iam();
    boolean  free();
    void     initMenuBar();

    ///////////////////////////////////////////////
    // Dialog menu demo methods
    ///////////////////////////////////////////////
    boolean test101(MenuItem*);
    boolean test102(MenuItem*);
    boolean test103(MenuItem*);
    boolean test201(MenuItem*);
    boolean test202(MenuItem*);
    boolean test203(MenuItem*);
};

extern Class *MyAppViewCls;
#endif
```

The names of the first three handlers must also be changed in the class implementation in MYAPPVW.CPP.

```
boolean MyAppView::test101(MenuItem*)
{
    Report::dialog("Test Stub", this, "101");
}

boolean MyAppView::test102(MenuItem*)
{
    Report::dialog("Test Stub", this, "102");
}

boolean MyAppView::test103(MenuItem*)
{
    Report::dialog("Test Stub", this, "103");
}

boolean MyAppView::test201(MenuItem*)
{
    Report::dialog("Test Stub", this, "201");
}

boolean MyAppView::test202(MenuItem*)
{
    Report::dialog("Test Stub", this, "202");
}
```

```
boolean MyAppView::test203(MenuItem*)
{
    Report::dialog("Test Stub", this, "203");
}
```

Now to create two menus, you need two name arrays and two method pointer arrays. The arrays for the first menu are shown again because of the modifications required when the names of the method handlers were changed.

```
//////////////////////////////////////////////////////////////
// MENU1 menu static data
//////////////////////////////////////////////////////////////
static char *MENU1names[] =
{
    "Choice 101",
    "Choice 102",
    "Choice 103",
    0
};

static method MENU1nameMthds[] =
{
    defMethod(MyAppView,test101),
    defMethod(MyAppView,test102),
    defMethod(MyAppView,test103),
};
```

The arrays for the second menu are similar.

```
//////////////////////////////////////////////////////////////
// MENU2 menu static data
//////////////////////////////////////////////////////////////
static char *MENU2names[] =
{
    "Choice 201",
    "Choice 202",
    "Choice 203",
    0
};

static method MENU2nameMthds[] =
{
    defMethod(MyAppView,test201),
    defMethod(MyAppView,test202),
    defMethod(MyAppView,test203),
};
```

The only remaining modification is the creation and addition of MENU2 to the top-level menu bar inside MyAppView::initMenuBar.

```
void MyAppView::initMenuBar()
{
        ///////////////////////////////////////////
        // create MENU1 and add to menu bar
        ///////////////////////////////////////////
        PopupMenu *MENU1pop = new PopupMenu("Menu 1  ");
        addPopup(MENU1pop);
        MENU1pop->addItems(MENU1names,
                          MENU1nameMthds,
                          this);

        ///////////////////////////////////////////
        // create MENU2 and add to menu bar
        ///////////////////////////////////////////
        PopupMenu *MENU2pop = new PopupMenu("Menu 2  ");
        addPopup(MENU2pop);
        MENU2pop->addItems(MENU2names,
                          MENU2nameMthds,
                          this);
}
```

You can now compile and run the program. No surprises here. Two
menus now can be activated from the top-level menu bar. The second
menu looks almost identical to the first.

MENUS AND EVENTS

Menus and events are not as closely associated in C++Views as they are in
Turbo Vision. The event-dispatching mechanism is more transparent in C++
Views. This is not to say that it is less powerful or flexible. In fact, the
event-dispatching mechanism of C++Views *is* the Microsoft Windows event
and message-passing system. C++Views bundles an encapsulated layer of
classes around Microsoft Windows to make it easy to handle events and
manage control of your application. It's amazing how little you need to
know about the event mechanism in C++Views, even when building sophisticated application programs.

Dispatching Events

There are no command events *per se* in C++Views. That is to say, selecting a
menu item does not create an event that is sent to an event handler, which,
in turn, directs control to the appropriate routine. Instead, only mouse
movement, mouse button press and release events, and keyboard

keypresses and releases are considered events. Resizing or moving a window is also an event that causes a "paint" message to be generated. In this respect, the event handlers provided in C++ Views are true handlers. They do not dispatch events themselves like TMyApp.EventHandler in a Turbo Vision program. While it is possible to explicitly generate events in C++ Views, you seldom need to. The only thing you need to worry about is whether a handler *consumes* an event or not. The dispatching of events is handled at a higher level, completely transparent to you if you would rather not pay attention to the mechanism.

Handling Events

Handling events from menus is done by providing a method that corresponds to the pointer specified in a MenuItem object. That's all there is to it. The only restriction is that the method must be a member of the view class to which the PopupMenu object and its child MenuItem object belong. You do not explicitly need to consume events that are dispatched through menus. The nice thing about the event handling provided by C++ Views is that it is completely compatible with the multitasking of Microsoft Windows. If you want to direct events to windows other than the one opened for your C++ Views application, you can do so without worry. In order to direct events to your C++ Views application, simply set the input focus to the views associated with the application using either the mouse pointer or the ALT-TAB key combination provided as standard task switching commands by Microsoft Windows.

SPECIAL MENU FEATURES

C++ Views, like Turbo Vision, provides a number of handy features for constructing and using menus. You can use shortcut keys to activate menus by specifying unique letters in the names of each of the top-level menu-bar entries. Within a menu you can also specify shortcut keys. When a menu is active, pressing a shortcut key causes the method associated with the key to be called. Accelerator keys allow you to bypass the menu altogether. You can use accelerator keys to directly invoke methods by pressing a single key or key combination.

Shortcut Keys

The next thing you'll want to do is add shortcut keys to activate the menus and select menu items in an active menu. In both cases, shortcuts are specified by inserting an ampersand (&) inside of the string specified for the menu or menu item. The & is placed in front of the character that you want to be the shortcut key. For example, to make ALT-1 activate the menu associated with "Menu 1" when the menu is created inside initMenuBar, put the ampersand before the *1*:

```
PopupMenu *MENU1pop = new PopupMenu("Menu &1   ");
```

If you want ALT-2 to activate the second menu, you could put an & in front of the 2 in "Menu &2". The entire definition for MyAppView::init-MenuBar now looks like this:

```
void MyAppView::initMenuBar()
{
        /////////////////////////////////////////
        // create MENU1 and add to menu bar
        /////////////////////////////////////////
        PopupMenu *MENU1pop = new PopupMenu("Menu &1   ");
        addPopup(MENU1pop);
        MENU1pop->addItems(MENU1names,
                           MENU1nameMthds,
                           this);

        /////////////////////////////////////////
        // create MENU2 and add to menu bar
        /////////////////////////////////////////
        PopupMenu *MENU2pop = new PopupMenu("Menu &2   ");
        addPopup(MENU2pop);
        MENU2pop->addItems(MENU2names,
                           MENU2nameMthds,
                           this);
}
```

You can do the same thing with the strings that appear inside of the menu as menu-item names.

```
static char *MENU1names[] =
{
    "Choice 10&1",
    "Choice 10&2",
    "Choice 10&3",
    0
};
```

```
    .
    .
    .
static char *MENU2names[] =
{
    "Choice 20&1",
    "Choice 20&2",
    "Choice 20&3",
    0
};
```

Accelerator Keys

Accelerator keys provide a direct way of invoking a method without ever activating the menu. For instance, with the shortcut keys specified above, you would still need to strike two keys to activate the third selection in the first menu (ALT-1, 3). However, a command might be invoked so frequently that pressing a single key would be preferable. You could assign F3 to this menu item as an accelerator key. Pressing F3 would then cause the dialog box associated with this menu item to appear without ever activating the menu. Accelerator keys can be specified as a third static array associated with the array of names and the array of method pointers. The array is declared as a static array of integers.

C++ Views defines a set of keyboard integer constants in the file WIN-TYPES.H. The symbolic constants for the keys F1, F2, and F3 are K_F1, K_F2, and K_F3. Other constants are defined. For instance, the letters for the standard ASCII keys *A* through *Z* are K_A, K_B, ... K_Z. You can use a bitwise OR operation to combine keyboard-modification keys along with these standard ASCII keys. Such combinations would allow you to specify keys such as ALT-A, CTRL-R, and ALT-F1. For example, to specify ALT-A, you would use the following expression:

```
    K_Mod_Meta2 | K_A,
```

CTRL-R is specified as

```
    K_Mod_Meta1 | K_R,
```

and to specify ALT-F1,

```
    K_Mod_Meta2 | K_F1,        // Alt-F1
```

The array of accelerator keys should have the same number of elements as the array of names in the array of method pointers for a given menu. The last entry in the array should be a 0, to indicate the end of the array. For example, the following array could be used to specify accelerator keys for Menu 2.

```
static int MENU2accelKeys[] =
{
    K_Mod_Meta2 | K_F1,      // Alt-F1
    K_Mod_Meta2 | K_F2,      // Alt-F2
    K_Mod_Meta2 | K_F3,      // Alt-F3
    0
};
```

Now when the menu is created inside initMenuBar, four arguments, rather than three, are given to PopupMenu::addItems.

```
/////////////////////////////////////////////
// create MENU2 and add to menu bar
/////////////////////////////////////////////
PopupMenu *MENU2pop = new PopupMenu("Menu &2  ");
addPopup(MENU2pop);
MENU2pop->addItems(MENU2names,
                   MENU2nameMthds,
                   MENU2accelKeys,
                   this);
```

The additional argument for the accelerator key array is inserted between the method pointer array and the pointer to the parent window.

Accelerator Key String Names

The last thing you'll want to do is add strings in a right column in the menus to inform users about available accelerator keys. When you specify the array of names for the menu items, you can insert a *tab character*. A tab character is interpreted as a division between the part of the string intended to align in the left column and the part of the string intended to align in the right column of the menu. Turbo Vision accomplished the same thing by looking at two different arguments, one for each column. The first argument was the string intended for the left column of the menu; the second argument was the string intended to align with the right column. Either one of these strings could be empty. This kind of effect can be achieved for the menu-item name strings in Menu 2 with the following array definition:

```
static char *MENU2names[] =
{
    "Choice 20&1\tAlt-F1",
    "Choice 20&2\tAlt-F2",
    "Choice 20&3\tAlt-F3",
    0
};
```

Menu Line Separators

As with Turbo Vision, it is possible to leave a menu-item entry empty, in which case a horizontal bar is drawn in place of the entry. This is a convenient way of visually grouping related menu elements. If you want to do this, a null menu entry must be specified in each of the three arrays. In the array of strings used for menu item names, you would specify a null string using a pair of double quotes with nothing between them.

```
"",
```

In the array of method pointers, you would specify that no method is to be called with the following constant:

```
NIL_METHOD
```

In the array of accelerator keys, you would specify:

```
K_NULL,
```

So, for example, if you wanted to construct the menu that appears in Figure 11-3, you would use the following three arrays to build the menu:

```
//////////////////////////////////////////////////////////////
// MENU1 menu static data
//////////////////////////////////////////////////////////////
static char *MENU1names[] =
{
    "Choice 10&1\tF1",
    "Choice 10&2\tF2",
    "Choice 10&3\tF3",
    "",
    "&About\tAlt-A",
    "E&xit\tAlt-X",
    0
};
```

```
static method MENU1nameMthds[] =
{
    defMethod(MyAppView,test101),
    defMethod(MyAppView,test102),
    defMethod(MyAppView,test103),

    NIL_METHOD,
    defMethod(MyAppView,testAbout),
    defMethod(MyAppView,exit),
};

static int MENU1accelKeys[] =
{
    K_F1,
    K_F2,
    K_F3,
    K_NULL,
    K_Mod_Meta2 | K_A,
    K_Mod_Meta2 | K_X,
    0
};
```

There are two methods referred to in the table of method pointers that have not yet been defined—MyAppView::testAbout and MyAppView::exit.

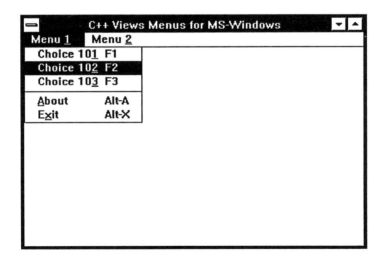

Figure 11-3. Menu with five menu items and a separator bar. Menus and menu items all include shortcut keys, which are underlined. Accelerator key string names appear in the right column of the menu.

Before you can define these methods, they must first be declared in a header file. The entire header file for MYAPPVW.H looks like this:

```
#ifndef MYAPPVW_H
#define MYAPPVW_H

#include "appview.h"
#include "popupmen.h"

class MyAppView : public AppView
{
public:
    MyAppView();
    ~MyAppView();
    Class    *iam();
    boolean  free();
    void     initMenuBar();

    /////////////////////////////////////////////////
    // Dialog menu demo methods
    /////////////////////////////////////////////////
    boolean test101(MenuItem*);
    boolean test102(MenuItem*);
    boolean test103(MenuItem*);
    boolean test201(MenuItem*);
    boolean test202(MenuItem*);
    boolean test203(MenuItem*);

    boolean testAbout(MenuItem*);
    boolean exit(MenuItem*);
};

extern Class *MyAppViewCls;
#endif
```

The definitions for the two new methods are as follows:

```
boolean MyAppView::testAbout(MenuItem *m)
{
    Report::dialog("Report", this, "Invoke About Dialog");
}

boolean MyAppView::exit(MenuItem  *m)
{
    enum yesNoCancel result =
    YesNo::dialog(this,                 // current window
                  FALSE,                // cancel button supplied
                  NoButton,             // default response
                  "Terminate program?" // prompt
                  );
    if (result == YesButton)
    {
```

```
        close();                        // exit application
    }
}
```

There's nothing new in testAbout. It's simply provided so that the final program in this chapter mimics the final program in Chapter 10. The exit method adds a new dimension to the program. It gives the user the option of canceling, in case the exit command was selected accidentally. The YesNo dialog is provided as a standard C++Views class. In order to use it, you must specify the following include statement at the top of the file:

```
#include "yesno.h"
```

YesNo::dialog is a static member function of the YesNo class. Recall that static member functions can be called directly and do not require an instance of the YesNo class to be associated with the call. The function YesNo::dialog can therefore be called directly and returns an enumerated type, which is one of YesButton, NoButton, or CancelButton. A CancelButton is a possible result of this dialog only if the second argument to YesNo::dialog is TRUE. If this argument is FALSE, no cancel button appears in the dialog. In this case, the user must press either Yes or No to terminate the dialog. The following six lines constitute a single statement from the exit method:

```
enum yesNoCancel result =
YesNo::dialog(this,                 // current window
            FALSE,                  // cancel button supplied
            NoButton,               // default response
            "Terminate program?"    // prompt
          );
```

The first line declares the variable, "result", which records the value of the button (selected by the user) that terminated the dialog. The first argument to YesNo::dialog is a pointer to the parent window, in this case, the single instance of MyAppView created when the program is run. The second argument, as already discussed, indicates whether or not a cancel button is included as a third button; a Yes button and a No button are always included. The third argument indicates the default button, which will have input focus when the dialog is activated. The No button becomes the default selection in the code above. This way, if the user inadvertently presses RETURN after selecting the Exit command, the dialog will assume a mistake was made and return to the program. This technique is frequently used in text editors in which the data buffer has been modified, but the changes have not been saved to a disk file when the user asks to quit. The fourth and final argument to YesNo::dialog is the prompt string that will appear in the dialog.

After the dialog terminates, the result variable is tested. Only if the user selects the Yes button is the inherited method AppView::close called, which closes the top-level window and terminates the application program.

The illustration here shows the YesNo dialog used to query the user before terminating the application.

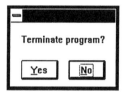

The entire listing for MYAPPVW.CPP is included here so you can ensure that all elements are included in the right order if you are following along on your computer.

```
#include "myappvw.h"
#include <stdio.h>
#include <string.h>

#include "report.h"
#include "yesno.h"

defineClass(MyAppView,AppView)
static char *WindowTitle="C++ Views Menus for MS-Windows";

//////////////////////////////////////////////////////////////
// MENU1 menu static data
//////////////////////////////////////////////////////////////
static char *MENU1names[] =
{
    "Choice 10&1\tF1",
    "Choice 10&2\tF2",
    "Choice 10&3\tF3",
    "",
    "&About\tAlt-A",
    "E&xit\tAlt-X",
    0
};
```

```
static method MENU1nameMthds[] =
{
    defMethod(MyAppView,test101),
    defMethod(MyAppView,test102),
    defMethod(MyAppView,test103),

    NIL_METHOD,
    defMethod(MyAppView,testAbout),
    defMethod(MyAppView,exit),
};

static int MENU1accelKeys[] =
{
    K_F1,
    K_F2,
    K_F3,
    K_NULL,
    K_Mod_Meta2 | K_A,
    K_Mod_Meta2 | K_X,
    0
};

//////////////////////////////////////////////////////////
// MENU2 menu static data
//////////////////////////////////////////////////////////
static char *MENU2names[] =
{
    "Choice 20&1\tAlt-F1",
    "Choice 20&2\tAlt-F2",
    "Choice 20&3\tAlt-F3",
    0
};

static method MENU2nameMthds[] =
{
    defMethod(MyAppView,test201),
    defMethod(MyAppView,test202),
    defMethod(MyAppView,test203),
};

static int MENU2accelKeys[] =
{
    K_Mod_Meta2 | K_F1,        // Alt-F1
    K_Mod_Meta2 | K_F2,        // Alt-F2
    K_Mod_Meta2 | K_F3,        // Alt-F3
    0
};
//////////////////////////////////////////////////////////

MyAppView::MyAppView()
{
    setTitle(WindowTitle);
    initMenuBar();
}
MyAppView::~MyAppView()
{
```

```
}

boolean MyAppView::free()
{
    delete this;
    return TRUE;
}

void MyAppView::initMenuBar()
{
        /////////////////////////////////////////////
        // create MENU1 and add to menu bar
        /////////////////////////////////////////////
        PopupMenu *MENU1pop = new PopupMenu("Menu &1  ");
        addPopup(MENU1pop);
        MENU1pop->addItems(MENU1names,
                           MENU1nameMthds,
                           MENU1accelKeys,
                           this);

        /////////////////////////////////////////////
        // create MENU2 and add to menu bar
        /////////////////////////////////////////////
        PopupMenu *MENU2pop = new PopupMenu("Menu &2  ");
        addPopup(MENU2pop);
        MENU2pop->addItems(MENU2names,
                           MENU2nameMthds,
                           MENU2accelKeys,
                           this);
}

boolean MyAppView::test101(MenuItem*)
{
    Report::dialog("Test Stub", this, "101");
}

boolean MyAppView::test102(MenuItem*)
{
    Report::dialog("Test Stub", this, "102");
}

boolean MyAppView::test103(MenuItem*)
{
    Report::dialog("Test Stub", this, "103");
}

boolean MyAppView::test201(MenuItem*)
{
    Report::dialog("Test Stub", this, "201");
}

boolean MyAppView::test202(MenuItem*)
{
    Report::dialog("Test Stub", this, "202");
}
```

```
boolean MyAppView::test203(MenuItem*)
{
    Report::dialog("Test Stub", this, "203");
}

boolean MyAppView::testAbout(MenuItem *m)
{
    Report::dialog("Report", this, "Invoke About Dialog");
}

boolean MyAppView::exit(MenuItem   *m)
{
    enum yesNoCancel result =
    YesNo::dialog(this,                     // current window
                FALSE,                      // cancel button supplied
                NoButton,                   // default response
                "Terminate program?"        // prompt
              );
    if (result == YesButton)
    {
        close();                            // exit application
    }
}
```

CHAPTER HIGHLIGHTS

Programming in Microsoft Windows with a standard C compiler can be quite painful, but using an application framework such as C++ Views does a lot of the dirty work for you and lets you concentrate on the more interesting and unique components of your application. Getting menus up and running is very easy. In fact, it is even easier to get menus and menu command event handlers up and running in C++ Views than it is in Turbo Vision.

In the next chapter you'll see how C++ Views handles dialog boxes. This is where C++ Views really shines. Once you start developing Microsoft Windows applications with a good application framework like C++ Views, you'll never be able to go back to a C compiler. You've been warned.

12

C++ VIEWS: DIALOGS AND CONTROL VIEWS

This chapter shows how to use a set of dialog boxes with C++ Views. The previous chapter showed how to construct menus for a C++ Views application program. You can use a single menu as a command dispatcher to test the dialogs described in this chapter. The first thing to do is to modify the menu developed in the previous chapter so that it can dispatch control to the following seven types of dialog boxes:

- About

- Report

- YesNo

- YesNoCancel

- Input

- ListSelect

- FileSelect

This is the order in which the menu entries appear in the menu. These same seven dialog boxes will also be developed to work with ObjectWindows using both C++ and object-oriented Pascal in Chapter 13, "ObjectWindows: A Language-Independent Application Framework". This common set of dialog boxes should provide grounds for comparing the features of ObjectWindows and C++ Views.

C++ Views provides each of the seven dialogs as a predefined class. You don't have to construct any new classes in order to use or understand these dialogs. Therefore, the presentation order of the dialogs in this chapter follows the order of the above list.

The first thing that you will need to do is adapt the C++ Views framework used to test menus in the previous chapter. A single menu, Dialogs, will be used to test each of the dialog classes.

A FRAMEWORK FOR TESTING DIALOG BOXES

The framework for building and testing dialog boxes in C++ Views is nearly identical to the framework used to test menus in the previous chapter. You need to specify a file containing the main function, and then you need to create the View class and methods for the top-level view. To keep things as consistent as possible, the same class name as that used in Chapter 11, MyAppView, will be used. The same filenames will also be used. This means you won't have to edit the program maintenance files, MAKEFILE, MYAPP.LNK, and MYAPP.DEF, that help build the executable file. If you want to preserve the files used to build the menu examples from the previous chapter, you might want to archive them with an archive utility or simply copy them to another subdirectory or a floppy disk.

In building the framework, you can therefore concentrate on three files: MYAPP.CPP, which contains the main function; MYAPPVW.H, which contains the class declaration for the MyAppView class; and MYAPPVW.CPP, which defines the class methods for MyAppView. MYAPP.CPP is unchanged from the listing specified in Chapter 11.

FILE: MYAPP.CPP

```
#include "notifier.h"
#include "myappvw.h"
```

```
char *CTWindow = __FILE__;

main()
{
        MyAppView *v = new MyAppView();
        v->show();
        notifier.start();
}
```

Before considering the declaration for MyAppView, look at the menu in Figure 12-1 that will be constructed by the view. A test method that is a member of MyAppView must be declared for each menu entry. That makes it easy to specify the class declaration for MyAppView directly from the menu. Here is the header file:

```
FILE: MYAPPVW.H

#ifndef MYAPPVW_H
#define MYAPPVW_H

#include "appview.h"
#include "popupmen.h"

class MyAppView : public AppView
```

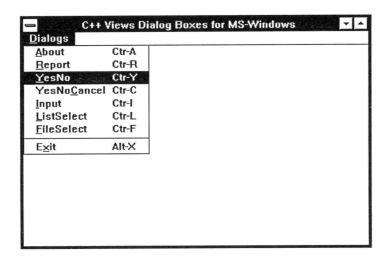

Figure 12-1.   Dialogs menu used to invoke MyAppView methods to test dialog boxes

```
{
public:
    MyAppView();
    ~MyAppView();
    Class    *iam();
    boolean  free();
    void     initMenuBar();

    //////////////////////////////////////////////
    // Dialog menu demo methods
    //////////////////////////////////////////////
    boolean testAbout(MenuItem*);
    boolean testReport(MenuItem*);
    boolean testYesNo(MenuItem*);
    boolean testYesNoCancel(MenuItem*);
    boolean testInput(MenuItem*);
    boolean testListSelect(MenuItem*);
    boolean testFileSelect(MenuItem*);
    boolean exit(MenuItem*);
};

extern Class *MyAppViewCls;
#endif
```

Now the only thing remaining to get a simplified version of the final program up and running is the creation of the menu and implementation of simple do-nothing methods for each of the dialogs.

The Menu, Menu Items, and Method Pointers

The menu and methods are defined in MYAPPVW.CPP. Here is what the static arrays look like for the Dialogs menu:

```
//////////////////////////////////////////////////////////////
// DEMO menu static data
//////////////////////////////////////////////////////////////
static char *DEMOnames[] =
{
    "&About\tCtr-A",
    "&Report\tCtr-R",
    "&YesNo\tCtr-Y",
    "YesNo&Cancel\tCtr-C",
    "&Input\tCtr-I",
    "&ListSelect\tCtr-L",
    "&FileSelect\tCtr-F",
    "",
    "E&xit\tAlt-X",
    0
};
```

```
static method DEMOnameMthds[] =
{
    defMethod(MyAppView,testAbout),
    defMethod(MyAppView,testReport),
    defMethod(MyAppView,testYesNo),
    defMethod(MyAppView,testYesNoCancel),
    defMethod(MyAppView,testInput),
    defMethod(MyAppView,testListSelect),
    defMethod(MyAppView,testFileSelect),

    NIL_METHOD,
    defMethod(MyAppView,exit),
};

static int DEMOaccelKeys[] =
{
    K_Mod_Metal | K_A,
    K_Mod_Metal | K_R,
    K_Mod_Metal | K_Y,
    K_Mod_Metal | K_C,
    K_Mod_Metal | K_I,
    K_Mod_Metal | K_L,
    K_Mod_Metal | K_F,
    K_NULL,
    K_Mod_Meta2 | K_X,
    0
};
//////////////////////////////////////////////////////////////
```

Remember from Chapter 11 that three arrays are required: one for the name strings, one for the method pointers, and one for the accelerator keys. Note also that C++ Views implements CTRL-key combinations (CTRL-A for About, for example) to invoke menu-item methods directly. It would be equally feasible to implement the accelerator keys using ALT-key combinations as another possible alternative. A quick-exit accelerator key is used in the Dialogs menu. Pressing ALT-X calls the exit method immediately without invoking the Dialogs menu.

Next you must define the constructor, the destructor, and a *free* method—a standard method name associated with a given class called when you want to free an object of the class that has been allocated on the heap.

```
MyAppView::MyAppView()
{
    setTitle(WindowTitle);
    initMenuBar();
}

MyAppView::~MyAppView()
{
```

```
}

boolean MyAppView::free()
{
    delete this;
    return TRUE;
}
```

These three methods have exactly the same definitions as their counterparts defined in the previous chapter.

Now you can define the method, initMenuBar, which creates the menu and inserts it into the top-level view.

```
void MyAppView::initMenuBar()
{
        ///////////////////////////////////////////
        // create menu and add menu bar
        ///////////////////////////////////////////
        PopupMenu *DEMOpop = new PopupMenu("&Dialogs");
        addPopup(DEMOpop);
        DEMOpop->addItems(DEMOnames,
                          DEMOnameMthds,
                          DEMOaccelKeys,
                          this);
}
```

Menu-Item Test Methods

Now you need a test stub for each of the seven types of dialogs tested by the framework. Here are the seven empty test stub definitions, which can be filled in later.

```
boolean MyAppView::testAbout(MenuItem *m)
{
}

boolean MyAppView::testReport(MenuItem *m)
{
}

boolean MyAppView::testYesNo(MenuItem *m)
{
}

boolean MyAppView::testYesNoCancel(MenuItem *m)
{
}
```

```
boolean MyAppView::testInput(MenuItem *m)
{
}

boolean MyAppView::testListSelect(MenuItem *m)
{
}

boolean MyAppView::testFileSelect(MenuItem *m)
{
}
```

Finally, you need a definition for MyAppView::exit.

```
boolean MyAppView::exit(MenuItem  *m)
{
    enum yesNoCancel result =
    YesNo::dialog(this,                 // current window
                FALSE,                  // cancel button supplied
                NoButton,               // default response
                "Terminate program?"   // prompt
               );
    if (result == YesButton)
    {
        close();                        // exit application
    }
}
```

This definition is unchanged from the menu test framework shown in the previous chapter. With all these definitions in place you should now be able to compile and run the program. When the program is run, the Dialogs menu can be activated; however, selecting any of the menu-item entries other than Exit will not produce any result.

USING DIALOGS PROVIDED BY C++ VIEWS

Now you can go through and implement the code for each type of dialog, one method at a time. This is a good incremental development strategy. It's always best to check your work as frequently as possible. Developing one method at a time and then testing it keeps you from passing errors in the implementation of one test method on to other methods.

All dialogs in this chapter are derived from the Dialog class defined in C++ Views. The Dialog class provides the common control mechanism and the basic view properties inherited by all C++ Views dialog classes.

In contrast to the standard dialogs provided by Turbo Vision, all C++ Views predefined dialogs are variable in size and adjust automatically to accommodate a prompt string. C++ Views provides a broad range of dialog box classes that will meet most general programming needs from reporting information, confirming command requests, selecting strings from lists, and opening files and changing directories—all the way through dialog box controls. The problem with C++ Views might be that it does too much work for you. You rarely need to develop your own dialog classes except where very specialized data is controlled by dialog box input. In this respect, this chapter teaches more about using existing C++ Views dialog classes rather than teaching how to build specialized dialog classes.

The following chapter will dig a little deeper into building specialized dialog boxes. For now, just think about the kinds of things you can do with the dialogs presented in this chapter.

Here is a partial branch of the C++ Views class hierarchy, showing that Dialogs are inherited from PopupWindows, which are inherited from Views.

```
Object
  Display
    Window
      View
        ControlView
        PopupWindow
          Dialog
            About
            YesNo
            Report
            Input
            ListSelect
            FileSelect
```

Notice that ControlViews are also inherited from PopupWindows. ControlViews provide a way of making controls such as buttons and list boxes visible. ControlViews define properties that are desirable for controls inserted into a dialog, such as having a title, being sizable, being movable, or possibly having a control-menu icon and control menu. ControlViews have a pointer to a Control class object as a member variable.

About

The About dialog invoked by testAbout appears in the following illustration. C++ Views provides an About class including a static member method, About::dialog, which can be used to implement testAbout.

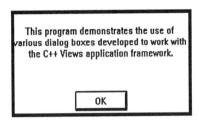

This program demonstrates the use of various dialog boxes developed to work with the C++ Views application framework.

OK

```
boolean MyAppView::testAbout(MenuItem *m)
{
    About::dialog( "\n"
                   "This program demonstrates the use of "
                   "various dialog boxes developed to "
                   "work with the C++ Views "
                   "application framework.",
                   this);
}
```

Only two arguments are passed to About::dialog. The first argument is a string, and the second argument is a pointer to the parent window for the dialog. The "this" pointer is used within the MyAppView class definition to indicate the single instance of MyAppView created when the program is run. It is this instance that owns the dialog created by the preceding method.

It might look like there are more arguments in the single statement in this method. However, as mentioned previously, both the Zortech and Turbo C++ compilers allow you to concatenate strings defined one right after another. For instance, the expression,

```
"one " "string"
```

is equivalent to

```
"one string"
```

This allows you to break up long strings over several lines and make program listings more readable. The preceding method definition therefore specifies a single string as the first argument to About::dialog. This string starts with a newline, \n, and is broken up over five lines.

Notice, when you look at the resulting dialog, that the string appears to have three newlines in addition to the preliminary one. As in Turbo Vision, strings are wrapped to fit into a given rectangle when printed. The difference is that strings printed inside an About dialog box are centered in C++ Views. Also note that no title box is provided by an About dialog. This means an About window cannot be moved around the screen and that no title string appears.

Report

As you can see here, Report dialogs are very similar to About dialogs.

Both display a prompt string, and both insert an OK control button in the center of the window near the bottom. The main difference is that a Report dialog includes a *title box*. The title box includes a menu control icon at the left, for activating the system control menu associated with the window, and it may include a title string. Any window with a title box may also be moved with the mouse by pointing to the title box, holding down the left mouse button, and dragging the window around the display. Keyboard keys may also be used if the "move menu" command is selected from the window's control menu.

Here is the definition for testReport:

```
boolean MyAppView::testReport(MenuItem *m)
{
    Report::dialog("Report Dialog",
```

```
              this,
              "Report dialogs expand automatically "
              "to accommodate long prompt strings."
              );
}
```

Report is another class provided by C++ Views that provides a static member method called dialog. In fact, all seven dialogs demonstrated in the chapter follow the same pattern. Each dialog is invoked by calling a static member method implemented in a class with the same name as the dialog:

```
About::dialog
Report::dialog
YesNo::dialog
YesNoCancel::dialog
Input::dialog
ListSelect::dialog
FileSelect::dialog
```

The first argument to Report::dialog is the string that is to appear in the title box. This second argument is a pointer to the parent view for the dialog. The third argument is the prompt string, again wrapped to fit into a rectangle. You can control the formatting of the prompt string by inserting tabs, \t, and newline characters, \n. Report dialogs will grow in size to accommodate long prompt strings.

YesNo

The YesNo dialog class was discussed briefly in the previous chapter. The following illustration shows a YesNo dialog. YesNo::dialog takes four arguments.

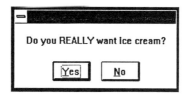

The first argument is a pointer to the parent window. The second argument is a boolean value indicating whether or not a Cancel button should be included in addition to the Yes and No buttons. The third argument indicates which of the buttons is the active, or default, button when the dialog is first invoked. The last argument is the prompt string displayed inside the dialog box. The testYesNo method looks like this:

```
boolean MyAppView::testYesNo(MenuItem  *m)
{
    enum yesNoCancel result =
    YesNo::dialog(this,          // current window
                  FALSE,         // cancel button NOT supplied
                  YesButton,     // default button
                  "Do you REALLY want ice cream?"
                 );
    String *ps;
    switch (result)
    {
        case YesButton:
                ps = new String("Yes");
                break;
        case NoButton:
                ps = new String("No");
                break;
        default:
                break;
    }
    char buf[10];
    ps->gets(buf, 10);
    Report::dialog("YesNo",      // window title
                   this,         // current window
                   "You selected: %s", buf);
    ps->free();
}
```

The button pressed to terminate this dialog is recorded in an enum type variable called "result". A pointer to a String, ps, is then assigned either "Yes" or "No" in a switch statement based on result.

Strings are interesting objects in C++ Views. Strings are a subclass of Container. String objects are not fixed in size like standard char arrays in C. Therefore, Strings can grow as new characters or as other strings are concatenated or copied into them. However, String objects cannot be passed to functions or methods, which expect standard C or C++ strings in the form of character arrays or character pointers (char *s). Therefore, the String class provides a method to copy the contents of a String object into a character array. The method is String::gets. The first argument to this method is the destination character array into which the contents of the string should be copied. The second argument is the maximum number of characters to be copied, not including the NULL character appended automatically to the end of the character array. Given a pointer to a String, ps, and a character array, buf, large enough to contain ten elements of type char, the following statement will copy up to the first ten characters in the String pointed to by ps into buf.

```
ps->gets(buf, 10);
```

The net result of all the code appearing after the call to YesNo::dialog in the testYesNo method is to create and display a Report dialog indicating which button was pressed to terminate the YesNo::dialog. For instance, the following illustration shows the Report dialog generated if the Yes button terminated the YesNo dialog.

YesNoCancel

The testYesNoCancel method is nearly identical to testYesNo, but contains a few twists.

```
boolean MyAppView::testYesNoCancel(MenuItem  *m)
{
    int warning = 999;
    String *ps = new String("DIALOG.CPP");
    enum yesNoCancel result =
    YesNo::dialog(this,            // current window
                  TRUE,            // cancel button supplied
                  YesButton,       // default response
                  "Warning: %d\n"
                  "File not saved %s\n"
                  "Save before quitting?",
                  warning, ps->gets()
                 );
    ps->free();
```

```
switch (result)
{
    case YesButton:
            ps = new String("Yes");
            break;
    case NoButton:
            ps = new String("No");
            break;
    case CancelButton:
            ps = new String("Cancel");
            break;
    default:
            break;
}
char buf[10];
ps->gets(buf, 10);
Report::dialog("YesNoCancel",
                this,
                "You selected: %s", buf);
ps->free();
}
```

The following illustration is the dialog that results from invoking this method:

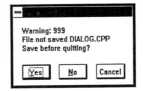

There are two main differences between this dialog and the YesNo dialog. Both call the static method YesNo::dialog. However, testYesNoCancel specifies TRUE for the second argument, indicating that a Cancel button is to be supplied.

The second twist is the use of C printf-style format strings. Most dialog boxes provided by C++ Views allow this type of formatting. As with printf, the prompt string may contain format specifiers such as %d and %s. For each format specifier in the prompt string, an additional argument must be appended to the argument list that is passed to the static dialog method. If no format specifiers are in the prompt string, then YesNo::dialog accepts exactly four arguments, the last of which is the prompt string. However, in the test method above, the prompt string contains two format specifiers: %d and %s. So in addition to the prompt string, two arguments are appended to the argument list:

```
warning, ps->gets()
```

The first argument is an integer variable set to the value of 999. This object is type-compatible with the %d format specifier in the prompt string. The value 999 is converted to a string and substituted for the %d in the prompt string before the string is printed in the dialog box. The second additional argument is actually a method call to String::gets(). This version of String::gets() receives no arguments; it therefore overrides the String:: gets method discussed previously, which expected two arguments.

The result of calling String::gets with no argument is a char* type pointer pointing to the first character inside the String object pointed to by ps. This is another way of saying that the expression,

```
ps->gets()
```

evaluates to a char* C string, which is compatible with the %s format specifier in the prompt string. The net result is that the String pointed to by ps ("DIALOG.CPP") is substituted for the %s in the prompt string before the prompt string is printed in the dialog box. You might use this type of format specification if you want to pass a variable string identifier to a warning or an error message dialog.

Notice also that in the above test method, the String, "DIALOG.CPP", is created on the heap using the C++ new operator.

```
String *ps = new String("DIALOG.CPP");
```

Any object created on the heap should be destroyed when it is no longer needed. String objects provide a method, String::free, which automatically deallocates String objects created on the heap.

```
ps->free();
```

This test method also uses a Report dialog to tell the user which button was pressed to terminate the YesNoCancel dialog.

Input

Input dialogs are useful for getting strings of text from the user. They are used frequently, for example, when filling out address forms in a database program or when typing filenames in a file management utility. The following illustration shows an Input dialog. An Input dialog has three controls—the input field itself where text is typed, the OK button, and the Cancel button.

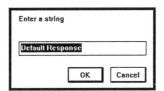

There is a label field equivalent to the prompt field discussed in previous dialogs. This label field can be used to prompt the user with directions for input. A default response string may also be specified. If the default response string is specified, it will appear in highlighted text when the Input dialog is first invoked. If any alphanumeric keys are typed before pressing a cursor control key, such as HOME, END, LEFT ARROW, or RIGHT ARROW, the highlighted text disappears and is replaced by the newly typed text. Pressing a cursor control key first will cause the highlighting to disappear, and any alphanumeric keys you press will insert the corresponding characters into the default response string at the current cursor position.

```
boolean MyAppView::testInput(MenuItem  *m)
{
    String  *response;
    String  *defaultResponse = new String("Default Response");
    response = Input::dialog("Enter a string",
                             defaultResponse,
                             this);
    if (response)
    {
        char buf[200];
        response->gets(buf, 200);
        Report::dialog("Input",
                       this,
                       "Response: %s", buf);
```

```
        response->free();
    }
}
```

The call to Input::dialog accepts three arguments. The first is the prompt string, containing directions to the user. The second argument is a pointer to a String object that contains the default response. In the event that the user immediately presses RETURN, this is the string returned by the dialog. The third argument is a pointer to the parent window for this dialog. The value returned by Input::dialog is a pointer to a String object. The prompt string for Input::dialog does not support C printf-style formatting.

The following illustration shows what happens if you type a very long input string and then press HOME to move the cursor back to the beginning of the string.

You can use the cursor control keys to scroll through the input. If the OK button is pressed, the input string is accepted and returned to the caller. In the next illustration, you see what the call to Report::dialog in the previous test method does with a long response string.

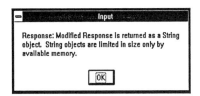

If Cancel is selected, the default response string is the value returned by the Input dialog and all editing changes are lost.

ListSelect

The ListSelect dialog allows you to display a list of strings in a view that includes a title box, an OK button, and a Cancel button. Such a list can be seen in Figure 12-2. If the number of the items in the list of strings was so great that the full list could not be displayed on the screen at once, a vertical scrollbar would appear to the right of the list, allowing the user to scroll up and down through the strings. The list of strings is passed to the static ListSelect::dialog method as an array of pointers to String objects. Such an array is declared as follows:

```
const strListSize = 20;
String *strList[strListSize];
```

Now strings can be added by assigning pointers to String objects to the elements of the array.

```
strList[0] = &String("Vanilla");
strList[1] = &String("Chocolate");
   .
   .
   .
```

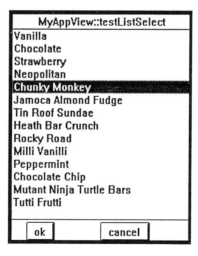

Figure 12-2.   A ListSelect dialog

There's a little trick you can use in the event that you will later want to change the order of pointers in the array. Simply use an integer, i, as an index into the strList array. Set this index to have an initial value of 0. You can use the C++ post-increment operator, + +, to automatically increase the index each time you add a new string pointer to the array.

```
int i=0;
strList[i++] = &String("Vanilla");
strList[i++] = &String("Chocolate");
    .
    .
    .
```

Once the strList array is created, you are ready to call ListSelect.

```
int index =                 // return index of selected
ListSelect::dialog(TRUE,    // item or -1 if canceled
                   "MyAppView::testListSelect",
                   strList, // list of String selections
                   this     // window
                  );
```

The value returned by ListSelect is the index number of the element in strList that was highlighted when the OK button is pressed. Since this is a 0-based array, a −1 return value is used to signal that the dialog was terminated with the Cancel button.

If the Cancel button has not been pressed, you can print out the selected String element by copying it into a buffer and displaying it in a Report dialog.

```
char buf[100];
if (index != -1)             // cancel NOT selected
    strList[index]->gets(buf, 100);
else
    strcpy(buf, "no selection");
Report::dialog("ListSelect",
               this,
               "Selected list item: %s", buf);
```

Again, this technique makes use of the two-argument String::gets method to copy the String pointed to by strList[index] into the character array buf.

```
strList[index]->gets(buf, 100);
```

Report::dialog is called with a prompt string containing a %s format specifier, and the corresponding string is passed as the extra argument, buf. Here's the entire definition for testListSelect:

```
boolean MyAppView::testListSelect(MenuItem *m)
{
    const strListSize = 20;
    String *strList[strListSize];
    int i=0;
    strList[i++] = &String("Vanilla");
    strList[i++] = &String("Chocolate");
    strList[i++] = &String("Strawberry");
    strList[i++] = &String("Neapolitan");
    strList[i++] = &String("Chunky Monkey");
    strList[i++] = &String("Jamoca Almond Fudge");
    strList[i++] = &String("Tin Roof Sundae");
    strList[i++] = &String("Heath Bar Crunch");
    strList[i++] = &String("Rocky Road");
    strList[i++] = &String("Milli Vanilli");
    strList[i++] = &String("Peppermint");
    strList[i++] = &String("Chocolate Chip");
    strList[i++] = &String("Mutant Ninja Turtle Bars");
    strList[i++] = &String("Tutti Frutti");
    strList[i++] = NIL;

    int index =                 // return index of selected
    ListSelect::dialog(TRUE,    // item or -1 if canceled
                    "MyAppView::testListSelect",
                    strList, // list of String selections
                    this     // window
                );

    char buf[100];
    if (index != -1)            // cancel NOT selected
        strList[index]->gets(buf, 100);
    else
        strcpy(buf, "no selection");
    Report::dialog("ListSelect",
                this,
                "Selected list item: %s", buf);
}
```

The next illustration shows the Report dialog that results from selecting OK with "Chunky Monkey" highlighted.

The selected string in a ListSelect dialog can be retrieved from the index value returned by ListSelect.

FileSelect

FileSelect dialogs are very powerful and can be used in many different situations. You can use such dialogs in a file manager, a paint program, an editor, or just about any program that needs to load, create, or save files on a disk. Figure 12-3 shows a FileSelect dialog. A FileSelect dialog has five control views:

1. A text edit box field, where the user can type a filename, including wildcards

2. A list box containing files that match the current filename specification

3. A list box containing directories immediately accessible from the current directory

4. An Open pushbutton

5. A Cancel pushbutton

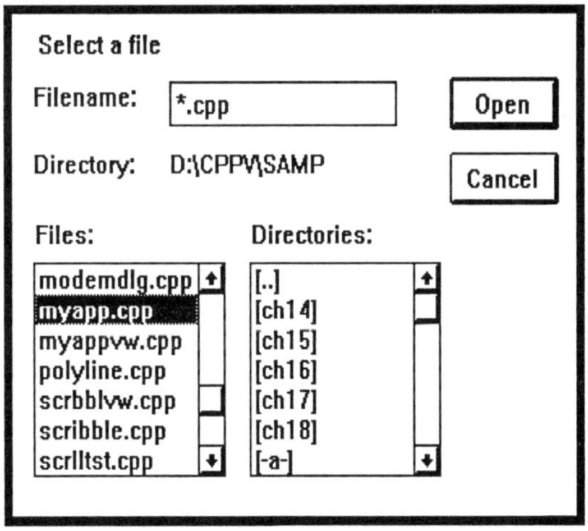

Figure 12-3.   A FileSelect dialog

In addition, a FileSelect dialog contains a prompt specified by the programmer, a text field indicating the currently logged directory, and labels for the Files and Directories list-selection boxes.

The user supplies four arguments in a call to the static method FileSelect:: dialog. The first argument is a pointer to the view that owns the dialog. The second argument is the prompt string that appears at the top of the FileSelect dialog box. The third argument is the initial file you wish to be selected within the Files list—this file will appear at the top of the list in inverse video. If the third argument is NIL, the initial file is the first file in the current directory that matches the file-filter specification in the fourth argument.

The fourth argument is the file-filter specification, which accepts standard MS-DOS wildcards such as ? to match any single character and * to match any sequence of characters. The list in the Files selection box will include only files in the current directory that match the filter specification. If filter is NIL, the filter specification is interpreted as "*.*". If you wanted the file list to only include files starting with *M* and having a .CPP extension, you could use the filter "M*.CPP". This filter must be a pointer to a String object. The following declaration creates such a filter for showing all files in the current directory with a .CPP extension.

```
String *filter = new String("*.cpp");
```

You can then use such a filter in a call to FileSelect::dialog:

```
String *result = FileSelect::dialog(this,
                            "Select a file",
                            NIL,
                            filter);
```

FileSelect returns a pointer to a String object corresponding to the string that is highlighted in the Files list when the Open button is pressed. If the dialog is terminated by pressing Cancel, the value of this pointer will be NIL. If a value other than NIL is returned, it means that FileSelect actually created a new String object on the heap. This object must be discarded to reclaim the heap memory with a statement like the following, when the object is no longer needed.

```
result->free();
```

It is an error to make this call if the value of result is NIL. Be sure to test the value of result before making the call, or the program may crash. The complete implementation of testFileSelect is shown here:

```
boolean MyAppView::testFileSelect(MenuItem  *m)
{
    String *filter = new String("*.cpp");
    String *result = FileSelect::dialog(this,
                                        "Select a file",
                                        NIL,
                                        filter);
    if (result)
    {
        char buf[100];
        result->gets(buf, 100);
        Report::dialog("FileSelect",
                       this,
                       "File selected: %s", buf);
        result->free();
    }
    filter->free();
}
```

A Report dialog is used to show the selected file as long as the FileSelect dialog is not terminated with the Cancel button. The following illustration shows the result string when the current working directory is D:\CPPV\SAMPLES\ and the file MYAPP.CPP is selected.

This final listing shows the complete implementation of MYAPP-VW.CPP, including all test methods for the seven types of dialogs presented in this chapter. This file also includes the specification for the application menu as well as all definitions for member methods of the MyAppView class.

```
FILE: MYAPPVW.CPP

#include "myappvw.h"
#include <stdio.h>
#include <string.h>
```

```
#include "about.h"
#include "report.h"
#include "input.h"
#include "yesno.h"
#include "listslct.h"
#include "fileslct.h"

defineClass(MyAppView,AppView)
static char *WindowTitle="C++ Views Dialog Boxes for MS-Windows";

//////////////////////////////////////////////////////////////
// DEMO menu static data
//////////////////////////////////////////////////////////////
static char *DEMOnames[] =
{
    "&About\tCtr-A",
    "&Report\tCtr-R",
    "&YesNo\tCtr-Y",
    "YesNo&Cancel\tCtr-C",
    "&Input\tCtr-I",
    "&ListSelect\tCtr-L",
    "&FileSelect\tCtr-F",
    "",
    "E&xit\tAlt-X",
    0
};

static method DEMOnameMthds[] =
{
    defMethod(MyAppView,testAbout),
    defMethod(MyAppView,testReport),
    defMethod(MyAppView,testYesNo),
    defMethod(MyAppView,testYesNoCancel),
    defMethod(MyAppView,testInput),
    defMethod(MyAppView,testListSelect),
    defMethod(MyAppView,testFileSelect),

    NIL_METHOD,
    defMethod(MyAppView,exit),
};

static int DEMOaccelKeys[] =
{
    K_Mod_Metal | K_A,
    K_Mod_Metal | K_R,
    K_Mod_Metal | K_Y,
    K_Mod_Metal | K_C,
    K_Mod_Metal | K_I,
    K_Mod_Metal | K_L,
    K_Mod_Metal | K_F,
    K_NULL,
    K_Mod_Meta2 | K_X,
    0
};
//////////////////////////////////////////////////////////////
```

```
MyAppView::MyAppView()
{
   setTitle(WindowTitle);
   initMenuBar();
}

MyAppView::~MyAppView()
{
}

boolean MyAppView::free()
{
    delete this;
    return TRUE;
}

void MyAppView::initMenuBar()
{
        //////////////////////////////////////////
        // create menu and add menu bar
        //////////////////////////////////////////
        PopupMenu *DEMOpop = new PopupMenu("&Dialogs");
        addPopup(DEMOpop);
        DEMOpop->addItems(DEMOnames,
                          DEMOnameMthds,
                          DEMOaccelKeys,
                          this);
}

boolean MyAppView::testAbout(MenuItem *m)
{
    About::dialog( "\n"
                   "This program demonstrates the use of "
                   "various dialog boxes developed to "
                   "work with the C++ Views "
                   "application framework.",
                   this);
}

boolean MyAppView::testReport(MenuItem *m)
{
    Report::dialog("Report Dialog",
                   this,
                   "Report dialogs expand automatically "
                   "to accomodate long prompt strings."
                   );
}

boolean MyAppView::testYesNo(MenuItem  *m)
{
    enum yesNoCancel result =
    YesNo::dialog(this,          // current window
                  FALSE,         // cancel button NOT supplied
                  YesButton,     // default button
                  "Do you REALLY want ice cream?"
                  );
```

```
    String *ps;
    switch (result)
    {
        case YesButton:
                ps = new String("Yes");
                break;
        case NoButton:
                ps = new String("No");
                break;
        default:
                break;
    }
    char buf[10];
    ps->gets(buf, 10);
    Report::dialog("YesNo",       // window title
                    this,          // current window
                    "You selected: %s", buf);
    ps->free();
}

boolean MyAppView::testYesNoCancel(MenuItem  *m)
{
    int warning = 999;
    String *ps = new String("DIALOG.CPP");
    enum yesNoCancel result =
    YesNo::dialog(this,            // current window
                    TRUE,          // cancel button supplied
                    YesButton,     // default response
                    "Warning: %d\n"
                    "File not saved %s\n"
                    "Save before quitting?",
                    warning, ps->gets()
                );
    ps->free();
    switch (result)
    {
        case YesButton:
                ps = new String("Yes");
                break;
        case NoButton:
                ps = new String("No");
                break;
        case CancelButton:
                ps = new String("Cancel");
                break;
        default:
                break;
    }
    char buf[10];
    ps->gets(buf, 10);
    Report::dialog("YesNoCancel",
                    this,
                    "You selected: %s", buf);
    ps->free();
}
```

```
boolean MyAppView::testInput(MenuItem  *m)
{
    String  *response;
    String  *defaultResponse = new String("Default Response");
    response = Input::dialog("Enter a string",
                                 defaultResponse,
                                 this);
    if (response)
    {
        char buf[200];
        response->gets(buf, 200);
        Report::dialog("Input",
                        this,
                        "Response: %s", buf);
        response->free();
    }
}

boolean MyAppView::testListSelect(MenuItem *m)
{
    const strListSize = 20;
    String *strList[strListSize];
    int i=0;
    strList[i++] = &String("Vanilla");
    strList[i++] = &String("Chocolate");
    strList[i++] = &String("Strawberry");
    strList[i++] = &String("Neapolitan");
    strList[i++] = &String("Chunky Monkey");
    strList[i++] = &String("Jamoca Almond Fudge");
    strList[i++] = &String("Tin Roof Sundae");
    strList[i++] = &String("Heath Bar Crunch");
    strList[i++] = &String("Rocky Road");
    strList[i++] = &String("Milli Vanilli");
    strList[i++] = &String("Peppermint");
    strList[i++] = &String("Chocolate Chip");
    strList[i++] = &String("Mutant Ninja Turtle Bars");
    strList[i++] = &String("Tutti Frutti");
    strList[i++] = NIL;

    int index =                  // return index of selected
    ListSelect::dialog(TRUE,     // item or -1 if canceled
                        "MyAppView::testListSelect",
                        strList, // list of String selections
                        this     // window
                        );

    char buf[100];
    if (index != -1)             // cancel NOT selected
        strList[index]->gets(buf, 100);
    else
        strcpy(buf, "no selection");
    Report::dialog("ListSelect",
                    this,
                    "Selected list item: %s", buf);
}
```

```
boolean MyAppView::testFileSelect(MenuItem  *m)
{
    String *filter = new String("*.cpp");
    String *result = FileSelect::dialog(this,
                                        "Select a file",
                                        NIL,
                                        filter);
    if (result)
    {
        char buf[100];
        result->gets(buf, 100);
        Report::dialog("FileSelect",
                        this,
                        "File selected: %s", buf);
        result->free();
    }
    filter->free();
}

boolean MyAppView::exit(MenuItem  *m)
{
    enum yesNoCancel result =
    YesNo::dialog(this,                     // current window
                    FALSE,                  // cancel button supplied
                    NoButton,               // default response
                    "Terminate program?"   // prompt
                 );
    if (result == YesButton)
    {
        close();                            // exit application
    }
}
```

CHAPTER HIGHLIGHTS

This chapter discussed the use of a standard set of dialog boxes provided by C++ Views. An application framework was set up with a menu used to call test methods for each of these dialogs. All of the dialogs used in this chapter are derived from a class called Dialog, which, in turn, is derived from the class PopupWindow, which is a form of View object.

There will be times when you will need to change the behavior of these dialog classes or implement more sophisticated dialogs with many different controls. C++ Views provides an easy way to build such dialogs. In fact, a utility is provided that allows you to take files generated by the Microsoft Windows Software Development Kit (SDK) Dialog Editor and generate C++ Views dialog classes directly from those files.

The next chapter discusses the creation of custom dialogs and shows how to get complex data into and out of dialog boxes.

13

DIALOGS AND DATA

Chapters 11 and 12 introduced the C++ Views application framework and showed how to create common menus and dialog boxes for Microsoft Windows application programs. Many applications require dialog boxes that are custom built to handle special types of data or to give a special look to an application. When you build a custom dialog box you have to provide a way to get data into the dialog before it is activated and a way to get data out of the dialog once it is accepted. This chapter demonstrates the construction of advanced dialog boxes and dialog controls.

Building dialogs from scratch allows you to position and size dialog controls anywhere you like inside the dialog box. An example dialog box used to control modem communication parameters demonstrates specification of buttons and button groups, including radio buttons and check boxes. To build the example programs in this chapter you need the C++ Views application framework from CNS, Inc., and either a Zortech C++ or Borland C++ compiler.

The discussion of dialog boxes so far has concentrated on how to use predefined dialog boxes. Building custom dialog boxes for C++ Views has not been discussed at all. Also, although the concept of model-view-controller has been discussed as a structuring technique, few of the programs have actually used models. That's because you need to learn to build user-interface components before you can learn how to make them work with an application model. This chapter introduces a model whose data is to be manipulated by a dialog box. Look again at the connections between model-view-controller components shown in the diagram in Figure 13-1.

In this model-view-controller context, a dialog box is a view. If a dialog is going to change or modify data, it must have a model associated with it. The way this frequently works in practice is to have the top-level view invoke one or more dialogs as subviews. The top-level view maintains an instance connection to the model for the entire application. Before invoking a specific dialog to manipulate some subset of the data for the entire program model, the top-level view passes a copy of the appropriate data to the dialog box. The user can then modify the data inside the dialog box and terminate the dialog when finished. If the user indicates the desire to accept the data modified in the dialog box (OK button pressed), the top-level view takes the modified copy of data, which has been altered by the dialog, and moves the modified data back to the program model.

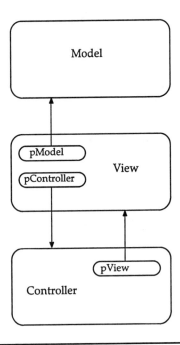

Figure 13-1.   Connections among top-level model, view, and controller components of an application program

BUILDING CUSTOM DIALOGS

Suppose, for example, you were developing a telecommunications program to work with a modem. One of the subsets of data that the program would need to maintain would be communications parameters: baud rate, parity, number of data bits, number of stop bits, and so forth. This set of data is large, but the elements of the data set are all related. It makes sense, therefore, to have a single dialog box, such as that in Figure 13-2.

The basic program structure in terms of the model-view-controller paradigm would be modified to look like Figure 13-3. There are two new components: the modem parameter object is a model controlled by the modem parameter dialog (a control view). The modem parameter model is a subset of all the data for the modem component of the system, which contains all the data necessary for a modem terminal program to operate. This would include text data on the screen, names of open files, and current program operating state, including phone numbers, current connection status, and incoming data buffers.

This chapter develops one element from the modem model—the part of the modem model that contains data controlling the current communications parameter settings. A modem dialog view is also developed in this chapter and is designed to work hand in hand with the modem model. These two subcomponents are typical of components you will find in a real working application program. Before looking at the details of the modem model or the ModemDialog view, consider the programming required to create a typical dialog view.

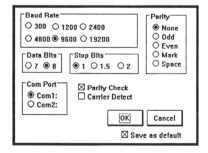

Figure 13-2.   A dialog box to control modem communications parameters

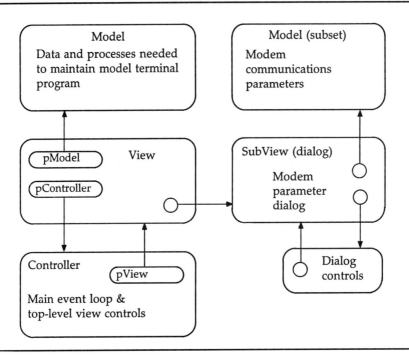

Figure 13-3. A model-view-controller diagram showing relationship between top-level view and dialog subview. Subviews, like their parents, also have models and controllers.

Typical Dialog View

A typical dialog view inherits its properties from the Dialog class.

```
class MyDialog : public Dialog
{
    ...
};
```

There are certain public methods that must be defined for Dialogs simply because Dialogs are a subclass of Objects. These include a class identifier, a constructor of no arguments, and a destructor.

```
class MyDialog : public Dialog
{
public:
    Class *iam();
    MyDialog();
    ~MyDialog();
};
```

Typically, C++Views dialogs will include three more methods. The first method will be an additional constructor receiving arguments. Usually, a minimum of two arguments is specified for such a constructor. The first argument is the data displayed in the dialog, often a character string. The second argument would be a pointer to the window that is a parent for the dialog view.

```
class MyDialog : public Dialog
{
public:
    ...
    MyDialog(char *, Window *w);
    ...
};
```

This is the format of the constructor used for the About dialog shown in Chapter 12. The first string is used as a prompt to be displayed inside of the dialog box. Also, a static member method is usually supplied for a dialog. This static member usually receives the same arguments as the constructor and possibly one or more additional arguments, usually pointers that are used to copy data into and out of the dialog. The declaration for such a static member function for MyDialog might be as follows:

```
class MyDialog : public Dialog
{
public:
    ...
    static void dialog(char *, Window *w);
    ...
};
```

Typically, such a static member function would create an instance of the dialog, pass control to it, and return the results, if any, to the calling routine. Static member functions make the calling syntax easier for the user. The previous method returns no value, since the dialog is intended to mimic an About dialog. You could call the method from a menu command handler routine such as the one defined here:

```
boolean MyAppView::testMyDialog(MenuItem *m)
{
    MyDialog::dialog("Dialog prompt string",
                     this);
}
```

The other two methods included in most dialog views are a private initialization method and at least one event handler. The event handler is necessary to handle the event required to terminate the dialog.

```
class MyDialog : public Dialog
{
    ...
    boolean init();          // private method
public:
    ...
    boolean ok(Button *);
};
```

Several private instance variables are then usually declared to point at the controls to be inserted into the dialog.

A dialog almost always includes one button, usually an OK button, pointed to by a private instance variable inside the dialog object. The button is then created by the private init initialization method, and the pointer is assigned to point to the newly created object. Also, if any type of text string is to be displayed it is necessary to declare a pointer to a TextBox object, which will also be created by init. The entire declaration for MyDialog, including private instance variable pointers, would look like this:

```
class MyDialog : public Dialog
{
    TextBox       *aTextBox;
    PushButton    *okButton;

    boolean init();
public:
    Class *iam();
    MyDialog();
    MyDialog(char *, Window *w);
    ~MyDialog();
    static void dialog(char *, Window *w);
    boolean ok(Button *);
};
```

Creating a Dialog Window

The first thing the constructor must do is create a new window for the dialog. This is done by calling the getWindow function. It's often easiest to work with dimensions that are multiples of the font width and the font height of the text to be displayed. It's easier to figure out how many lines of text a window needs to accommodate than to figure out how many pixels high a window should be. For this reason, C++ Views provides access to the fontSize routine. The fontSize routine accepts two pointer arguments, both pointing to integers. The function returns the width and the height of the current system font in the variables pointed to by these arguments.

Next, the constructor calls the private init method. The init method is simply a convenient way to separate the code used to create control objects in the dialog. Often this code can become quite long. The code is usually not complicated, but it may take many lines to insert a large number of controls into a complex dialog box. Breaking this code off into a private method makes the constructor more readable. Here's the code for a typical constructor:

```
MyDialog::MyDialog(char *prompt, Window *win)
{
    int w, h;
    fontSize(&w, &h);
    if (!getWindow(50, 50, 40*w, 10*h, win) || !init())
        return;                     // can't open window
    if(prompt)
        aTextBox->putText(prompt);
    show();
    okButton->takeFocus();
    modal();
}
```

Consider the code in more detail. First, the window is created and the private initialization method is called in a single statement. If either one of these calls fails, they will return 0. The if statement will be true, and the constructor will return without ever passing control to the dialog.

```
    if (!getWindow(50, 50, 40*w, 10*h, win) || !init())
        return;                     // can't open window
```

Next, if the prompt string passed to the constructor is not NULL, the prompt string is printed inside the TextBox. Although you have not seen it yet, the code that creates the text box control object and the OK button control object is found in init.

Before looking at init, consider the last three statements in the constructor. The inherited method, show, is called to make the newly created window visible. The OK button is given input focus, and finally, modal is called giving *modal input control* to the dialog box. Any one of the controls within a dialog box can be given input focus. The dialog window keeps a list of all controls within the dialog that can have input focus. Pressing the TAB key shifts the input focus to the next control in the list.

A TextBox cannot have input focus unless it is a special subclass of text box called EditBox. Because the MyDialog view only contains two controls, and because the TextBox control cannot take focus, explicitly directing input focus to the OK button is not necessary. However, most dialogs have more than one control that will accept input focus, so most constructors do indicate which control is to be active when the dialog is invoked. The modal control established by dialog boxes prevents the user from sending events to any views within the application other than the active dialog view. The techniques for starting and ending modal control will be discussed in the section titled "Modal Control".

Adding Dialog Controls

Although it would be possible to add the controls for a dialog in the constructor, most C++ Views dialogs, by convention, create and insert controls in the private method, init, which is called from the constructor. Here's a typical definition for init:

```
boolean MyDialog::init()
{
    int w, h;
    fontSize(&w, &h);
    int windowWidth, windowHeight;
    sizeOfImage(&windowWidth, &windowHeight);

    int xCenter = windowWidth / 2;
    int buttonWidth = w*10;
    int buttonHeight = 2*h;
    int x = xCenter - (buttonWidth/2);
    int y = windowHeight - (buttonHeight+int(0.5*h));
    okButton = new PushButton(x,              y,
                              buttonWidth, buttonHeight,
                              this);
    okButton->setTitle("OK");
    okButton->setDefault(TRUE);
    okButton->uponClick(this,methodOf(MyDialog,ok));

    aTextBox = new TextBox(2*w,h,windowWidth-(4*w),2*h,this);
    return TRUE;  // successful initialization
}
```

If you look carefully at this method, you will only find two statements containing the operator, new.

```
okButton = new PushButton(x,           y,
                          buttonWidth, buttonHeight,
                          this);
...
aTextBox = new TextBox(2*w,h,windowWidth-(4*w),2*h,this);
```

These statements both create new control objects. The first statement creates a new PushButton object and assigns it to the private instance variable pointer, okButton. The second statement creates a new TextBox control object and assigns the private instance variable aTextBox to point to it.

The rest of the code involves calculations used to determine where to place the controls within the window. The exception includes three lines of code used to specify options for the okButton. First, the string title to be printed inside the button is set:

```
okButton->setTitle("OK");
```

The next statement simply draws a dark border around the button to indicate to the user that this button is the default control.

```
okButton->setDefault(TRUE);
```

This statement does not have anything to do with directing input focus; it merely gives a visual emphasis to the button.

The third statement establishes a callback method for the button. The callback method must be a member of the class of object that owns the button. In other words, this method must be a member of MyDialog class.

```
okButton->uponClick(this,methodOf(MyDialog,ok));
```

This statement establishes that the method MyDialog::ok will be called from the MyDialog object that owns the OK button. This method will be called whenever the OK button is activated inside the dialog box. This form of callback method is necessary to terminate the modal control of input established when the dialog box is activated from the constructor. This will be discussed in detail in the section, "Callback Methods".

Modal Control

The last thing the constructor does is call the inherited method Dialog::modal, which puts the dialog in *modal operation*. When a dialog is in modal operation, it disables all keyboard and mouse events to windows within the application. The exception is the currently active dialog. As long as the dialog box remains in the modal state, all input is directed to the dialog.

This condition persists until the inherited method Dialog::endModal is called. The problem, then, is how to call endModal. First, consider the flow of control inside a hypothetical constructor for a dialog view.

```
MyDialog::MyDialog(char *prompt, Window *win)
{
    //statement 1
    modal();
    //statement 2
}
```

Statements 1 and 2 might represent one or more program statements within the constructor. All the code represented by statement 1 is executed before the call to modal. This code usually initializes and displays the dialog view. When modal is called, program control stops inside this constructor and is passed to a dialog event loop routine invisible to the programmer. This event loop traps all input to the application and sends it directly to the now-active dialog view. Control remains inside this routine until the method Dialog::endModal is called. This is where callback methods are required. Program control as understood in typical structured programming is now out of the hands of the programmer. All input is now being handled and dispatched by the modal dialog event loop. The application program therefore needs to intercept certain specified events and direct program control to a method that invokes Dialog::endModal.

Callback Methods

The method MyDialog::ok is a *callback method*. All button objects have a private instance variable that can be used to point to a callback method. By default, this method pointer points at the NIL_METHOD. As long as this pointer is not changed nothing happens when the button is pressed.

However, if the programmer changes the value of this pointer by using the Button::uponClick method, pressing the button will pass control to the assigned method. Recall that MyDialog::init assigns such a callback method for okButton.

```
okButton = new PushButton(x,          y,
                          buttonWidth, buttonHeight,
                          this);
...
okButton->uponClick(this,methodOf(MyDialog,ok));
```

The last statement establishes the method MyDialog::ok as the method to be called when okButton is pressed.

The definition for MyDialog::ok is as follows:

```
boolean MyDialog::ok(Button *b)
{
    endModal();
    return TRUE;
}
```

This is how endModal gets called. The prototype for a callback method must meet certain criteria. It must return a boolean value and must accept as an argument a pointer to a Button object. Button objects include push-buttons, radio buttons, and check boxes. Here is the C++ Views class hierarchy for common buttons:

```
Button
  PushButton
  CheckBox
    RadioButton
```

All objects from this type hierarchy are considered buttons. The callback method is a form of event handler. Event handlers are called from the main event loop, and the handlers need to tell the main event loop whether or not they have handled, or consumed, an event. A handler that returns the value of TRUE tells the main event loop that it has handled or responded to the event. This means the main event loop does not need to look for other objects to handle the event. Once endModal is called from MyDialog::ok, control returns to the statement following the call to Dialog::modal in the constructor. This would be the statements represented by statement 2 in the following listing:

```
MyDialog::MyDialog(char *prompt, Window *win)
{
    //statement 1
    modal();
    //statement 2
}
```

In the definition of the constructor presented earlier, there is no state-ment following modal. Execution control, therefore, returns immediately from the constructor to the routine that created the MyDialog object that invoked the constructor.

DIALOGS AND DATA

Now that you know how to create custom dialogs, you need to be able to associate a given set of data with a dialog. Such a set of data is often referred to as a *model*. A dialog box can then be associated with the model using the model-view-controller paradigm. In this context, the data is the model and the dialog is the view. The controller is the set of commands that can be activated through the controls contained inside of the dialog when the dialog is active.

Model-View-Controller Considerations

Remember that the purpose of using a model-view-controller structure is to make application data (the model) as independent as possible of the way in which data is displayed (the view), and the way in which input is used to manipulate the data (the controller). This structure upholds the general principle and goal of object-oriented programming: to minimize the num-ber of connections among system components. Make everything as simple as possible.

Creating a Model

For the sake of simplicity, the class name for the model developed in this chapter will be called Modem. It might be more accurate to call the model ModemParameters since only a subset of all the data and processes needed for a modem application will be managed by the model. However, to avoid long identifier names like ModemParametersDialog, the shorter versions Modem and ModemDialog will be used. The first thing to do when building a new class is to declare the private instance variables. These can be found easily enough by listing each of the control parameters in the dialog box in Figure 13-2.

Most methods for Modem objects are defined inline in the declaration for Modem found in MODEM.H.

```
FILE: MODEM.H

#ifndef MDMPARAM_H
#define MDMPARAM_H

#include "object.h"

enum baudEnum
{
    baud300,
    baud1200,
    baud2400,
    baud4800,
    baud9600,
    baud19200,
};

enum dataEnum
{
    data7,
    data8
};

enum stopEnum
{
    stop1,
    stop1_5,
    stop2
};

enum comPortEnum
{
    comPort1,
    comPort2
};

enum parityEnum
{
    parityNone,
    parityOdd,
    parityEven,
    parityMark,
    paritySpace
};
```

```
class Modem : public Object
{
    baudEnum    _baud;
    dataEnum    _data;
    stopEnum    _stop;
    comPortEnum _comPort;
    parityEnum  _parity;
    boolean     _parityCheck;
    boolean     _carrierDetect;
public:
    Modem();
    void baud(baudEnum value)         { _baud = value; }
    baudEnum baud()                   { return _baud; }

    void data(dataEnum value)         { _data = value; }
    dataEnum data()                   { return _data; }

    void stop(stopEnum value)         { _stop = value; }
    stopEnum stop()                   { return _stop; }

    void comPort(comPortEnum value)   { _comPort = value; }
    comPortEnum comPort()             { return _comPort; }

    void parity(parityEnum value)     { _parity = value; }
    parityEnum parity()               { return _parity; }

    void parityCheck(boolean value)   { _parityCheck = value; }
    boolean parityCheck()             { return _parityCheck; }

    void carrierDetect(boolean value){ _carrierDetect = value; }
    boolean carrierDetect()           { return _carrierDetect; }
};

#endif
```

Only the constructor for Modem objects is defined in a separate .CPP file. Here's a possible definition:

```
FILE: MODEM.CPP

#include "modem.h"

Modem::Modem()
{
    baud(baud9600);
    data(data8);
    stop(stop1);
    comPort(comPort1);
    parity(parityNone);
    parityCheck(TRUE);
    carrierDetect(FALSE);
}
```

This listing actually shows more than the definition. It shows the entire file, MODEM.CPP. Only one method is defined in the file.

Connections Among Model-View-Controller Components

Figure 13-3 shows that the model-view-controller relationship that holds for the top-level view can also be applied to subviews. An application program usually has many subviews. At all levels, views are the central components that manage the relationships between themselves and their associated models and controllers.

Figure 13-4 shows how controls added to a subview interact with the subview. Various types of controls are added to a dialog box, for example. These controls include radio buttons, check boxes, pushbuttons, and text editing fields. The user communicates with the view by activating these controls. When a control is activated, the main event manager issues messages associated with a given control object. The message is a callback method loosely similar to an event. The callback method associated with a control usually invokes an event handler defined inside of the view that owns the control.

When a view contains a model, event handler methods (defined in the view) respond to control messages by sending messages, in turn, to manipulate data within the model. The view must subsequently read data back from the model and update the display.

CREATING A DIALOG VIEW FOR THE MODEM MODEL

It's often easiest, when building a class, to start by listing the private instance variables. After that, the public methods can be defined to manipulate the values of these variables. Because of the complexity of the modem parameter dialog, the presentation order will be slightly different. The best way to generate a dialog box such as that found in Figure 13-2 is to use a dialog resource editor, such as the Whitewater Resource Toolkit or the SDK (Software Development Kit) dialog editor. The SDK dialog editor is a standard Microsoft Windows tool provided with the toolkit that must be purchased in order to develop Windows applications. If you have Borland C++, you'll probably be using the Whitewater dialog editor.

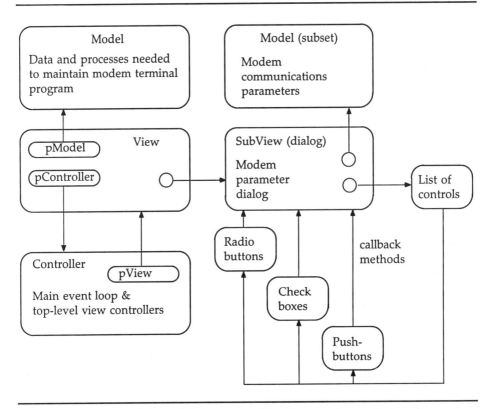

Figure 13-4.   Expanded model-view-controller diagram shows that a view such as a dialog contains a number of control objects in a list, which point to callback methods in the view. Selecting a control object invokes the associated callback method.

C++ Views provides a way to take the files generated by the SDK and Whitewater dialog editors (.DLG files) and from these files create class declarations and method definitions for the dialog view. This utility is called MKDLG.EXE and is provided with C++ Views. This utility will generate a header file (.H) and a C++ source code file (.CPP) for each type of dialog. The name of the dialog class associated with the Modem model is ModemDialog. The files generated through the dialog editor and C++ conversion utility are MODEMDLG.H and MODEMDLG.CPP.

For instance, the dialog source file generated by the SDK dialog editor for the dialog in Figure 13-2 looks like this:

```
FILE: MODEMDLG.DLG

MODEMDIALOG DIALOG LOADONCALL MOVEABLE DISCARDABLE 24, 23, 208, 136
STYLE WS_DLGFRAME | WS_POPUP
BEGIN
     CONTROL "OK",            100, "button", BS_PUSHBUTTON |
                                             WS_TABSTOP |
                                             WS_CHILD,
                                             105, 102, 41, 16
     CONTROL "Baud Rate",     104, "button", BS_GROUPBOX |
                                             WS_TABSTOP |
                                             WS_CHILD,
                                             6, 2, 133, 38
     CONTROL "Parity",        126, "button", BS_GROUPBOX |
                                             WS_TABSTOP |
                                             WS_CHILD,
                                             149, 3, 46, 63
     CONTROL "Data Bits",     102, "button", BS_GROUPBOX |
                                             WS_TABSTOP |
                                             WS_CHILD,
                                             8, 42, 45, 23
     CONTROL "Stop Bits",     127, "button", BS_GROUPBOX |
                                             WS_TABSTOP |
                                             WS_CHILD,
                                             62, 42, 78, 24
     CONTROL "Com Port",      122, "button", BS_GROUPBOX |
                                             WS_TABSTOP |
                                             WS_CHILD,
                                             8, 71, 51, 36
     CONTROL "300",           105, "button", BS_RADIOBUTTON |
                                             WS_GROUP |
                                             WS_TABSTOP |
                                             WS_CHILD,
                                             11, 12, 28, 12
     CONTROL "1200",          106, "button", BS_RADIOBUTTON |
                                             WS_TABSTOP |
                                             WS_CHILD,
                                             42, 13, 28, 12
     CONTROL "2400",          107, "button", BS_RADIOBUTTON |
                                             WS_TABSTOP |
                                             WS_CHILD,
                                             73, 13, 28, 12
     CONTROL "4800",          111, "button", BS_RADIOBUTTON |
                                             WS_TABSTOP |
                                             WS_CHILD,
                                             11, 25, 28, 12
     CONTROL "9600",          110, "button", BS_RADIOBUTTON |
                                             WS_TABSTOP |
                                             WS_CHILD,
                                             41, 25, 28, 12
     CONTROL "19200",         108, "button", BS_RADIOBUTTON |
                                             WS_TABSTOP |
                                             WS_CHILD,
                                             74, 25, 32, 12
```

```
CONTROL "7",            117, "button", BS_RADIOBUTTON ¦
                                       WS_GROUP ¦
                                       WS_TABSTOP ¦
                                       WS_CHILD,
                                       11, 52, 15, 12
CONTROL "8",            114, "button", BS_RADIOBUTTON ¦
                                       WS_TABSTOP ¦
                                       WS_CHILD,
                                       32, 52, 15, 12
CONTROL "1",            123, "button", BS_RADIOBUTTON ¦
                                       WS_GROUP ¦
                                       WS_TABSTOP ¦
                                       WS_CHILD,
                                       65, 52, 17, 12
CONTROL "1.5",          116, "button", BS_RADIOBUTTON ¦
                                       WS_TABSTOP ¦
                                       WS_CHILD,
                                       86, 52, 23, 12
CONTROL "2",            124, "button", BS_RADIOBUTTON ¦
                                       WS_TABSTOP ¦
                                       WS_CHILD,
                                       116, 52, 23, 12
CONTROL "None",         128, "button", BS_RADIOBUTTON ¦
                                       WS_GROUP ¦
                                       WS_TABSTOP ¦
                                       WS_CHILD,
                                       156, 15, 30, 9
CONTROL "Odd",          129, "button", BS_RADIOBUTTON ¦
                                       WS_TABSTOP ¦
                                       WS_CHILD,
                                       156, 24, 27, 9
CONTROL "Even",         130, "button", BS_RADIOBUTTON ¦
                                       WS_TABSTOP ¦
                                       WS_CHILD,
                                       156, 33, 33, 9
CONTROL "Mark",         131, "button", BS_RADIOBUTTON ¦
                                       WS_TABSTOP ¦
                                       WS_CHILD,
                                       156, 42, 34, 9
CONTROL "Space",        132, "button", BS_RADIOBUTTON ¦
                                       WS_TABSTOP ¦
                                       WS_CHILD,
                                       156, 51, 33, 9
CONTROL "Com1:",        125, "button", BS_RADIOBUTTON ¦
                                       WS_GROUP ¦
                                       WS_TABSTOP ¦
                                       WS_CHILD,
                                       14, 83, 33, 9
CONTROL "Com2:",        133, "button", BS_RADIOBUTTON ¦
                                       WS_TABSTOP ¦
                                       WS_CHILD,
                                       14, 92, 33, 9
CONTROL "Parity Check", 136, "button", BS_CHECKBOX ¦
                                       WS_TABSTOP ¦
                                       WS_CHILD,
                                       72, 75, 63, 9
```

```
    CONTROL "Carrier Detect",   134, "button", BS_CHECKBOX │
                                                WS_TABSTOP │
                                                WS_CHILD,
                                                72, 84, 63, 9
    CONTROL "Save as default", 135, "button", BS_CHECKBOX │
                                                WS_TABSTOP │
                                                WS_CHILD,
                                                121, 121, 86, 11
    CONTROL "Cancel",          113, "button", BS_PUSHBUTTON │
                                                WS_TABSTOP │
                                                WS_CHILD,
                                                150, 102, 41, 16
END
```

You can tell which buttons are which by the labels that appear as strings for each of the button definitions. The C++ Views conversion utility picks out the following button names and declares each button as a pointer object that is a private instance variable inside the declaration for the ModemDialog class.

USING MODEMDIALOG

The primary method of ModemDialog requiring explanation is the static method, ModemDialog::dialog.

```
enum yesNoCancel ModemDialog::dialog(Window *pWin, Modem *pModem)
{
    enum yesNoCancel e = CancelButton;
    ModemDialog aModemDialog(pModem, &e, pWin);
    return e;
}
```

The static function provides a convenient way to invoke the dialog. Instead of having to worry about getting the response from the dialog by passing a pointer to the response object, you can let the static member function do this for you. First, the function creates an enumerated variable, e, which it sets to a default value, CancelButton. Next, the function creates a Modem-Dialog object, passing a pointer to e as a second argument. Creating a ModemDialog object automatically invokes the dialog and passes modal control to the dialog, because of the call to Dialog::modal in the constructor for ModemDialog.

Other arguments passed to the constructor are a pointer to the Modem model to be manipulated by the dialog and a pointer to the parent window that owns the dialog view. These two arguments are passed to the static member function. The variable e is modified by the constructor. When the dialog terminates, e contains the value assigned to the static variable TerminateButton by either ModemDialog::ok or ModemDialog::cancel. The value of e is then returned by the static member function.

A typical use of ModemDialog would be to call the static member function ModemDialog::dialog from a top-level view. This would probably be done from a method intended to respond to the selection of a menu item associated with the top-level view. For instance, a top-level view called MyAppView, which has a Modem object as its model, could define a method, setParameters, intended to be invoked in response to a menu selection.

```
boolean MyAppView::setParameters(MenuItem *m)
{
    Modem modem(*((Modem*)model));
    enum yesNoCancel e =
      ModemDialog::dialog(this, &modem );
    if (e == YesButton)
    {
        (*((Modem*)model)) = modem;
        update();
    }
}
```

This method retrieves a copy of the model contained by the top-level view. All views inherit a variable called model, which points to the view's model. This variable must be cast to the appropriate type before it can be used. The expression,

```
(Modem*)model
```

takes the model pointer and casts it as a pointer to a Modem object.

Preceding the entire expression with an asterisk (*) dereferences the pointer and produces a copy of the object pointed to. This object can then be used to initialize a newly declared Modem object.

```
Modem modem(*((Modem*)model));
```

Note that modem is an independent copy of the model and not a pointer to the model. This gives the programmer a chance to reject the modifications made by the dialog in the event the dialog is terminated with a Cancel button. The modem dialog is already designed not to do this, but it is still wise to take precautions. The modem dialog is invoked through the static member function ModemDialog::dialog, which is passed a pointer to modem as one of its arguments. The button used to terminate the dialog is recorded in the variable, e. The setParameters method then tests to see if the dialog was terminated with the YesButton. If so, the value of modem now reflects the modifications made to it while the modem dialog was active. The instance variables in the modem variable can be copied back into the original model with a simple assignment operation.

```
(*((Modem*)model)) = modem;
```

The current view is then updated. The update is necessary because the Modem program constantly shows the values of the modem parameters at the bottom of the screen. If this were not the case, the call to updated would not be required.

The question remains, how does the model get assigned to the top-level view? The model is actually assigned to the view when the view is created in the main function for the entire application.

```
FILE: MYAPP.CPP

#include "notifier.h"
#include "modem.h"
#include "myview.h"

char *CTWindow = __FILE__;

main()
{
        Modem    *m;
        MyAppView *v;

        m = new Modem();
        v = new MyAppView(m);
        v->show();
        notifier.start();
}
```

This definition of main requires that the modem class be declared by first including the header file MODEM.H. The class declaring MyAppView must also be declared by including the file MYVIEW.H. A pointer to the model is then passed as an argument to the constructor for MyAppView.

```
v = new MyAppView(m);
```

A corresponding constructor must be defined for MyAppView inside the file MYVIEW.CPP.

```
MyAppView::MyAppView(id aModel)
{
    model = aModel;
    setTitle(WindowTitle);
    createMenus();
}
```

ACCESSING THE MODEL DIRECTLY

There are a number of reasons why you would want to access the Modem model assigned to MyAppView. You might want to call a Report dialog that shows the values contained in the Modem object. Such a Report dialog is shown here:

The Report dialog might be produced by selecting a menu entry that, in turn, calls the command handler MyAppView::displayParameters. Such a method would require the support of some global string arrays used to convert the enumerated values of the modem parameters into strings that make sense to the user.

```
////////////////////////////////////////////////////////
                            // **** strings used to
                            // **** show internal
                            // **** values of Modem
                            // **** parameters
                            ////////////////////////////
char *baudStrings[] =    {  "300", "1200", "2400",
                         "4800", "9600", "19200" };
```

```
char *dataStrings[] =     { "7 bits", "8 bits" };

char *stopStrings[] =     { "1 bits", "1.5 bits", "2 bits" };

char *comPortStrings[] = { "Com1", "Com2" };

char *parityStrings[] =   { "None", "Odd", "Even",
                            "Mark", "Space" };

char *booleanStrings[] = {   "OFF", "ON" };

//////////////////////////////////////////////////////
                        // **** methods unique to
                        // **** this application
                        /////////////////////////////

boolean MyAppView::displayParameters(MenuItem  *m)
{
    Modem modem(*((Modem*)model));
    Report::dialog("Modem Settings",
                    this,
                    "baud: \t\t%s\n"
                    "parity: \t\t%s\n"
                    "data: \t\t%s\n"
                    "stop: \t\t%s\n"
                    "comPort: \t%s\n"
                    "parityCheck: \t%s\n"
                    "carrierDetect: \t%s\n",

                    baudStrings[modem.baud()],
                    parityStrings[modem.parity()],
                    dataStrings[modem.data()],
                    stopStrings[modem.stop()],
                    comPortStrings[modem.comPort()],
                    booleanStrings[modem.parityCheck()],
                    booleanStrings[modem.carrierDetect()]
                );
}
```

Another reason to provide access to the Modem model pointed to by MyAppView would be to constantly show the value of certain parameters at the bottom of the screen in the form of a status line. You can see such a status line at the bottom of the application window in Figure 13-5.

All views inherit a method called Window::paint. This is a virtual method. If your view overrides the definition of this method, you can control the detailed output of the entire top-level view. This method requires a fair amount of code to display modem-parameter status values at the bottom of the screen. The nice thing, however, is that you do not need to worry about calling MyAppView::paint directly. Calls to this method are managed by C++ Views and Microsoft Windows. This method is invoked whenever an exposure event that affects your application's top-level view is

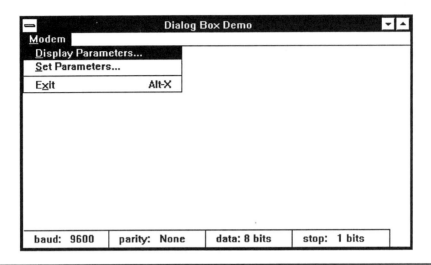

Figure 13-5. The top-level application view continuously displays modem settings in the status line at the bottom of the screen by overriding the Window::paint method.

generated. Calling the Window::update method automatically generates an exposure event for the entire window. Here's the definition of MyApp-View::paint:

```
boolean MyAppView::paint()
{
    Modem modem(*((Modem*)model));
    int w, h, tw, th;

    fontSize(&tw,&th);
    sizeOfImage(&w, &h);

    ////////////////////////////////////
    // Port objects are used for
    // graphics support such
    // as drawing lines.
    ////////////////////////////////////
    Port port(this);
    port.open();
```

```
/////////////////////////////////
// Now print four different
// status strings separated
// from each other by vertical
// lines.
/////////////////////////////////
char buf[200];
int x = 0;
int yText = h-(th+th/4);
int yStatLine = h-(th+th/2);

/////////////////////////////////
// constant defines # of chars
// between strings and vertical
// separator lines.
/////////////////////////////////
const margin=2;

/////////////////////////////////
// 1 BAUD
/////////////////////////////////
sprintf(buf, "baud: %6s", baudStrings[modem.baud()]);
x += margin*tw;
wrtText(buf, x,yText);
x += tw*(strlen(buf)+margin);
port.moveTo(x, yStatLine);
port.lineTo(x, h);            // vertical separator

/////////////////////////////////
// 2 PARITY
/////////////////////////////////
sprintf(buf, "parity: %6s", parityStrings[modem.parity()]);
x += margin*tw;
wrtText(buf, x,yText);
x += tw*(strlen(buf)+margin);
port.moveTo(x, yStatLine);
port.lineTo(x, h);            // vertical separator

/////////////////////////////////
// 3 DATA BITS
/////////////////////////////////
sprintf(buf, "data: %6s", dataStrings[modem.data()]);
x += margin*tw;
wrtText(buf, x,yText);
x += tw*(strlen(buf)+margin);
port.moveTo(x, yStatLine);
port.lineTo(x, h);            // vertical separator

/////////////////////////////////
// 4 STOP BITS
/////////////////////////////////
sprintf(buf, "stop: %8s", stopStrings[modem.stop()]);
x += margin*tw;
wrtText(buf, x,yText);
x += tw*(strlen(buf)+margin);
```

```
    port.moveTo(x, yStatLine);
    port.lineTo(x, h);            // vertical separator

    /////////////////////////////////////
    // Now draw a horizontal line
    // above the status text
    // connecting the vertical
    // seperators.
    /////////////////////////////////////
    port.moveTo(x, yStatLine);    // from last separator
    port.lineTo(0, yStatLine);    // to left edge of window

    port.close();
    return TRUE;
}
```

The paint callback method defined for each view in a C++ Views application determines what the user will see when the view is active.

CHAPTER HIGHLIGHTS

You've seen some advanced examples of custom dialog boxes and control components. When you build a custom dialog, it's your responsibility to provide the mechanism for getting data into and out of the dialog. C++ Views applies the model-view-controller structure to dialog boxes, which are a special type of view. The pushbuttons, radio buttons, and check boxes within a dialog box are controllers and views at the same time because they are controllers that need to be made visible. For this reason, they're given the name *control views*.

The following highlights the features of the model-view-controller paradigm when applied to setting and retrieving data inside custom dialog boxes built with C++ Views.

Connections Among Model-View-Controller Components

- Models maintain application data.

- Views read data from models.

- Views write data to models.

- Views get input from controls.

- Users interact with views through visible controls.

Dialog Views and Data Models

- Dialogs are views with built-in controls.

- Dialog views manage dialog data.

- Top-level views invoke dialog views.

- Subviews manage subsets of data.

- Models are controlled by views.

- Views extract and display data from models.

For complex dialog boxes, it's not recommended that you build entire classes from scratch. Instead, use a dialog editor such as that provided by SDK. Then use a utility to convert the dialog resource into files that declare and implement classes in a manner consistent with your application framework. Next, modify these files to include event handlers and initialization code that is unique to the model that the dialog view is intended to manipulate.

Two files were generated in this chapter through the process just described. Even though most of the code is generated automatically, it's still useful to display the code here in the event that you wish to borrow some of it or if you want to see the declarations and definitions in context. The files generated are MODEMDLG.H and MODEMDLG.CPP. You can learn a great deal by studying both of these files, but remember—if you have to implement dialogs as complex as the modem dialog, a dialog editor is the place to start.

Here's the header file:

```
FILE: MODEMDLG.H

#ifndef Modemdlg_h
#define Modemdlg_h
#include "dialog.h"
#include "yesno.h"

extern class CheckBox;
extern class RadioButton;
extern class PushButton;
extern class ExclusiveGroup;
extern class Button;
extern class Modem;

class ModemDialog : public Dialog
{
    Modem *pModem;      // model manipulated by this dialog
```

```
    PushButton *button100;
    ExclusiveGroup *button104;
    ExclusiveGroup *button126;
    ExclusiveGroup *button102;
    ExclusiveGroup *button127;
    ExclusiveGroup *button122;
    RadioButton *button105;
    RadioButton *button106;
    RadioButton *button107;
    RadioButton *button111;
    RadioButton *button110;
    RadioButton *button108;
    RadioButton *button117;
    RadioButton *button114;
    RadioButton *button123;
    RadioButton *button116;
    RadioButton *button124;
    RadioButton *button128;
    RadioButton *button129;
    RadioButton *button130;
    RadioButton *button131;
    RadioButton *button132;
    RadioButton *button125;
    RadioButton *button133;
    CheckBox *button136;
    CheckBox *button134;
    CheckBox *button135;
    PushButton *button113;

    void init();
public:
    Class *iam();
    boolean free();
    ModemDialog();
    ModemDialog(Modem *, enum yesNoCancel *, Window *);
    ~ModemDialog();
    static enum yesNoCancel dialog(Window *, Modem *);

    ///////////////////////////
    // event handlers
    ///////////////////////////
    boolean ok(Button *b);
    boolean cancel(Button *b);
};

extern Class *ModemDialogCls;

#endif
```

The method definitions for ModemDialog are shown next.

```
FILE: MODEMDLG.CPP

#include "winclass.h"
```

```
#include "Modemdlg.h"
#include "pushbttn.h"
#include "exclgrp.h"
#include "radibttn.h"
#include "checkbox.h"
#include "pushbttn.h"

#include "modem.h"

///////////////////////////////////////
// Exclusive Group Control Buttons
///////////////////////////////////////
#define baudGroupButton       button104
#define dataGroupButton       button102
#define stopGroupButton       button127
#define comPortGroupButton    button122
#define parityGroupButton     button126


///////////////////////////////////////
// Check Box Buttons
///////////////////////////////////////
#define parityCheckButton     button136
#define carrierDetectButton   button134
#define saveAtDefaultButton   button135

defineClass(ModemDialog,Dialog)

#define xcnv(n) ((n*tw+3)/4)
#define ycnv(n) ((n*th+7)/8)
ModemDialog::ModemDialog()
{
}

enum yesNoCancel ModemDialog::dialog(Window *pWin, Modem *pModem)
{
    enum yesNoCancel e = CancelButton;
    ModemDialog aModemDialog(pModem, &e, pWin);
    return e;
}

///////////////////////////////////////////////////////////
// TerminateButton is the value returned by the constructor
// and by ModemDialog::dialog. This is made a static
// local variable so it can be shared by the constructor
// and two other methods in ModemDialog. The constructor
// sets the default value of this variable to CancelButton
// before the dialog enters modal input control. Modal
// input control is terminated when the user presses either
// the OK or Cancel buttons within the dialog box. Either
// ModemDialog::ok or ModemDialog::cancel is called
// accordingly. Both of these set the appropriate value
// for Terminate button, and then call endmodal to pass
// control back to the constructor which in turn passes
// control back to the calling routine.
///////////////////////////////////////////////////////////
static enum yesNoCancel TerminateButton;
```

```
void ModemDialog::init()
{
    int tw,th;
    fontSize(&tw,&th);

    button100 = new PushButton(xcnv(105),ycnv(102),
                               xcnv(41),ycnv(16),this);
    button100->putText("OK");
    button100->uponClick(this,methodOf(ModemDialog,ok));

    button104 = new ExclusiveGroup(xcnv(6),ycnv(2),
                                   xcnv(133),ycnv(38),this);
    button104->putText("Baud Rate");

    button126 = new ExclusiveGroup(xcnv(149),ycnv(3),
                                   xcnv(46),ycnv(63),this);
    button126->putText("Parity");

    button102 = new ExclusiveGroup(xcnv(8),ycnv(42),
                                   xcnv(45),ycnv(23),this);
    button102->putText("Data Bits");

    button127 = new ExclusiveGroup(xcnv(62),ycnv(42),
                                   xcnv(78),ycnv(24),this);
    button127->putText("Stop Bits");

    button122 = new ExclusiveGroup(xcnv(8),ycnv(71),
                                   xcnv(51),ycnv(36),this);
    button122->putText("Com Port");

    button105 = new RadioButton(xcnv(5),ycnv(10),
                                xcnv(28),ycnv(12),button104);
    button105->putText("300");
    button104->addButton(button105);
    button106 = new RadioButton(xcnv(36),ycnv(11),
                                xcnv(28),ycnv(12),button104);
    button106->putText("1200");
    button104->addButton(button106);
    button107 = new RadioButton(xcnv(67),ycnv(11),
                                xcnv(28),ycnv(12),button104);
    button107->putText("2400");
    button104->addButton(button107);
    button111 = new RadioButton(xcnv(5),ycnv(23),
                                xcnv(28),ycnv(12),button104);
    button111->putText("4800");
    button104->addButton(button111);
    button110 = new RadioButton(xcnv(35),ycnv(23),
                                xcnv(28),ycnv(12),button104);
    button110->putText("9600");
    button104->addButton(button110);
    button108 = new RadioButton(xcnv(68),ycnv(23),
                                xcnv(40),ycnv(12),button104);
    button108->putText("19200");
    button104->addButton(button108);

    button117 = new RadioButton(xcnv(3),ycnv(10),
                                xcnv(15),ycnv(12),button102);
    button117->putText("7");
```

```
button102->addButton(button117);
button114 = new RadioButton(xcnv(24),ycnv(10),
                            xcnv(15),ycnv(12),button102);
button114->putText("8");
button102->addButton(button114);
button123 = new RadioButton(xcnv(3),ycnv(10),
                            xcnv(17),ycnv(12),button127);
button123->putText("1");
button127->addButton(button123);
button116 = new RadioButton(xcnv(24),ycnv(10),
                            xcnv(23),ycnv(12),button127);
button116->putText("1.5");
button127->addButton(button116);
button124 = new RadioButton(xcnv(54),ycnv(10),
                            xcnv(23),ycnv(12),button127);
button124->putText("2");
button127->addButton(button124);
button128 = new RadioButton(xcnv(7),ycnv(12),
                            xcnv(30),ycnv(9),button126);
button128->putText("None");
button126->addButton(button128);
button129 = new RadioButton(xcnv(7),ycnv(21),
                            xcnv(27),ycnv(9),button126);
button129->putText("Odd");
button126->addButton(button129);
button130 = new RadioButton(xcnv(7),ycnv(30),
                            xcnv(33),ycnv(9),button126);
button130->putText("Even");
button126->addButton(button130);
button131 = new RadioButton(xcnv(7),ycnv(39),
                            xcnv(34),ycnv(9),button126);
button131->putText("Mark");
button126->addButton(button131);
button132 = new RadioButton(xcnv(7),ycnv(48),
                            xcnv(33),ycnv(9),button126);
button132->putText("Space");
button126->addButton(button132);
button125 = new RadioButton(xcnv(6),ycnv(12),
                            xcnv(33),ycnv(9),button122);
button125->putText("Com1:");
button122->addButton(button125);
button133 = new RadioButton(xcnv(6),ycnv(21),
                            xcnv(33),ycnv(9),button122);
button133->putText("Com2:");
button122->addButton(button133);
button136 = new CheckBox(xcnv(72),ycnv(75),
                         xcnv(63),ycnv(9),this);
button136->putText("Parity Check");
button134 = new CheckBox(xcnv(72),ycnv(84),
                         xcnv(63),ycnv(9),this);
button134->putText("Carrier Detect");
button135 = new CheckBox(xcnv(121),ycnv(121),
                         xcnv(86),ycnv(11),this);
button135->putText("Save as default");
button113 = new PushButton(xcnv(150),ycnv(102),
                           xcnv(41),ycnv(16),this);
button113->putText("Cancel");
button113->uponClick(this,methodOf(ModemDialog,cancel));
```

```
    /////////////////////////////////////////////////////////////
    // Set default values for buttons
    // from pModem instance variable.
    /////////////////////////////////////////////////////////////
    baudGroupButton->setCurrent(pModem->baud());
    dataGroupButton->setCurrent(pModem->data());
    stopGroupButton->setCurrent(pModem->stop());
    comPortGroupButton->setCurrent(pModem->comPort());
    parityGroupButton->setCurrent(pModem->parity());
    parityCheckButton->check(pModem->parityCheck());
    carrierDetectButton->check(pModem->carrierDetect());
    saveAtDefaultButton->check(TRUE);
}

ModemDialog::ModemDialog(Modem *m,
                         enum yesNoCancel *pResponse,
                         Window *pWin)
{
    int x,y,w,h,tw,th;
    int fw,fh;

    fontSize(&tw,&th);
    x = xcnv(24);
    y = ycnv(23);
    w = xcnv(208);
    h = ycnv(136);
    fw = GetSystemMetrics(SM_CXDLGFRAME);
    fh = GetSystemMetrics(SM_CYDLGFRAME);
    x -= fw; y -= fh; w += 2*fw; h += 2*fh;
    getWindow(x,y,w,h,pWin);
    pModem = m;  // must precede call to init
    init();

    /////////////////////////////////////////////////////////////
    // Default value of TerminateButton is CancelButton.
    // This value will be returned to the caller through
    // the constructor's argument, *pResponse.
    // TerminateButton can be changed by the callback
    // methods ModemDialog::cancel and ModemDialog::ok.
    // Both cancel and ok call endmodal to terminate
    // modal control of input by dialog box.
    /////////////////////////////////////////////////////////////
    TerminateButton = CancelButton;
    modal();
    *pResponse = TerminateButton;
}

boolean ModemDialog::free()
{
    delete this;
    return TRUE;
}

ModemDialog::~ModemDialog()
{
```

```
        button100->free();
        button104->free();
        button126->free();
        button102->free();
        button127->free();
        button122->free();
        button136->free();
        button134->free();
        button135->free();
        button113->free();
}

boolean ModemDialog::ok(Button *b)
{
        /////////////////////////////////////
        // Transfer current button group
        // and check box button
        // values from dialog box to
        // Modem object pointed to by
        // instance variable, pModem.
        /////////////////////////////////////
        pModem->baud((baudEnum)baudGroupButton->getCurrent());
        pModem->data((dataEnum)dataGroupButton->getCurrent());
        pModem->stop((stopEnum)stopGroupButton->getCurrent());
        pModem->comPort((comPortEnum)comPortGroupButton->getCurrent());
        pModem->parity((parityEnum)parityGroupButton->getCurrent());
        pModem->parityCheck(parityCheckButton->checked());
        pModem->carrierDetect(carrierDetectButton->checked());

        /////////////////////////////////////
        // TerminateButton is the value
        // returned by the constructor
        // in the pointer argument,
        // pResponse. This is the same
        // value that is returned by the
        // static method,
        // ModemDialog::dialog
        /////////////////////////////////////
        TerminateButton = YesButton;
        endModal();
        return TRUE;
}

boolean ModemDialog::cancel(Button *b)
{
        /////////////////////////////////////
        // TerminateButton is the value
        // returned by the constructor
        // in the pointer argument,
        // pResponse. This is the same
        // value that is returned by the
        // static method,
        // ModemDialog::dialog
        /////////////////////////////////////
        TerminateButton = CancelButton;
        endModal();
        return TRUE;
}
```

14

OBJECTWINDOWS: A LANGUAGE-INDEPENDENT APPLICATION FRAMEWORK

ObjectWindows is an application framework that works with Actor, Turbo Pascal for Windows, and Borland C++. The beauty of using an application framework that supports a variety of languages is that you can do development in the language of your choice and later translate your program to other languages as required. ObjectWindows programs written in Borland C++ and Turbo Pascal for Windows match one another almost exactly on a line-for-line basis. Now with Borland's integrated development environments operating directly under Microsoft Windows, Actor and Smalltalk no longer provide the only development platforms that eliminate switching back and forth between Windows and DOS when constructing and testing programs. In addition, ObjectWindows takes much of the grief out of developing Windows programs. With ObjectWindows, it's just as easy to write programs for Windows as for DOS.

This chapter looks at the ObjectWindows application framework and shows sample programs for ObjectWindows in both Turbo Pascal and Borland C++. Where the ideas are general or the code is nearly identical in both Pascal and C++, sample listings are shown in Pascal. Only C++ listings and programs that highlight important differences between C++ and Pascal are presented directly in this chapter. To keep from cluttering the chapter, the final C++ program (DIALOG.CPP) is shown in Appendix B, "C++

Program for Chapter 14". A discussion of the differences between C++ and
Pascal implementations of the ObjectWindows example programs is available on disk and includes complete listings of resource files, project file lists,
and a generalized make file used to build the programs.

A SIMPLE OBJECTWINDOWS PROGRAM

The structure of an ObjectWindows program is nearly identical to the
structure of a Turbo Vision program. Recall the simplest possible Turbo
Vision program presented in Chapter 10, "Turbo Vision: Constructing
Menus for a Character-Oriented Application Framework".

```
program template;

uses App;

type
  TMyApp = object(TApplication)
  end;

var
  MyApp: TMyApp;

begin
  MyApp.Init;
  MyApp.Run;
  MyApp.Done;
end.
```

This produces a single application window that works with a standard IBM
PC character-oriented screen.

Compare this with the simplest possible program for ObjectWindows
using Turbo Pascal for Windows.

```
program template;

uses WObjects;

type
  TMyApp = object(TApplication)
  end;

var
  MyApp: TMyApp;
```

```
begin
  MyApp.Init('Application Name');
  MyApp.Run;
  MyApp.Done;
end.
```

The programs are nearly identical. The primary difference is the name specified for the Turbo Pascal unit. Instead of the App unit, ObjectWindows programs use the WObjects unit.

The constructor for TApplication now takes an argument.

```
MyApp.Init('Application Name');
```

This argument is the name of the application stored in an instance variable of the single TApplication object created when the program is run. This string can be anything you want and can be used internally by methods that you write. For example, you might want to specify a string containing the version number of a program or the spoken language of the user for a given application. The Name instance variable for the application could then be used to specify alternative features or output.

```
MyApp.Init('French');
  .
  .
  .
  if (MyApp.Name = 'English') then
      ...
  else if (MyApp.Name = 'French') then
      ...
```

You can always specify nil if you don't plan to use the name.

```
MyApp.Init(nil);
```

The C++ version of a simple ObjectWindows template has exactly the same components as the Pascal version. A user-defined class called TMy-App is derived from the class TApplication. An instance of this class, called MyApp, is created and initialized. MyApp then receives a Run message, which opens the application and transfers control to the main event loop. When the user closes the window, control passes to the last statement in the main routine. C++ sends a Status message to the application and returns the resulting value to the operating environment. Pascal sends a Done message to the application object. Here's the C++ version:

```
#include <owl.h>
//================================================================//
// TMyApp class                                                   //
//================================================================//
class TMyApp : public TApplication
{
public:
  TMyApp(LPSTR   AName,            //---------------------------//
         HANDLE  hInstance,        // constructor               //
         HANDLE  hPrevInstance,    // argument                  //
         LPSTR   lpszCmdLine,      // declarations              //
         int     nCmdShow)         //---------------------------//
    : TApplication(AName,          //---------------------------//
               hInstance,          // Inline method definition: //
               hPrevInstance,      //    constructor initializer //
               lpszCmdLine,        //    calls parent constructor //
               nCmdShow)           //                           //
               {};                 //    empty function body    //
                                   //---------------------------//
};

//================================================================//
// WinMain   (main Windows function)                              //
//================================================================//
#pragma argsused
int PASCAL WinMain(HANDLE   hInstance,        //---------------//
                   HANDLE   hPrevInstance,    // WinMain       //
                   LPSTR    lpszCmdLine,      // declaration   //
                   int      nCmdShow)         //---------------//
{
  TMyApp MyApp("Application Name",            //---------------//
               hInstance,                     // create MyApp  //
               hPrevInstance,                 // and call      //
               lpszCmdLine,                   // constructor   //
               nCmdShow);                     //---------------//
  MyApp.Run();
  return MyApp.Status;
}
```

When reading C++ programs in this chapter, it's helpful to be familiar with some of the common type definitions declared in the header file WINDOWS.H. For instance, a HANDLE is a synonym for an unsigned int, and an LPSTR is a long or far pointer to a char object. These are declared with standard C typedef statements. Other important Windows types include general handles (HANDLE) and window handles (HWND).

```
typedef char far        *LPSTR;
typedef unsigned int    WORD;
typedef WORD            HANDLE;
typedef HANDLE          HWND;
```

The above program template produces a no-frills window that looks like this:

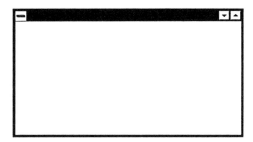

You probably want more than a no-frills window, so you'll need to add a title.

Adding a Window Title

First you need to override the InitMainWindow virtual method defined for all TApplication objects. Add the declaration,

```
type
  TMyApp = object(TApplication)
    procedure InitMainWindow; virtual;
  end;
```

then add the definition:

```
procedure TMyApp.InitMainWindow;
begin
  MainWindow :=
    New(PWindow,
        Init(nil, 'Hello ObjectWindows'));
end;
```

In C++, you can define a method at the point where it is declared inside the class. A C++ method defined inside the class where it is declared is treated like an inline macro, eliminating the overhead of a function call whenever the method is invoked.

```
class TMyApp : public TApplication
{
public:
  TMyApp(LPSTR  AName,
         HANDLE hInstance,         HANDLE hPrevInstance,
         LPSTR  lpszCmdLine,       int    nCmdShow)
    : TApplication(AName,
                   hInstance,      hPrevInstance,
                   lpszCmdLine,    nCmdShow) {};
  virtual void InitMainWindow(void)
  {
    MainWindow = new TWindow(NULL, "Hello ObjectWindows");
  }
};
```

Now when you run the program, you'll get a window with a title. The following illustration shows the window created by InitMainWindow, specifying the window title in the TWindow constructor.

Creating a Simple Menu

Creating menus is a little more complicated in ObjectWindows than in Turbo Vision. ObjectWindows menus are created as resources in a separate program file. This is standard Microsoft Windows practice. First create the source or script file for the resource (.RC). Then compile the script with the resource compiler to produce a compiled resource file (.RES) that can be used by any Windows application program.

For instance, you could create a file called MENU1.RC that looks like this:

```
100 MENU
BEGIN
    POPUP "Menu 1"
    BEGIN
        MENUITEM "Choice &1", 101
        MENUITEM "Choice &2", 102
        MENUITEM "Choice &3", 103
    END

END
```

You would then create a resource file called MENU1.RES by invoking the resource compiler with the -r option (-*r* means create .RES file).

```
>rc -r menu1
```

There are two different approaches to using resources in a program. If you don't specify -r, the resource compiler looks for an .EXE file with the same name as the resource file (.RES) and actually compiles the resources into the executable file. The C++ programs in this chapter use this first technique for binding resources to the executable file. For example,

```
rc menu1
```

will bind the resources in the compiled resource file, MENU1.RES, to the executable file MENU1.EXE. If the resource file has a different name than the executable, both names are specified with the resource first.

```
rc menu1.res menu2.exe
```

The -r flag is not specified in either case. The resource compiler is actually invoked twice for a given program: the first time with the -r flag and an .RC file as an argument; the second time without the -r flag with a .RES file as an argument and either an implicit or explicit .EXE file as the second argument. The resource compiler is invoked for the second time only after all .OBJ files are linked together to create the executable .EXE file.

The Pascal programs in this chapter use a different technique. Instead of compiling resources into the executable file, a separate .RES file is generated, which is then loaded by the program when it is compiled and linked by including a special compiler directive in the program source code. This technique is unique to Turbo Pascal and is not available for C++ programs. If you use this technique, you must remember to specify the appropriate resource file in the program source code.

The *Windows Programming Guide* that comes with Turbo Pascal for Windows provides a chapter called "Resources in Depth", which gives a detailed explanation of using the resource compiler and the resources toolkit to build common resources such as menus, dialog boxes, icons, cursors, keyboard accelerators, bitmaps, and character strings.

The resulting MENU1.RES file created with the -r resource compiler option can now be included in Turbo Pascal for Windows programs that contain the following compiler directive:

```
{$R MENU1.RES}
```

The menu resource, now bound into the executable image, must be associated with a window when the program is run. A good way to do this is to load the resource into a window when it is constructed.

```
constructor TMyWindow.Init(AParent: PWindowsObject; ATitle: PChar);
begin
    TWindow.Init(AParent, ATitle);
    Attr.Menu := LoadMenu(HInstance, PChar(100));
end;
```

The first argument to LoadMenu is the handle of the window that owns the resource. The second argument is a numeric constant cast as a Windows-compatible string. This string is used to identify the menu resource from candidates in all the resource files specified for a program. For this reason, each menu resource must be given a unique identification number or string. This number is associated with the resource definition in the resource script file.

```
100 MENU
BEGIN
    ...
END
```

Here's a Pascal program that adds the preceding menu to its main window.

```
FILE: MENU2.PAS

{ Pascal }

program Menu;

uses WObjects, winTypes, WinProcs;

{$R MENU1.RES}

{===============================================================}
{ INTERFACE: CLASS DECLARATIONS                                 }
{===============================================================}

{------------------------}
{ Application (interface) }
{------------------------}

type
  TMyApp = object(TApplication)
    procedure InitMainWindow; virtual;
  end;

{------------------------}
{ Main Window (interface) }
{------------------------}

type
  PMyWindow = ^TMyWindow;
  TMyWindow = object(TWindow)
    constructor Init(AParent: PWindowsObject; ATitle: PChar);
  end;

{===============================================================}
{ IMPLEMENTATION: METHOD DEFINITIONS                            }
{===============================================================}

{----------------------------}
{ Application (implementation) }
{----------------------------}

procedure TMyApp.InitMainWindow;
begin
  MainWindow :=
    New(PMyWindow,
        Init(nil, 'ObjectWindows Menus'));
end;

{----------------------------}
{ Main Window (implementation) }
{----------------------------}

constructor TMyWindow.Init(AParent: PWindowsObject; ATitle: PChar);
begin
  TWindow.Init(AParent, ATitle);
    Attr.Menu := LoadMenu(HInstance, PChar(100));
```

```
end;

{==============================================================}
{ MAIN PROGRAM                                                 }
{==============================================================}

var
  MyApp: TMyApp;

begin
  MyApp.Init('Menu');
  MyApp.Run;
  MyApp.Done;
end.
```

Now when you run the program the main window will have a menu like the one shown here, which uses the menu resource from MENU1.RC as a top-level menu:

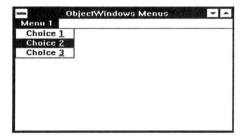

Though the menu will now appear when the program is run, nothing will happen when you select commands from the menu. In order to see something happen, you need to define callback methods to respond to the Windows messages that are generated by selecting a menu command.

Specifying Callback Methods

Callback methods have a number associated with them that matches the number specified in the menu resource. The constants associated with the menu items in the menu in MENU1.RC are 101, 102, and 103. If the window using this menu is a TMyWindow object, you would have to declare three virtual methods in the TMyWindow class to handle the menu commands 101, 102, and 103. Here's a possibility:

```
type
  PMyWindow = ^TMyWindow;
  TMyWindow = object(TWindow)
    constructor Init(AParent: PWindowsObject; ATitle: PChar);
    procedure Choice101(var Msg: TMessage);
      virtual cm_First + 101;
    procedure Choice102(var Msg: TMessage);
      virtual cm_First + 102;
    procedure Choice103(var Msg: TMessage);
      virtual cm_First + 103;
  end;
```

The compiler, together with the ObjectWindows library, automatically binds messages generated by these menu commands to the methods you define for the above handler declarations. The C++ method declarations are very similar.

```
class TMyWindow : public TWindow
{
public:
  TMyWindow(PTWindowsObject AParent, LPSTR ATitle);

  virtual void Choice101 (TMessage& Msg) = [CM_FIRST + 101];
  virtual void Choice102 (TMessage& Msg) = [CM_FIRST + 102];
  virtual void Choice103 (TMessage& Msg) = [CM_FIRST + 103];
};
```

In both cases, callback methods are assigned to respond to Windows command messages by assigning a unique, user-defined command identifier to the desired method. These command identifiers are symbolic integer constants, which must be the same number in both the menu resource that generates the Windows commands and in the application program that handles or responds to the commands.

Technically, this is a modification of the standard C++ language definition. There is some precedence for assigning an integer value to virtual methods. In standard C++, abstract virtual functions can be assigned a value of 0 to indicate that the function is a *pure virtual function*.

```
class MyClass
{
  ...
  virtual void f() = 0;  // pure virtual function
  ...
}
```

Pure virtual functions should not be called directly in normal C++ programs. Typically, derived classes override virtual function definitions and these derived versions are invoked automatically through polymorphic message dispatch. Borland C++ changes this restriction by allowing virtual functions to be assigned a value other than 0 and by allowing these functions to be invoked directly as callback methods when the appropriate Windows command message is received by the application.

Here is a program that specifies complete definitions for the callback methods, which are sometimes called *message handlers*. First, the Pascal version:

```pascal
FILE: MENU3.PAS

{ Pascal }
program Menu;

uses WObjects, winTypes, WinProcs;
{$R MENU1.RES}

{===============================================================}
{ INTERFACE: CLASS DECLARATIONS                                 }
{===============================================================}

{------------------------}
{ Application (interface) }
{------------------------}

type
  TMyApp = object(TApplication)
    procedure InitMainWindow; virtual;
  end;

{------------------------}
{ Main Window (interface) }
{------------------------}

type
  PMyWindow = ^TMyWindow;
  TMyWindow = object(TWindow)
    constructor Init(AParent: PWindowsObject; ATitle: PChar);
    procedure Choice101(var Msg: TMessage);
      virtual cm_First + 101;
    procedure Choice102(var Msg: TMessage);
      virtual cm_First + 102;
    procedure Choice103(var Msg: TMessage);
      virtual cm_First + 103;
  end;


{===============================================================}
{ IMPLEMENTATION: METHOD DEFINITIONS                            }
{===============================================================}
```

```
{----------------------------}
{ Application (implementation) }
{----------------------------}

procedure TMyApp.InitMainWindow;
begin
  MainWindow :=
    New(PMyWindow,
        Init(nil, 'ObjectWindows Menus'));
end;

{----------------------------}
{ Main Window (implementation) }
{----------------------------}

constructor TMyWindow.Init(AParent: PWindowsObject; ATitle: PChar);
begin
  TWindow.Init(AParent, ATitle);
    Attr.Menu := LoadMenu(HInstance, PChar(100));
end;

procedure TMyWindow.Choice101(var Msg: TMessage);
begin
  MessageBox(HWindow, 'Choice 1 selected',
    'Message Box Title: Menu1', mb_Ok);
end;

procedure TMyWindow.Choice102(var Msg: TMessage);
begin
  MessageBox(HWindow, 'Choice 2 selected',
    'Message Box Title: Menu1', mb_Ok);
end;

procedure TMyWindow.Choice103(var Msg: TMessage);
begin
  MessageBox(HWindow, 'Choice 3 selected',
    'Message Box Title: Menu1', mb_Ok);
end;


{============================================================}
{ MAIN PROGRAM                                               }
{============================================================}

var
  MyApp: TMyApp;

begin
  MyApp.Init('Menu');
  MyApp.Run;
  MyApp.Done;
end.
```

Each handler simply invokes a message dialog with a prompt string that identifies the method being invoked. If you run the program and select the second menu choice, you'll see a message box dialog like the one in the following illustration. Callback methods, resources, and message dialogs will be covered in more detail shortly.

Here's the C++ version of MENU3:

```
#include <owl.h>

//=============================================================//
// INTERFACE: CLASS DECLARATIONS                               //
//=============================================================//

//-----------------------//
// Application (interface) //
//-----------------------//

class TMyApp : public TApplication
{
public:
  TMyApp(LPSTR  AName,
         HANDLE hInstance,      HANDLE hPrevInstance,
         LPSTR  lpszCmdLine,    int    nCmdShow)
  : TApplication(AName,
                 hInstance,     hPrevInstance,
                 lpszCmdLine,   nCmdShow) {};
  virtual void InitMainWindow(void);
};

//-----------------------//
// Main Window (interface) //
//-----------------------//

class TMyWindow : public TWindow
{
public:
  TMyWindow(PTWindowsObject AParent, LPSTR ATitle);

  virtual void Choice101 (TMessage& Msg) = [CM_FIRST + 101];
  virtual void Choice102 (TMessage& Msg) = [CM_FIRST + 102];
  virtual void Choice103 (TMessage& Msg) = [CM_FIRST + 103];
};

typedef TMyWindow *PMyWindow;
```

```
//=============================================================//
// IMPLEMENTATION: METHOD DEFINITIONS                          //
//=============================================================//

//----------------------------//
// Application (implementation) //
//----------------------------//

void TMyApp::InitMainWindow(void)
{
  MainWindow = new TMyWindow(NULL, "ObjectWindows Menus");
}

//------------------------------//
// Main Window (implementation) //
//------------------------------//

TMyWindow::TMyWindow(PTWindowsObject AParent, LPSTR ATitle)
  : TWindow(AParent, ATitle)
{
  AssignMenu(100);
}

#pragma argsused
void TMyWindow::Choice101(TMessage& Msg)
{
  MessageBox(HWindow, "Choice 1 selected",
        "Message Box Title: Menu1", MB_OK);
}

#pragma argsused
void TMyWindow::Choice102(TMessage& Msg)
{
  MessageBox(HWindow, "Choice 2 selected",
        "Message Box Title: Menu1", MB_OK);
}

#pragma argsused
void TMyWindow::Choice103(TMessage& Msg)
{
  MessageBox(HWindow, "Choice 3 selected",
        "Message Box Title: Menu1", MB_OK);
}

//=============================================================//
// MAIN PROGRAM                                                //
//=============================================================//

#pragma argsused
int PASCAL WinMain(HANDLE hInstance, HANDLE hPrevInstance,
                   LPSTR lpszCmdLine, int nCmdShow)
{
  TMyApp MyApp("Menu1",
               hInstance,       hPrevInstance,
               lpszCmdLine,     nCmdShow);
  MyApp.Run();
  return MyApp.Status;
}
```

DIALOGS, MENUS, AND RESOURCES

Chapter 12, "C++Views: Dialogs and Control Views", showed you how to build and use seven common types of dialog boxes.

- About

- Report

- YesNo

- YesNoCancel

- Input

- ListSelect

- FileSelect

It's just as easy to implement these dialogs in ObjectWindows. First you need to build a menu to test the dialogs. Start by creating a resource file called DIALOG.RC. Resource files allow you to define symbolic constants using a #define directive just like the directive provided by the C and C++ preprocessors. It's easier to remember the meaning of symbolic constants than numbers, so resource files frequently include C or C++ header files to share constants with programs.

Since C-style header files are not compatible with Pascal, you will have to define the constants in both the resource file,

```
#include "windows.h"

#define szAppName "StandardDialogs"

#define menuTestDialogs 100
#define cmAbout         101
#define cmReport        102
#define cmYesNo         103
#define cmYesNoCancel   104
#define cmInput         105
#define cmListSelect    106
#define cmFileSelect    107
#define cmQuit          108

#define idOk              1
#define idCancel          2
#define idListBox       201
```

and in the Pascal program:

```
program StandardDialogs;
    .
    .
    .
const
  menuTestDialogs = 100;
  cmAbout         = 101;
  cmReport        = 102;
  cmYesNo         = 103;
  cmYesNoCancel   = 104;
  cmInput         = 105;
  cmListSelect    = 106;
  cmFileSelect    = 107;
  cmQuit          = 108;

  idListBox       = 201;
    .
    .
    .
```

Now you can define the top-level menu for the application. Most top-level menus have more than one menu item, like the one defined in the previous menu. The following menu has two items at the top level, Test Dialogs and About. Test Dialogs, when selected, invokes a pop-up menu, while About will immediately respond by sending a command message with the symbolic constant cmAbout as its argument.

```
menuTestDialogs MENU
BEGIN
    POPUP "&Test Dialogs"
    BEGIN
        .
        .
        .
    END
    MENUITEM "&About"              cmAbout
END
```

Nested Menus

Menus can have entries that are either POPUP or MENUITEM. POPUPs invoke submenus when selected, MENUITEMs send command messages to Windows. It's possible to nest POPUP entries so that submenus can have their own submenus. The test framework for the standard dialogs uses such a nested menu.

```
menuTestDialogs MENU
BEGIN
    POPUP "&Test Dialogs"
    BEGIN
        MENUITEM "&Report"          cmReport
        MENUITEM "&YesNo"           cmYesNo
        MENUITEM "YesNo&Cancel"     cmYesNoCancel
        MENUITEM "&Input"           cmInput
        POPUP    "&List Dialogs"
        BEGIN
            MENUITEM "&ListSelect"      cmListSelect
            MENUITEM "&FileSelect"      cmFileSelect
        END
        MENUITEM  SEPARATOR
        MENUITEM "E&xit"            cmQuit
    END
    MENUITEM "&About"               cmAbout
END
```

Such a menu could be made the top-level menu for a user-defined application object by specifying the menu in the application's constructor.

```
constructor TMyWindow.Init(AParent: PWindowsObject; ATitle: PChar);
begin
  TWindow.Init(AParent, ATitle);
  Attr.Menu := LoadMenu(HInstance, PChar(menuTestDialogs));
end;
```

In C++ the member function, TWindow::AssignMenu, is used instead of calling LoadMenu directly.

```
TMyWindow::TMyWindow(PTWindowsObject AParent, LPSTR ATitle)
  : TWindow(AParent, ATitle)
{
    AssignMenu(menuTestDialogs);
}
```

The following illustration shows the menus that are built when the above menu resource is loaded into an application.

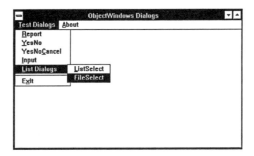

Callback Methods Handle Windows Events

Let's look again at the bare-bones template for an ObjectWindows program.

```
program template;

uses WObjects;

type
  TMyApp = object(TApplication)
    procedure InitMainWindow; virtual;
    end;

procedure TMyApp.InitMainWindow;
begin
  MainWindow :=
    New(PWindow,
        Init(nil, 'Hello ObjectWindows'));
end;

var
  MyApp: TMyApp;

begin
  MyApp.Init('Application Name');
  MyApp.Run;
  MyApp.Done;
end.
```

This is the program that produced the window illustrated earlier in the chapter with the window title, "Hello ObjectWindows". Much of the work of handling a windows event is taken care of when you use resources such as menus and dialogs to generate events through the Windows main event dispatcher. You already saw how to handle the events generated by menus. Simply declare virtual methods that attach the appropriate menu command constants.

```
{ Pascal }

type
  TMyWindow = object(TWindow)
    ...
    procedure Choice101(var Msg: TMessage);
      virtual cm_First + 101;
    ...
  end;

// C++

class TMyWindow : public TWindow
```

```
{
public:
  ...
  virtual void Choice101 (TMessage& Msg)
                 = [CM_FIRST + 101];
  ...
};
```

ObjectWindows automatically takes care of binding the Windows messages generated by the menu to the command handler you designate in the declaration. All you need to do is define the code for the previous declaration of TMyWindow.Choice101, and whenever command number 101 is generated inside a TMyWindow object, your routine is called by Object-Windows.

Mouse events are even easier. Before moving on to mouse events let's look at dialogs and simple text output to windows to help see what's going on inside a running program.

Dialog Resources

You can also specify dialog boxes in resource files. Dialogs are typically composed of other resources such as buttons, list boxes, and text input fields. A dialog could be defined as follows in a resource file:

```
LISTBOXDIALOG DIALOG  30, 10, 188, 100
STYLE WS_POPUP | WS_DLGFRAME
BEGIN
    .
    .
    .
END
```

This code defines a dialog to be referred to in a program with the symbolic name, LISTBOXDIALOG. The arguments represent the position and size of the dialog box (relative to the parent window) and the window style for the dialog box. The components of the dialog are specified between the BEGIN and END resource statements.

```
LISTBOXDIALOG DIALOG  30, 10, 188, 100
STYLE WS_POPUP | WS_DLGFRAME
BEGIN
   CONTROL "OK"      idOk, "BUTTON",
                           WS_CHILD | WS_VISIBLE | WS_TABSTOP,
                           111, 13, 68, 12
```

```
CONTROL "Cancel"  idCancel, "BUTTON",
                    WS_CHILD | WS_VISIBLE | WS_TABSTOP,
                    112, 66, 68, 12
CONTROL "LISTBOX" idListBox, "LISTBOX",
                    WS_CHILD | WS_VISIBLE | WS_BORDER |
                    WS_VSCROLL | 0x3L,
                    8, 8, 83, 73
END
```

This definition specifies two buttons and a list box and would appear as illustrated here. No data appears in a dialog until specified by the programmer. Such a dialog would be used in association with an ObjectWindows PDialog object.

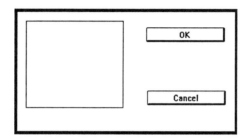

LISTBOXDIALOG is a dialog resource containing a list box and two pushbuttons. The list box is filled with a collection of strings at run time.

```
{ Pascal }

var
  theDialog       : PDialog;
  ...
begin
  theDialog := new(PDialog, Init(@Self, 'LISTBOXDIALOG'));
  ...

// C++

  ...
  TDialog *theDialog = new TDialog(this, "LISTBOXDIALOG");
  ...
```

Following is the entire definition file for DIALOG.RC, which specifies the menu resource and the dialog resource required for the standard dialog demonstration program. The nice thing about defining resources in a separate file is that they can be used by other programs and in programs written in other languages, including Actor and C++. Also, menus can be changed without recompiling the main program, so you can provide alternative menus for different languages and skill levels.

```
FILE: DIALOG.RC

#include "windows.h"

#define szAppName "StandardDialogs"

#define menuTestDialogs 100
#define cmAbout         101
#define cmReport        102
#define cmYesNo         103
#define cmYesNoCancel   104
#define cmInput         105
#define cmListSelect    106
#define cmFileSelect    107
#define cmQuit          108

#define idOk              1
#define idCancel          2
#define idListBox       201

menuTestDialogs MENU
BEGIN
    POPUP "&Test Dialogs"
    BEGIN
        MENUITEM "&Report"          cmReport
        MENUITEM "&YesNo"           cmYesNo
        MENUITEM "YesNo&Cancel"     cmYesNoCancel
        MENUITEM "&Input"           cmInput
        POPUP    "&List Dialogs"
        BEGIN
            MENUITEM "&ListSelect"    cmListSelect
            MENUITEM "&FileSelect"    cmFileSelect
        END
        MENUITEM  SEPARATOR
        MENUITEM "E&xit"            cmQuit
    END
    MENUITEM "&About"              cmAbout
END

LISTBOXDIALOG DIALOG  30, 10, 188, 100
STYLE WS_POPUP | WS_DLGFRAME
BEGIN
  CONTROL "OK"      idOk, "BUTTON",
                        WS_CHILD | WS_VISIBLE | WS_TABSTOP,
                        111, 13, 68, 12
  CONTROL "Cancel"  idCancel, "BUTTON",
                        WS_CHILD | WS_VISIBLE | WS_TABSTOP,
                        112, 66, 68, 12
  CONTROL "LISTBOX" idListBox, "LISTBOX",
                        WS_CHILD | WS_VISIBLE | WS_BORDER |
```

```
                    WS_VSCROLL | 0x3L,
                    8, 8, 83, 73
END
```

Build the resource by invoking the resource compiler on DIALOG.RC.

```
rc -r -i\tpw\owl dialog
```

This creates the resource file DIALOG.RES, which can be used in a Pascal program that includes the following line:

```
{$R DIALOG.RES}
```

The -i flag for the resource compiler is followed by an argument that tells the compiler what directory to look in to find header files specified by the #include directive.

The dialogs for About, Report, YesNo, and YesNoCancel all use the MessageBox function. MessageBox invokes a dialog with a title, a prompt string, and at least one button. You can add a number of predefined buttons to get different responses from the user. Here is the About dialog:

The definition for testing the About dialog follows. (See Appendix B for C++ method definitions to invoke equivalent dialogs.)

```
procedure TMyWindow.testAbout(var Msg: TMessage);
begin
  MessageBox(HWindow,
            'This program demonstrates the use of '  +
                'various dialog boxes developed to '  +
                'work with the ObjectWindows '        +
                'application framework.',
            'About',
            mb_Ok);
end;
```

The last argument is a flag in which each of the bits specifies a button or an icon to be included in the dialog. By ORing these flags you can include any combination of predefined buttons and icons in your dialog. For instance, if you wanted both an OK and a Cancel button, you would specify the following:

```
mb_Ok or mb_Cancel
```

The Report dialog is just like the About dialog, but it adds an exclamation point icon by ORing mb _ IconExclamation with mb _ Ok.

```
procedure TMyWindow.testReport(var Msg: TMessage);
begin
  MessageBox(HWindow,
             'The MessageBox function is used '          +
                  'to create a variety of dialogs '       +
                  'in ObjectWindows. MessageBox constants, '   +
                  'like mb_IconExclamation, let you include '  +
                  'special bit-mapped symbols in your message ' +
                  'dialogs.',
             'ObjectWindows Report Dialog',
             mb_Ok or mb_IconExclamation);
end;
```

The exclamation point can be seen in this illustration:

Symbolic constants defined for messages boxes all start with *mb _*. Certain constants set one or more flags for commonly used combinations. For instance,

```
mb_Yes or mb_No
```

can be specified with the single constant:

```
mb_YesNo
```

This can save typing and space in listings.

The following dialog poses a Yes/No question, including two buttons and a question mark icon.

```
procedure TMyWindow.testYesNo(var Msg: TMessage);
var
  Selection : Integer;
  response : PChar;
begin
  Selection :=
  MessageBox(HWindow,
             'Do real programmers drink Jolt?',
             'YesNo Dialog',
             mb_YesNo or mb_IconQuestion);
  case Selection of
    id_Yes    : response := 'Yes';
    id_No     : response := 'No';
  end;
  MessageBox(HWindow,
             response,
             'You selected:',
             mb_ok);
end;
```

MessageBox returns the value of the button pressed by the user to terminate the dialog.

The resulting dialog can be seen here:

Specifying three buttons, Yes, No, and Cancel can be done with a single constant,

```
mb_YesNoCancel
```

as well as by ORing together three constants.

```
mb_Yes  or  mb_No  or  mb_Cancel
```

The following code shows how to include string and integer variables in the prompt string for a dialog and how to test for the button pressed by the user in response to the dialog. Three buttons and a warning, or stop, icon are specified.

```
procedure TMyWindow.testYesNoCancel(var Msg: TMessage);
var
  selection : Integer;
  argList   : array[0..2] of Word;
  s         : array[0..100] of Char;
  fileName  : String;
  response  : PChar;
begin
  fileName := 'DIALOG.PAS';
  argList[0] := 999;
  wvSprintf(s, 'Warning: %d %'#13'File not saved: ', argList);
  strPCopy(StrEnd(s), fileName + #13'Save before quitting?');
  selection :=
  MessageBox(HWindow,
             s,
             'Warning',
             mb_YesNoCancel or mb_IconStop);
  case Selection of
    id_Yes    : response := 'Yes';
    id_No     : response := 'No';
    id_Cancel : response := 'Cancel';
  end;

  MessageBox(HWindow,
             response,
             'You selected:',
             mb_ok);
end;
```

The resulting dialog is shown here:

MessageBox does not allow text input fields. If you need to get information typed by the user into a dialog, you should use the predefined dialog
TInputDialog. Such a dialog can be created from a pointer to a TInputDialog object declared as PInputDialog.

```
ptrDialog := New(PInputDialog,
                 Init(@Self,
                      'Input Dialog',
                      'Enter some text: ',
                      buf,
                      SizeOf(buf) ));
```

The constructor, TInputDialog.Init, expects five arguments. The first is a pointer to the parent window that owns the dialog window. The second argument is the title for the dialog window, and the third argument is the prompt string. The fourth and fifth arguments represent the data buffer to hold the text typed by the user and the maximum number of characters allowed to be typed into this buffer.

If you copy a string into the buffer, it will appear as the default response when the dialog is invoked.

The previous statement merely creates the TInputDialog object and assigns ptrDialog to point to it. To invoke the dialog, you need to execute the following statement:

```
Application^.ExecDialog(ptrDialog);
```

Note that the two statements in the previous two listings are assumed to be defined in methods associated with a class derived from TWindow. This class would be the *parent* of the dialog window. The following method definition shows how to use a TInputDialog with a default response string:

```
procedure TMyWindow.testInput(var Msg: TMessage);
var
  buf : array[0..255] of Char;
begin
  StrPCopy(buf, 'Default response');
  Application^.ExecDialog(New(PInputDialog,
                          Init(@Self,
                               'Input Dialog',
                               'Enter some text: ',
                               buf,
                               SizeOf(buf)  )));
  MessageBox(HWindow, buf, 'Response:', mb_Ok);
end;
```

The resulting dialog is shown in this illustration:

These simple forms of dialog boxes are all variations on the theme of using the Windows MessageBox function supplied with different arguments and flag settings. Selection of items from lists is more complicated.

Before digging into that subject, let's prepare by looking at callback methods for handling Windows messages and then see how simplified I/O in Turbo Pascal for Windows makes porting standard Pascal programs a breeze.

Handling Mouse Events with Callback Methods

Mouse events are easy because you don't need to set up a menu or a dialog box to generate events. Windows automatically reacts to mouse events and sends the events to the appropriate windows. All you need to do is tell ObjectWindows that you want a particular type of window to respond to certain mouse events. The main mouse events you'll be concerned with are mouse button presses and releases. First you need to declare the type for the window that will respond to mouse events.

```
{ Pascal }

type
  PTestWindow = ^TTestWindow;
  TTestWindow = object(TWindow)
  end;

// C++

class TTestWindow : public TWindow
{
  ...
public:
  ...
};

typedef TTestWindow *PTestWindow;
```

Now declare a method inside this window object that will respond to a left mouse button press.

```
{ Pascal }

  ...
  procedure WMLButtonDown(var Msg: TMessage);
    virtual wm_First + wm_LButtonDown;
  ...
```

```cpp
// C++

    ...
    virtual void WMLButtonDown (TMessage& Msg)
                = [WM_FIRST + WM_LBUTTONDOWN];
    ...
```

The method must be virtual and must have a message identifier constant in the range $0000-$7FFF. The constant wm_First is defined as $0000. Adding the specific Windows message, wm_LButtonDown, to this constant assures that the result will be in the appropriate range. It might seem silly at first to add a constant to a constant that is 0, but different types of identifiers must fall in other ranges. For example, command messages, such as those generated by menus, must fall in the range $A000-$FFFF. The first command constant is at $A000, so this is the value assigned to cm_First. The beginnings of other identifier ranges are specified by id_First ($8000-$8FFF) for child id messages and by nf_First ($9000-$9FFF) for notification messages.

Now you can define the method for handling the mouse event. The simplest possibility is to pop up a report dialog to indicate that the message has been received and handled.

```pascal
{ Pascal }
procedure TTestWindow.WMLButtonDown(var Msg: TMessage);
begin
  MessageBox(HWindow,
             'Left button pressed',
             'Callback method: TTestWindow.WMLButtonDown',
             mb_Ok);
end;
```

```cpp
// C++
void TTestWindow::WMLButtonDown(TMessage& Msg)
{
  MessageBox(HWindow,
             "Left button pressed",
             "Callback method: TTestWindow::WMLButtonDown",
             MB_OK);
}
```

You need to make one more modification before the program will work. You need to tell TMyApp.InitMainWindow to use your newly defined

TTestWindow class for the main application window instead of using TWindow. For Pascal, change the line,

```
New(PWindow,
```

to read:

```
New(PTestWindow,
```

A similar change is made in the C++ version. The entire definition for TMyApp.InitMainWindow now looks like this:

```
{ Pascal }

procedure TMyApp.InitMainWindow;
begin
  MainWindow :=
    New(PTestWindow,
        Init(nil, 'Hello ObjectWindows'));
end;

// C++

void TMyApp::InitMainWindow(void)
{
  MainWindow = new TTestWindow(NULL, "Hello ObjectWindows");
}
```

When you run the program and press the left mouse button while pointing at the TTestWindow containing the title "Hello ObjectWindows", a Report dialog will appear. You will have to click on the OK button to make the report disappear. It would be handy if you could test mouse keypresses simply by sending output to another window, rather than having to invoke and close a dialog box each time a mouse button is pressed. Turbo Pascal provides a snappy way to do this that should make DOS programmers already familiar with Turbo Pascal very happy.

Turbo Pascal for Windows Programs Can Use DOS-Compatible I/O Routines

Turbo Pascal provides an interesting transitional tool for programmers moving from DOS to Windows. You can take any Turbo Pascal program written for DOS that is based on the standard Crt unit, and transfer the program directly to work with Turbo Pascal for Windows. This means programs that use write and writeln statements and restrict themselves to the character-oriented subroutines provided by the Crt unit (gotoXY, clrScr, clrEol, whereX, whereY, keyPressed, readKey, and so on) will run directly under ObjectWindows without changes. Any program that does this must specify use of the WinCrt unit in addition to any others required by the program.

```
uses WObjects,   { Required by all ObjectWindows applications. }
     WinTypes,   { Required to use constants like
                   mb_Ok or wm_LButtonDown. }
     WinProcs,   { Required to use Windows procedures
                   like MessageBox }
     WinCrt;     { Required to use Write and Writeln procedures
                   which by default write to a global
                   ObjectWindows window referred to by
                   the handle, CrtWindow. Handy for porting
                   character-oriented programs written for
                   standard Turbo Pascal to run under Ms-Windows }
```

While using the WinCrt unit is not exactly in the spirit of object-oriented programming, it does provide some interesting possibilities for debugging and sending state information to an output window for monitoring program execution. You can use the CrtWindow for output much the way that Smalltalk uses its Transcript window for system messages, compiler error messages, and user-specified output for debugging stubs.

The CrtWindow object is opened automatically the first time output is sent to it and stays open until you explicitly close it. All you need to do to send output to the CrtWindow instead of to a pop-up dialog is change the definition of TTestWindow.WMLButtonDown:

```
procedure TTestWindow.WMLButtonDown(var Msg: TMessage);
begin
  writeln('Left  button pressed');
end;
```

That's all there is to it. Now each time the left mouse button is pressed in the main application window, the string "Left button pressed" will be printed in the CrtWindow followed by a new line. When the window is full, it will scroll automatically just like output to the Crt when using DOS.

C++ Programmer's Note

You could build your own class that provides the same sort of conveniences for C++ applications. You would have to build a window class containing a text buffer and include instance variables to keep track of the window state, such as window size and current cursor position. You could then implement methods equivalent to writeln, clrScr, clrEol, gotoXY, whereX, and whereY. You might want to use output conventions closer to C++ streams by defining an output operator, <<, for each data type you want to print in the CRT window. The program WINCRT.CPP on the available source code disk, provides a rough start in this direction by implementing a text buffer based on an array of String objects. You can change the output for any line in the CRT window by replacing the associated String in the text buffer array. WINCRT.CPP shows mouse callback and monitoring methods roughly equivalent to the Pascal examples in this chapter. The program also clarifies the distinction between printing temporary text and permanent text in a window. *Temporary text* is wiped out by the next exposure event, such as resizing the window, while *permanent text* is not. The secret is in defining routines to repaint the screen in response to Windows Paint messages.

By default the screen is large enough to contain 80 columns and 25 rows just as in DOS. You can override the default size and position for the CrtWindow if your output will not take much space.

```
WindowOrg.X := 0;
WindowOrg.Y := 0;
ScreenSize.X := 30;   { Set global screen window to 40    }
ScreenSize.Y := 10;   { characters wide, 10 lines high.}
```

This code sets the origin of the CrtWindow to the upper-left screen corner and makes a window big enough to hold 10 lines of text with up to 40 characters in each line. Notice that these values are in character units as opposed to the pixel units used with most ObjectWindows and Microsoft Windows procedures.

The best place to put this code is in the constructor for the main application window.

```
constructor TTestWindow.Init(AParent: PWindowsObject; ATitle: PChar);
begin
  { First call parent's constructor }
  TWindow.Init(AParent, ATitle);

  { Set position and size for instance of TTestWindow }
  Attr.X := 100;
  Attr.Y := 100;
  Attr.W := 200;
  Attr.H := 200;

  WindowOrg.X := 0;
  WindowOrg.Y := 0;
  ScreenSize.X := 40;   { Set global screen window to 40 }
  ScreenSize.Y := 10;   { characters wide, 10 lines high. }
end;
```

Of course, before you can define the constructor, you must declare it.

```
type
  TTestWindow = object(TWindow)
    constructor Init(AParent: PWindowsObject;
                     ATitle : PChar);
    .
    .
    .
  end;
```

While you're at it, you might as well include a method to handle right-button presses for the mouse. You could also add a handler to report when the left mouse button is released. The declaration would look like this:

```
type
  PTestWindow = ^TTestWindow;
  TTestWindow = object(TWindow)
    constructor Init(AParent: PWindowsObject;
                     ATitle: PChar);
    procedure WMLButtonDown(var Msg: TMessage);
      virtual wm_First + wm_LButtonDown;
```

```
  procedure WMRButtonDown(var Msg: TMessage);
    virtual wm_First + wm_RButtonDown;
  procedure WMLButtonUp(var Msg: TMessage);
    virtual wm_First + wm_LButtonUp;
end;
```

The methods for handling the messages WMRButtonDown and WML-ButtonUp need to be defined. The right-button press handler prints a message to CrtWindow.

```
procedure TTestWindow.WMRButtonDown(var Msg: TMessage);
begin
  writeln('Right button pressed');
end;
```

You could do something a little more useful with the left mouse button release handler. You could have this callback method report the position at which the mouse button is released. This is not necessarily the same position where the left mouse button was pressed.

```
procedure TTestWindow.WMLButtonUp(var Msg: TMessage);
var
  xPos, yPos : Integer;
begin
  xPos := Msg.LParamLo;
  yPos := Msg.LParamHi;
  write('Left  button released at: ');
  writeln(xPos, ' @ ', yPos);

end;
```

The message that is passed to the handler contains the position at which the event occurred. A TMessage object is a record containing a window handle, as well as other data parameters. In the case of mouse events, the data parameters hold the x and y positions of the mouse when the event was triggered.

The entire program follows. (See WINCRT.CPP on the companion disk for a rough equivalent in C++.)

```
FILE: WINCRT.PAS

program Callback;

uses WObjects,  { required by all ObjectWindows applications }
     WinTypes,  { required to use constants like mb_Ok or wm_LButtonDown}
```

```
    WinProcs,   { required to use Windows procedures like MessageBox }
    WinCrt;     { required to use Write and Writeln procedures
                  which by default write the global ObjectWindows
                  object called Screen. Handy for porting character-
                  oriented programs written for standard Turbo Pascal
                  to run under Ms-Windows }

{-------------------------------}
{ Declare your application here. }
{-------------------------------}
type
  TMyApp = object(TApplication)
    procedure InitMainWindow; virtual;
  end;

{--------------------------------}
{ Declare special types of windows }
{ used by your application here.    }
{--------------------------------}
type
  PTestWindow = ^TTestWindow;
  TTestWindow = object(TWindow)
    constructor Init(AParent: PWindowsObject;
                                  ATitle: PChar);
    procedure WMLButtonDown(var Msg: TMessage);
      virtual wm_First + wm_LButtonDown;
    procedure WMRButtonDown(var Msg: TMessage);
      virtual wm_First + wm_RButtonDown;
    procedure WMLButtonUp(var Msg: TMessage);
      virtual wm_First + wm_LButtonUp;
  end;

{-----------------------}
{ Define methods for    }
{ your application here. }
{-----------------------}
procedure TMyApp.InitMainWindow;
begin
  MainWindow :=
    { New(PWindow, { Change when to specify your own type of window }
    New(PTestWindow,
        Init(nil, 'Hello ObjectWindows'));
end;

{--------------------------}
{ Define methods for your  }
{ special window types here. }
{--------------------------}
constructor TTestWindow.Init(AParent: PWindowsObject; ATitle: PChar);
begin
  { First call parent's constructor }
  TWindow.Init(AParent, ATitle);

  { Set position and size for instance of TTestWindow }
  Attr.X := 300;
  Attr.Y := 100;
```

```
  Attr.W := 200;
  Attr.H := 200;

  WindowOrg.X := 0;
  WindowOrg.Y := 0;
  ScreenSize.X := 40;   { Set global screen window to 40  }
  ScreenSize.Y := 10;   { characters wide, 10 lines high. }
end;

procedure TTestWindow.WMLButtonDown(var Msg: TMessage);
begin
  writeln('Left  button pressed');
end;

procedure TTestWindow.WMRButtonDown(var Msg: TMessage);
begin
  writeln('Right button pressed');
end;

procedure TTestWindow.WMLButtonUp(var Msg: TMessage);
var
  xPos, yPos : Integer;
begin
  xPos := Msg.LParamLo;
  yPos := Msg.LParamHi;
  write('Left  button released at: ');
  writeln(xPos, ' @ ', yPos);
end;

{------------------}
{ Main application }
{------------------}
var
  MyApp: TMyApp;

begin
  MyApp.Init('Callback Methods');
  MyApp.Run;
  MyApp.Done;
end.
```

When run, this program responds each time either mouse button is pressed by printing a string to the CrtWindow. In addition, each time the left mouse button is released the position of the mouse and a string announcing the release are shown. Typical output is shown in Figure 14-1.

You could add one final twist to the program that takes advantage of the WinCrt procedures, gotoXY and clrEol. Instead of having the output to the CrtWindow scroll, always print the text for the left mouse button in the first line of the window. When the button is pressed, report it with a string and include the mouse position. When the left mouse button is released, clear the first line. A method is also added to handle the release of the right

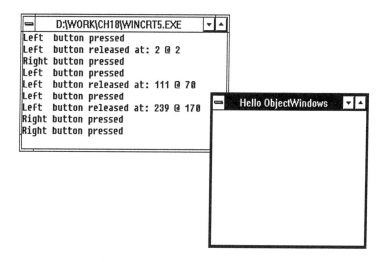

Figure 14-1.   An ObjectWindows application with mouse event callback routines. Turbo Pascal for Windows allows use of writeln statements to send output to a global CrtWindow object.

mouse button to clear the second line. When the right mouse button is pressed, a string appears on the second line of the CrtWindow. When the right mouse button is released, the string is erased. Here's the declaration for the main window class:

```
{--------------------------------}
{ Declare special types of windows }
{ used by your application here.    }
{--------------------------------}
type
  PTestWindow = ^TTestWindow;
  TTestWindow = object(TWindow)
    constructor Init(AParent: PWindowsObject;
                                ATitle: PChar);
    procedure WMLButtonDown(var Msg: TMessage);
      virtual wm_First + wm_LButtonDown;
    procedure WMLButtonUp(var Msg: TMessage);
      virtual wm_First + wm_LButtonUp;
    procedure WMRButtonDown(var Msg: TMessage);
      virtual wm_First + wm_RButtonDown;
    procedure WMRButtonUp(var Msg: TMessage);
      virtual wm_First + wm_RButtonUp;
  end;
```

Here are the callback method definitions:

```
procedure TTestWindow.WMLButtonDown(var Msg: TMessage);
var
  xPos, yPos : Integer;
begin
  xPos := Msg.LParamLo;
  yPos := Msg.LParamHi;
  GotoXY(1,1);
  write('Left  button pressed at: ');
  writeln(xPos, ' @ ', yPos);

end;

procedure TTestWindow.WMLButtonUp(var Msg: TMessage);
begin
  GotoXY(1,1);
  ClrEol;
end;

procedure TTestWindow.WMRButtonDown(var Msg: TMessage);
begin
  GotoXY(1,2);
  writeln('Right button pressed');
end;

procedure TTestWindow.WMRButtonUp(var Msg: TMessage);
begin
  GotoXY(1,2);
  ClrEol;
end;
```

If you run this program and press both mouse buttons simultaneously, you will see output similar to Figure 14-2. Using the CrtWindow is a good way to check to see if your callback event handlers are being called when you think they should be. The next section will use the CrtWindow to test the contents of a collection of sorted strings to see that it is being built properly before passing it as data for a List box dialog.

DATA AND DIALOGS

For all the dialogs shown so far, only simple types of data such as strings and button identification constants have been sent to or retrieved from dialog boxes. List boxes require that you specify more complex information.

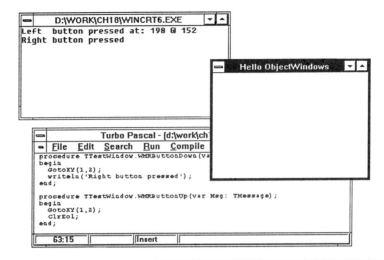

Figure 14-2. The Turbo Pascal for Windows development environment showing part of the source code for the ObjectWindows application that covers it. The WinCrt unit allows use of gotoXY and clrEol in a CrtWindow.

List boxes keep track of two pieces of data: a list of strings from which a selection is to be made and the integer index of the currently selected string.

Before worrying about transferring these two pieces of data to or from an ObjectWindows dialog object, consider the smaller problem of creating a collection of sorted strings.

```
var
  ListStrings : PCollection;
begin
  {-------------------------------- --}
  { Collection starts with 10 elements }
  { and grows dynamically by 5         }
  { elements each time it is filled     }
  { to capacity.                        }
  {--------------------------------}
  ListStrings := new(PStrCollection, Init(10, 5));

  with ListStrings^ do
  begin
    Insert(StrNew('Vanilla'));
    Insert(StrNew('Chocolate'));
    Insert(StrNew('Strawberry'));
```

```
    Insert(StrNew('Neapolitan'));
    Insert(StrNew('Chunky Monkey'));
    Insert(StrNew('Jamoca Almond Fudge'));
    Insert(StrNew('Tin Roof Sundae'));
    Insert(StrNew('Heath Bar Crunch'));
    Insert(StrNew('Rocky Road'));
    Insert(StrNew('Milli Vanilli'));
    Insert(StrNew('Peppermint'));
    Insert(StrNew('Chocolate Chip'));
    Insert(StrNew('Mutant Ninja Turtle Bars'));
    Insert(StrNew('Tutti Frutti'));
  end;
```

Note: The complete C++ implementation of the final dialog application can be found in Appendix B under the name DIALOG.CPP.

You can take advantage of the simplified I/O provided by the WinCrt unit to print out the collection. With the new type of PChar strings used by Turbo Pascal to create and manipulate strings compatible with Microsoft Windows, you can easily become confused. You don't want to start building complex dialog boxes without testing the contents of your string collection. If you give a collection of normal Pascal strings (first byte of string is length count), your program will crash if you invoke a List box dialog to work on the collection. Here's a simple way to test your collection of strings. After specifying the collection as in the previous listing, define a global procedure to print the collection.

```
{-------------------------}
{ print a collection of   }
{ Strings in the CrtWindow }
{-------------------------}
procedure printCollection(c: PCollection);

  {---------------------------------------}
  { Local procedure: prints one string.   }
  { Procedures passed as arguments to     }
  { iterators must be declared as far.    }
  {---------------------------------------}
  procedure printString(p : PChar); far;
  begin
    writeln(P);
  end;

begin { printCollection }
  writeln;
```

```
        c^.ForEach(@printString);      {-------------------------------}
                                       { The ForEach iterator is       }
                                       { a TCollection method which    }
                                       { calls the specified procedure }
                                       { (printString) for each element }
                                       { of the collection (c).        }
                                       {-------------------------------}
    end;
```

This procedure takes a collection as an argument and iterates over the collection using the ForEach iterator method defined for all TCollection and descendant classes. Output is sent directly to the CrtWindow using writeln.

The entire program for printing the collection follows. A sorted string collection is tested by printing it to the CrtWindow.

```
FILE: LISTSTR.PAS

program ListOfStrings;

uses WObjects, WinCrt, Strings;

{-------------------------}
{ print a collection of   }
{ Strings in the CrtWindow }
{-------------------------}
procedure printCollection(c: PCollection);

   {-------------------------------------}
   { Local procedure: prints one string. }
   { Procedures passed as arguments to    }
   { iterators must be declared as far.  }
   {-------------------------------------}
   procedure printString(p : PChar); far;
   begin
     writeln(P);
   end;

begin { printCollection }
  writeln;
  c^.ForEach(@printString);      {-------------------------------}
                                 { The ForEach iterator is       }
                                 { a TCollection method which    }
                                 { calls the specified procedure }
                                 { (printString) for each element }
                                 { of the collection (c).        }
                                 {-------------------------------}
end;

var
  ListStrings : PCollection;
begin
```

```
{-----------------------------------}
{ Collection starts with 10 elements }
{ and grows dynamically by 5         }
{ elements each time it is filled    }
{ to capacity.                       }
{-----------------------------------}
ListStrings := new(PStrCollection, Init(10, 5));

with ListStrings^ do
begin
  Insert(StrNew('Vanilla'));
  Insert(StrNew('Chocolate'));
  Insert(StrNew('Strawberry'));
  Insert(StrNew('Neapolitan'));
  Insert(StrNew('Chunky Monkey'));
  Insert(StrNew('Jamoca Almond Fudge'));
  Insert(StrNew('Tin Roof Sundae'));
  Insert(StrNew('Heath Bar Crunch'));
  Insert(StrNew('Rocky Road'));
  Insert(StrNew('Milli Vanilli'));
  Insert(StrNew('Peppermint'));
  Insert(StrNew('Chocolate Chip'));
  Insert(StrNew('Mutant Ninja Turtle Bars'));
  Insert(StrNew('Tutti Frutti'));
end;
                              {----------------------}
                              { Set attributes for   }
                              { CrtWindow.           }
                              {----------------------}
ScreenSize.X := 40;
ScreenSize.Y := ListStrings^.Count + 2;
StrPCopy(WindowTitle,   'Ice Cream');
StrPCopy(InactiveTitle, 'Program Terminated');

InitWinCrt;                   {----------------------}
                              { Opens CrtWindow. Not }
                              { really necessary to  }
                              { call InitWinCrt since}
                              { it is called         }
                              { automatically the    }
                              { first time output is }
                              { sent to CrtWindow.   }
                              {----------------------}

printCollection(ListStrings);

readKey;                      {----------------------}
                              { CrtWindow stays active }
                              { as long as program has }
                              { not terminated. Once   }
                              { the program terminates,}
                              { the WindowTitle is     }
                              { replaced by the        }
                              { InactiveTitle in the   }
                              { title box.             }
                              {----------------------}
```

```
    dispose(ListStrings, Done);     { release heap memory }
    DoneWinCrt;                     {----------------------}
                                    { Include this line only }
                                    { if you want the window }
                                    { to close automatically }
                                    { when the program       }
                                    { terminates.            }
                                    {----------------------}
end.
```

The output is shown here:

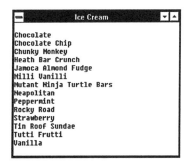

Once you know the collection is being built properly, you're ready to hand it off to the List box dialog.

Transferring Data to and from List Box Dialogs

Like Turbo Vision, ObjectWindows uses data structures to transfer data to and from dialog boxes. The transfer-record fields need to be exactly the right size and specified in the same order as the corresponding control objects defined for the dialog resource. Pushbuttons don't require any data inside a transfer record, so for the list box resource specified in DIA-LOG.RC, all you need to worry about is the collection of strings to be manipulated by the dialog. Transfer records for ObjectWindows list box collections require a pointer to the string collection and an index to keep track of the currently selected string. Such a data record could be declared as follows:

```
type
  TransferRecord = record
    ListStrings   : PStrCollection;   { list box strings      }
    ListSelection : Integer;          { index of              }
                                      {    selected string    }
  end;
```

You then create an instance of this data record and set the ListStrings field to point to the desired collection.

```
var
   theBuffer       : TransferRecord;       { data transfer buffer   }
   ...
begin
   ...
   theBuffer.ListStrings := New(PStrCollection, Init(10,5) );
   theBuffer.ListSelection := 0;
   ...
```

Next, add the string elements to the collection.

```
   ...
   with theBuffer.ListStrings^  do
   begin
     Insert(StrNew('Vanilla'));
     Insert(StrNew('Chocolate'));
     ...
   end;
   ...
```

Now you need to create a dialog from the dialog resource called 'LISTBOXDIALOG'.

```
var
   theDialog : PDialog;
   ...
begin
   ...
   theDialog := new(PDialog, Init(@Self, 'LISTBOXDIALOG'));
   ...
```

You also have to create the list box object contained inside the dialog box.

```
var
   theListBox      : PListBox;
   ...
begin
   ...
   new(theListBox, InitResource(theDialog, idListBox ));
   ...
```

As if that isn't enough to remember, you now need to specify that the variable, theBuffer, is to be used by the dialog to transfer data into and out of the dialog.

```
theDialog^.TransferBuffer := @theBuffer;
```

Now when the dialog is invoked, it will use the PStrCollection pointer inside theBuffer to initialize the contents of the list box. When the dialog is terminated, you can check the value of theBuffer.ListSelection to see which item was highlighted when the dialog was terminated. You can also check the contents of the string collection by looking at the variable, theBuffer.List-Strings. Some List box dialogs actually add or remove collection elements. The test dialog doesn't change the contents of the collection, so you can still use theBuffer.ListStrings along with the index theBuffer.ListSelection to retrieve the string for the selected element.

```
index          := theBuffer.ListSelection;
stringSelected := theBuffer.ListStrings^.at(index);
MessageBox(HWindow, stringSelected, 'You selected:', mb_OK);
```

Here's a method definition for the user-defined window class, TMyWindow, that puts everything together:

```
procedure TMyWindow.testListSelect(var Msg: TMessage);
                                   {------------------------}
                                   { TransferRecord is a   }
                                   { local type for        }
                                   { creating a data       }
                                   { transfer buffer to    }
                                   { move list box data    }
                                   { into and out of a     }
                                   { list box dialog.      }
                                   {------------------------}
type
  TransferRecord = record
    ListStrings   : PStrCollection;   { list box strings     }
    ListSelection : Integer;          { index of selection   }
  end;
var
  theListBox     : PListBox;
  theDialog      : PDialog;
  theBuffer      : TransferRecord;    { data transfer buffer }
  index          : Integer;
  buttonPressed  : Integer;
  stringSelected : PChar;
```

```
begin
                                        {----------------------}
                                        { 'LISTBOXDIALOG' is   }
                                        {   the name of the    }
                                        {   dialog specified in }
                                        {   the resource file. }
                                        {----------------------}

    theDialog := new(PDialog, Init(@Self, 'LISTBOXDIALOG'));
    new(theListBox, InitResource(theDialog, idListBox ));

                                        {----------------------}
                                        { Create the sorted    }
                                        { string collection for }
                                        { the list of strings. }
                                        { Set the data transfer }
                                        { buffer for the dialog. }
                                        {----------------------}

    theBuffer.ListStrings := New(PStrCollection, Init(10,5) );
    theBuffer.ListSelection := 0;
    theDialog^.TransferBuffer := @theBuffer;

                                        {----------------------}
                                        { Add the strings to the }
                                        { collection in the    }
                                        { data transfer buffer. }
                                        {----------------------}
    with theBuffer.ListStrings^  do
    begin
      Insert(StrNew('Vanilla'));
      Insert(StrNew('Chocolate'));
      Insert(StrNew('Strawberry'));
      Insert(StrNew('Neapolitan));
      Insert(StrNew('Chunky Monkey'));
      Insert(StrNew('Jamoca Almond Fudge'));
      Insert(StrNew('Tin Roof Sundae'));
      Insert(StrNew('Heath Bar Crunch'));
      Insert(StrNew('Rocky Road'));
      Insert(StrNew('Milli Vanilli'));
      Insert(StrNew('Peppermint'));
      Insert(StrNew('Chocolate Chip'));
      Insert(StrNew('Mutant Ninja Turtle Bars'));
      Insert(StrNew('Tutti Frutti'));
    end;
                                        {----------------------}
                                        { Invoke the dialog and }
                                        { record the button used }
                                        { to end the dialog.   }
                                        {----------------------}

    buttonPressed := Application^.ExecDialog(theDialog);

    if buttonPressed = id_Ok then
    begin
```

```
                                        {----------------------}
                                        { Get the index and use }
                                        { it to retrieve the    }
                                        { associated string out }
                                        { of the collection in  }
                                        { the data transfer     }
                                        { buffer. Show the      }
                                        { result.               }
                                        {----------------------}
    index          := theBuffer.ListSelection;
    stringSelected := theBuffer.ListStrings^.at(index);
    MessageBox(HWindow, stringSelected, 'You selected:', mb_OK);
  end
  else
  begin
                                        {----------------------}
                                        { Dialog terminated with }
                                        { Cancel button          }
                                        {----------------------}
    MessageBox(HWindow, 'Cancel', 'You selected:', mb_OK);
  end;
end;
```

The dialog that is invoked on execution of this method is shown here:

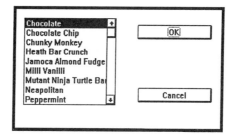

FILE SELECTION DIALOGS

Since getting user input to specify a filename is so common in Windows programs, ObjectWindows provides a standard dialog class called TFileDialog. The constructor for TFileDialog takes three arguments. The first is a pointer to the parent window. The second argument is a constant that is cast as a string to specify the specific type of File selection dialog: sd_FileOpen or sd_FileSave. You get a slightly different dialog, depending on which type you specify. The third argument to the constructor is an array of characters that, on input, contains the default filename or filename template (for example, '*.pas' or '*.cpp'). When the dialog is terminated, the buffer passed as the third argument will contain the complete path name of the selected file.

Here's a test method for TMyWindow that invokes a TFileDialog as an sd_FileOpen dialog with '*.pas' as the filename template.

```
procedure TMyWindow.testFileSelect(var Msg: TMessage);
var
    fileName : array[0..fsPathName] of Char;
begin
  StrPCopy(fileName, '*.pas');
  Application^.ExecDialog(
                New(PFileDialog,
                Init(@Self,
                    PChar(sd_FileOpen),
                    fileName
                    )));
  MessageBox(HWindow, fileName, 'Response:', mb_Ok);
end;
```

The resulting dialog is shown here:

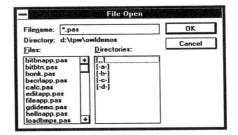

If you substitute sd_FileSave for sd_FileOpen in the above listing, you'll see the dialog shown in the following illustration. It has a different title box and leaves out the list box of filename strings matching the template specified in the filename text field.

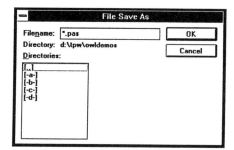

Here is the entire listing for a program framework to test each of the seven dialogs. (See Appendix B for the equivalent C++ program. Alternative ways of constructing List box dialogs are provided on the companion disk.)

```
FILE: DIALOG.PAS

{ Pascal }
program StandardDialogs;

uses WObjects, winTypes, WinProcs, Strings, StdDlgs, WinDos;
{$R DIALOG.RES}

const
  menuTestDialogs = 100;
  cmAbout         = 101;
  cmReport        = 102;
  cmYesNo         = 103;
  cmYesNoCancel   = 104;
  cmInput         = 105;
  cmListSelect    = 106;
  cmFileSelect    = 107;
  cmQuit          = 108;

  idListBox       = 201;


{=============================================================}
{ INTERFACE: CLASS DECLARATIONS                               }
{=============================================================}


{------------------------}
{ Application (interface) }
{------------------------}
```

```
type
  TMyApp = object(TApplication)
    procedure InitMainWindow; virtual;
  end;

{------------------------}
{ Main Window (interface) }
{------------------------}

type
  PMyWindow = ^TMyWindow;
  TMyWindow = object(TWindow)
    constructor Init(AParent: PWindowsObject; ATitle: PChar);
    procedure testAbout(var Msg: TMessage);
              virtual cm_First + cmAbout;
    procedure testReport(var Msg: TMessage);
              virtual cm_First + cmReport;
    procedure testYesNo(var Msg: TMessage);
              virtual cm_First + cmYesNo;
    procedure testYesNoCancel(var Msg: TMessage);
              virtual cm_First + cmYesNoCancel;
    procedure testInput(var Msg: TMessage);
              virtual cm_First + cmInput;
    procedure testListSelect(var Msg: TMessage);
              virtual cm_First + cmListSelect;
    procedure testFileSelect(var Msg: TMessage);
              virtual cm_First + cmFileSelect;
    procedure testQuit(var Msg: TMessage);
              virtual cm_First + cmQuit;
  end;

{============================================================}
{ IMPLEMENTATION: METHOD DEFINITIONS                         }
{============================================================}

{---------------------------}
{ Application (implementation) }
{---------------------------}

procedure TMyApp.InitMainWindow;
begin
  MainWindow :=
    New(PMyWindow,
        Init(nil, 'ObjectWindows Dialogs'));
end;

{---------------------------}
{ Main Window (implementation) }
{---------------------------}

constructor TMyWindow.Init(AParent: PWindowsObject; ATitle: PChar);
begin
  TWindow.Init(AParent, ATitle);
    Attr.Menu := LoadMenu(HInstance, PChar(menuTestDialogs));
  end;
```

```
procedure TMyWindow.testAbout(var Msg: TMessage);
begin
  MessageBox(HWindow,
            'This program demonstrates the use of '    +
              'various dialog boxes developed to '      +
              'work with the ObjectWindows '               +
              'application framework.',
            'About', mb_Ok);
end;

procedure TMyWindow.testReport(var Msg: TMessage);
begin
  MessageBox(HWindow,
            'The MessageBox function is used ' +
              'to create a variety of dialogs ' +
              'in ObjectWindows. MessageBox constants, ' +
              'like mb_IconExclamation, let you include ' +
              'special bit-mapped symbols in your message ' +
              'dialogs.',
            'ObjectWindows Report Dialog',
            mb_Ok or mb_IconExclamation);
end;

procedure TMyWindow.testYesNo(var Msg: TMessage);
var
  Selection : Integer;
  response : PChar;
begin
  Selection :=
  MessageBox(HWindow, 'Do programmers still drink Jolt?',
    'YesNo Dialog', mb_YesNo or mb_IconQuestion);
  case Selection of
    id_Yes    : response := 'Yes';
    id_No     : response := 'No';
  end;

  MessageBox(HWindow,
            response,
            'You selected:',
            mb_ok);
end;


procedure TMyWindow.testYesNoCancel(var Msg: TMessage);
var
  Selection : Integer;
  Params: array[0..2] of Word;
  S : array[0..100] of Char;
  fileName : String;
  response : PChar;
begin
  fileName := 'DIALOG.PAS';
  Params[0] := 999;
  wvSprintf(S, 'Warning: %d %'#13'File not saved: ', Params);
  strPCopy(StrEnd(S), fileName + #13'Save before quitting?');
  Selection :=
```

```
    MessageBox(HWindow,
              S,
              'Warning',
              mb_YesNoCancel or mb_IconStop);
    case Selection of
      id_Yes    : response := 'Yes';
      id_No     : response := 'No';
      id_Cancel : response := 'Cancel';
    end;

    MessageBox(HWindow,
               response,
               'You selected:',
               mb_ok);
end;

procedure TMyWindow.testInput(var Msg: TMessage);
var
    buf : array[0..255] of Char;
begin
  StrPCopy(buf, 'Default response');
  Application^.ExecDialog(New(PInputDialog,
                          Init(@Self,
                               'Input Dialog',
                               'Enter some text: ',
                               buf,
                               SizeOf(buf)
                               )));
  MessageBox(HWindow, buf, 'Response:', mb_Ok);
end;

procedure TMyWindow.testListSelect(var Msg: TMessage);
type
  TransferRecord = record
    ListStrings : PStrCollection; { list box strings }
    ListSelection : Integer;      { index of selected string }
  end;
var
  theListBox     : PListBox;
  theDialog      : PDialog;
  theBuffer      : TransferRecord;
  index          : Integer;
  buttonPressed  : Integer;
  stringSelected : PChar;
begin
                                    { 'LISTBOXDIALOG' is
                                      the name of dialog
                                      specified in resource
                                      file               }
  theDialog := new(PDialog, Init(@Self, 'LISTBOXDIALOG'));
  new(theListBox, InitResource(theDialog, idListBox ));
  theBuffer.ListStrings := New(PStrCollection, Init(10,5) );
  theBuffer.ListSelection := 0;
  theDialog^.TransferBuffer := @theBuffer;

  with theBuffer.ListStrings^  do
```

```
begin
  Insert(StrNew('Vanilla'));
  Insert(StrNew('Chocolate'));
  Insert(StrNew('Strawberry'));
  Insert(StrNew('Neapolitan'));
  Insert(StrNew('Chunky Monkey'));
  Insert(StrNew('Jamoca Almond Fudge'));
  Insert(StrNew('Tin Roof Sundae'));
  Insert(StrNew('Heath Bar Crunch'));
  Insert(StrNew('Rocky Road'));
  Insert(StrNew('Milli Vanilli'));
  Insert(StrNew('Peppermint'));
  Insert(StrNew('Chocolate Chip'));
  Insert(StrNew('Mutant Ninja Turtle Bars'));
  Insert(StrNew('Tutti Frutti'));
end;

                                        {-----------------------}
                                        { Invoke the dialog and }
                                        { record the button used }
                                        { to end the dialog.    }
                                        {-----------------------}
buttonPressed := Application^.ExecDialog(theDialog);

if buttonPressed = id_Ok then
begin
  index         := theBuffer.ListSelection;
  stringSelected := theBuffer.ListStrings^.at(index);
  MessageBox(HWindow, stringSelected, 'You selected:', mb_OK);
end
else
begin
  MessageBox(HWindow, 'Cancel', 'You selected:', mb_OK);
end;
end;

procedure TMyWindow.testFileSelect(var Msg: TMessage);
var
    fileName : array[0..fsPathName] of Char;
begin
  StrPCopy(fileName, '*.pas');
  Application^.ExecDialog(
                          New(PFileDialog,
                          Init(@Self,
                               PChar(sd_FileOpen),
                               fileName
                               )));
  MessageBox(HWindow, fileName, 'Response:', mb_Ok);
end;

procedure TMyWindow.testQuit(var Msg: TMessage);
var
  Selection : Integer;
begin
  Selection :=
  MessageBox(HWindow, 'Exit program?',
```

```
    'Goodbye', mb_YesNo or mb_IconQuestion);
  if Selection = id_Yes then
    PostQuitMessage(0);
end;

{==============================================================}
{ MAIN PROGRAM                                                 }
{==============================================================}
var
  MyApp: TMyApp;

begin
  MyApp.Init('StandardDialogs');
  MyApp.Run;
  MyApp.Done;
end.
```

CHAPTER HIGHLIGHTS

Turbo Pascal

- If you are already a Pascal programmer, Turbo Pascal for Windows is by far the easiest way to transfer existing knowledge and programs from a DOS environment to a Microsoft Windows environment.

  If you're more interested in getting programs up and running quickly than in learning about objects, Turbo Pascal for Windows could be your best choice. Turbo Pascal for Windows is also probably the least expensive way to get all the tools required to develop sophisticated Windows programs.

  Even for C or C++ programmers, Pascal provides a very easy transition to Windows because it is close enough to C++ in syntax and procedural structure. The speed of the Pascal compiler almost gives the feel of working with an interpreted language. Windows programs of several hundred lines compile and link in less than five seconds on a 25 MHz 386 machine. Turbo Pascal for Windows is a very solid choice for a prototyping environment, as well as for a delivery language.

C++

- C++ is an important language and the most widely distributed object-oriented language. If you need a standard, have a lot of existing C or

C++ code, or work on a large team and plan to build complex programs consisting of many modules, you'll want the power of C++.

Be forewarned that you will pay a significant penalty in compile time for selecting C++ over Pascal. C++ is not recommended for prototyping.

Actor and Smalltalk

- Actor has been touted as the easiest way to learn how to program in Windows because it provides an interactive development environment, but you still have to learn the Actor language. Since Actor is a "pure" object-oriented language, learning Actor is no small accomplishment. However, Actor is no more difficult to learn than Smalltalk, and it is highly recommended that you learn either Smalltalk or Actor, even if you plan to program in Pascal or C++.

  Actor is a little more comprehensible for those familiar with procedural languages. Actor lacks some of the power of Smalltalk, but newcomers won't notice. Also, Actor provides compatibility with classes available for C++ and Pascal. When you buy Actor 4.0, the Object-Windows class library comes with it at no extra cost. The class library that came with Actor 3.0 was the foundation on which ObjectWindows for C++ and Pascal was built as a joint effort of Borland and the group Whitewater.

  Smalltalk is the best choice for prototyping. Learning the language can take a while, but the rewards are well worth the effort. Microsoft Windows programs written in Smalltalk compare favorably with execution speeds of C++ and Pascal programs and can be developed in a fraction of the time.

If, after weighing your options, C++ still seems like the best choice, you'll be in good company, and you'll still enjoy the support of tools not available for standard Windows programming. With the power extended to you by the ObjectWindows class library, the integrated development environment running under Windows, and Turbo Debugger for Windows, you'll be way ahead of anyone trying to do Windows program development with a standard C or Pascal compiler.

IV

APPENDIXES

Janie Wooldridge

A

ROTATE SHAPES IN PASCAL, SMALLTALK, AND ACTOR

The only complete listing of the rotate shapes program in this appendix is shown in Turbo Pascal. A QuickPascal version is available on disk. For Smalltalk and Actor, only classes that are not already listed in Chapter 7, "Language Support for User-Defined Types", and Chapter 8, "Language Support for Object-Oriented Programming", are listed here. Complete Smalltalk, Actor, and C++ versions of rotate shapes are provided on disk as well. See the coupon in the front of the book for ordering information.

ROTATE SHAPES IN OBJECT-ORIENTED PASCAL

The term *object-oriented Pascal* applies to three varieties of Pascal: Object Pascal from Apple Computer, QuickPascal from Microsoft, and Turbo Pascal (versions 5.5 and later) from Borland International.

When language features are discussed in Chapters 7 and 8, the example programs generally apply to all three versions of object-oriented Pascal. However, in the discussions of more advanced features, such as constructors, destructors, and heap management for polymorphic objects, Turbo

Pascal is used. This is because Turbo Pascal is the only Pascal that provides constructors and destructors and gives the programmer a choice regarding allocating objects *statically* (in the same data areas as normal Pascal variables) or *dynamically* (on the heap using pointers). All objects in Object Pascal and QuickPascal are allocated dynamically on the heap using new and must be discarded when no longer needed using dispose. Object Pascal and QuickPascal do not allow static objects. Turbo Pascal is also the only version of Pascal to provide a choice regarding whether object methods use static binding or dynamic binding. The keyword *virtual* has no meaning in Object Pascal or QuickPascal, since all methods are dynamically bound, and static binding is not possible.

Object Pascal was not intended to provide some of the more powerful features of object-oriented programming. Class variables and class methods were purposely excluded from the language because designers did not want to overwhelm Pascal programmers with an abundance of features. As its inventors indicated, Object Pascal was intended as a bare-bones object-oriented language, allowing programmers to use standard Pascal programming techniques and ease slowly into the object-oriented paradigm. QuickPascal followed in the footsteps of Object Pascal and is essentially the same language with different class libraries for a different computing environment (MS-DOS, as opposed to the Macintosh operating environment). Consequently, Object Pascal and QuickPascal can show neither examples of constructors and destructors nor the distinction between managing object memory on the heap and allowing the compiler to manage static memory allocation automatically.

Turbo Pascal also extends the features of the standard Pascal routines new and dispose for managing memory allocated on the heap using object types as well as object pointer variables. The Turbo Pascal extensions to new and dispose allow these heap management routines to work more easily with constructors and destructors so that object creation, initialization, and assignment can be performed in a single Pascal statement without the need for temporary variables. These combined features make it much easier to create polymorphic objects and place them in polymorphic collections.

The source code shown in this appendix takes advantage of the object-oriented extensions to Object Pascal provided only in Turbo Pascal. Use of these extensions is limited to situations where they make code easier to read and maintain. If you can read code in Object Pascal or QuickPascal, you will have no problem following the Turbo Pascal code. The first thing you will notice is fewer uses of new and dispose, since static objects are used by default in Turbo Pascal, eliminating the need to manage heap memory. The other thing you will notice is the absence of the "self" qualifier in references to instance variables and methods inside object definitions.

Turbo Pascal Units

The main program source file for the object-oriented Pascal version of rotate shapes is ROTATE.PAS. This source file must be compiled and linked together with three Turbo Pascal Unit (TPU) files to create the executable program, ROTATE.EXE. The .TPU files are

```
point.tpu
shapes.tpu
screen.tpu
```

The source files that generate each of these .TPU files have the same file name as the .TPU files, but with a .PAS extension.

```
point.pas
shapes.pas
screen.pas
```

The compiler is able to tell that these files are the source code for units (TPUs) rather than for executable programs (EXEs) because the first line of source code in each file contains the keyword *unit*, followed by the name of the unit.

```
FILE: POINT.PAS

    unit Point;
    .
    .
    .

FILE: SHAPES.PAS

    unit Shapes;
    .
    .
    .

FILE: SCREEN.PAS
```

```
unit Screen;
    .
    .
    .
```

Contrast the use of *unit* with the use of the keyword *program* found in the main program module. If a .PAS file contains source code for an executable file, it typically has a line that starts with the keyword, *program*, followed by the name of the program.

FILE: ROTATE.PAS

```
program RotateShapes;
    .
    .
    .
```

Some versions of Pascal allow *program* to be omitted. In such cases, as long as *unit* does not appear, the file is considered the main program source module.

Another distinguishing feature of units is that they are divided up into an interface section and an implementation section.

FILE: POINT.PAS

```
unit Point;
    .
    .
    .
interface
    .
    .
    .
    { ---------------------------------------------------}
    { Declare the names of constants, variables,         }
    { procedures, and functions that can be accessed     }
    { by other units or programs that indicate use of    }
    { the Point unit. For example, the Screen            }
    { unit makes use of the Point unit by                }
    { declaring the following statement in its           }
    { interface section.                                 }
    {                                                    }
    {     uses Graph, Point;                             }
    {                                                    }
    { ---------------------------------------------------}
    .
    .
    .
```

```
implementation

  { ------------------------------------------------}
  { Implementation of functions and procedures      }
  { declared in the public interface section        }
  { ------------------------------------------------}
      .
      .
      .
end.              { end of unit definition }
```

The *interface section* of a Turbo Pascal unit source file is like a header file (for example, POINT.H) for a C or C++ program, which declares all constants, variables, function prototypes, and classes for a corresponding C or .CPP file. The *implementation section* of a Turbo Pascal Unit source file includes the procedure, function, and class definitions that would be found in the corresponding C or .CPP file (for example, POINT.CPP). Note that the keyword *end* followed by a period declares the end of the source code for the unit, just as it declares the end of the source code for the program in the main program file.

Compile and Link Instructions for Turbo Pascal

The easiest way to compile the program in Turbo Pascal is from inside the integrated development environment. Start the IDE with the main program file as an argument.

```
turbo rotate
```

The desktop will appear with an edit window open on the file RO-TATE.PAS. Now select the command Compile | Make from the top-level menu. The compiler will look at the "uses" statement in ROTATE.PAS to determine that it needs to link in the .TPU files POINT.TPU, SHAPES.TPU, and SCREEN.TPU.

```
uses Crt, Point, Shapes, Screen;
```

If the .TPU files do not already exist, the compiler will look for the source code files POINT.PAS, SHAPES.PAS, and SCREEN.PAS and compile these files into .TPU files before compiling ROTATE.PAS. Be sure that your

Unit directories specification is set for the proper directories for the standard Turbo Pascal units. This specification is set automatically when you install the compiler and only needs to be altered with the Options | Directories command if you have moved or renamed .TPU directories or files since the installation.

Turbo Pascal will compile and link all source files in less than three seconds on a 25 MHz 386 computer. You can run the program from the integrated environment by selecting the Run | Run menu command.

You can also compile the program using the Turbo Pascal command-line compiler, TPC.EXE. You can compile each of the source files separately in the following order:

```
tpc point
tpc shapes
tpc screen
tpc rotate
```

Alternatively, you can have the compiler build all source files automatically by using the /B flag and specifying only the main source-program file:

```
tpc /B rotate
```

You can run the program from the command line by typing:

```
rotate
```

Pascal Source-File Listings

The four source code files required to build ROTATE.EXE follow. ROTATE.PAS contains the main program:

```
FILE: ROTATE.PAS
program RotateShapes;

{$N+}
{$E+}

uses Crt, Point, Shapes, Screen;

procedure wait;
var
  junk : Char;
begin
```

```
    junk := ReadKey;
end;

var
  p1, p2     : TPoint;
  i, j       : Integer;
  shapeArray : Array[0..9] of PShape;
  size       : Integer;

begin

  Display.initialize;

  {----------------------------------------------------------}
  { POLYMORPHISM                                             }
  {   Rotate and display an array of shapes                  }
  {----------------------------------------------------------}
                                    { First create an      }
                                    { array of TShape      }
                                    { objects.             }
                                    {                      }
                                    { These objects have}
                                    { no names because     }
                                    { they are created     }
                                    { with New, which      }
                                    { returns a pointer.}
                                    {                      }
                                    { Therefore,           }
                                    { shapeArray is an     }
                                    { array of pointers }
                                    { to TShape objects.}
                                    {-------------------}
  size := 0;                        { size keeps track
                                      of the number of
                                      items in array.
                                      Increment size
                                      each time a new
                                      shape is added to
                                      the array.         }

  {----------------------------------------------------------}
  { Create the array                                         }
  {----------------------------------------------------------}
  p1.init(60, 6);
  shapeArray[size] := New(PCircle, init(p1, 4));
  inc(size);

  p1.init(70, 6);
  p2.init(8,8);
  shapeArray[size] := New(PRectangle, init(p1, p2));
  inc(size);

  p1.init(80, 6);
  p2.init(8,8);
  shapeArray[size] := New(PTriangle, init(p1, p2));
```

```
  inc(size);

  {-----------------------------------------------------------}
  { Draw and rotate the shape array 9 times                   }
  {-----------------------------------------------------------}
  for i := 0 to 8 do
  begin
    for j := 0 to size-1 do
    begin
      shapeArray[j]^.draw;
      shapeArray[j]^.rotate(10);
    end;
  end;

  wait;
  Display.cleanup;
end.
```

POINT.PAS defines the TPoint class:

```
FILE: POINT.PAS

unit Point;

interface

type

  {-----------------------------------------------------------}
  { TPoint class (interface)                                  }
  {-----------------------------------------------------------}
  PPoint = ^TPoint;
  TPoint = object
    constructor init(x, y: Integer);
    function  getX: Integer;
    function  getY: Integer;
    procedure initFrom(p :TPoint);
    procedure initAdd      (p1, p2: TPoint);
    procedure initSubtract(p1, p2: TPoint);
    procedure initMultiply(p1 : TPoint; i : Integer);
    procedure initDivide  (p1 : TPoint; i : Integer);
    procedure print;
  private
    xVal, yVal: Integer;
  end;



implementation

  {-----------------------------------------------------------}
  { TPoint class (implementation)                             }
  {-----------------------------------------------------------}
  constructor TPoint.init(x, y: Integer);
```

```
begin
  xVal := x;
  yVal := y;
end;

function TPoint.getX: Integer;
begin
  getX := xVal;
end;

function TPoint.getY: Integer;
begin
  getY := yVal;
end;

procedure TPoint.initFrom(p :TPoint);
begin
  xVal := p.getX;
  yVal := p.getY;
end;

procedure TPoint.initAdd      (p1, p2: TPoint);
begin
  xVal := p1.getX + p2.getX;
  yVal := p1.getY + p2.getY;
end;

procedure TPoint.initSubtract(p1, p2: TPoint);
begin
  xVal := p1.getX - p2.getX;
  yVal := p1.getY - p2.getY;
end;

procedure TPoint.initMultiply(p1 : TPoint; i : Integer);
begin
  xVal := p1.getX * i;
  yVal := p1.getY * i;
end;

procedure TPoint.initDivide(p1 : TPoint; i : Integer);
begin
  xVal := p1.getX div i;
  yVal := p1.getY div i;
end;

procedure TPoint.print;
begin
write(xVal, ' @ ', yVal);
end;

end.
```

The SHAPES.PAS module defines the abstract class, TShape, as well as the classes TCircle, TRectangle, and TTriangle. This module also defines private utility routines in its implementation section to convert degrees to radians and to rotate a point a given number of degrees in relation to the origin of the screen coordinate system.

```pascal
FILE: SHAPES.PAS

unit Shapes;

interface

uses Point;

type

  {-----------------------------------------------------------}
  { TShape class (interface)                                  }
  {-----------------------------------------------------------}
  PShape = ^TShape;
  TShape = object
    constructor init(p: TPoint);
    procedure    setAngle(a: Integer);
    function     getAngle : Integer;
    procedure    position(var p : TPoint);
    procedure    moveTo(p : TPoint);
    procedure    draw; virtual;
    procedure    rotate(a : Integer);
    procedure    print; virtual;
  private
    center : TPoint;
    color  : Integer;
    angle  : Integer;
  end;

  {-----------------------------------------------------------}
  { TCircle class (interface)                                 }
  {-----------------------------------------------------------}
  PCircle = ^TCircle;
  TCircle = object(TShape)
    constructor init(p : TPoint; r : Integer);
    procedure    setRadius(r : Integer);
    function     getRadius : Integer;
    procedure    draw; virtual;
    procedure    print; virtual;
  private
    radius : Integer;
  end;

  {-----------------------------------------------------------}
  { TRectangle class (interface)                              }
  {-----------------------------------------------------------}
  PRectangle = ^TRectangle;
  TRectangle = object(TShape)
    constructor init(ctr : TPoint; ext : TPoint);
    procedure    setExtent(ext : TPoint);
```

```
    procedure   getExtent(var ext : TPoint);
    procedure   draw; virtual;
    procedure   print; virtual;
  private
    extent : TPoint;
  end;


  {-----------------------------------------------------------}
  { TTriangle class (interface)                               }
  {-----------------------------------------------------------}
  PTriangle = ^TTriangle;
  TTriangle = object(TRectangle)
    procedure   draw; virtual;
  end;




implementation

uses Screen;

{----------------------------------------------------------}
{ Utility routines used by methods of                      }
{ classes descended from TShape                            }
{                                                          }
{      degreesToRadians                                    }
{      rotateAboutOrigin                                   }
{                                                          }
{----------------------------------------------------------}
function degreesToRadians(a : Integer) : Real;
begin
  degreesToRadians := (a*ArcTan(1)/45);
end;
procedure rotateAboutOrigin(var p            : TPoint;
                                angle        : Integer);
var
  x, y : Integer;
  theta : Real;
  cosTheta, sinTheta: Real;
begin
  theta := degreesToRadians(angle);
  cosTheta := cos(theta);
  sinTheta := sin(theta);
  x := Round(p.getX*cosTheta - p.getY*sinTheta);
  y := Round(p.getX*sinTheta + p.getY*cosTheta);
  p.init(x, y);
end;

{---------------------------------------------------------}
{ TShape class (implementation)                           }
{---------------------------------------------------------}
constructor TShape.init(p: TPoint);
begin
  center.initFrom(p);
```

```
    angle := 0
end;

procedure TShape.setAngle(a: Integer);
begin
     angle := a;
end;

function  TShape.getAngle : Integer;
begin
     getAngle := angle;
end;

procedure TShape.position(var p : TPoint);
begin
     p.initFrom(center);
end;

procedure TShape.moveTo(p : TPoint);
begin
     center.initFrom(p);
end;

procedure TShape.draw; { virtual method }
begin
end;

procedure TShape.rotate(a : Integer);
begin
     angle := angle + a;
end;

procedure TShape.print;
begin
    write('center: ');
    center.print;
    write(', angle: ', angle);
end;

{----------------------------------------------------------}
{ TCircle class (implementation)                           }
{----------------------------------------------------------}
constructor TCircle.init(p : TPoint; r : Integer);
begin
    TShape.init(p);
    radius := r;
end;

procedure   TCircle.setRadius(r : Integer);
begin
    radius := r;
end;

function    TCircle.getRadius : Integer;
begin
  getRadius := radius;
```

```
end;

procedure   TCircle.draw; { virtual procedure }
var
  p : TPoint;
begin
  position(p);
  rotateAboutOrigin(p, getAngle);
  Display.circle(p, radius);
end;

procedure TCircle.print;
begin
  write('center: '); center.print;
  write(', radius: ', radius);
  write(', angle: ', angle);
end;

{----------------------------------------------------------}
{ TRectangle class (implementation)                        }
{----------------------------------------------------------}
constructor TRectangle.init(ctr : TPoint; ext : TPoint);
begin
  TShape.init(ctr);
  extent.initFrom(ext);
end;

procedure   TRectangle.setExtent(ext : TPoint);
begin
  extent.initFrom(ext);
end;

procedure   TRectangle.getExtent(var ext : TPoint);
begin
  ext.initFrom(extent);
end;

procedure   TRectangle.draw; { virtual procedure }
var
  a, b, c, d : TPoint;
  extentDiv2 : TPoint;
begin
  extentDiv2.initDivide(extent, 2);
  a.initSubtract(center, extentDiv2);
  c.initAdd(a, extent);
  b.init(c.getX, a.getY);
  d.init(a.getX, c.getY);

  rotateAboutOrigin(a, getAngle);
  rotateAboutOrigin(b, getAngle);
  rotateAboutOrigin(c, getAngle);
  rotateAboutOrigin(d, getAngle);

  Display.moveTo(a);
  Display.lineTo(b);
  Display.lineTo(c);
  Display.lineTo(d);
```

```
    Display.lineTo(a);
end;

procedure    TRectangle.print;
begin
  write('center: ');    center.print;
  write(', extent: '); extent.print;
  write(', angle: ', angle);
end;

{-----------------------------------------------------------}
{ TTriangle class (implementation)                          }
{-----------------------------------------------------------}
procedure    TTriangle.draw; { virtual procedure }
var
  a, b, c : TPoint;
  extentDiv2 : TPoint;
  w2, h2 : Integer;
  p : TPoint;
begin
  extentDiv2.initDivide(extent, 2);
  w2 := extentDiv2.getX;
  h2 := extentDiv2.getY;

  p.init( 0,  h2); a.initAdd(center, p);
  p.init( w2, -h2); b.initAdd(center, p);
  p.init(-w2, -h2); c.initAdd(center, p);

  rotateAboutOrigin(a, getAngle);
  rotateAboutOrigin(b, getAngle);
  rotateAboutOrigin(c, getAngle);

  Display.moveTo(a);
  Display.lineTo(b);
  Display.lineTo(c);
  Display.lineTo(a);
end;

end.
```

The SCREEN.PAS module defines an abstract TScreen class that supports only the methods required to draw and rotate TShape objects. This unit also declares a public instance of TScreen called Display. Only one instance of the TScreen class should be created in a program. This particular implementation of TScreen maps the abstract coordinate system and shape manipulation methods to Borland's BGI graphics library.

```
FILE: SCREEN.PAS

unit Screen;

interface
```

```
uses Graph, Point;

type

  {----------------------------------------------------------}
  { TScreen class (interface)                                }
  {----------------------------------------------------------}
  TScreen = object
    procedure translate(    initialPoint : TPoint;
                        var resultPoint : TPoint);
    function translateX(x : Integer) : Integer;
    function translateY(y : Integer) : Integer;
    procedure initialize;
    procedure cleanup;
    procedure moveTo(p : TPoint);
    procedure lineTo(p : TPoint);
    procedure circle(p : TPoint; radius : Integer);
    procedure clear;
  private
    maxX : Integer;
    maxY : Integer;
    virtualMaxX : Integer;
    virtualMaxY : Integer;
  end;

{---------------------------------------------------------}
{ Display is a global instance of TScreen               }
{ used to access virtual display screen.                }
{---------------------------------------------------------}
                              { TShape and descendent }
                              { class methods need     }
                              { access to the global  }
                              { Display object.        }
                              {----------------------}
var
  Display : TScreen;
{---------------------------------------------------------}




implementation

const                         {-----------------------------}
  PathToDrivers = '\TP60\BGI'; { Default path of *.BGI files. }
                              { Be sure to change this      }
                              { to the appropriate directory }
                              { for your installation. Or   }
                              { you can copy all the BGI     }
                              { drivers into the directory   }
                              { where you plan to run any    }
                              { programs that use            }
                              { SCREEN.TPU.                  }
                              {-----------------------------}
```

```
{----------------------------------------------------------}
{ TScreen class (implementation)                           }
{----------------------------------------------------------}
procedure TScreen.translate(    initialPoint : TPoint;
                             var resultPoint : TPoint);
begin
  resultPoint.init(translateX(initialPoint.getX),
                   translateY(initialPoint.getY));
end;

function TScreen.translateX(x : Integer) : Integer;
begin
  translateX := Integer((LongInt(maxX) * LongInt(x))
                        div virtualMaxX);
end;

function TScreen.translateY(y : Integer) : Integer;
begin
  translateY := maxY -
                Integer((LongInt(maxY) * LongInt(y))
                        div virtualMaxY);
end;

procedure TScreen.initialize;
var
  GraphDriver: Integer;
  GraphMode: Integer;
  ErrorCode: Integer;
begin
  GraphDriver := Detect;             { autodetect BGI driver }
  DetectGraph(GraphDriver, GraphMode);
  InitGraph(GraphDriver, GraphMode, PathToDrivers);
  if GraphResult <> GrOK then
  begin
    Writeln(GraphErrorMsg(GraphDriver));
    if GraphDriver = grFileNotFound then
    begin
      Writeln('in ', PathToDrivers,
              '. Modify "PathToDrivers" in SCREEN.TPU.');
      Writeln;
    end;
    Writeln('Press Enter...');
    Readln;
    Halt(1);
  end;
  virtualMaxX := 100;
  virtualMaxY := 100;
  maxX := GetMaxX;
  maxY := GetMaxY;
end;

procedure TScreen.cleanup;
begin
  CloseGraph;
end;
```

```
procedure TScreen.moveTo(p : TPoint);
var
  p2 : TPoint;
begin
  translate(p, p2);
  Graph.MoveTo(p2.getX, p2.getY);
end;

procedure TScreen.lineTo(p : TPoint);
var
  p2 : TPoint;
begin
  translate(p, p2);
  Graph.LineTo(p2.getX, p2.getY);
end;

procedure TScreen.circle(p : TPoint; radius : Integer);
var
  p2 : TPoint;
  xr, yr, r : Integer;
begin
  translate(p, p2);
                              {-------------------------}
                              { Set r to the average of }
                              { the x and y translations }
                              { for radius.             }
                              {-------------------------}
  xr := (LongInt(maxX) * LongInt(radius)) div virtualMaxX;
  yr := (LongInt(maxY) * LongInt(radius)) div virtualMaxY;
  r  := (xr + yr) div 2;

  Graph.circle(p2.getX, p2.getY, r);
end;

procedure TScreen.clear;
begin
  ClearDevice;
end;

end.
```

THE ABSTRACT TSCREEN CLASS FOR SMALLTALK

The TScreen class provides the basic functionality of an abstract or virtual screen class to help make rotate shapes as portable as possible. A single instance of this class, called Screen, is created as a global variable. The classes TCircle, TRectangle, and TTriangle assume the existence of Screen and use its methods for drawing circles and lines.

```
FILE: TSCREEN.CLS

Object subclass: #TScreen
  instanceVariableNames:
    'maxX maxY virtualMaxX virtualMaxY pen sinTable
  classVariableNames: "
  poolDictionaries: " !

!TScreen class methods !

new
        "create new object, initialize variables"
    ^super new initialize.! !

!TScreen methods !

circle: centerPoint radius: theRadius
        "draw a circle"
    ¦ c r xr yr¦
    c := self translate: centerPoint.
    xr := theRadius * maxX / virtualMaxX.
    yr := theRadius * maxY / virtualMaxY.
    r := (xr + yr) // 2.
    pen up.
    pen goto: c.
    pen ellipse: r aspect: 1.!

cleanup
        "Pause by using a menu"
        "with a single menu item."
        "Restore desktop after"
        "user selects menu item."
    Menu message: 'continue'.
    Scheduler systemDispatcher redraw.!

clear
        "Replace programming environment"
        "desktop with white screen."
    Display white.!

cos: angle
        "Return a Fraction object (a ratio)
        representing the cos of angle, which
        should be an integer in the range
        0-90."

    ¦ numerator ¦
    numerator := sinTable at:
                  (91 - angle).
    ^numerator / 10000.!

demoDrawShapes
        "Demonstration program to
        draw TShape objects."
    ¦ shapeArray ¦
    shapeArray := OrderedCollection new.
```

```
    shapeArray add:
        (TCircle center: 50 @ 50
                radius: 20).
    shapeArray add:
        (TRectangle center: 50 @ 50
                    extent: 40 @ 40).
    shapeArray add:
        (TTriangle center: 50 @ 50
                    extent: 40 @ 40).
    self clear.
    shapeArray do: [ :shape | shape draw.].
    self cleanup.!

demoRotateShapes
        "Demonstration program to rotate objects of class
        TShape about the origin of the virtual screen."

    | shapeArray |
    shapeArray := OrderedCollection new.
    shapeArray add:
        (TCircle center: 60 @ 6
                radius: 4).
    shapeArray add:
        (TRectangle center: 70 @ 6
                    extent:  8 @ 8).
    shapeArray add:
        (TTriangle center: 80 @ 6
                    extent:  8 @ 8).
    self clear.
    shapeArray do: [ :shape | shape draw.].
    1 to: 8 do: [ :i |
        shapeArray do: [ :shape | shape rotate: 10.
                                  shape draw.].].
    self cleanup.!

initialize
        "initialize a virtual screen object"

    maxX := Display width.
    maxY := Display height.
    virtualMaxX := 100.
    virtualMaxY := 100.
    pen := Pen new.

"Build an integer based sine table
 with entries for angles 0 - 91
 and assign it to the variable,
 sinTable"

sinTable := #(
       0     174     348     523     697     871    1045    1218
    1391    1564    1736    1908    2079    2249    2419    2588
    2756    2923    3090    3255    3420    3583    3746    3907
    4067    4226    4383    4539    4694    4848    4999    5150
    5299    5446    5591    5735    5877    6018    6156    6293
    6427    6560    6691    6819    6946    7071    7193    7313
```

```
7431    7547    7660    7771    7880    7986    8090    8191
8290    8386    8480    8571    8660    8746    8829    8910
8987    9063    9135    9205    9271    9335    9396    9455
9510    9563    9612    9659    9702    9743    9781    9816
9848    9876    9902    9925    9945    9961    9975    9986
9993    9998    10000 ).!
```

```
lineTo: aPoint
        "Draw line between current pen location
        and point indicated by argument."
    ¦ newPoint ¦
    newPoint := self translate: aPoint.
    ^pen down; goto: newPoint; up.!
```

```
moveTo: aPoint
        "Move the screen pen to the virtual
        point indicated by the argument."
    ¦ newPoint ¦
    newPoint := self translate: aPoint.
    ^pen up; goto: newPoint.!
```

```
rotateAboutOrigin: thePoint angle: theAngle
        "Return a Point object resulting
        from rotating thePoint about
        the origin by theAngle."
    ¦ x y x2 y2 sinTheta cosTheta ¦
    x := thePoint x.
    y := thePoint y.
    sinTheta := self sin: theAngle.
    cosTheta := self cos: theAngle.
    x2 := (((x * cosTheta) - (y * sinTheta)))truncated.
    y2 := (((x * sinTheta) + (y * cosTheta)))truncated.
    ^(x2 @ y2).!
```

```
sin: angle
        "Return a Fraction object (a ratio)
        representing the sin of angle, which
        should be an integer in the range
        0-90."

    ¦ numerator ¦
    numerator := sinTable at:
                (angle + 1).
    ^numerator / 10000.!
```

```
translate: aPoint
        "Translate aPoint from virtual to
        real display coordinates."
    ¦ x y ¦
    x := self translateX: aPoint x.
    y := self translateY: aPoint y.
    ^x @ y.!
```

```
translateX: anInteger
        "Translate an x value from
        virtual to screen coordinates."
```

```
        ^((anInteger * maxX) / virtualMaxX) truncated.!

translateY: anInteger
        "Translate a y value from
         virtual to screen coordinates."
    ^(maxY - ((anInteger * maxY) / virtualMaxY)truncated).! !
```

THE TDEMOWINDOW AND TSCREEN CLASSES FOR ACTOR

The TDEMOWIN.CLS file contains the definition for the TDemoWindow class. A single instance of this class called DemoWindow is created in order to run the program.

```
FILE: TDEMOWIN.CLS

/* Actor */

/* TDemoWindow class */!!

/* The TDemoWindow class is used to create
 * a window and provide a paint method to
 * respond to the Windows paint message.
 * The main program for rotate shapes is
 * found inside the paint method and is called
 * each time Windows generates an exposure
 * event for the rotate shapes window. Exposure
 * events are generated when a window is resized
 * or uncovered.
 */!!

inherit(Window, #TDemoWindow, nil, 2, nil)!!

now(class(TDemoWindow))!!

now(TDemoWindow)!!

/* Handle Windows paint message
 * by creating a shape array,
 * adding 3 shapes, and
 * rotating them about the origin.
 */
Def paint(self, hDC | shapeArray)
{
  init(Screen, self, hDC);
  if isInitialized(Screen)
  then
```

```
    /* Create and draw shapes */
    shapeArray := new(OrderedCollection, 10);
    add(shapeArray, new(TCircle, 60@6, 4));
    add(shapeArray, new(TRectangle, 70@6, 8@8));
    add(shapeArray, new(TTriangle, 80@6, 8@8));
    do(shapeArray, {using(shape) draw(shape); });
    do(over(0,9), {using(i)
      do(shapeArray, {using(shape)
        rotate(shape,10);
        draw(shape);
      });
    });
  endif;
  cleanup(Screen);
}
!!
```

The TSCREEN.CLS file contains the definition for the TScreen class. This is the abstract screen that is provided by each of the other versions of the rotate shapes program. As with the Pascal, Smalltalk, and C++ versions of this program, a single instance of the TScreen class is created called Screen.

```
FILE: TSCREEN.CLS

/* Actor */

/* TScreen class */!!

inherit(Object,
        #TScreen,
        #(hWin hDC maxX maxY virtualMaxX virtualMaxY),
        2,
        nil)!!

now(class(TScreen))!!

now(TScreen)!!

/* Utility routine to rotate
 * a point about the screen
 * origin by a given angle.
 */
Def rotateAboutOrigin(self, thePoint, theAngle | x y x2 y2)
{
  x  := x(thePoint);
  y  := y(thePoint);
  x2 := asInt(x * cos(degToRad(theAngle))
          - y * sin(degToRad(theAngle)));
  y2 := asInt(x * sin(degToRad(theAngle))
          + y * cos(degToRad(theAngle)));
  ^point(x2, y2);
}
```

```
!!
/* Move current drawing
 * position to specified point
 * after translating coordinates.
 */
Def moveTo(self aPoint | p)
{
  p := translate(self, aPoint);
  moveTo(p, hDC);
}
!!

/* Draw line from current
 * drawing position to
 * specified point.
 */
Def lineTo(self aPoint | p)
{
  p := translate(self, aPoint);
  lineTo(p, hDC);
}
!!
/* Return true if TScreen
 * object has been initialized,
 * otherwise return false.
 */
Def isInitialized(self)
{
  if hWin ~= nil
  then
    ^true;
  else
    ^false;
  endif
}
!!

/*  Reset TScreen object
 *  to uninitialized state.
 */
Def cleanup(self)
{
  hWin := nil;
  hDC  := nil;
}
!!

/* Draw a circle of the
 * specified radius at the
 * specified center point.
 */
Def circle(self, centerPoint, radius | p xr yr r theEllipse)
{

  p  := translate(self, centerPoint);
  /* average the radius when translating coordinates */
```

```
  xr := (maxX * radius) / virtualMaxX;
  yr := (maxY * radius) / virtualMaxY;
  r  := (xr + yr) / 2;

  theEllipse := new(WinEllipse);
  init(theEllipse, x(p) - r,
                   y(p) - r,
                   x(p) + r,
                   y(p) + r);

  /* Draw ellipse using the device context handle */
  draw(theEllipse, hDC);

}
!!

/* Translate a point from virtual
 * coordinate system to real
 * coordinate system.
 */
Def translate(self, aPoint | x y)
{ x := translateX(self, x(aPoint));
  y := translateY(self, y(aPoint));
  ^point(x, y);
}
!!

/* Translate y coordinate from
 * virtual coordinate system to
 * real coordinate system.
 */
Def translateY(self, y)
{ ^(maxY - asInt((y * maxY) / virtualMaxY));
}
!!

/* Translate x coordinate from
 * virtual coordinate system to
 * real coordinate system.
 */
Def translateX(self, x)
{ ^asInt((x * maxX) / virtualMaxX);
}
!!

/* Initialize TScreen object
 */
Def init(self, handle, deviceContext)
{ hWin := handle;
  hDC := deviceContext;
  maxX := width(clientRect(handle));
  maxY := height(clientRect(handle));
  virtualMaxX := 100;
  virtualMaxY := 100;
}
!!
```

B

C++ PROGRAM FOR CHAPTER 14

The file DIALOG.CPP shows the complete C++ ObjectWindows implementation of the seven standard dialogs you have seen implemented in Pascal for Turbo Vision and ObjectWindows, and in C++ for C++ Views. At the end of the listing, modifications are suggested for the List box dialog.

```
#include <owl.h>
#include <stdio.h>
#include <stdlib.h>
#include <array.h>
#include <abstarry.h>
#include <strng.h>

#pragma hdrstop        /////////////////////////////////////
                       // Turn off precompiled headers    //
                       // from this point on.             //
                       // Precompiled-headers             //
                       // significantly reduce compile    //
                       // time, but must always appear    //
                       // in the same order for           //
                       // each file in a project          //
                       // which uses them.                //
                       /////////////////////////////////////
#include <sortarry.h>
#include <listbox.h>
#include <inputdia.h>
#include <filedial.h>
```

```
#define menuTestDialogs 100
#define cmAbout         101
#define cmReport        102
#define cmYesNo         103
#define cmYesNoCancel   104
#define cmInput         105
#define cmListSelect    106
#define cmFileSelect    107
#define cmQuit          108

#define idOk              1
#define idCancel          2
#define idListBox       201


//===========================================================//
// INTERFACE: CLASS DECLARATIONS                             //
//===========================================================//


//------------------------//
// Application (interface) //
//------------------------//

class TMyApp : public TApplication
{
public:
  TMyApp(LPSTR  AName,
         HANDLE hInstance,        HANDLE hPrevInstance,
         LPSTR  lpszCmdLine,      int    nCmdShow)
   : TApplication(AName,
                  hInstance,      hPrevInstance,
                  lpszCmdLine,    nCmdShow) {};
  virtual void InitMainWindow(void);
};


//------------------------//
// Main Window (interface) //
//------------------------//

class TMyWindow : public TWindow
{
public:
  TMyWindow(PTWindowsObject AParent, LPSTR ATitle);

  virtual void testAbout        (TMessage& Msg)
                              = [CM_FIRST + cmAbout];
  virtual void testReport       (TMessage& Msg)
                              = [CM_FIRST + cmReport];
  virtual void testYesNo        (TMessage& Msg)
                              = [CM_FIRST + cmYesNo];
  virtual void testYesNoCancel (TMessage& Msg)
                              = [CM_FIRST + cmYesNoCancel];
  virtual void testInput        (TMessage& Msg)
                              = [CM_FIRST + cmInput];
  virtual void testListSelect  (TMessage& Msg)
                              = [CM_FIRST + cmListSelect];
  virtual void testFileSelect  (TMessage& Msg)
```

```
                                      = [CM_FIRST + cmFileSelect];
  virtual void testQuit        (TMessage& Msg)
                                      = [CM_FIRST + cmQuit];
};

typedef TMyWindow *PMyWindow;

//============================================================//
// IMPLEMENTATION: METHOD DEFINITIONS                         //
//============================================================//

//-----------------------------//
// Application (implementation) //
//-----------------------------//

void TMyApp::InitMainWindow(void)
{
  MainWindow = new TMyWindow(NULL, "ObjectWindows Dialogs");
}

//-----------------------------//
// Main Window (implementation) //
//-----------------------------//

TMyWindow::TMyWindow(PTWindowsObject AParent, LPSTR ATitle)
  : TWindow(AParent, ATitle)
{
    AssignMenu(menuTestDialogs);
}

#pragma argsused
void TMyWindow::testAbout(TMessage& Msg)
{
  MessageBox(HWindow,
         "This program demonstrates the use of "
           "various dialog boxes developed to "
           "work with the ObjectWindows "
           "application framework.",
         "About", MB_OK);
}

#pragma argsused
void TMyWindow::testReport(TMessage& Msg)
{
  MessageBox(HWindow,
         "The MessageBox function is used "
           "to create a variety of dialogs "
           "in ObjectWindows. MessageBox constants, "
           "like MB_ICONEXCLAMATION, let you include "
           "special bit-mapped symbols in your message "
           "dialogs.",
         "ObjectWindows Report Dialog",
         MB_OK | MB_ICONEXCLAMATION);
}

#pragma argsused
void TMyWindow::testYesNo(TMessage& Msg)
```

```
{
  int   Selection;
  LPSTR response;

  Selection =
    MessageBox(HWindow, "Do real programmers drink Jolt?",
      "YesNo Dialog", MB_YESNO | MB_ICONQUESTION);
  switch(Selection)
  {
    case IDYES : response = "Yes"; break;
    case IDNO  : response = "No"; break;
  }

  MessageBox(HWindow,
        response,
        "You selected:",
        MB_OK);
}

#pragma argsused
void TMyWindow::testYesNoCancel(TMessage& Msg)
{
  int        Selection;
  char       S [100];
  LPSTR      fileName;
  LPSTR      response;

  fileName = "DIALOG.CPP";
  wsprintf(S,
    "Warning: %d\nFile not saved: %s\nSave before quitting?",
    999, fileName);
  Selection =
  MessageBox(HWindow,
        S,
        "Warning",
        MB_YESNOCANCEL | MB_ICONSTOP);
  switch(Selection) {
    case IDYES    : response = "Yes"; break;
    case IDNO     : response = "No"; break;
    case IDCANCEL : response = "Cancel"; break;
  }

  MessageBox(HWindow,
        response,
        "You selected:",
        MB_OK);
}

#pragma argsused
void TMyWindow::testInput(TMessage& Msg)
{
  char buf[255];

  strcpy(buf, "Default response");
  if(GetApplication()->ExecDialog(new TInputDialog(
        this,
          "Input Dialog",
```

```
              "Enter some text: ",
              buf,
              sizeof(buf)
          )) == IDOK)
      MessageBox(HWindow, buf, "Response:", MB_OK);
}

#pragma argsused
void TMyWindow::testListSelect(TMessage& Msg)
{
              //----------------------------------//
              // Create a sorted array of String  //
              // objects to be used in the        //
              // ListBox object inside the dialog //
              //----------------------------------//

    SortedArray a(14);
    a.add(*new String("Vanilla"));
    a.add(*new String("Chocolate"));
    a.add(*new String("Strawberry"));
    a.add(*new String("Neapolitan"));
    a.add(*new String("Chunky Monkey"));
    a.add(*new String("Jamoca Almond Fudge"));
    a.add(*new String("Tin Roof Sundae"));
    a.add(*new String("Heath Bar Crunch"));
    a.add(*new String("Rocky Road"));
    a.add(*new String("Milli Vanilli"));
    a.add(*new String("Peppermint"));
    a.add(*new String("Chocolate Chip"));
    a.add(*new String("Mutant Ninja Turtle Bars"));
    a.add(*new String("Tutti Frutti"));

              //----------------------------------//
              // "LISTBOXDIALOG" is the name of   //
              // the dialog defined in DIALOG.RC  //
              //----------------------------------//

    TDialog      *pDialog  = new TDialog(this,    "LISTBOXDIALOG");

              //----------------------------------//
              // The symbolic constant, idListBox,//
              // identifies the ListBox defined in//
              // the resource file DIALOG.RC      //
              //----------------------------------//

    TListBox     *pListBox = new TListBox(pDialog, idListBox);

              //----------------------------------//
              // Create a transfer buffer and set //
              // it to contain a pointer to the   //
              // sorted array of Strings created  //
              // above. The default selection is  //
              // highlighted when the dialog is   //
              // invoked.                         //
              //----------------------------------//
```

```
TListBoxData  *pBuffer  = new TListBoxData;
pBuffer->Strings = (Array*)(&a);
pBuffer->SelCount = 0;
pBuffer->SelStrings = new Array(10, 0, 10);
char firstString[100];
strcpy(firstString, (String&)a[0]);
pBuffer->SelectString(firstString);

            //----------------------------------//
            // Set the transfer buffer for      //
            // the dialog                       //
            //----------------------------------//

pDialog->SetTransferBuffer(&pBuffer);
pListBox->EnableTransfer();
pDialog->Transfer(pBuffer, TF_GETDATA);

            //----------------------------------//
            // Invoke the dialog and record the //
            // button used to end the dialog    //
            //----------------------------------//

int buttonPressed =
  GetApplication()->ExecDialog(pDialog);

if(buttonPressed == idOk )
{
  if (pBuffer->SelCount <= 0)
  {
    MessageBox(HWindow,
               "No item selected",
               "Terminated with OK",
               MB_OK);
    return;
  }
            //----------------------------------//
            // Get a copy of the selected       //
            // String from the transfer buffer  //
            //----------------------------------//

  char      s[100];
  pBuffer->GetSelString(s, 100);
  MessageBox(HWindow,
             s,
             "You selected:",    // message box title
             MB_OK);
}
else
{
  MessageBox(HWindow, "Cancel", "You selected:", MB_OK);
}
}

#pragma argsused
void TMyWindow::testFileSelect(TMessage& Msg)
{
  char fileName[MAXPATH];
```

```
    strcpy(fileName, "*.cpp");
    if(GetApplication()->ExecDialog(new TFileDialog(
            this,
              SD_FILEOPEN,
              fileName
            )) == IDOK)
    {
      MessageBox(HWindow, fileName, "Response:", MB_OK);
    }
}

#pragma argsused
void TMyWindow::testQuit(TMessage& Msg)
{
  int Selection =
    MessageBox(HWindow, "Exit program?",
      "Goodbye", MB_YESNO | MB_ICONQUESTION);
  if(Selection == IDYES)
    PostQuitMessage(0);
}

//============================================================//
// MAIN PROGRAM                                               //
//============================================================//

#pragma argsused
int PASCAL WinMain(HANDLE hInstance, HANDLE hPrevInstance,
                   LPSTR lpszCmdLine, int nCmdShow)
{
  TMyApp MyApp("StandardDialogs",
               hInstance,      hPrevInstance,
               lpszCmdLine,    nCmdShow);
  MyApp.Run();
  return MyApp.Status;
}
```

INDEX

T